# THE A. W. MELLON LECTURES IN THE FINE ARTS

DELIVERED AT THE
NATIONAL GALLERY OF ART, WASHINGTON, D.C.

1952. CREATIVE INTUITION IN ART AND POETRY *by* Jacques Maritain

1953. THE NUDE: A STUDY IN IDEAL FORM *by* Kenneth Clark

1954. THE ART OF SCULPTURE *by* Herbert Read

1955. PAINTING AND REALITY *by* Etienne Gilson

1956. ART AND ILLUSION: A STUDY IN THE PSYCHOLOGY OF PICTORIAL REPRESENTATION *by* E. H. Gombrich

1957. THE ETERNAL PRESENT: I. THE BEGINNINGS OF ART II. THE BEGINNINGS OF ARCHITECTURE *by* S. Giedion

1958. NICOLAS POUSSIN *by* Anthony Blunt

1959. ON DIVERS ARTS *by* Naum Gabo

1960. HORACE WALPOLE *by* Wilmarth Sheldon Lewis

1961. CHRISTIAN ICONOGRAPHY: A STUDY OF ITS ORIGINS *by* André Grabar

1962. BLAKE AND TRADITION *by* Kathleen Raine

1963. THE PORTRAIT IN THE RENAISSANCE *by* John Pope-Hennessy

1964. ON QUALITY IN ART *by* Jakob Rosenberg

1965. THE ORIGINS OF ROMANTICISM *by* Isaiah Berlin

1966. VISIONARY AND DREAMER: TWO POETIC PAINTERS, SAMUEL PALMER AND EDWARD BURNE-JONES *by* David Cecil

1967. MNEMOSYNE: THE PARALLEL OF LITERATURE AND THE VISUAL ARTS *by* Mario Praz

# BLAKE
## and TRADITION

THE A. W. MELLON LECTURES IN THE FINE ARTS · 1962

THE NATIONAL GALLERY OF ART · WASHINGTON, D. C.

# *Blake*

# *and Tradition*

Volume II

## KATHLEEN RAINE

ROUTLEDGE & KEGAN PAUL · LONDON

FIRST PUBLISHED IN ENGLAND BY ROUTLEDGE & KEGAN PAUL, LTD.
BROADWAY HOUSE, 68-74 CARTER LANE, LONDON E. C. 4
1969


THIS TWO-VOLUME WORK IS THE ELEVENTH VOLUME OF
THE A. W. MELLON LECTURES IN THE FINE ARTS,
WHICH ARE DELIVERED ANNUALLY
AT THE NATIONAL GALLERY OF ART, WASHINGTON.
PUBLISHED IN THE UNITED STATES OF AMERICA
FOR BOLLINGEN FOUNDATION, NEW YORK
BY PRINCETON UNIVERSITY PRESS, PRINCETON, NEW JERSEY


SBN   7100   6151   X

PRINTED IN THE UNITED STATES OF AMERICA
DESIGNED BY ANDOR BRAUN

# Contents

## *Part V:*   The Zoas of Reason

## *Part VI:*   The Zoas of Perception

## *Part VII:*   What Is Man?

# List of Illustrations

An asterisk indicates a color reproduction. For a note on sources, see I, p. xxiii. Unless otherwise noted, the *Jerusalem* pictures are from the Mellon copy.

# Part V

# The Zoas of Reason

In the figure of Urizen and the myths that belong to him Blake has personified conceptual or discursive reason, διάνοια; or, rather, he has given form and expression to the state of the soul governed by the belief that all knowledge is based upon the ratio of the five senses. But Urizen is not presented through his arguments: we are not given to read those "books" that he writes with his "iron pen"; he is presented to us as a mode of being. The final argument against the positivist is not the breaking down of his own arguments but the clear perception of his disastrous limitations, his monstrosity. Urizen, wise in his own estimation, is consistent by his own standards; but "he who defines himself is not therefore clear." Urizen is revealed, by Blake, in all his limitations, anxious and unhappy in himself and a tyrant when he governs a soul or a society.

CHAPTER *16*

# The Tyger

The question of good and evil, which forms the theme of the *Marriage*, was likewise the inspiration of *The Tyger*, written about the same time. That grand incantation of rhetorical questions which makes up the substance of Blake's most famous poem may seem to require no answer. Those tremendous questions that evoke in our imagination the very forge of creation, while seeming to lead up to some supreme affirmation, lead only to the unanswered question: "Did he who made the Lamb make thee?" Belief in a creator seems to demand the answer yes, but leaves us then in extreme doubt about the nature of that God. If we may call him good, must we also call him evil? A God beyond good and evil seems certainly to be implied in the *Marriage*—Boehme's Father, with his creative "wrath-fires," without whose energy there can be no life. A Proverb of Hell, "The tygers of wrath are wiser than the horses of instruction," seems to make the Tyger a spirit of the irrational "Hell" that Blake opposes to the rational "Heaven." Yet the answer might equally be no, leading, in that case, to the conclusion that, at least in a certain sense, there is more than one creator.

There is much to be said in support of the first view. Is Blake in the antithesis of Tyger and Lamb already foreshadowing those gods of double aspect, Urthona-Los, Orc-Luvah, and the rest, who in eternity are serene and beautiful, and in the world of generation terrible and angry? The *Marriage* is a vindication of the energy of life in whatever form: "The roaring of lions, the howling of wolves, the raging of the stormy sea, and the destructive sword, are portions of eternity, too great for the eye of man." [1]

Tigers were a fashionable subject of painting at the end of the century; wild beasts in their untamed energy and beauty expressed one aspect of the romantic revolt of imagination against reason. The vogue was introduced in England by Stubbs, and followed by Morland and other

[123]

painters, until the time of Landseer. Stubbs's famous Tiger (now in the Tate Gallery) was exhibited at the Society of Artists of Great Britain, in Somerset Street, in 1769. Blake at this time was twelve years old, and in his second year as a student at Pars's drawing school, which was held in the same house where the Society (at which Stubbs regularly exhibited) was lodged. Is *The Tyger* a tribute to a boy's enthusiasm for Stubbs's glorious beast, seen at that impressionable age? If this is so, has Stubbs communicated to Blake something of that sense of the glory of wild beasts that was his own contribution, as a forerunner of the romantics, to the rise of energy against reason?

Much evidence might also be brought to prove that the Tyger is indeed an emblem of evil. In *The Four Zoas* the song of triumph in praise of the natural creation declares that "the Human form is no more," and expands this statement in the lines ". . . The Tyger fierce / Laughs at the Human form . . ." [2] The tigers and lions are here created by Urizen; they are called "dishumaniz'd men." In a horrific passage Blake describes this dishumanization, as the spectral warriors enter "the beastial state." (It will be remembered that animal forms, in the *Lyca* poems, symbolize what is below the human, a state to which mankind may revert.)

*Troop by troop the beastial droves rend one another . . .*

. . .

> *. . . those that remain*
> *Return in pangs & horrible convulsions to their beastial state;*
> *For the monsters of the Elements, Lions or Tygers or Wolves,*
> *Sound loud the howling music . . . terrific men*
> *They seem to one another, laughing terrible among the banners.*[3]

Neither of these answers is wholly excluded from a final understanding of the poem. There are several levels upon which different answers may be envisaged, and Blake in leaving the question unanswered is aware of this. If a sense of the relative is part and parcel of the meaning of the poem, there is another question implicit in its paradox: If Lamb and Tyger are alike expressions of the divine energy, under what conditions does the Tyger come into existence? If the "fires" are the First Principle of the Divine Essence (as Boehme taught), does some agency other than the supreme God impose a form of evil upon the primal energy? [4]

Before attempting to answer the question, "Did he who made the Lamb make thee?" we may simplify it by answering one part of it: Who made the Lamb? The poet's answer in an earlier poem, *The Lamb*, seems at first sight naïve:

> *He is called by thy name,*
> *For he calls himself a Lamb.*
> *He is meek, & he is mild;*
>
> *He became a little child.*
> *I a child, & thou a lamb,*
> *We are called by his name.*[5]

Blake is not giving a sentimentally childish answer but making a theological statement: lamb and child are made by the Son, the Logos incarnate in Jesus the Imagination, the Lamb. He was surely here thinking in Boehme's terms, of the world of the Son, or Light, the spiritual principle which is man's eternal dwelling place; and the abyss of the Father is the place of the Tyger, that mysterious hell of evil or energy which is nevertheless the ground from which the spiritual principle of the Son is eternally generated. In *The Lamb* Blake is describing the eternal world of light, in *The Tyger* the dark world of "Hell, or energy"—"nature," as Boehme understood it. The tiger is one of "the terrors of the Abyss," the "horrid shapes & sights of torment." [6] It roams "the forests of the night"—the forests that Blake knew from Taylor as the classical symbol of natural existence, and the "night" of the Hades of the temporal world, far removed from the light of the spiritual sun. The Lamb, we are told, feeds "By the stream & o'er the mead"—Vergil's landscape of Elysium. Vala, the goddess Nature, is described as roaming in "forests of eternal death, shrieking in hollow trees." [7] We read of "forests of affliction where lions and tigers roam"; and the blind tyrant Tiriel is led by his daughter "to the covert of a wood . . . where wild beasts resort . . . but from her cries the tygers fled. All night they wander'd thro' the wood." [8] We find everywhere the same consistent combination of imagery—darkness, forests, and beasts of prey—as in *The Tyger*.

These forests of nature Blake equates with the multiplication of the one tree, called by him "The Tree of Mystery." Associated with the image of this ramifying tree, or the resulting forest, is the image of "smoke" or "fire," and with smoke, the tiger.

The "Tree of Mystery" originates, it seems, in Paracelsus, who writes of nature as the "Great Mystery," and whose images for this natural creation in its constant flux are a forest and smoke: "Briefly, whatsoever hath a body is nothing but curdled smoke. . . . For all bodies shall passe away and vanish into nothing but smoke, they shall all end in a fume." [9] The origin of all subsequent images of material nature as a cloud or smoke is, of course, the Hermetic cloud of dark moisture. Nature is also likened by Paracelsus to a great forest that will be consumed away:

> And as all the things of the creatures are wip'd away, minished and do perish with the mystery, as a forrest which the fire burns into a little heap of ashes, out of which ashes but a little glasse is made and that glass is brought into a small beryll, which beryll vanisheth into wind: in like manner we also shall be consumed, still passing from one thing into another, til there be nothing of us left. Such as the beginning such is the end of the creatures. If the Cypres tree can spring out of a little graine, surely it may be brought into as small a quantity as that little kernell was at first.[10]

Such is the Great Mystery, nature; it is a forest that vanishes in smoke; even as it grows it consumes, for a natural body is only "curdled smoke." Therefore Blake writes that, in this natural mystery, lions and tigers "roam in the redounding smoke In forests of affliction." [11] The forests are themselves the "redounding smoke" of Paracelsus' splendid image of mutability; they are synonymous. Vala, as goddess of nature, is called "the Demoness of smoke," [12] for this describes her nature. In *The Last Judg-*

*ment* [13] Mystery (who is both goddess – "the shadowy female" – and tree) is consumed in flames:

> *In the fierce flames the limbs of Mystery lay consuming . . .*
>
> .     .     .
>
> *. . . The tree of Mystery went up in folding flames*

And in his description of the symbols of the Last Judgment, Blake wrote of

> Two Beings each with three heads; they Represent Vegetative Exist-    [124, 125]
> ence; as it is written in Revelations, they strip her [Mystery] naked
> & burn her with fire; it represents the Eternal Consummation of

124 Figures with wreathed torches: detail of Blake's sketch (1810?) for the Last Judgment [176]

On the analogy of Hecate the vegetative principle is represented with three heads.

125 The Triple Hecate:
oil painting (1794?)

Vegetable Life & Death with its Lusts. The wreathed Torches in
their hands represents Eternal Fire which is the fire of Generation or
Vegetation; it is an Eternal Consummation. Those who are blessed
with Imaginative Vision see This Eternal Female & tremble at what
others fear not, while they despise & laugh at what others fear.[14]

Thus we have the Tyger as a denizen of the forests of nature,
themselves that fire; and in this context we see the image of the Tyger
"burning bright" as more than a description of the flaming beauty of the
living creature (though it is that also): the Tyger is itself part of that ever-
burning, ever-consuming Great Mystery of nature and her "progeny of
fires."

There is a passage in *Europe* that illuminates many of the themes of
*The Tyger*. The shadowy female, who is nature, laments that she must
generate, in the "nether abyss" of the alchemists, creatures who are the
progeny of the "Starres Above." This alchemical marriage of the "Above"
and the "Beneath" is a betrayal, she complains, of a heavenly progeny into
a world of darkness:

> *Unwilling I look up to heaven, unwilling count the stars:*
> *Sitting in fathomless abyss of my immortal shrine*

*I sieze their burning power*
*And bring forth howling terrors, all devouring fiery kings,*

*Devouring & devoured, roaming on dark and desolate mountains,*
*In forests of eternal death, shrieking in hollow trees.*
*Ah mother Enitharmon!*
*Stamp not with solid form this vig'rous progeny of fires.*

*I bring forth from my teeming bosom myriads of flames* [15]                    [126, 177]

Blake is returning yet again to the question that troubled Thel: Why should
spirit be forced to mingle with the evil dark principle of matter?

The landscape is that of *The Tyger:* the stars above, the nether abyss,
the "forests of eternal death." The forms that shriek in hollow trees suggest
Dante's wood of self-slayers punished by metamorphosis into a form not only
below the human but below the animal—"vegetated," as Blake himself
constantly writes of the lowest degradation possible to life. If we are in doubt
as to the literalness of the "burning" of the Tyger, we are left in none here, of
the "progeny of fires" and "myriads of flames," who are the creatures of
nature and tiger-like, for they are roamers and devourers, "devouring fiery
kings" and "howling terrors," "consumed and consuming." [16]

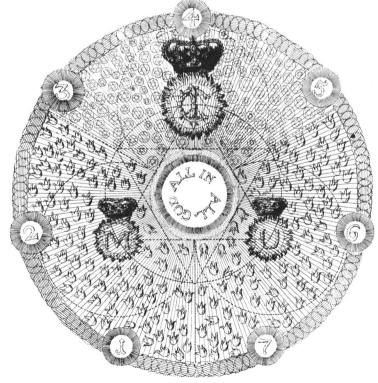

126 Cosmological table by
D. A. Freher in Law's Boehme
(1764), vol. 2, plate XIII

The seven fountain spirits, and
"myriads of flames" within the
primal creative fires of the
Father. The seals of Solomon
may illustrate the *Signatura
Rerum*, the stamping with
solid form to which Blake refers. (See above, l. 6.) Cf.
[188].

So strange an image as the "fire" and "smoke" of vegetation is explicable in terms of Paracelsus' natural philosophy; and behind Paracelsus lies Heraclitus' comparison of nature to an everlasting fire, parts kindling, parts going out—an image used so finely by Yeats to describe the Tree of Attis:

> *A tree there is that from its topmost bough*
> *Is half all glittering flame and half all green.*[17]

The "forests of the night" are not described as burning; but if we follow the theme of tiger and forest into other contexts, we find that the forests are consumed in smoke, and that tigers are denizens of these forests, called the "fire" of vegetation, because they are ever-consuming. The combined "torch" and "wreath" in the hands of the vegetative spirits says the same. The Tyger himself is "burning bright"; he is a "fiery king," one of nature's "progeny of fires"; and in view of this consistent grouping of the images of fire, forest, and tiger, it may not be fanciful to suggest that the image implies not only the fiery splendor of the Tyger but its participation in the natural world forever kindling and consuming.

From the speech of the shadowy female it is clear that the "myriads of flames" are of heavenly origin, and that the stamping of this "vig'rous progeny" with "solid form" is an evil; for the "fire" is holy, being nothing less than the divine essence. The flames are Boehme's fires of the father; they are also that fiery essence which to the alchemical tradition as a whole was held to be the indestructible spirit which incarnates in pneumatic and hylic bodies—garments or envelopes. Berkeley's *Siris* is a philosophic essay on this solar principle in all things; without this fire, says Berkeley, there can be no creation.[18]

But in *The Tyger* Blake asks, "What the hand dare sieze the fire?" By implication, the fire has been seized, or stolen, by the creator of the Tyger; therefore, that creator cannot be the supreme God. The theft of fire is one of the oldest and most universal of all myths; for that theft Prometheus was punished by Zeus. Fire is the divine essence, and whoever would become a creator must possess himself of it. This is the cosmic crime, to create, by perversion of a principle that in itself remains incorruptible and divine, a world apart from God. For this Zeus punished the Titan who placed such power in the hands of man; and Blake writes that Milton's Messiah (who is the Satan of his own mythology) "Formed a heaven with what he stole from the abyss." We are not told in this passage what he stole; but from

*Europe*, from *The Tyger*, and from *The Book of Urizen* we may deduce that it was fire.

In *Europe* it is the shadowy female herself who seizes the "burning power"; *The Book of Urizen* tells of the mastery of the eternal fires by Urizen; and in *The Tyger* the Creator is unnamed:

> *In what distant deeps or skies*
> *Burnt the fire of thine eyes?*
> *On what wings dare he aspire?*
> *What the hand dare sieze the fire?*

The "daring" aspiration of the thief suggests both Prometheus and Milton's winged Satan, "coasting the wall of Heaven." The conclusion is inescapable: the creator of the Tyger is this thief.

Boehme himself in the *Aurora* describes at great length the corruption of the fountain-spirits, the creative powers of the Father, each in turn. While retaining their essential nature and their creative powers, they manifest themselves, after their corruption by Lucifer, in evil forms. He even describes the coming into existence, through this corruption, of evil beasts not intended in the divine plan, but originating in the corruption of the world by Lucifer and his Host. If there had been no fall, there would have been no evil creatures in nature—no serpents, toads, or venomous insects:

> For the whole *Salitter* should be a House of Pleasure and *Delight* for angelical Bodies, and all should rise up according to the Delight of their Spirit, and image themselves so, that they should never at all have *any* Displeasure in any Figure, Shape, or Creature . . . If they had but continued in their meek Birth or Geniture, according to the *divine Right* . . . nothing had been among them and in them, but merely the Joy of Love, to speak after an earthly Manner, as it were an *eternal Laughing*, and a perpetual Rejoicing in an eternal hearty Delight. For God and the Creatures had been one Heart and one Will.

Blake's *Laughing Song* suggests such a state of innocence; but after Lucifer's fall it was otherwise:

> But when *Lucifer* exalted himself, and kindled his qualifying or fountain Spirits, then the animated or soulish Spirit went forth. . . . as a fiery Serpent, or *Dragon*, and imaged and framed all Manner of

fiery and poisonous Forms and Images, like to wild, cruel, and evil
Beasts.

And from hence the wild, fierce, and evil Beasts have their
Original in this World. For the Host or Army of *Lucifer* had kindled
the Salitter of the Stars and of the Earth, and half killed, spoiled
and destroyed it. . . .

And that Beast, which had most of the Fire, or the bitter, or the
astringent *Quality*, in the *Mercurius*, that became also a bitter, hot,
and fierce Beast, all according as the Quality was predominant or
*chief* in the Beast.[19]

Is Blake's Tyger Boehme's "Beast, which had most of the Fire"?

Blake wrote *The Tyger* in 1793, it is supposed. Why was Blake
asking, at just this time, such questions concerning the creator?

It would be foolish to pretend that in or about 1793 Blake, as a man of
thirty-six, living an active, practical life as a London craftsman, noticed for
the first time that there are evils—or is evil—in the world.[20] He had written
robustly about such things in *Poetical Sketches*, and his *Songs of Innocence*
imply a full awareness of evils of many kinds: *The Chimney Sweeper* can
scarcely be said to show an unawareness of evil; rather it expresses a vision
of innocence that can make the worst evils tolerable. What is new in *Songs
of Experience* is not the knowledge that evil exists, or some personal struggle
with it (the poems on the theme of evil are all strikingly impersonal), but
the intellectual excitement of a new imaginative realization of its place in the
order of things. We know that before the writing of the *Marriage* he had
been reading Boehme and Paracelsus; he was by now familiar, under a
variety of forms, with a more subtle tradition of thought on the nature of
evil. But the thought of *The Tyger* is not to be explained by Boehme
alone.

The epithet "Gnostic" was first applied to Blake by Crabb Robinson.
Whether Blake himself would have accepted the term as a description of his
system of thought we do not know. No Gnostic texts had been published
during Blake's lifetime: the Codex Brucianus (the *Pistis Sophia*) was lying
untranslated in the Bodleian,[21] and the Askew Codex in the British Museum;
so that whatever Blake may have known of Gnostic thought came to him at
third hand, from the writings of ecclesiastical historians drawing solely
upon the fragments of Gnostic thought preserved, or attributed, by their
enemies the Church Fathers. Sources available to Blake were Mosheim's

127 Creation of Adam: tempera color printed monotype (1795)

Adam is the natural man or "mortal worm" made of clay; his creator is the Elohim or demiurge. Compare this figure with Satan, in *Job*, plate 11 [143].

*Ecclesiastical History*,[22] Lardner, and Priestley's *Early Opinions concerning Jesus Christ*. From these, however, Blake must have been aware that the Gnostic systems all held that the creator of the temporal world was not the supreme God; so that Crabb Robinson was so far justified in his report on his conversation with Blake:

> The eloquent descriptions of Nature in Wordsworth's poems were conclusive proof of atheism, for whoever believes in Nature said B. disbelieves in God. For Nature is the work of the Devil. On my obtaining from him the declaration that the Bible was the work of God, I referred to the commencement of *Genesis*—"In the beginning God created the Heaven & the Earth." But I gained nothing by this, for I was triumphantly told that this God was not Jehovah, but the Elohim, & the doctrine of the Gnostics repeated with sufficient consistency to silence one so unlearned as myself.[23]

So Crabb Robinson concludes with the assurance of the plain man who knows the answer to so simple a question as how the world was created and by whom. Nevertheless, the diarist has recorded nothing that is not confirmed in Blake's own writings. In *Jerusalem* he wrote that "in his

[127]

Chaotic State of Sleep" into which Albion, the universal humanity, is fallen, "Satan & Adam & the whole World was Created by the Elohim." [24]

Blake had probably read both Mosheim and Priestley. Mosheim gives a fair and coherent account of the principal beliefs of the Gnostics. Chief of these—and common to all schools of Gnosticism—is the affirmation that the creator of the temporal world is not the supreme God; this view was common to oriental and Egyptian Gnostics, and to the Jewish schools: Mosheim calls cabalism a form of Jewish Gnosticism. According to the Jewish Gnostics, the God of the Old Testament is this lesser divinity. Those Gnostics who adopted Christianity believed that Christ, son of the supreme God, came to end the power of the inferior deity. Yet the demiurge also has his origin in the supreme God: he has "descended" from the pleroma (the eternal world)

> either by a fortuitous impulse, or in consequence of a divine com-
> mission, reduced to order this unseemly mass [matter], adorned it
> with a rich variety of gifts, created men, and inferior animals of dif-
> ferent kinds to store it with inhabitants, and corrected its malignity
> by mixing with it a certain portion of light, and also of a matter
> celestial and divine. This creator of the world is distinguished from
> the supreme deity by the name of *demiurge*. His character is a com-
> pound of shining qualities, and insupportable arrogance; and his
> excessive lust of empire effaces his talents and his virtues. He claims
> dominion over the new world he has formed, as his sovereign right;
> and, excluding totally the supreme deity from all concernment in it,
> he demands from mankind, for himself and his associates, divine
> honours. . . . the imperious *demiurge* exerts his power in opposition
> to the merciful purpose of the supreme being, resists the influence of
> those solemn invitations, by which he exhorts mankind to return to
> him, and labours to efface the knowledge of God in the minds of
> intelligent beings.[25]

This striking characterization of the demiurge may very well be a source of the "Prince of Light," Urizen, who "descends" from his place in eternity to create the temporal world, his "horrible chaos of futurity":

> *Indignant, muttering low thunders, Urizen descended,*
> *Gloomy sounding: "Now I am God from Eternity to Eternity."* [26]

Cerinthus, a Jew converted to Christian Gnosticism, taught

> that the creator of this world, whom he considered also as the sover-

eign and lawgiver of the Jewish people, was a *being* endowed with the greatest virtues, and derived his birth from the *Supreme God;* that this *being* fell, by degrees, from his native virtue, and his primitive dignity; that the *Supreme God,* in consequence of this, determined to destroy his empire, and sent upon earth, for this purpose, one of the ever-happy and glorious *aeons,* whose name was CHRIST.[27]

Blake would have found substantially the same account of the principal systems of Gnosticism in the works of Priestley.

It is just possible that Blake, with his predisposition to read white where the orthodox read black, might have reconstructed for himself, and imaginatively adopted, a framework of Gnostic thought from the fragments he came to know through two screens of detraction, those of their ancient and modern commentators. But he had learned enough from other sources to give him a motive for gleaning what he could of these ancient myths from the uninspired and uninspiring pages of Priestley and of the *Ecclesiastical History.* He was already familiar with allied forms of thought from the Christian cabalists Fludd and Agrippa, from Paracelsus, and from the Hermetica. The view that the creation was the work of a demiurge was also held by Paracelsus, who writes of the "mortal God" as the author of nature—the "Great Mystery":

> Sith the things created are divided into *eternall* and *mortall;* the reason whereof is, because there was another creator of the mysteries, besides the chiefest and most high. For the most high (Creator) ought to be the Judge and corrector of all the creatures, who should know how much was bestowed on them whereby they might do either good or evil, though they had it not (immediately) from him. Moreover, the creatures are alway egged on and provoked rather to evil, compeled thereto by the fates, stars, and by the infernall one; which by no means could have bin, if they had proceeded out of the most high himself, that we should be forced into those properties of good and evill.[28]

The elaborate cabalistic hierarchy of emanations Blake knew probably both from Fludd and from Agrippa, who give substantially the same account: the world of nature is created not by the supreme God but mediately by the *Elohim* (eight in number). If we read *The Tyger* not in the light of Boehme but of the Gnostic philosophy, we shall say that *The Lamb* describes the eternal, *The Tyger* the temporal, order. Weight is given to this view by the fact that nature, the Tree of Mystery, is constantly associated with the demiurge Urizen and his fallen world, which is not Boehme's hell or ground of primal fires but a world of illusion or *maya*. "Error, or Creation" began in the "sleep" of fallen man; and at the Last Judgment "Error, or Creation, will be Burned up, & then, & not till Then, Truth or Eternity will appear. It is Burnt up the Moment Men cease to behold it." The Tyger is one of "the horrid shapes & sights of torment" who live in a state of mutual destructiveness because they are bound and imprisoned within the temporal order: "Beyond the bounds of their own self their senses cannot penetrate." [28a]

There is reason to believe that *The Tyger* was written under the immediate excitement and delight occasioned by Blake's reading of Everard's translation of the Hermetica, *The Divine Pymander of Hermes Trismegistus*. The poem reflects a passage in the fifth book, "That God is not manifest and yet most manifest." The book as a whole is in praise of God as creator, throughout this tractate named the Workman (demiurge).

On the *Laocoön* group he wrote: "What can be Created Can be Destroyed. Adam is only The Natural Man & not the Soul or Imagination." Adam was created from "the Female, the Adamah" or red clay; and the Tyger, like the natural Adam, is molded in clay:

*In what clay & in what mould*
*Were thy eyes of fury roll'd?* [29]

To Blake this distinction was quite clear; and the passage from the *Pymander* is also an account of the natural creation:

> And if thou wilt see and behold this Workman, even by mortal things that are upon earth, and in the deep, consider, O Son, how *Man* is made and framed in the Womb; and examine diligently the skill and cunning of the Workman, and learn who it was that wrought and fashioned the beautiful and Divine shape of *Man;* who circumscribed and marked out his eyes? Who bored his nostrils and ears? Who opened his mouth? who stretched out and tied together his sinews? Who channelled the veins? Who hardened and made strong the bones? Who clothed the flesh with skin? Who divided the fingers and

128 Los (and specter) with hammer, anvil, and furnace: *Jerusalem* (1804–1820), plate 6, detail

See also [1, 93].

the joints? Who flatted and made broad the soles of the feet? who digged the pores? who stretched out the spleen? who made the heart like a *Pyramis?* [30]

The rhetorical form – the series of questions which in being asked are answered – and the many details of resemblance in the imagery seem to leave no doubt that Blake had this passage in mind. Compare:

> . . . *what art*
> *Could twist the sinews of thy heart?*

with "who stretched and tied together his sinews? Who channelled the veins?" The heart "like a *Pyramis*" (a "furnace"), the eyes "circumscribed and marked out," the strange image, "Who flatted and made broad the soles of the feet," so skillfully turned by Blake into the "dread feet" of the Tyger. In the line "What dread hand? & what dread feet?" Blake leaves us in doubt whether either, or both, belong to the maker or the made.

The Workman of *The Tyger* is (so we deduce from the early drafts)  [128] both potter and blacksmith: he molds the eyes in clay; he also works with hammer, anvil, and furnace (for nothing can be made without fire), forging chains like the Hephaestus of Aeschylus (himself, in the Orphic tradition, identified with the Demiurge):

> *Where the hammer? Where the chain?*
> *In what furnace was thy brain?*
> *What the anvil? What dread grasp?* [31]

This potter and blacksmith becomes, in the Prophetic Books, expanded into the figure of Los with his "Furnaces," hammer, and anvil, who binds Urizen and Orc with the chain of time that he hammers out in heartbeats upon his anvil. Los's furnaces are also potters' furnaces, for they are called in one passage "the Potter's Furnace among the Funeral Urns of Beulah." [32] The "Funeral Urns" (molded, of course, in clay) are the mortal bodies of those who descend into incarnation, an image likewise taken from the *Pymander*, where the body is compared to "the sensible Carcass, the Sepulchre, carried about with us." The Old Testament also abounds in metaphorical comparison of God's creation of man to the work of a potter.

The association of "Nostrils, Eyes, & Ears" in the later poem *To Tirzah* is still reminiscent of the passage quoted above—"who . . . marked out his eyes? Who bored his nostrils and ears?"

> *Thou, Mother of my Mortal part,*
> *With cruelty didst mould my Heart,*
> *And with false self-decieving tears*
> *Didst bind my Nostrils, Eyes, & Ears:*
>
> *Didst close my Tongue in senseless clay,*
> *And me to Mortal Life betray.* [33]

This poem makes clear the point left in doubt in *The Tyger*—that Blake regards the incarnation of man "in clay" as an evil, the work of "a very cruel being." The molding of the body in clay recurs in many passages in the later Prophetic Books that more or less directly echo this poem. In the account of Urizen's "dens" [34] the "dishumaniz'd men" are called tigers and lions, serpents and monsters, and then this same image describes the closing of their senses:

> *. . . their Ears*
> *Were heavy & dull, & their eyes & nostrils closed up.*

Animal forms, for Blake, fall short, always, of the human form, the perfect expression of the Logos.

The character of the demiurge, as Blake derived his knowledge of this being from the various sources available to him, is not so much evil as ambiguous; and this ambiguity is most clearly conveyed in the second canceled draft of *The Tyger* in the Rossetti Manuscript:

> *Burnt in distant deeps or skies*
> *The cruel fire of thine eyes?*
> *Could heart descend or wings aspire?* [35]

These lines make clear a point obscured (no doubt deliberately) in the final draft—that the deeps and the skies are contrasted. Did "heart descend" or did "wings aspire," did the Workman draw forth his Tyger from above or from beneath? In the final version,

> *In what distant deeps or skies*
> *Burnt the fire of thine eyes?*
> *On what wings dare he aspire?* [36]

Blake, thinking of the Smaragdine Table, no doubt intended this equivocal identification and contrast. It may seem to be laboring the point to say that it makes a great difference to our understanding of Blake's implicit identification of "deeps" and "skies" in the finished draft, if we consider that his starting point is their opposition. But if we overlook this point and read "deeps or skies" merely as a piece of cosmic landscape-painting, we shall miss the whole point of the paradox which suggests that heaven and hell may, after all, in the final reckoning, be one and the same:

> *Heaven Above, Heaven Beneath;*
> *Starres Above, Starres Beneath;*
> *All that is Above, is also Beneath.*[37]

The "nether sky" of the fourth *Memorable Fancy* of the *Marriage* is, again, the "Heaven Beneath" of alchemy; here Blake is prepared to commit himself to this void, "and see whether providence is here also."

The image of "Starres Beneath" appears again in the *Introduction* to *Songs of Experience:*

> *The starry floor,*
> *The wat'ry shore,*
> *Is giv'n thee till the break of day.*[38]

[I, 67; II, 179]

Starry floor and watery shore link the alchemical with the Platonic sources of the poem; water, as a symbol of matter and, as such, of the lowest of the planes of being, is common to all traditions. Paracelsus writes that "God created Water the first matter of Nature," [39] and also that "In the first Creation, the things above, and the things below, the upper and lower Heaven or Water, the Superiour Coagulated Nature or Stars, and the inferiour Terrestrial Nature were all commixt in one, and were but one thing." [40] The "separation" (this is the term employed by Paracelsus to account for the origin of the elements from the "one thing") of "the Waters of the Valley of darkness"—from which earth originates—from the "superior Terrestrial Bodies or Stars" gives rise to the "Above" and the "Beneath," which nevertheless retain a "concordancy and affinity." The waters below are feminine in relation to the heavenly bodies, the stars, which are masculine. Earth's starry floor and watery shore suggest the "Starres Beneath" of Vaughan, and also the "Waters of the Valley of darkness," which constitute the "Heaven Beneath," according to Paracelsus. In the *Marriage* "the nether deep grew black as a sea," as Leviathan appeared in the waves and raging foam of the "black deeps."

It is hard to say precisely what response the lines are meant to evoke. "Giv'n thee" seems neither a promise of good nor a doom of evil. It is simply a statement of the conditions "below." There is a perfect coldness and stillness in the presentation of the image, which contrasts with the dynamic energy of *The Tyger;* but in both poems the poet leaves us with an open question. "Giv'n thee till the break of day" has no more finality than "Did he who made the Lamb make thee?" In both poems he presents us with a dilemma in the highest degree seeming to demand a solution, and then withholds that solution. *The Tyger* is, from beginning to end, an unanswered question; and in the *Introduction*, where we would expect the speaker (the Bard, or the Holy Word) to follow up the call to Earth to awake, by summoning her to leave the starry floor and watery shore, we find instead what seems to be an acquiescence, a divine permission (if the speaker is the Holy Word) of the conditions of the nether world that Earth must for the time endure.

Starry Jealousy of *Earth's Answer* is, it is true, presented as wholly evil; yet the traditional demiurge is neither wholly good nor wholly evil, and this ambiguity of his nature (and of his creation therefore) is never altogether forgotten by Blake. Urizen himself (who is a developed form of Starry Jealousy) is not wholly evil and is redeemable. This ambiguous

129 "God blessing the seventh day" (the seven creative spirits): water color (1803?)

relation of the Workman to the supreme God is described, for example, in the second book of the Hermetica. Nature is, as Plato taught in the *Timaeus*,[41] an "imitation" of eternity; the eternal world is the work of the Logos, the copy is the work of the demiurge:

> For the *Mind* being God, *Male and Female*, *Life and Light*, brought forth by his *Word* another *Mind* or *Workman;* which being God of the *Fire*, and the *Spirit*, fashioned and formed seven other *Governors*, which in their circles contain the *Sensible World*, whose Government or disposition is called *Fate* or *Destiny*.    [129]
>
> *Straightway* leaped out, or exalted itself from the downward Elements of God, *The Word of God*, into the clean and pure Workmanship of Nature, and was united to the *Workman*, *Mind*, for it was *Consubstantial* . . . But the *Workman*, *Mind*, together with the *Word*, containing the circles, and whirling them about, turned round as a wheel, his own Workmanships; and suffered them to be turned from an indefinite Beginning to an indeterminable end, for they always begin where they end.[42]

Here is the Workman who frames the natural universe, who, as in the Gnostic texts, "descends" from the supreme God, and yet who in part is carrying out the divine plan and works "together with the Word." Here we have, also, mention of the seven planetary spirits who labor together with the

130 David delivered out of many waters: water color

The angelic figure above appears surrounded by seven spirits, clearly differentiated according to the traditional qualities.

[130, 126, 131, 132, 192]

Workman. Most Gnostic systems make mention of the "Seven angelic architects," who are, of course, also Plato's seven planetary spirits, those who turn the circles of destiny.[43] The whirling circles of the *Pymander* are no doubt Plato's spindle of necessity from the myth of Er. The seven are found, also, in the Hebrew tradition[44] and have passed into Christian mythology as the sevenfold gifts or qualities of the Holy Ghost. In the writings of Boehme they figure prominently as the "fountain spirits" of the Father. The seven may be regarded as an ogdoad, if the Workman is regarded as an eighth spirit. In astronomical symbolism he corresponds to the sphere of the fixed stars, within which turn the seven planetary spheres.[45] Blake, in his later mythology, developed an ogdoad of the four Zoas and their four feminine emanations. These persons Blake calls the "eight immortal starry ones" because they are "of the Elohim," the demiurgic planetary governors or qualifying spirits. Blake, when he wrote *The Tyger*, had not completed his system, nor did the Zoas yet exist in his mind otherwise than in the most vague foreshadowing. But here are the roots of much that was later to grow.

It is difficult, even, to say with certainty that the Workman of *The Tyger* is wholly the later Urizen, for in some respects he resembles the later Los; both are demiurgic, and supremacy in the creative process is, in the later books, contested between the two. The seven furnaces of Los are clearly the seven spirits. They retain, moreover, an affinity with the planetary spheres, for we are told that they are "sevenfold, each within the other," like the concentric spheres of the wheel turned by the Workman, or Plato's spindle of necessity.[46] The furnaces have a close relation to the "starry wheels"—the circles of the seven planetary governors:

> *. . . Los roll'd furious*
> *His thunderous wheels from furnace to furnace . . .*[47]

and again:

> *Then wondrously the Starry Wheels felt the divine Hand. Limit*
> *Was put to Eternal Death. Los felt the Limit & saw*
> *The Finger of God touch the Seventh furnace in terror . . .*
> *And Los beheld the hand of God over his furnaces*[48]

Yet in making Los lord of the furnaces, Blake felt the necessity of overcoming some confusion of function between Los and Urizen, which he does in characteristically perfunctory fashion by stating that Los's furnaces were "given over to him" by Urizen. This clue is not to be overlooked; for it does unmistakably indicate that for Blake, Urizen, ruler of destiny and of the stars, was pre-eminently the demiurge, as responsible for the fallen world, whereas Los's task, as the time-spirit, is its recovery:

> *Then Los with terrible hands siez'd on the Ruin'd Furnaces*
> *Of Urizen: Enormous work, he builded then anew,*
> *Labour of Ages . . .*[49]

The Hermetic Workman, like Prometheus, was called "god of the fire, and the Spirit"; for "the Mind which is the Workman of all, useth the fire as his instrument in his Workmanship; and he that is Workman of all, useth it in the making of all things." It is now Los's hand that dares "sieze the fire" and labors at "the furnaces of affliction."

The furnaces are also akin to the Athanor of which Paracelsus wrote in mystical terms: "Who seeth not the form and frame of the universal created World, to bear the similitude and likeness of a Furnace: or, that I may speak more reverently, containing the Matrix of a Womb; that is to say, the Elements wherein the Seeds of the Sun and Moon, by their various astral influences are corrupted, concocted and digested, for the Generation of all things?" [50] It is in the Athanor that the base Mercurius, named by Boehme in a passage quoted above,[51] is "resolved into the First Matter of Sol," the principle of fire, which is the spiritual essence of creation. This Paracelsus gives as the secret of the power of the Athanor: "the first actual, is the Fire; the first local Instrument is the Furnace, which by the Ancients is called by this Chymical Name, *Athanor:* this referreth to the Womb in the Spagyric Generation. . . . the Spagyric *Athanor* ought to be built from the imitation of the Foundation of Heaven and Earth." [52]

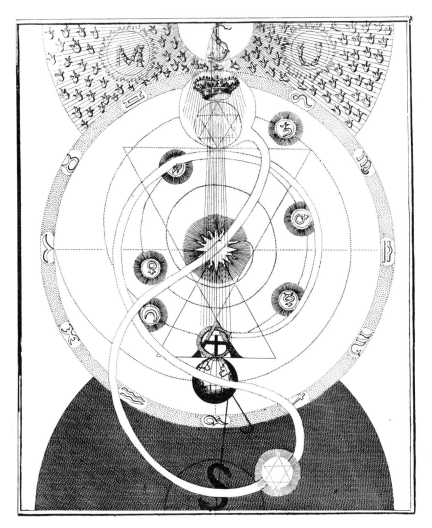

131 Cosmological table by Freher in Law's Boehme (1764), vol. 2, plate XI

The seven spirits within the zodiac; the serpentine curve illustrates the track by which Jesus entered creation. (Cf. "Miltons Track" [1, 68].)

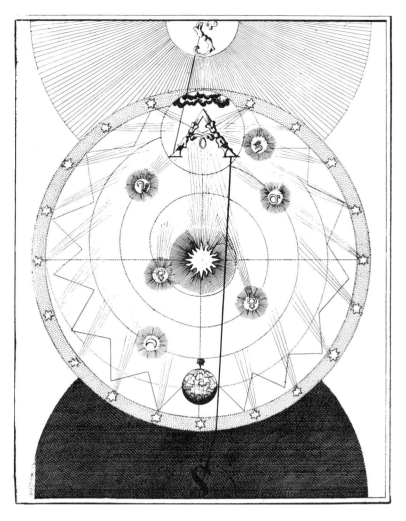

132 Cosmological table by Freher in Law's Boehme (1764), vol. 2, plate VIII
The stars in the round globe of heaven, raining down influences, the planets each in their sphere. Cf. [1, 100].

"The male is a furnace of beryll," Blake wrote in *Jerusalem;* and Paracelsus' account of the Athanor suggests that Blake means by this a great deal more than Shakespeare's "lover, sighing like furnace." [53] The male as a furnace is the agent of the creative principle.[54]

The furnaces are also Boehme's seven fountain-spirits, which are also the qualifying or planetary principles. We can be sure that Blake's furnaces are Boehme's fountains, for at the end of the time process,

> . . . *the Furnaces became*
> *Fountains of Living Waters flowing from the Humanity Divine.*[55]

This is Boehme's imagery, and it is also Boehme's thought; for unfallen, the seven qualifying spirits are the eternal rejoicing of creation in the Father.

[132]     The stars, then, for Blake, signify the planetary governors of destiny, or the Elohim. Blake calls his Zoas "the starry eight." "Los was the fourth immortal starry one," [56] because the sun is traditionally the fourth of the seven planets. Boehme's Sol is likewise the fourth of his fountain-spirits. Urizen is the ruler of the eighth sphere, that of the fixed stars of the firmament enclosing the universe; he is called "prince of the starry wheels"—the wheels being the orbits of the planets over whom he rules. He is the "Starry Jealousy" of *Earth's Answer* and "the starry king" of *A Song of Liberty*, leader of "the starry hosts"; and we may say that Blake never writes of the stars without intending us to think not of the landscape of the sky but of the rulers of destiny. Blake's references to stars and the night sky suggest spiritual darkness and the government of destiny; never are they intended to evoke an image of the beautiful and serene "waters on a starry night" of Wordsworth, or the rapture of Hopkins' "Look at the stars!"

Boehme's Father—whose part is also demiurgic—is also described as ruler of the stars:

> When we consider the whole Nature and its Property, then we see the Father.
>
> When we behold Heaven and the Stars, then we behold his eternal *Power* and Wisdom: So many Stars as stand in the whole Heaven, which are innumerable and incomprehensible to *Reason*, and some of them are not visible, so manifold and *various* is the Power and Wisdom of God the Father.
>
> But every Star in Heaven differs in its Power and *Quality*, which also makes so many Distinctions in and among the Creatures upon the Earth, and in the whole Creation.
>
> . . . Therefore if a Man would liken the Father to any thing, he should liken him to the round Globe of Heaven.
>
> You must not conceive here, that every Power which is in the Father, stands in a peculiar severed or divided Part and *Place* in the Father, as the Stars do in Heaven.
>
> No, but the Spirit shows that *all* the Powers in the Father are one in another as one Power.[57]

Boehme is still speaking the old language according to which the stars rule destiny; his Father, like the older demiurge, is likened to the eighth sphere, and so Blake also conceived the stars and Urizen their ruler.

"The starry pole" of the *Introduction* is to be understood in association with "Starry Jealousy," who rules the circles of the stars, which revolve about the pole as Plato's circles about the spindle of necessity. Later—and perhaps already in these poems—Blake identified this government of the demiurge with Newton's "astronomical telescopic heavens," a modern version of "error, or Creation," which presented, from a symbolic point of view, apt affinities with the ancient picture of the demiurge as ruler of the "stars" and as, therefore, a nocturnal ruler of a universe from which the sun of spiritual light is for a time withdrawn. Newton's nocturnal landscape is a major theme of Young's *Night Thoughts;* an imagery of stars is there associated with the Newtonian philosophy by what might seem coincidence, but which to Blake could only seem an inherent fitness in the nature of things: the very landscape (skyscape) of Newton's universe proclaims itself, by "divine analogy," as the work of the demiurgic ruler of the stars.

In *Earth's Answer* "Starry Jealousy" controls the universe; in the later poem, *Introduction,* Blake is reminding Earth that this rule is the condition only of her fallen state: there is another ruler who "might controll / The starry pole."

This statement seems to refer to just that cosmic situation described in the passage from the *Pymander* quoted on page 21 above. The circles of the stars are turned by the second mind, the Workman; but this mind was brought forth by the first mind, "the Word"; the Word is also the essence of the soul itself. The passage from the *Pymander* which describes, in eloquent terms, this identity of the divine mind with the essential "self" is quoted at length in a later section (p. 110).[58]

The syntax of the first verses of the *Introduction* is profoundly ambiguous; nor does Blake's own erratic punctuation, which I have here restored, help in any way:

> *Hear the voice of the Bard!*
> *Who Present, Past, & Future sees*
> *Whose ears have heard,*
> *The Holy Word.*
> *That walk'd among the ancient trees.*
>
> *Calling the lapsed Soul*
> *And weeping in the evening dew:*
> *That might controll*
> *The starry pole:*
> *And fallen, fallen light renew!* [59]

Who is "Calling the lapsed Soul"? Is it the Bard or the Holy Word or both? And who is it "That might controll / The starry pole"? Is it the Bard, the Holy Word, or the lapsed Soul? The voice of the Bard is the voice of imagination; the voice of imagination is the voice of the Holy Word, as might be proved from any number of later passages, in which Jesus and the Imagination are used synonymously. The Holy Word is the divine Logos, God as manifested to man and within man; Adam, unfallen in the Garden of Eden, communed continually with this divine presence among "the ancient trees" (of life and of knowledge?). If it is the lapsed Soul herself who "might controll / The starry pole," this also would be true because the Logos dwells within the soul, whose own nature is divine: "We are all coexistent with God, Members of the Divine body. We are all partakers of the divine nature." [60] The Pymander tells Hermes: "*I am that Light*, the *Mind*, *thy God. . . . that bright and lightful Word from the mind is the Son of God. . . . That which in thee seeth and heareth, the Word of the Lord, and the Mind the Father, God*, differ not one from the other." [61] Did not Blake intentionally leave the syntax ambiguous because he intended all these meanings?

A passage written much later, in *Jerusalem*,[62] uses the same image of the Saviour ("the Holy Word") "weeping in the evening dew" and calling "the lapsed Soul," here Albion, the fallen Man. Albion

> . . . *must have died, but the Divine Saviour descended*
> *Among the infant loves & affections, and the Divine Vision wept*
> *Like evening dew on every herb upon the breathing ground.*

In both passages the "evening" and the "dew" are likewise symbolic, not descriptive. The image is one of sorrow; for the "evening" is the onset of spiritual night, and the "dew" is the enveloping moisture of hyle gathering upon all things in the fallen world—as the Little Boy Lost was "wet with dew."

Unfallen man (Adam walking in Eden hearing the voice of God, the Platonic soul before she enters the Kingdom of Pluto through the northern gate of the Zodiac) are not subject to the rule of Starry Jealousy. Nor can the tyranny of the demiurge of the natural world have any power over the awakened soul, "That might controll / The starry pole" if she could, in the Platonic language, remember again what in her sleep she has forgotten: her divine nature.

Thus prepared, we can turn to the stars as they appear in *The Tyger*. What is the meaning of the lines:

*When the stars threw down their spears*
*And water'd heaven with their tears,*
*Did he smile his work to see?*

The stars, we can assume, are the planetary spirits or governors of destiny, subject to the demiurge. But we can go further than this; for in "Night the Fifth" of *The Four Zoas* the demiurge himself (Urizen) uses the same phrase, "the stars threw down their spears," and extends its meaning. Urizen is describing—and lamenting—his fall:

*I went not forth: I hid myself in black clouds of my wrath;*
*I call'd the stars around my feet in the night of councils dark;*
*The stars threw down their spears & fled naked away.*
*We fell. I siez'd thee, dark Urthona. In my left hand falling.*

*I siez'd thee, beauteous Luvah; thou art faded like a flower*
*And like a lilly is thy wife Vala wither'd by winds.*[63]

Here the stars throwing down their spears are unmistakably associated with the fall of the demiurge, and the meaning is made still more clear by the naming of some of the "starry ones" who fell with Urizen and because of him—Urthona, Luvah, and Vala. We can conclude, since Blake has used the same words, that he is here giving a fuller account of the episode so mysteriously described in *The Tyger*. When the demiurge Urizen fell, he drew down with him his seven planetary spirits, and with their fall, the creation of the temporal world comes to pass and the Tyger is created in the dark forests of nature. "Did he smile?" He may have done so; for Urizen's fall was a voluntary "descent"; but from the long lament from which the above lines are quoted we know that remorse followed.

The throwing down of the spears echoes Milton's account of the fall of the rebel angels, driven out of heaven by the onset of the Messiah's chariot:

[133]

133 Four fallen starry ones (the Zoas?): *Jerusalem* (1804–1820), plate 54, bottom detail

> *. . . they astonisht all resistance lost,*
> *All courage; down thir idle weapons drop'd;*
> *O're Shields and Helmes, and helmed heads he rode.*[64]

They flee,

> *. . . witherd all their strength,*
> *And of thir wonted vigour left them draind,*
> *Exhausted, spiritless, afflicted, fall'n.*[65]

There is an echo of the "witherd" and "exhausted" Seraphim of Milton in the lines that described Luvah and Vala as "faded" and "wither'd." It is the same stars who in the illustrations to the Book of Job are shown as risen again in their brightness, "When the morning Stars sang together, and all the sons of God shouted for joy."

What, then, in the light of all this, is the answer we are to give to the final question of *The Tyger:* "Did he who made the Lamb make thee?" Are we to answer it in some such words as Boehme used: "The God of the holy World, and the God of the dark World, are *not two* Gods; there is but *one* only God. He himself is the whole Being, He is Evil and Good; Heaven and Hell; Light and Darkness; Eternity and Time; Beginning and End. Where his love is *hid* in any Thing, there his anger is *manifest*. In many a Thing Love and Anger are in equal Measure and Weight; as is to be understood in this outward World's Essence." [66] Such a God is beyond good and evil. The abyss and the heavens are the two eternal contraries that make up the unity of the "one thing."

If the answer is not yes but no, then we must imagine not one world but two—the eternal and the temporal. This would be the Platonic answer—Thel's answer. To the eternal world, Eden, belongs all selfless innocence—lamb, child, and the Lamb himself, Jesus or Imagination or the Divine Humanity. To the time-world belongs the principle of the selfhood that preys upon other lives—the Tyger. Only at the deepest level of all might the answer again be yes, since the creation of the demiurge, with his world of good and evil, itself exists by the permission of the supreme God. Blake, I believe, left his question unanswered not because he did not know the answer or was in doubt, but because the answer is itself a no and yes of such depth and complexity.

Nor must we overlook, in analyzing the meaning of the text, all that is conveyed by the powerful exaltation of the meter, by the fiery grandeur of the images. If the discoverable meaning of the poem is that the Tyger is the work of a being ambiguous or evil, the emotive force of meter and image is all affirmation, praising the fiery might, the energy, and the intelligence of the mortal God; and *The Tyger* is in the mood of the *Marriage* (written about the same time), with its vindication of the fiery energies wrongly condemned as evil.

Instead of seeking to find a yes or a no, we will be nearest to the truth if we see the poem rather as an utterance of Blake's delight not in the solution but in the presentation of the problem of evil as he found it in the Hermetic and Gnostic tradition. Instead of the uncompromising, unimaginative, and closed dualism of the conventional picture of heaven and hell, Blake had discovered a world of profounder perspectives, a tradition that makes possible the simultaneous contemplation of the perfection of an eternal world and the imperfection of the temporal, as modes of being simultaneously possible within one harmonious whole.

134 Device from Bryant's *Mythology*, vol. 1 (1764), plate VIII

CHAPTER *17*

# The Ancient Trees

The tree of Mystery, which plays so great a part in the Prophetic Books, first makes its appearance in two poems in *Songs of Experience: The Human Abstract* and *A Poison Tree. A Poison Tree,*[1] under the title of *Christian Forbearance*, is Number 10 of the poems and fragments in the Rossetti manuscript,[2] and *The Human Abstract* [3] — in its early draft called *The Human Image*—Number 28.[4] We may assume that the poison tree and the "tree of Mystery" are the same; for the first bears "an apple bright" that kills the foe who steals it; the second,

[135]

> . . . *the fruit of Deceit*
> *Ruddy and sweet to eat.*

Both trees are tended with fears and tears and deceit; of the poison tree Blake writes:

> *And I water'd it in fears,*
> *Night & morning with my tears;*
> *And I sunned it with smiles,*
> *And with soft deceitful wiles*

and of "the Mystery":

> *He sits down with holy fears,*
> *And waters the ground with tears*

The "deceit" in the second poem is transferred to the "fruit of Deceit." Most striking of all, both trees exist within the human mind. The poison tree is "my wrath," which grows into a tree and bears an apple; and the tree of Mystery is nowhere to be found in nature:

> *The Gods of the earth and sea*
> *Sought thro' Nature to find this Tree;*

135 "A Poison Tree" from *Songs of Experience* (1789–94)

*But their search was all in vain:*
*There grows one in the Human Brain.*

"Tree of Mystery" carries the special meaning Paracelsus gives the words: the natural creation, which Blake conceives as the single and indivisible whole of manifested being. Paracelsus writes of the manifestation of nature out of "the Mystery" in terms that suggest the Indian philosophic concept of *Samsara*, the phenomenal universe of appearance, or "that which is become, born, made, and formed": [5] "Most manifest it is, that out of one seed the root sprouteth into many sprigs, then into the stalk, afterwards the boughs shoot out, lastly the flower, fruit and seed put forth. Just so is it in the various procreations out of the four Elements." [6]

The Mystery is also personified as a woman, "the onely mother of all perishing things"; Blake's Vala is also called "Mystery" and "Nature, mother of all."

33

Vala herself, therefore, is (by the logic of symbolism) sometimes represented as a tree,[7] she being the Great Mystery, from whom all creatures are generated. She speaks in the person of the tree when she says:

*My roots are brandish'd in the heavens, my fruits in earth beneath*
*Surge, foam and labour into life, first born & first consum'd!*
*Consumed and consuming!* [8]

But whence comes this fantastic image of an inverted tree whose fruits "Surge, foam" like water? The surging foam suggests a fountain: nature according to the Orphic tradition is the "fountain of forms." Proclus has a fine image of nature as a tree reflected in water and, in this sense, inverted; this is in keeping with the Platonic philosophy that sees generated nature as a shadow or reflected image of eternity: "the corporeal world is in a continual state of flowing and formation, but never possesses real being; and is like the image of a lofty tree seen in a rapid torrent, which has the appearance of a tree without the reality; and which seems to endure perpetually the same, yet is continually renewed by the continual renovation of the stream." [9]

The inverted tree immediately brings to mind the cabalistic Tree of God, which is emblematically so represented, for the root ("above") is in God's highest and most hidden essence, and the twigs and branches ("below") in nature (the garden of Malkuth). Although Blake probably knew the Tree of God from the writings of Fludd, the description given in the *Mosaicall Philosophy* makes no mention of the *inversion* of the tree, the central point of Blake's image. He may nevertheless have known this emblem of cabalism [10] from conversation, if not from a written source; yet we need not assume this, for there is a book in the Bhagavad-Gita which opens with a comparison of the phenomenal creation to an inverted tree. This is

the tree *Aswattha*, whose root is above and whose branches are below. . . . Its branches growing from the three *Goon* or qualities, whose lesser shoots are the objects of the organs of sense, spread forth some high and some low. . . . When a man hath cut down this *Aswattha*, whose root is so firmly fixed, with the strong ax of disinterest, from that time that place is to be sought from whence there is no return for those who find it; and I make manifest that first *Pooroosh* from whom is produced the ancient progression of all things.[11]

Krishna is instructing Arjuna in the illusory nature of manifested being. The tree is creation. Maya, according to the Vedas, is but a sorrowful illusion of which the clear mind must be purged. The lines

> *Let us agree to give up Love,*
> *And root up the infernal grove;*
> *Then shall we return & see*
> *The worlds of happy Eternity* [12]

are strongly reminiscent of this passage. Blake is using the word "Love" in a sense akin to the Vedic scriptures, as the desire through which the soul is held in a state of attachment to illusory things; and Eternity is "that place from whence there is no return." Again we are reminded that Blake did not exalt sexual love.

The symbol of the infernal grove is further developed in *The Four Zoas:*

> *For Urizen fix'd in envy sat brooding & cover'd with snow;*
> *His book of iron on his knees, he trac'd the dreadful letters*
>
> .        .        .
>
> *Age after Age, till underneath his heel a deadly root*    [145]
> *Struck thro' the rock, the root of Mystery accursed shooting up*
> *Branches into the heaven of Los: they, pipe form'd, bending down*
> *Take root again where ever they touch, again branching forth*
> *In intricate labyrinths o'erspreading many a grizly deep.*
>
> *Amaz'd started Urizen when he found himself compass'd round*
> *And high roofed over with trees; he arose, but the stems*
> *Stood so thick he with difficulty & great pain brought*
> *His books out of the dismal shade. . . .*[13]

The sinister enrooting of the tree (Blake does not distinguish between animal and vegetable "vegetation") is based on Milton's description of the fig tree from which fallen Adam and Eve gathered the leaves to hide their shame after their fall:

> *. . . both together went*
> *Into the thickest Wood, there soon they chose*
> *The Figtree, not that kind for Fruit renown'd,*
> *But such as at this day to* Indians *known*
> *In* Malabar *or* Decan *spreds her Armes*

*Braunching so broad and long, that in the ground*
*The bended Twigs take root, and Daughters grow*
*About the Mother Tree, a Pillard shade*
*High overarch't. . . .*[14]

This wood is nature, in whose recesses and "labyrinths" man attempts to
hide from God. "Satan's labyrinth" is another name he gives to this "infernal
grove." [15] Thus the tree of Mystery becomes the forest of nature, the forests
of the night. The multiplication is implicit in the symbol of the tree as such.
Boehme writes of Adam's tree, the human race:

[136, 137, 173]

. . . a delightful *Tree of* the *Life* of divine Wisdom and Contemplation ingrafted into the Paradise of God, *viz.* into Heaven, and
into the Time of this World, standing in both; fit to generate again
and propagate, and from *his Like* out of himself; as out of one Tree
many Twigs, Boughs, Branches and Fruits grow; where every Fruit
has a Grain, Kernel or Pippin in it, fit to produce a *new* Stock and
Tree; the like we are also to understand concerning the Tree of
*Mankind*.[16]

136 Raphael conversing with Adam and Eve,
with the Tree in the background: water color
(1808) illustrating *Paradise Lost*
See also [1, 29, 64].

137 "I found him beneath a Tree": *For Children: The Gates of Paradise* (1793), plate 8
The female figure draws the child from the ground like a mandrake.

Boehme writes of the tree of nature, or tree of this world, in terms closely reminiscent of Paracelsus, as vanishing into nothing at the end of time: "I have told you before, out of what Power the Tree is grown; *viz.* that it grew out of the Earth, and has wholly had the Nature of the Earth in it, as at this Day all Earthly Trees are so, wherein Corruptibility stands, as the earth is corruptible, and shall pass away in the End, when all shall go into its Ether, and nothing else shall remain of it besides the Figure." [17] He writes not of one but of two trees—the tree of nature, which is Paracelsus' Mystery, and the tree of life.[18] Here we have the ever-recurring theme of the eternal and temporal orders, presented under the symbols of the two trees, the one eternal, the other the mortal tree of good and evil, nature.

In reality, so Boehme understood, these two trees are one and the same: [19]

> But that *Moses* says, *The Tree of Life stood in the Midst of the Garden*, and presently, the next after sets down, *And the Tree of Knowledge of Good and Evil:* Here lies the Vail before his Eyes, that the earthly sinful Man cannot behold him . . . The precious Pearl lies in [the Knowledge of] the Difference of *the two Trees;* and yet it is but only *one*, but manifest in two Kingdoms [20]

—that is to say, in eternity and in time,

for *the Tree of Life Standeth* wholly *in the Midst of the Garden*, for it stands in two Principles, in the *Midst*, *viz.* in the holy World, between the eternal dark World of God's Anger, where God is an angry zealous God, and a consuming Fire, and the outward visible World. The *holy* Power of God in the Tree was the middlemost Kingdom; for the Middlemost penetrated the Outermost, and manifested itself with the Outward; this was the *Knowledge of the Good*, which *Adam* should have as little known, in its Original, as the Evil.

Evil, as well as good, lay hidden from man's comprehension within the archetypal tree from the beginning:

> Now *the Tree of the Knowledge of Evil* was the dark World, which also was manifest on this Tree . . . therefore *Moses* distinguishes the Tree, and says, *the Tree of Life;* thereby he understands the Property of the eternal *Life* in the Tree, *viz.* the second Principle; and by the Words *of the Tree of the Knowledge of Good and Evil* he understands the Wrath of the Anger of God, which was manifest by the Essence of the outward World in Earthliness in *this Tree*, of which *Adam* should not eat; for he should have eaten with the inward Mouth, and not with the earthly Desire, but with the heavenly, for he had such Fruit growing for him, which the inward Mouth could *enjoy;* indeed the outward Mouth did also eat thereof, but not into the Worms *Carcase.*

Adam, instead of feeding upon the bread of heaven, the "fruits of Life" (so Boehme calls them), ate the earthly nature of the tree, in which was the hidden wrath of God the Father. This is the old story of the descent of the soul from an eternal to a temporal world. In the classical myth the lure is the honey of generation; in the Hebraic, the apple on the tree of nature: the meaning is the same.

Two words in *A Poison Tree*, "wrath" and "poison," point to Boehme. The fact that the words "wrath," "poison," and "anger" do not appear to stand in a mythological context should not mislead us; for in this poem the mythological symbolism, which is by no means simple, is kept in the background of a human theme that is not at all obscure. We do not need any special knowledge to recognize the force of Blake's argument that it is better to clear the air by an honest expression of anger than to accumulate the far more deadly and insidious poison of concealed wrath which goes under the name of "Christian forbearance." But this purely human truth is illustrated by an implicit analogy with the behavior of the God of Genesis, who planted "the Tree of the Knowledge of Good and Evil," and made it "pleasant to the eye and to be desired," yet hid within it what Boehme calls "the Wrath of the Anger of God." This wrath is invisible, hidden within the fair-seeming tree of nature; and this God, Blake implies, conceals his evil intentions toward man, and awaits what he knows is bound to follow: man, whom he hates (he can do no less to have set such a snare), is lured by the brightness of the apple, steals the forbidden fruit, and dies:

> *In the morning Glad I see*
> *My foe outstretch'd beneath the tree.*

*A Poison Tree*, while seeming to criticize only human behavior, gives Blake occasion for a more far-reaching criticism of this God. Boehme raises a common, human question: "Reason says, *Why* did God suffer this Tree to grow, seeing Man should not eat of it? Did he not bring it forth for the *Fall* of Man? And must it not needs be the *Cause* of Man's Destruction?"[21]

The words "wrath" and "poison" occur many times in Boehme's writings about the tree and its fruit—"Mother Eve's Wrath Apples": "as before the Time of the Wrath it had brought forth heavenly Fruits, which had a *holy*, pure heavenly Body, and were the Food of Angels, so now it brought forth Fruits, according to its comprehensible, palpable, hard, evil, wrathful, poisonous, venomous, *half*-dead Kind."[22]

Blake's expression "fruits of life" is also frequent in Boehme, who writes of the paradisiacal trees, which were intended for man's food in Eden, that they bear "fruits of life," which are contrasted with the "Wrath Apples." Blake is writing a text from the Bible of hell when he declares:

> *Abstinence sows sand all over*
> *The ruddy limbs & flaming hair,*
> *But Desire Gratified*
> *Plants fruits of life & beauty there.*[23]

It is morality, says Blake, not desire, that causes man's Paradise to become a sandy and sterile desert (Paradise taken here in the sense of man's body, according to Boehme's teaching that the "gross Garden of *Eden*" is our earthly flesh).[24]

The poison apples, then, grow from the principle of "wrath." Boehme attributes the kindling of the poison in the tree to the wrath fires of the Father; and when Blake writes of human wrath, the figure of this God is implicit, for he it was who planted the apple tree:

> . . . *my wrath did grow*
>
> .          .          .
>
> *And it grew both day and night,*
> *Till it bore an apple bright*

That the tree grows up in man's own mind is also to be found in the works of his master, Boehme: "in thyself thou shall find the Tree of the Temptation, and also the Will to have it, which made it spring up; yea the Source whence it sprung up, stands in thee, and not in God." [25] *A Poison Tree* is generated from an angry thought: "But the Question is: Wherefore grew the earthly Tree of the Knowledge of Good and Evil? For if that had not been, *Adam* had not eaten of it: or why must *Adam* be tempted? Hearken, ask your Mind about it, wherefore it so suddenly generates and conceives in itself a Thought of Anger, and then of Love? . . . the Center of the Mind is free, and it generates the Will from Hearing and Seeing, out of which the Imagination and Lust arises." [26]

Boehme imagines the generation of the tree from man's desire for it, very much as Blake has described it in *A Poison Tree:* "seeing *Adam's Spirit* longed after that Fruit which was of the Quality of the corrupted Earth, *therefore* also Nature formed or framed such a Tree for him as was *like* the corrupted Earth. For *Adam* was the Heart in Nature, and therefore his animated or soulish Spirit *helped* to image, fashion, or form *this Tree*, of which he would fain eat." [27]

> *And I water'd it in fears,*
> *Night & morning with my tears;*
> *And I sunned it with smiles,*
> *And with soft deceitful wiles*
>
> *And it grew both day and night,*
> *Till it bore an apple bright;*
> *And my foe beheld it shine,*
> *And he knew that it was mine.*

As there is no god, so there is no serpent in Blake's poison tree; but there are "soft deceitful wiles." The later development of the symbol produces, in due course, the serpent. The venomous fruit of the two *Songs* is described at greater length in *The Four Zoas*, Night VIIa, and we now are told what the poison is: it is "the poison of sweet Love":

> ,. . . *the tree of Mystery, which in the dismal Abyss*
> *Began to blossom in fierce pain, shooting its writhing buds*
> *In throes of birth; & now, the blossoms falling, shining fruit*
> *Appear'd of many colours & of various poisonous qualities,*
> *Of Plagues hidden in shining globes that grew on the living tree.*
>
> .        .        .
>
> *Redd'ning, the demon strong prepar'd the poison of sweet Love.*[28]

The "sweet Love" is plainly "female Love," source of the infernal grove; and the falling blossoms suggest "Blossoms show'ring all around" of the "lovely mirtle tree" of marriage,[29] which we see, by implication, ripening into the poison apples; and now some creature is "writhing" in "throes of birth"—a latent serpent.

Here another element has been added to the symbolic aggregate, from yet another tree, the Myrrh. Ovid, in his *Cinyras and Myrrha*, describes the [138] birth of the god Adonis from the bark of his mother-tree, who had lost her human form as a punishment for her incest. Like Vala, who is also the tree of mystery, Myrrha is "vegetated" and accursed. The birth of a child from the bark of a tree does not, so far as I know, occur elsewhere:

> *Mean time the mis-begotten Infant grows,*
> *And, ripe for Birth, distends with deadly Throws*
> *The swelling Rind, with unavailing Strife,*
> *To leave the wooden Womb, and pushes into Life.*
> *The Mother-Tree, as if oppress'd with Pain,*
> *Writhes here, and there, to break the Bark, in vain;*
> *And, like a lab'ring Woman wou'd have pray'd,*
> *But wants a Voice to call* Lucina's *Aid.*
> *The bending Bole sends out a hollow Sound,*
> *And trickling Tears fall thicker on the Ground.*
> *The mild* Lucina *came uncall'd, and stood*
> *Beside the strugling Boughs, and heard the groaning Wood.*

138 Daphne turning into a laurel: from Blake's Notebook, p. 2

This drawing illustrates Blake's knowledge of Ovid's *Metamorphoses*.

.     .     .

*The Bark divides, the living Load to free,*
*And safe delivers the Convulsive Tree.*[30]

In *A Poison Tree* we had only a bright poisoned apple; but in the passage above, already the pestilential and many-colored fruits of the writhing tree begin to suggest the serpent-formed Orc and his sinister beauty. This strange symbolic process is brought to completion in a third passage. The venom of the tree has now engendered the serpent Orc, and the poison-bright beauty of the wrath apples has transferred itself to the serpent. The serpent is Love himself, and he is serpent-formed because he is now earthborn from the tree, and compelled to feed on its pestilential fruit. Thus, by the logic of the symbol, it is the divine anger that secretes the poison; the buds and blossoms of "female Love" initiate the growth of the poison apple, which in its turn generates the wily deceiver, the serpent. Thus does Blake interpret the Genesis myth, laying the radical guilt upon the god whose anger is the latent poison in the tree:

*. . . for Orc augmented swift*
*In fury a Serpent wondrous among the Constellations of Urizen*

*A crest of fire rose on his forehead red as the carbuncle*
*Beneath down to his eyelids scales of pearl then gold & silver*
*Immingled with the ruby overspread his Visage down*
*His furious neck writhing contortive in dire budding pains*
*The scaly armour shot out. Stubborn down his back & bosom*
*The Emerald Onyx Sapphire jasper beryl amethyst*
*Strove in terrific emulation which should gain a place*
*Upon the mighty Fiend the fruit of the mysterious tree*
*Kneaded in Uveths kneading trough. Still Orc devourd the food*
*In raging hunger Still the pestilential food in gems & gold*
*Exuded round his awful limbs Stretching to serpent length*
*His human bulk While the dark shadowy female brooding over*
*Measurd his food morning & evening . . .*

*With tears of sorrow incessant she labourd the food of Orc*
*Gathring the fruit of that mysterious tree circling its root*
*She spread herself thro all the branches in the power of Orc* [31]

The "writhing buds" of the previous passage have now given birth to the serpent, to whom the "budding pains" are transferred. The "poisonous qualities" of the fruits and their shining colors now appear in the splendors of the venomous serpent-form of Orc. By omitting any punctuation, Blake makes the serpent himself "the fruit of that mysterious tree," perhaps intentionally. The emerald, onyx, sapphire, jasper, beryl, and amethyst of the serpent are by the same grammatical ambiguity attributed to the fruit. What Orc eats as food appears in the jeweled beauty of his scales. He becomes a serpent because he feeds on the "pestilential food."

As if it were not enough that we should follow the transformation of Orc through the eating of poisoned food, we are asked to envisage the scene "among the constellations of Urizen." But even this is justified by the logic of the symbol; the metamorphosis necessarily occurs in the planetary circles of destiny ruled by the demiurge. The meaning is the same as the line "When the night had veil'd the pole," in *A Poison Tree*, and serves the same symbolic purpose of stating that this event can occur only in the night of the temporal world, when the polar center of the soul has become obscured, not in the day of eternity. Uveth is one of Urizen's three daughters—Blake's Fates; and the "dark Shadowy female" who broods over all is the Mystery herself, Vala.

*The Human Abstract* only briefly refers to the poison apples. The concentration in this poem is, rather, upon the tree itself.

This is the tree of the knowledge not of evil but of "Good and Evil." It is the inextricable admixture of the two qualities that characterizes the temporal world; and this paradox is the theme of *The Human Abstract:* [32]

> *Pity would be no more*
> *If we did not make somebody Poor;*
> *And Mercy no more could be*
> *If all were as happy as we.*
>
> *And mutual fear brings peace,*
> *Till the selfish Loves increase*

In an earlier draft these words were spoken by a Swedenborgian devil, who utters them as a "curse," but who has disappeared from the finished version of the poem; Blake with good reason exchanged the figure of a mere "devil" for that of "Cruelty" himself; for duality is the condition of the world of the demiurge. The subject of the four last verses of *The Human Abstract* is "Cruelty," who is introduced as the deceiver, immediately following these [139] paradoxes:

> *Then Cruelty knits a snare,*
> *And spreads his baits with care.*
>
> *He sits down with holy fears,*
> *And waters the ground with tears;*
> *Then Humility takes its root*
> *Underneath his foot.*[33]
>
> *Soon spreads the dismal shade*
> *Of Mystery over his head;*
> *And the Catterpiller and Fly*
> *Feed on the Mystery.*[34]

There is an accompanying design showing an aged, anxious, white-bearded figure, recognizably an early version of Urizen, entangled in a snare of heavy ropes that he himself is setting. It needs little ingenuity to associate with this drawing an epigram in the Notebook, *Lacedemonian Instruction:*

> *"Come hither, my boy, tell me what thou seest there."*
> *"A fool tangled in a religious snare."* [35]

139 *The Human Abstract* from *Songs of Experience* (1789–94)

The god of the Mystery was not content to tempt man with the apple of nature; he had also to trap him with the tangled complexities of the moral law.

A similar figure is illustrated in *The Book of Urizen;* and more is written there about the religious snare:

> . . . *a Web, dark & cold, throughout all*
> *The tormented element stretch'd*
> *From the sorrows of Urizen's soul.*
> *And the Web is a Female in embrio.*
> *None could break the Web, no wings of fire,*
>
> *So twisted the cords, & so knotted*
> *The meshes, twisted like to the human brain.*
>
> *And all call'd it The Net of Religion.*[36]

In *The Human Abstract* the tree is said to grow in the human brain; both the temporal creation and the moral law owe their birth to man's own complex errors. The "Female in embrio" is Vala, and the web her veil of maya. Web and veil and tree are all symbols of the Mystery. "The little female spreads her nets in every path," as Vala catches the specters in her veil, lowered like a fishing net into the "Atlantic Sea."

The image of the fowler's snare is common in the Old Testament, especially in the Book of Job and in the Psalms; but the specifically religious snare seems to have found its way from a Swedenborgian *Memorable Relation:*

> "O foolish and carnal People, your Faith hath seduced you, and become in your Hands like a Snare to catch Doves." On hearing these Words, a certain Magician formed as it were a Snare, or Gin, after the Image of that Faith, and hung it in a tree, saying, Observe, and see how I shall catch that Dove; and just as he spoke, a Hawk flew towards the Snare, and entangled his Neck in it, and was taken; whilst the Dove, seeing the Hawk, flew past, and escaped.[37]

There is a strong suggestion in this fable, as there is in the design accompanying *The Human Abstract* and in the similar design in *The Book of Urizen*, that the religious snare only catches the man who sets it. This situation is realized in *Vala*, in a passage that brings together all the related symbols of the tree of Mystery, the shadowy female, the Net of Religion,[38] tears, and the serpent Orc:

> *Urizen . . . saw the shadow[39] underneath*
> *His woven darkness; & in laws & deceitful religions,*
> *Beginning at the tree of Mystery, circling its root*
> *She spread herself thro' all the branches in the power of Orc:*
> *A shapeless & indefinite cloud, in tears of sorrow incessant*
> *Steeping the direful Web of Religion; swagging heavy, it fell*
> *From heaven to heav'n, thro' all its meshes, altering the Vortexes,*
> *Misplacing every Center; hungry desire & lust began*
> *Gathering the fruit of that Mysterious tree, till Urizen,*
> *Sitting within his temple, furious, felt the numming stupor,*
> *Himself tangled in his own net, in sorrow, lust, repentance.[40]*

Blake's symbolist thought, in such passages as this, reveals its dangerous tendency toward obscure, arbitrary, and abstract constructions, inexplicable

140 "Thou waterest him with tears": *For Children: The Gates of Paradise* (1793), plate 2

without knowledge of many elements not implicit in the poetry itself. Yet no poet but Blake could have written anything like it; the symbols are used like words in a sentence of complex and ambiguous grammar.

The watering of the ground with tears calls for explanation, because the phrase is one that Blake has used in several contexts, and because "weeping" is one of the constant attributes of the later figure, Urizen. In *The Tyger* the fallen stars "water'd heaven with their tears," and under one of the emblems of *The Gates of Paradise*, illustrating the figure called *Utha* (the Gaelic word for water, as Blake no doubt discovered from the footnotes of his Ossian), is the text "Thou waterest him with tears." In *A Poison Tree* it is the demiurge himself who says of the tree:

> *And I water'd it in fears*
> *Night & morning with my tears.*

The source of the phrase is Isaiah 16:9 (R.V.): "I will water thee with my tears, O Heshbon, and Elealeh: for upon thy summer fruits and upon thy harvest the battle shout is fallen. And gladness is taken away, and joy out of the fruitful field; and in the vineyards there shall be no singing, neither joyful noise." This forms part of a prophecy of the overthrow of Moab. Here the god who is about to overthrow the land also weeps for it; and with a certain justice Blake sees hypocrisy in the deity who pretends to weep for what he is about to destroy. According to Swedenborg, Moab is the state of

[140]

"natural goodness." It is the vineyards, the harvest fields, the gardens of innocence, of Eden, that are dedicated to this mournful vengeance of a moralistic and self-deluded tyrant. When Blake speaks of the demiurge watering the ground with tears, or speaks, in general, of weeping (Urizen often weeps), it is never with an implication of regeneration through penitence, but rather as the prelude to the destruction of the happy fields of Eden and the advent of the reign of the mortal god; for joy belongs to eternity. In *The Tyger* the tears of the fallen stars water the soil from which spring the forests of the night and their denizens; in the present poem the tears shed by Cruelty have the same result: they cause the tree of Mystery to grow.

The tree makes its final exit in the regeneration of man, in the last pages of *Jerusalem*. In this passage Blake's Cruelty, or Urizen, appears as the Patriarch Druid (a tree-priest also); he is the Specter Satan, the Accuser:

> *Where is the Covenant of Priam, the Moral Virtues of the Heathen?*
> *Where is the Tree of Good & Evil that rooted beneath the cruel heel*
> *Of Albion's Spectre, the Patriarch Druid? Where are all his Human*
> *Sacrifice*
> *For Sin in War & in the Druid Temples of the Accuser of Sin,*
> *beneath*
> *The Oak Groves of Albion that cover'd the whole earth beneath his*
> *Spectre?* [41]

This episode repeats, in a more explicit symbolic statement, the earlier consummation of the Great Mystery, in the "folding flames" of Paracelsian fires. Is the tree "rooted beneath the heel" of the Mortal God (an image Blake uses in several passages) intended to evoke the image of the cabalistic inverted Tree of manifested being, whose roots are in God and whose mysterious ramifications are experience "Beneath"?

## *Appendix I*

Boehme's tree was threefold, standing in the principles of wrath, of love, and of nature; and the tree of life stands in the eternal world where the tree of good and evil stands in the temporal. Blake seldom writes of the tree of life, but when he does it is in the tradition of Boehme. *The Marriage of Heaven and Hell* marks the strongest influence of Boehme on Blake; and it seems that Blake, in the account he gives there of the restoration of the tree of life, is reversing Boehme's account of man's fall through perceiving the temporal and not the eternal tree. The finite and corrupt will disappear, the infinite and holy will once again emerge: "For the cherub with his flaming sword is hereby commanded to leave his guard at tree of life; and when he does, the whole creation will be consumed and appear infinite and holy, whereas now it appears finite & corrupt."

This passage is a fair conclusion drawn from Boehme's account of the original nature of the tree that stood in both time and eternity. Adam, because he ate with his "outward mouth," perceived only the bodily tree; he must learn again to eat with his "inward mouth," well described by Blake as a cleansing of the doors of perception and an improvement of sensual enjoyment. In perceiving the outward tree only, Adam fell into the error of supposing that man has a body distinct from his soul. A reversal of that error will show man that there was, from the first, but the one tree. Sensual enjoyment, it is to be noted, is "improved" when it becomes spiritual.

Blake returned to this theme in 1810, in his notes on *The Vision of the Last Judgment;* and there is no essential change of belief:

> The Temple stands on the Mount of God; from it flows on each side the River of Life, on whose banks Grows the tree of Life, among whose branches temples & Pinnacles, tents & pavilions, Gardens & Groves, display Paradise with its Inhabitants walking up & down in Conversations concerning Mental Delights.[42]

> Here they are no longer talking of what is Good & Evil, or of what is Right or Wrong, & puzzling themselves in Satan's Labyrinth, But are Conversing with Eternal Realities as they Exist in the Human Imagination.[43]

The tree of life is the world of Imagination, whereas good and evil belong to the "error" of the tree of Creation. Satan's labyrinth is the forest of entangled nature created by the ramification of the tree of Mystery. Nature, imaginatively apprehended as the *magia*, the "wonders" of God, no longer has over man the destructive power possessed by nature and misconceived as "substance and principle."

## *Appendix II*

The often reiterated image of the tree of Mystery springing up *under the foot* of Cruelty is a strange one. In *The Book of Ahania* (1795) Cruelty is already called Urizen; and the event described is an exact repetition of that in *The Human Abstract*, with the addition of two details, a "rock" and a "book of iron."

> *For when Urizen shrunk away*
> *From Eternals, he sat on a rock*
> *Barren: a rock which himself*
> *From redounding fancies had petrified.*
> *Many tears fell on the rock,*
> *Many sparks of vegetation.*
> *Soon shot the pained root*
> *Of Mystery under his heel:*
>
> *It grew a thick tree: he wrote*
> *In silence his book of iron,*
> *Till the horrid plant bending its boughs*
> *Grew to roots when it felt the earth,*
> *And again sprung to many a tree.*
>
> .    .    .
>
> *The Tree still grows over the Void*
> *Enrooting itself all around,*
> *An endless labyrinth of woe!* [44]

The same insistence on the tree springing underneath the heel is repeated in the passage from *The Four Zoas* quoted on page 35, above.

Here the images are exactly repeated from the earlier poem – the watering tears, the seated figure with the tree shooting under his heel. The book of iron – the law – is so called no doubt because the Mosaic law belongs to the Iron Age of the world, the lowest of the four legendary periods of history. The rock is also the rock of the law; but it may have its visual origin in a passage of Swedenborg that seems to throw some light on the symbolism of the foot. Every part of the human body has, for Swedenborg, its spiritual correspondence; and there are infernal regions underfoot. In one of these, "The antediluvians who perished are in a certain hell under the heel of the left foot; there is a kind of cloudy rock with which they are covered, which bursts forth from their direful phantasies." [45] This, Blake is possibly echoing when he writes that Urizen sat on a rock "which himself / From redounding fancies had petrified."

There is another, perhaps even more relevant, description of a hell underfoot, this time relating the image to natural religion, and thus perhaps giving a logical justification for the springing up of the tree of Mystery from that region:

> Beneath the left foot . . . are such as have attributed all things to nature, yet still have confessed an ens of the universe from which come all things appertaining to nature; but exploration was made whether they believed in any ens of the universe or highest deity, as having created all things, but it was perceived . . . that what they believed in was as somewhat inanimate. . . . they did not acknowledge the creator of the universe, but nature. [46]

These Blake would have understood as the deists, responsible for "Natural Religion."

# *Appendix III*

Miss Piloo Nanavutty has pointed out [47] that the Indian creator, Brahma, is not exempt from the general denunciation of the demiurge included within the myth of Urizen. It is from Brahma that Urizen takes his spider's web, "the Net of Religion." The passage in question occurs in Priestley, and for the sake of completeness I quote it here:

> The production of all things from the substance of the Divine Being is thus represented by some of the Bramins. Comparing the first cause to a spider, they say the universe was produced by that insect spinning out of its own entrails and belly; so that it brought forth first the elements, and then the celestial globes, &c., and that things are to continue in this state till the end of ages, when this spider will draw into its body the several threads, which had issued from it, when all things will be destroyed, and the world no longer exist, but as in the belly of the spider.[48]

Blake attributes the web to Urizen:

> *. . . where ever he wander'd, in sorrows*
> *Upon the aged heavens,*
> *A cold shadow follow'd behind him*
> *Like a spider's web, moist, cold & dim,*
> *Drawing out from his sorrowing soul* [49]

The image of the web is repeated in *Vala:*

> *. . . wherever he travel'd a dire Web*
> *Follow'd behind him, as the Web of a Spider, dusky & cold,*
> *Shivering across from Vortex to Vortex, drawn out from his mantle*
> *of years* [50]

But Blake has apparently combined two notions, the cobweb of Brahma and the Swedenborgian Net of Religion.

141 Emblems of the psyche: Bryant's *Mythology*, vol. 2 (1774), plate x

# CHAPTER 18

# Governor of the Unwilling

There was never a time when the aged figure of Urizen did not inhabit Blake's imagination. He is already foreshadowed in the figure of Winter, who "hath rear'd his sceptre o'er the world"–a living presence who already steps beyond the static bounds of allegory:

> *Lo! now the direful monster, whose skin clings*
> *To his strong bones, strides o'er the groaning rocks:*
> *He withers all in silence, and his hand*
> *Unclothes the earth, and freezes up frail life.*[1]

There is something of Urizen in the aged tyrant Tiriel; he is the "old Man grey" who haunted Blake at Felpham in the form of a thistle,[2] and he is everywhere present in *Songs of Experience*. He is the "father white" whose "loving look / Like the holy book" blasts the innocent love of *A Little Girl Lost*. He is Starry Jealousy of *Earth's Answer*, Cruelty of *The Human Abstract*, and the priest who burns the Little Boy Lost on his altar. He is Aged Ignorance of *The Gates of Paradise*, and it is he who, unnamed, advances in pursuit of Oothoon's bright spirit, on the title page of *Visions of the Daughters of Albion*.

Urizen, as at first conceived, is Blake's Satan; later a distinction is made between Urizen, who is the Zoa of reason, and "Satan the Selfhood"; but since reason is the agent chiefly responsible for "error or creation," we know Urizen best in his fallen and satanic phase; as the Prince of Light and the husbandman, he is hardly realized.

Blake understood well that as God resides in man, so does Satan; man creates his own world by his manner of perceiving it. The world of the positivist philosophy is a hell created by fallen reason; it is the kingdom cut off from God, and in it the usurper passes for God. In the well-known cold hypocritical features of Urizen we see Satan appearing "like the most high,"

53

142 The poet pulling down the clay image of the false God with Tables of the Law: *Milton* (after 1804), plate 18

[142]  in the words of Isaiah. He is aged, white-bearded, partriarchal, sorrowful, "holy," and righteous; cloven-footed, he threatens Job with the heavy tables of the law. It is he whom the poet Milton, as "the inspired man," drags down like a clay image:[3]

> *Tho' thou art Worship'd by the Names Divine*
> *Of Jesus & Jehovah, thou art still*
> *The Son of Morn in weary Night's decline,*
> *The lost Traveller's Dream under the Hill.*[4]

The last line refers surely to Dante's hells, under the hill of purgatory, "Those deadly dreams that the soul falls into when it leaves Eden following

54

143 Satan with cloven hoof: engraving for *Job* (1826), plate 11

Compare the demiurge creating Adam [127].

the Serpent." Only Jesus the Imagination can perceive the limitations of the rational mind, and refuses to worship the God of this world:

> He had only to say that God was the devil, [143]
> And the devil was God, like a Christian Civil:
> Mild Christian regrets to the devil confess
> For affronting him thrice in the Wilderness [5]

*The First Book of Urizen* (he must have thought that others—many others perhaps—could be written) was evidently intended to form a part of that "Bible of Hell" promised to the world "whether they will or no," in *The Marriage of Heaven and Hell*. Whatever tributaries may before and after have enlarged the figure of Urizen, he is, in this book above all, Milton's God according to "the devil's account"; for Milton himself, as Blake believed, had fallen under the spell of the new science: "in Milton, the Father is Destiny, the Son a Ratio of the five senses, the Holy-ghost Vacuum." [6] His Father is "Newton's Pantocrator weaving the woof of Locke"; he is "destiny" because the laws of nature form an immutable mechanistic system, external to "the divine bosom," life, or mind. Thus the hell cut off from God is the universe as conceived by the scientific philosophy. Blake's purpose in writing *The First Book of Urizen* was to denounce and expose the fallacy of this pseudo-creation.

The name Urizen derives from οὐρίζειν, "to bound" or "limit," "with the cognate form Uranus, signifying Lord of the Firmament, or that first self-imposed set of bounds." [7] He is the *horizon*, and the overtone of "reason" that echoes in his name implies that reason is the setter of the bounds of the universe, for "Reason is the bound or outward circumference of energy." In Taylor's early writings, especially in his essays and notes to Proclus' *Commentaries on Euclid*, there is much said on the subject of the "bound" and the "infinite": the former is the generated, as the latter is the intellectual, order. As Saturn rules the intelligible "golden" world where the many are comprehended as one, so does Zeus the demiurge create the generated world. For Blake there is no "second creator," no demiurge, but in man's own mind; the divine creation, "truth, or eternity," is untouched by human "error, or creation," which is "burnt up the moment men cease to behold it." The name must have come to Blake out of his damning reflections on Milton's "Almighty Maker," and was perhaps suggested by the grand opening passage of the account of the Creation, illustrated in his composition *The Ancient of Days*, engraved in 1794, in the same year as *The Book of Urizen:*

[144]              . . . *in his hand*
                   *He took the golden Compasses, prepar'd*
                   *In Gods Eternal store, to circumscribe*
                   *This Universe, and all created things:*
                   *One foot he center'd, and the other turn'd*
                   *Round through the vast profunditie obscure,*
                   *And said, thus farr extend, thus farr thy bounds,*
                   *This be thy just Circumference, O World.*[8]

This creator with his golden compasses becomes Urizen:

144 The Ancient of Days: color print (1794)

The Creator (of the temporal world) is leaning out of the sphere of eternity or the soul in order to measure out in "the void" a universe external to mind or intellect. Cf. [158, 174].

> *He formed golden compasses,*
> *And began to explore the Abyss;*
> *And he planted a garden of fruits.*[9]

We know what kind of fruits grew in that garden planted for man: the tree of Eden is the "poison tree."

The Ancient of Days leans out from a sphere. Plato described the soul as a sphere, and in his depiction of Plato, in the Dante illustrations and elsewhere, Blake so represents it; this phase is eternity. From the *plenum* the demiurge leans out into a void—"the void outside existence" of physical space.

In *The Book of Urizen* Orc does not appear; but the "Eternals" are, like Orc, the fiery energies of "hell," condemned by the Prince of this world to live in chains. Like Milton, Blake claims inspiration for his poem; but his inspirers are the energies, the vanquished:

> *Eternals! I hear your call gladly.*
> *Dictate swift winged words & fear not*
> *To unfold your dark visions of torment.*[10]

Blake makes it clear in the first line—one may say in the first word—that he is writing an answer to Milton: the story to be told is not "*Of* man's first disobedience" but "*Of*" Urizen's tyranny:

> *Of the primeval Priest's assum'd power,*
> *When Eternals spurn'd back his religion*
> *And gave him a place in the north,*
> *Obscure, shadowy, void, solitary.*[11]

These lines tell us by a combination of allusions, which Blake certainly intended us to identify, both that he is answering Milton and whom he takes Milton's God to be. The usurper is given "a place in the north." Here we find Blake involving us in the confusion of his own eclecticism; for the "north" here has nothing to do with Porphyry's northern gate, the symbolism of Los-Urthona, and the gate of generation. In "eternity" Urthona's place is the north; but Urizen's "eternal" place is "in the South." He is placed in the north because he is the fallen Lucifer, "fallen, fallen light." The key to his location and to the history of Urizen that is to follow is to be found in Isaiah 14:12–17.

How art thou fallen from heaven, O Lucifer, son of the morning!

how art thou cut down to the ground, which didst weaken the nations!

For thou hast said in thine heart, I will ascend into heaven, I will exalt my throne above the stars of God: I will sit also upon the mount of the congregation, in the sides of the north:

. . . I will be like the most High.

Yet thou shalt be brought down to hell, to the sides of the pit.

They that see thee shall narrowly look upon thee, and consider thee, saying, Is this the man that made the earth to tremble . . .

That made the world as a wilderness, and destroyed the cities thereof; that opened not the house of his prisoners?

This is Urizen's nature (he is a travesty of God, "like" the most High) and his story.

It is by constant double allusion, to the story of Lucifer and to Milton, that Blake builds up his theme. *The Book of Urizen* is a satirical work. If we read as mere "influence" the Miltonic echoes that are everywhere apparent, Blake must seem the crudest of imitators. The "battles dire," "combustion, blast, vapour and cloud," "ocean of voidness unfathomable," the "terrible crash" as "Eternity roll'd wide apart" can seem nothing less than disastrous, so long as we fail to notice that the poem is written in a style of burlesque, in the high spirits of the *Marriage* with its *Memorable Fancies*. What these are to Swedenborg, this poem is to Milton—satire containing a serious argument and able to shift its mood to a graver and more direct speech.

Milton's symbolic landscape had already provided Blake with many of the points of allusion in the *Marriage*, where his own quarrel with Milton's God is first formulated. A Swedenborgian "angel" of Reason threatens the poet with destruction in the nether abyss of hell, where the Leviathan of revolution advances through the smoke of burning cities, "with all the fury of a spiritual existence." This angel is shown, in turn, the eternal lot of Reason as the poet's imagination conceives it; and the symbolic landscape is Miltonic. Blake, catching the angel in his arms,

. . . flew westerly thro' the night, till we were elevated above the earth's shadow; then I flung myself with him directly into the body of the sun; here I clothed myself in white, & taking in my hand Swedenborg's volumes, sunk from the glorious clime, and passed all the planets till we came to saturn: here I stay'd to rest, & then leap'd into the void between saturn & the fixed stars. "Here," said I, "is your lot, in this space—if space it may be call'd." [12]

This is, in reverse, the course of Milton's Satan as he approached the earth from outside the sphere of the fixed stars. Blake soars into the region "elevated above Newton's shadow" as Satan approached the sun,

> *So high above the circling Canopie*
> *Of Nights extended shade.*[13]

He then continues his flight to the bounds of the universe, to the cheerless void between the orbit of Saturn, the outermost planet, and the "first convex" of the fixed stars of the Ptolemaic universe. The space, "if space it may be call'd," is an accurate enough description of Milton's

> *Illimitable Ocean without bound,*
> *Without dimension, where length, breadth, and highth,*
> *And time and place are lost. . . .*[14]

Blake is never merely fanciful, and does not waste words: his allusion, here as elsewhere, is precise; for in that region are found "All things transitory and vain" and especially the erroneous opinions of the religious:

> *. . . the fruits*
> *Of painful Superstition and blind Zeal* [15]

We recognize Blake's landscape in Milton's regions consigned to wearers of "cowls, hoods and habits," and all the trappings of religious error:

> *Embryos, and Idiots, Eremits and Friers*
> *White, Black and Grey, with all thir trumperie.*[16]

The aptness of this relation becomes at once apparent when we have recognized where and in what company Blake has placed his rejected master:

> *. . . all these upwhirld aloft*
> *Fly o're the backside of the World farr off*
> *Into a* Limbo *large and broad, since calld*
> *The Paradise of Fools, to few unknown.*[17]

This, when we grasp Blake's allusion, is a very shrewd dig indeed at Swedenborg, himself a great space-traveler to other planets in the solar system. Milton's Satan, leaping into that space, ascends into the sun, where he assumes the disguise of an angel. Blake, traveling in reverse direction, also assumes angelic disguise in the body of the sun ("here I clothed myself in white") but with contrary results, since the assumption of angelhood (in the Swedenborgian sense) and the taking up of Swedenborg's heavy volumes only serve to weigh him down, and the Angel of Reason with him, into the fool's paradise. But if Swedenborg was the immediate butt of Blake's satire, *The Book of Urizen* carries the attack beyond Swedenborg to Milton himself.

For Urizen's "enormous labours" of creation, described in the first chapter, were never necessary at all; the building of Satan's kingdom "out of mind or thought" is the cosmic crime; the universe of science is "in fallacy": "Many suppose that before the Creation All was Solitude & Chaos. This is the most pernicious Idea that can enter the Mind, as it . . . Limits All Existence to Creation and to Chaos, To the Time & Space fixed by the Corporeal Vegetative Eye." [18]

Before Urizen began his labors there was no finite world, only "Eternity." There all creatures were "Eternals," who, like Los and Enitharmon, possessed not finite but "infinite senses"; the Newtonian universe had no existence "in the beginning":

> *Earth was not: nor globes of attraction;*
> *The will of the Immortal expanded*
> *Or contracted his all flexible senses;*
> *Death was not, but eternal life sprung.*[19]

Urizen labors to create the natural universe and to compel the Eternals to look "with not through" their senses; and they become "caverned men":

> *All the myriads of Eternity,*
> *All the wisdom & joy of life*
> *Roll like a sea around him,*
> *Except what his little orbs*
> *Of sight by degrees unfold.*
>
> *And now his eternal life*
> *Like a dream was obliterated.*[20]

Enclosed within their senses they become deformities, "serpent-forms," since the serpent is the earthborn eater of dust:

> *Till the shrunken eyes, clouded over,*
> *Discern'd not the woven hipocrisy;*

*But the streaky slime in their heavens,*
*Brought together by narrowing perceptions,*
*Appear'd transparent air; for their eyes*
*Grew small like the eyes of a man,*
*And in reptile forms shrinking together,*
*Of seven feet stature they remain'd.*[21]

In the opening passages of the poem we see Urizen creating the scientific abstraction of space-time, and measuring its bounds:

*Lo, a shadow of horror is risen*
*In Eternity! Unknown, unprolific,*
*Self-clos'd, all-repelling: what Demon*
*Hath form'd this abominable void,*
*This soul-shudd'ring vacuum? Some said*
*"It is Urizen." But unknown, abstracted,*
*Brooding, secret, the dark power hid.*

*Times on times he divided & measur'd*
*Space by space in his ninefold darkness* [22]

Urizen's "dark power" points to Milton's Messiah, "gloomie as night," and "That solitary one in Immensity," to Milton's Father, whose attributes, Blake thought, were those of the quantitative philosophy of Galileo's new science:

*. . . Omnipotent,*
*Immutable, Immortal, Infinite,*
*Eternal King: thee Author of all being,*
*Fountain of Light, thy self invisible*
*Amidst the glorious brightness where thou sit'st . .*
*Thron'd inaccessible. . . .*[23]

This is "Nobodaddy," to whom Blake addresses the question:

*Why art thou silent & invisible,*
*Father of Jealousy?*
*Why dost thou hide thyself in clouds*
*From every searching Eye?*

*Why darkness & obscurity*
*In all thy words & laws,*

> *That none dare eat the fruit but from*
> *The wily serpents jaws?*
> *Or is it because Secresy gains females' loud applause?* [24]

Urizen is a dark negative printed in reverse from Milton's inaccessible Godhead. He speaks from "the depths of dark solitude, From The eternal abode in my holiness, Hidden, set apart." [25]

He is:

> *A self-contemplating shadow,*
> *In enormous labours occupied.*
>
> .    .    .
>
> *Age on ages he lay, clos'd, unknown,*
> *Brooding shut in the deep; all avoid*
> *The petrific, abominable chaos.*[26]

The "Eternal King" of Milton's vision Blake saw to be a god of mere Newtonian duration—"ages on ages"; for the heavens in which he sits are "astronomical" and "telescopic." [27] Urizen is "the Almighty Power" who defeated the fallen angels,

> *Hurld headlong flaming from th' Ethereal Skie*
> *With hideous ruine and combustion down*
> *To bottomless perdition, there to dwell*
> *In Adamantine Chains and penal Fire,*
> *Who durst defie th' Omnipotent to Arms.*[28]

The underlying Miltonic pattern is clear when presently Urizen emerges in battle array:

> *. . . his ten thousands of thunders,*
> *Rang'd in gloom'd array, stretch out across*
> *The dread world; & the rolling of wheels,*
> *As of swelling seas, sound in his clouds.*[29]

This is a simple abridgment of Milton's description of the Messiah in his chariot:

> *. . . his fierce Chariot rowl'd, as with the sound*
> *Of torrent Floods, or of a numerous Host.*
> *Hee on his impious foes right onward drove,*
> *Gloomie as Night; under his burning Wheeles*
> *The stedfast Empyrean shook throughout,*

145 Urizen with tables and book of
the law beneath the enrooted tree of
nature: title page of *Urizen* (1794)

> . . . *Full soon*
> *Among them he arriv'd; in his right hand*
> *Grasping ten Thousand Thunders, which he sent*
> *Before him, such as in thir Souls infix'd*
> *Plagues. . . .*[30]

[145]      The plates add meaning to the text. On the title page we see Urizen,
with his two stone tables of the law like tombstones. There follow illustrations of "eternal" life—a woman teaching an infant soul to fly; an "eternal"
rejoicing in the "fires" of energy. In contrast there comes a sorrowful figure
on the oozy sea-floor of hyle—that same sea-floor on which Blake's Newton

sits drawing his diagrams of the "telescopic heavens." As the conditions of creation are imposed, there follow worse states: we see the Eternals enwrapped by serpents, hanging suspended in the "Abyss," and on later pages, peering down in fear and horror into "the endless Abyss of space." The creator of Adam, who is "the natural man, and not the soul or imagination," is Urizen. The "worm of sixty winters" [31] is man in serpent form, earthbound.

[146; 1, 17]

Urizen's "petrific, abominable chaos," his "space undivided by existence," is Milton's

> . . . *hoarie deep, a dark*
> *Illimitable Ocean without bound. . .*[32]

In this chaos Milton describes monstrous shapes, where

> . . . *Nature breeds,*
> *Perverse, all monstrous, all prodigious things,*
> *Abominable, inutterable, and worse*
> *Than Fables yet have feign'd, or fear conceiv'd,*
> Gorgons, *and* Hydra's, *and* Chimera's dire.[33]

We recognize the Miltonic echoes in Blake's

146 Immortals enwrapped by serpents, falling into mortality: *Urizen* (1794), plate 7, detail
Cf. above, [127].

147 The Four Elements: *Urizen*
(1794), plate 24

*For he strove in battles dire,*
*In unseen conflictions with shapes*
*Bred from his forsaken wilderness*
*Of beast, bird, fish, serpent & element,*
*Combustion, blast, vapour and cloud.*[34]

    The "shapes" are monstrous because they are not "Eternals" but
"elementals." All creatures are, so Blake believed, given form by the "influx"
of spirit, and to conceive them otherwise is to people the world with an "army
of horrors." Again the accompanying designs leave us in no doubt of Blake's
meaning: Plate 25 shows human-faced serpent-chimeras writhing in misery,

and Plate 24, the Four Elements, the "sons" of Urizen materializing in tortured protest: [147]

> . . . *First Thiriel appear'd,*
> *Astonish'd at his own existence,*
> *Like a man from a cloud born; & Utha,*
> *From the waters emerging, laments:*
> *Grodna rent the deep earth, howling*
> *Amaz'd; his heavens immense cracks*
> *Like the ground parch'd with heat, then Fuzon*
> *Flam'd out, first begotten, last born;* [35]

This account of Urizen's deformities is the prototype of similar accounts in *The Four Zoas* of endless warfare between creator and created; for the spirit of life cannot endure his laws, based not on reality but on a mistaken theory:

> . . . *he saw*
> *That no flesh nor spirit could keep*
> *His iron laws one moment.*[36]

"All the seven deadly sins of the soul" are "fallen fiends of heavenly birth" become violent through the tyranny of Urizen, who has dragged them down into the "hell" of his world of quantity.[37]

Urizen's triumph is a victory won over the holy essence of life. Of this victory he boasts that he has mastered "the fire"; his is the hand that dared to "sieze the fire" of the first principle of the divine essence; and he has bound the wind of the spirit, that "bloweth where it listeth":

> *First I fought with the fire, consum'd*
> *Inwards into a deep world within:*
> *A void immense, wild, dark & deep,*
> *Where nothing was: Nature's wide womb;*
> *And self balanc'd, stretch'd o'er the void,*
> *I alone, even I! the winds merciless*
> *Bound . . .*[38]

Here Blake implies that Milton's "earth self-balanc'd on its center hung" is one of Newton's "globes of attraction." To call the earth "self-balanc'd" is contrary to tradition, which sees the phenomenal world as suspended upon a "golden chain" of prior causes. So Plato taught, so Swedenborg's "influx" implies, so the Hermetic doctrine of emanation and the Orphic theogony of the generations of the gods all variously state, and above all, for Blake, so "Jesus the Imagination" reveals.

In Urizen's "I alone, even I!" echoes his boast that

> *Here alone I, in books form'd of metals,*
> *Have written the secrets of wisdom* [39]

And in the egoistic form of all his utterances, "*my* holiness" and "*my* stern counsels," Blake is implicitly criticizing Milton's Messiah:

> *Therefore to mee thir doom he hath assign'd;*
> *That they may have thir wish, to trie with mee*
> *In Battel which the stronger proves, they all,*
> *Or I alone against them. . . .*[40]

This is the voice of "Satan the Selfhood"—no longer the law of life, "every thing that lives is Holy," but "One Law for the Lion & Ox,"

> *Laws of peace, of love, of unity,*
> *Of pity, compassion, forgiveness*

These are "the selfish virtues of the natural heart," for they are external and imposed by "natural law":

> *One command, one joy, one desire,*
> *One curse, one weight, one measure,*
> *One King, one God, one Law.*[41]

With this is contrasted the law of life,

> *. . . yet are their habitations*
> *And their pursuits as different as their forms and as their joys.*[42]

The Eternals, whose law is energy, muster their forces in rebellion:

> *. . . Rage siez'd the strong,*

> *Rage, fury, intense indignation,*
> *In cataracts of fire, blood, & gall,*
> *In whirlwinds of sulphurous smoke,*
> *And enormous forms of energy,*
> *All the seven deadly sins of the soul* [43]
> *In living creations appear'd,*
> *In the flames of eternal fury.*[44]

These are Milton's hosts of hell, who presently are cast out of "Heav'n" through the breached wall:

> *Sund'ring, dark'ning, thund'ring,*
> *Rent away with a terrible crash,*
> *Eternity roll'd wide apart,*
> *Wide asunder rolling;*
> *Mountainous all around*
> *Departing, departing, departing* [45]

So Milton's Messiah

> *Drove them before him Thunder-struck, pursu'd*
> *With terrors and with furies to the bounds*
> *And Chrystal wall of Heav'n, which op'ning wide,*
> *Rowld inward, and a spacious Gap disclos'd*
> *Into the wastful Deep*
>
> .    .    .
>
> *Hell heard th' unsufferable noise, Hell saw*
> *Heav'n ruining from Heav'n. . . .* [46]

At such cost the energies of life are overcome.

The rewriting of Milton's story of the Fall according to the devil's account continues in *Vala* throughout all the passages that concern Urizen. The original poem opened [47] with the present "Night the Second," the fall of the Eternal Man into "deadly sleep," and the usurpation of Urizen:

> *. . . Man calld Urizen & said: "Behold these sick'ning Spheres,*
>
> .    .    .
>
> *Take thou possession! take this Scepter! go forth in my might,*
> *For I am weary & must sleep in the dark sleep of Death."* [48]

The sickening spheres are Newton's astronomical worlds; and in this account the usurpation of Urizen consists in the elevation of the phenomena to a status they do not properly possess. Urizen's function is that of "saving" (that is, accounting for) "the appearances." [49] This, philosophers of antiquity and the Middle Ages regarded as the proper function of scientific thought; and the formulae found to account for the phenomena were so regarded, and not, as in the modern world, as real laws governing substantially existent entities. "Accident they formed into Substance and Principle by the cruelties of Demonstration."

The phenomena, whose ordering is Urizen's proper task, have their origin in man's mind:

> *Tho' in the Brain of Man we live & in his circling Nerves,*
> *Tho' this bright world of all our joy is in the Human Brain*
> *Where Urizen & all his Hosts hang their immortal lamps* [50]

When Urizen proclaims "Now I am God from Eternity to Eternity," [51] he is usurping a place in the divine hierarchy that in reality belongs to "Jesus the Imagination," and is attributing to the phenomena substantial existence that belongs to the eternal forms of which they are only shadows; for "There Exist in that Eternal World the Permanent Realities of Every Thing which we see reflected in this Vegetable Glass of Nature." [52] A passage added in *The Four Zoas* to Urizen's blasphemous claim makes this point clear. To Los he says:

> *Art thou a visionary of Jesus, the soft delusion of Eternity?*
> *Lo I am God, the terrible destroyer, & not the Saviour.*
>
> .     .     .
>
> *The Spectre is the Man. The rest is only delusion & fancy.*[53]

The positivist philosophy has never been more succinctly stated.

Blake's account of Urizen's creation of the Newtonian solar system takes up the theme of the Bible of Hell, and describes the building of a heaven by the Messiah of Reason with "what he stole from the Abyss." None among the eighteenth-century poets whose fancy, like Young's, was fired by Newton's thought ever gave so splendid an imaginative expression to the scientific conception of the astronomical heavens as did Blake in his "devil's account."

Saurat [54] suggests that Blake was of Urizen's party without knowing it; but this is to underrate the thoroughness of his thought. Certainly he appreciated the magnificence of the natural creation and of its laws; but in the unfallen state Urizen understands that the earths, Newton's "self-balanced" globes, are not rolling through voidness, but upheld by anterior spiritual causes:

> *On clouds the Sons of Urizen beheld Heaven walled round;*
> *They weigh'd & ordered all, & Urizen comforted saw*
> *The wondrous work flow forth like visible out of the invisible;*

> *Thus were the stars of heaven created like a golden chain*
> *To bind the Body of Man to heaven from falling into the Abyss.*
> *Each took his station & his course began with songs and joy* [55]

Blake's stars are here the biblical morning stars that "sang together" when "the sons of God shouted for joy." "Songs and joy" occurs in the *Vala* manuscript, to be changed in *The Four Zoas* to "sorrow & care." In the earlier picture Blake is evoking the astronomic heavens upheld by "influx," "like visible out of the invisible." Urizen delights in the appearances and regulates them without forgetting their origin.

Milton's Pandemonium, which

> *Anon out of the earth a Fabrick huge*
> *Rose like an Exhalation, with the sound*
> *Of Dulcet Symphonies and voices sweet,*
> *Built like a Temple, where* Pilasters *round*
> *Were set, and Doric pillars overlaid*
> *With Golden Architrave* [56]

is the model of Urizen's beautiful golden building (with its pillars and "Exhalations" and Miltonic "many a . . .") , cut off from heaven, like Pandemonium, and a place of eternal lamentation:

> *But infinitely beautiful the wondrous work arose*
> *In sorrow & care, a Golden World whose porches round the heavens*
> *And pillar'd halls & rooms reciev'd the eternal wandering stars.*
> *A wondrous golden Building, many a window, many a door.*
> *And many a division let in & out into the vast unknown.*
> *Circled in infinite orb immoveable, within its walls & cielings*
> *The heavens were clos'd, and spirits mourn'd their bondage night*
>               *& day,*
>
> *Sorrowing went the Planters forth to plant, the Sowers forth to sow;*
> *They dug the channels for the rivers, & they pour'd abroad*
> *The seas & lakes; they rear'd the mountains & the rocks & hills*
> *On broad pavilions, on pillar'd roofs & porches & high towers,*
> *In beauteous order; thence arose soft clouds & exhalations*
> *Wandering even to the sunny orbs of light & heat.* [57]

Urizen's superb achievement dazzles with its splendor; but we are not permitted to forget that it is built in the void, and that it is a prison for the mourning spirits. Urizen knows this, even as he builds it:

> *Repining he contemplated the past in his bright sphere,*
> *Terrified with his heart & spirit at the visions of futurity*
> *That his dread fancy form'd before him in the unform'd void.*[58]

For this building is erected in the nonentity of duration and extension, not in the eternal world of imagination:

> *Terrific Urizen strode above in fear & pale dismay.*
> *He saw the indefinite space beneath & his soul shrunk with horror,*
> *His feet upon the verge of Non Existence; his voice went forth:*
>
> *Luvah & Vala trembling & shrinking beheld the great Work master*
> *And heard his Word: "Divide, ye bands, influence by influence.*
> *Build we a Bower for heaven's darling in the grizly deep."* [59]

We are left in no doubt about the illusory and fallen nature of this glorious universe. It is built in the "grizly deep" of Newtonian space-time by the "workmaster," as Blake translated the word "demiurge."

In *Paradise Lost* it is Satan who laments in "this dark opprobrious Den of shame":

> *Is this the Region, this the Soil, the Clime*
>
> .    .    .
>
> *That we must change for Heav'n, this mournful gloom*
> *For that celestial light?* [60]

Now it is Urizen who echoes Milton's "O how unlike the place from whence they fell":

> *Ah! how shall Urizen the King submit to this dark mansion?*
> *Ah! how is this! Once on the heights I stretch'd my throne sublime.*[61]

Milton's Satan laments the change in those who have fallen with him:

> *. . . But O how fall'n! how chang'd*
> *From him, who in the happy Realms of Light*
> *Cloth'd with transcendent brightness didst out-shine*
> *Myriads though bright.*[62]

Urizen laments the change in Luvah, "faded like a flower":

*Thy children smote their fiery wings, crown'd with the gold of*
                                                    *heaven.*

*Thy pure feet step'd on the steps divine, too pure for other feet,*
*And thy fair locks shadow'd thine eyes from the divine effulgence,*
*Then thou didst keep with Strong Urthona the living gates of*
                                                    *heaven,*
*But now thou art bow'd down with him, even to the gates of hell* [63]

and admits his responsibility for the fall of all the rebel "starry ones" who
followed him.

But unlike Milton's Satan—or indeed, any other Christian account of
the evil principle—Urizen repents. He admits, in his contrition, that his
world is an image or reflection of the world of Imagination, the Son or
Logos:

*O Fool! could I forget the light that filled my bright spheres*
*Was a reflection of his face who call'd me from the deep!* [64]

Urizen's late repentance restores due order to the hierarchies.


The place of the Creator of the Bible is also said to be the north. In the Book
of Job it is said that "He stretcheth out the north over the empty place, and
hangeth the earth upon nothing." [65] From the Bible, therefore, Blake might
have formed the frost-bound landscape of Urizen's "cold horrors silent":

*In his hills of stor'd snows, in his mountains*
*Of hail & ice . . .* [66]

But it is not possible to see how from the Bible alone he could have
elaborated Urizen's strange attribute of creation through the solidifying
action of cold. He creates "a petrific abominable chaos," "a solid without    [148]
fluctuation"; in *Milton* the north is called a place of "solid unfathomable
without end."

Boehme describes how, with the fall of Satan, the seven qualifying
spirits also fell, to become the seven "murderers" of man, and the contractive, constrictive property of the first spirit (Saturn) is likened to freezing:
"The astrigent Quality is a very horrible, tart, hard, dark, and cold Attraction or Drawing together, like *Winter*, when there is a fierce, bitter, cold
Frost, When water is frozen into Ice." [67] This spirit draws together "its

whole Region, Circuit, or Circumference," keeping it fast, as a "stern severe Lord." Swedenborg also sees solidification and fixity as an attribute of objects in the natural world: "the lowest Substances of Nature which constitute Earths are dead, and are not mutable and various according to the State of the Affections and Thoughts, as in the spiritual World, but immutable and fixed." [68] Urizen creates the "Mundane Shell" by the Swedenborgian process of "Petrifying all the Human Imagination into rock & solid."

It is impossible to read the accounts of the Elohim Ruach in Fludd's *Mosaicall Philosophy* and not be struck by the many resemblances of this figure to Blake's Urizen. In Fludd we find richly personified those cabalistic abstractions that in Agrippa remain mere tabulations and diagrams, the divine names and numerations.

Fludd's winds, clouds, rivers, lightnings, and snows are all, like Blake's "cloud, meteor and star," animated with spiritual agencies comparable in energy and grandeur with the Zoas: "not only the Clouds, the Thunder, and Lightnings, are moved by the windy ministers or Angels of the Lord; but also that Divinity it self, being compassed about with dark clowds in the middle region of the aire, is carried upon the airy Cherubin, and useth the wings of the winds as organs to move on." [69] For Blake the problem was metaphysical; but for Fludd the focus of interest was on effects rather than causes. His preoccupation was with the lodestone and its powers of attraction toward a center—speculations which ally him to Newton. Thus, looking to the Bible for his authority, he speculates upon the manner in which the god who "moved upon the face of the water"—the hyle or *prima materia*—brought into being a world of solid; and he postulates the constrictive, contractive action of cold:

> God in his hidden or latent property, doth by his essentiall action of cold, contract unto the center those things, which were before dilated towards the circumference. Secondly, that the property of cold is attributed or ascribed unto God, in his northern action, and therefore it is said, *Who is able to resist his cold?* For which reason it is evident, that it is an essential vertue in the divine puissance. Thirdly, That it must be the act of unity in his dark, hidden, and privative property. . . . I conclude therefore, that cold is the essential act of the divine puissance, or eternall sapience, shrowding it self in its mantle of darkness . . . in that it draweth from the circumference unto

the center, and therefore is the occasion of congregating of things, as well hetero- as homogeniall, and by consequence, the onely essentiall agent or efficient cause of inspissation, contraction, constriction, fixation, immobility, ponderosity, rest, obteneration or darkness, of mortification, privation, stupefaction, and such like.[70]

The power that Fludd calls here "the eternall sapience" (the rational mind, in contrast with one eternal wisdom) is the Elohim Ruach:

> By vertue of this *ELOHIM* Ruach, the dry land did appear out of the waters, as *Moses* telleth us . . . The spirits of the northern wind wax vigorous, and contract by congelation the catholick element of the aire, insomuch that by sucking together the dispersed element of air, they contract it into the solid and dense mass of snow, frost, hail, & ice. Whereby we may learn, that the earth was a thin water first, but by the breath of *ELOHIM* it was turned into an earthly substance by contraction.[71]

The Elohim Ruach (the Elohim are the creators) is the third of the ten divine names or numerations in the cabalistic Tree of God, and corresponds to Binah. Traditionally, the planet Saturn agrees with this potency, as being the planet of cold and constriction.[72] Each of these ten *Sefiroth* represents some aspect or potency of the Divine Being, which circulates as the life of all the tree. The ten are divided into three higher and seven lower

148 "The petrific abominable chaos": *Urizen* (1794), plate 12, detail

Sefiroth, corresponding respectively to the Platonic trinity of the supreme deity, the Logos, and the "Workman," and to the seven planetary spirits. The highest is Kether, "the Crown"; Hochmah, the second numeration, is Sophia, the divine wisdom; and the third, Binah, the Elohim Ruach, is *sapientia*, or reason. In Binah there is a condensation of force into form. The lower seven are subject to Binah, as in other systems the "starry ones" or "fountain spirits" are subject to the demiurge. The mysticism of the cabala envisages, moreover, both a fall, within the divine hierarchy, of the "seven," and also elements within the deity that may be called "evil."

There are astonishing images of Urizen creating the world by a sudden freezing of the waters:

> . . . *strong I repell'd*
> *The vast waves, & arose on the waters*
> *A wide world of solid obstruction.*[73]

And again, in *Vala*, he is called by Tharmas "Cold Demon," for he freezes all before him:[74]

> . . . *froze to solid were his waves,*
> *Silent in ridges he beheld them stand round Urizen,*
> *A dreary waste of solid waters . . .*
>
> .     .     .
>
> . . . *Silent on the ridgy waves he took*
> *His gloomy way . . .*[75]

Blake combines Fludd's strange gloss upon the Mosaic creation with the Platonic "lapse of the Soul" into the "sleep" of generation—more ingeniously than happily—when he writes:

> . . . *Urizen slept in a stoned stupor in the nether Abyss,*
> *A dreamful, horrible state in tossings on his icy bed*
> *Freezing to solid all beneath . . .*[76]

Urizen's whiteness is a diabolical travesty of the white garment and beard of the traditional figure of God; for it is the satanic whiteness of death and the north:

> . . . *a white woof cover'd his cold limbs from head to feet,*
> *Hair white as snow cover'd him in flaky locks terrific*
> *Overspreading his limbs. . . .*[77]

Orc, addressing Urizen, describes the ice, snowy wind, and hail that accompany him; he asks "Art thou the cold attractive power that holds me in this chain?" Orc says:

> *Yet my fierce fires are better than thy snows. Shudd'ring thou*
> *sittest.*
> *Thou art not chain'd. Why shouldst thou sit, cold grovelling*
> *demon of woe,*
> *In tortures of dire coldness? now a Lake of waters deep*
> *Sweeps over thee freezing to solid; still thou sits't clos'd up*
> *In that transparent rock as if in joy of thy bright prison,*
> *Till, overburden'd with its own weight drawn out thro' immensity,*
> *With a crash breaking across, the horrible mass comes down*
> *Thund'ring, & hail & frozen iron hail'd from the Element*
> *Rends thy white hair; yet thou dost, fix'd obdurate brooding, sit*
> *Writing thy books. Anon a cloud, fill'd with a waste of snows*
> *Covers thee, still obdurate, still resolv'd & writing still;*
> *Tho' rocks roll o'er thee, tho' floods pour, tho' winds black as the sea*
> *Cut thee in gashes, tho' the blood pours down around thy ankles,*
> *Freezing thy feet to the hard rock, still thy pen obdurate*
> *Traces the wonders of Futurity . . .*[78]

The tree of Mystery grows about Urizen "for a shelter from the tempests of Void and Solid" created by his own restrictive operations.

The Elohim creates not only "the world of rocky destiny" from the generative waters by contraction, but also all creatures, as Fludd affirms. He is the cause "in all the separating creation and formation, not onely of the simple heavens and elements, but also of the creatures composed of them, both in heaven and in earth . . . when the elements were compacted by congelation, into the compound creatures of the sea and land; for all this was the work of ELOHIM." [79]

Blake seems to be following Fludd literally, and attempts to imagine the creation of animals by "hardening":

> *. . . the Earth & all the Abysses feel his fury*
> *When as the snow covers the mountains, oft petrific hardness*
> *Covers the deeps, at his vast fury moving in his rock,*
> *Hardens the Lion & the Bear; trembling in the solid mountain*
> *They view the light & wonder; crying out in terrible existence,*
> *Up bound the wild stag & the horse . . .*[80]

A similar image occurs in *Milton:*

*How are the Beasts & Birds & Fishes & Plants & Minerals*
*Here fix'd into a frozen bulk subject to decay & death?*
*Those Visions of Human Life & Shadows of Wisdom & Knowledge*
*Are here frozen to unexpansive deadly destroying terrors.*[81]

In *Jerusalem* this concept is retained:

*To Create the lion & wolf, the bear, the tyger & ounce,*
*To Create the wooly lamb & downy fowl & scaly serpent,*
*The summer & winter, day & night, the sun & moon & stars,*
*The tree, the plant, the flower, the rock, the stone, the metal*
*Of Vegetative Nature by their hard restricting condensations.*

> .     .     .

*Where Luvah's World of Opakeness grew to a period, It*
*Became a Limit, a Rocky hardness without form & void,*
*Accumulating without end . . .*[82]

The phrases applied respectively to Satan (the selfhood) and to Adam (the natural man), "limit of opacity" and "limit of contraction," also seem to come from Fludd. The alternate action of the north and south winds determines expansion and contraction: "in blowing and breathing from the North, the same thin and rarified aire is made thick, dense, and visible, which was through rarifaction made invisible, and that which by dissipating of parts was made transparent light and diaphan, is now by the Northern properties contractive vertue, reduced into an opake or dark substance, and no way perspicuous." [83]

Opacity and contraction are the work of the Elohim; the world of Hochmah (the Logos or Jesus, according to the Christian cabalists) is rare and "diaphan"—translucent, as Blake says. Blake is therefore entirely in harmony with the tradition of the Christian cabalists in making his Jesus the Imagination the setter of the limits to opacity and contraction:

*The Saviour mild & gentle bent over the corse of Death,*
*Saying, "If ye will Believe, your Brother shall rise again."*
*And first he found the Limit of Opacity, & nam'd it Satan,*

> .     .     .

*And next he found the Limit of Contraction, & nam'd it Adam.*[84]

The terms "opacity" and "contraction" constantly recur in Fludd. The

Elohim pours out "beams of attraction or contraction by the port of *Binah* or *Prudentia*":

> . . . the fountain of this attractive and contractive property, is in the divine Attribute ELOHIM, which . . . is the head of the northern property, namely, of cold, drought, opacity, congelation, incrassation, and rest, which is caused in the center, because it is the *terminus ad quem, the point unto the which the contraction or attraction is chiefly made, beyond the which, there can be no further penetration* . . . for it is at that centrall butt that the property of ELOHIM doth aime, and the Divinity which dwelleth in the earth's center, is the divine essence under the name and property of ELOHIM.[85]

Perhaps Blake's emphatic condemnation of "the selfish centre" alludes to the Elohim that "dwelleth in the earth's center," operating his constrictive power. The center of Satan's world, the "white dot," is the point, the most finite of finite things, the *terminus ad quem* of the contractive power. This is the antithesis of the "eternal centre" or punctum, whose powers are infinite.[86] Blake had the more reason to welcome Fludd's conception of constriction and contraction because it must have seemed to him that this law governed Newton's "globes of attraction." With satisfaction he could point to the theory of gravitation as the work of the Elohim. He had probably read Newton's own definition of the motive force as "an endeavor and propensity of the whole towards a centre," and of "the Accelerative force to the Place of the body, as a certain power or energy diffused from the centre to all places around to move the bodies that are in them: and the Absolute force to the Centre, as indued with some cause . . . whether that cause is some central body, (such as is the Loadstone, in the centre of the force of Magnetism, or the Earth in the centre of the gravitating force) or any thing else that does not yet appear." [87] To Blake it was quite apparent: the force in the center was Urizen, or Satan, the constrictive Elohim.

But Urizen is able to repent and to relinquish his obscuring and constricting hold upon the energy of imagination. When he does so, he too is able to share the soul's unbounded vision:

> *Urizen said: "I have Erred, & my Error remains with me.*
> *What Chain encompasses? in what Lock is the river of light confin'd*
> *That issues forth in the morning by measure & in the evening by*
> *carefulness?*

*Where shall we take our stand to view the infinite & unbounded?*
*Or where are human feet? for Lo, our eyes are in the heavens."* [88]

The conclusion of this speech is explicable only in terms of Fludd's characterization of the restrictive Elohim:

*He ceas'd, for riv'n link from link, the bursting Universe explodes.*
*All things revers'd flew from their centers . . .*

The god who "dwelleth in the earth's centre," there exercising his constrictive contractive power, ceases to exert the force of gravity, releasing all that was held and bound into imaginative liberty and expansiveness by "rarifaction" and "dissipating of parts." Newton's laws cease to operate upon the "globes of attraction."

The "Vortexes" over which Urizen travels in his arduous exploration of his world come from another system of scientific speculation, now all but forgotten. The Cartesian vortexes find their last expression in Blake's Prophetic Books; yet while Descartes described them at length in his *Principles of Philosophy*, it seems likely that Blake made their acquaintance in a work of popular science, written originally in French, but translated into English in 1682 under the title *A Voyage to the World of Cartesius*.

The *Voyage* takes the form of a journey through space, made by a group of philosophers, to a series of imaginary Cartesian worlds. The guide of the party is called "the Old Gentleman," and this early figure of the space-traveling scientist is almost certainly compounded into the figure of Urizen. The party find Descartes occupied, in the vast regions of space, in building worlds. "As soon as I set Footing in those vast Regions, I descry'd indeed the finest and most advantagious Place possible to be imagin'd for the Building of a *World* in, nay for the Construction of *Millions* and *Infinite Worlds*." Descartes describes the nature of the vortexes: each is "a kind of *Firmament*, at whose Centre will be an *Astre* or fix'd Star." [89] The poles of one vortex are always terminated at the ecliptic of another, and the vortexes being of unequal size, it sometimes happens that smaller ones, like that of the earth or the planets, are swept round in the vortex of the great sun. The vortexes (in contrast with Fludd's constrictive centers) are centrifugal in their operation:

that which preserves a *Vortex* in the midst of several others, is that impulse caused by the Matter of the Star in its attempt to obtain a remove from the Centre towards the Circumference: For the Star, by that Impulse, pushing and supporting the Matter of its *Vortex* keeps the other Vortexes within their Bounds, and loses no Ground in the Dimensions of its Circuit. For, we must consider all these *Vortexes*, as so many *Antagonists* that dispute it to an Inch, and so long as their Forces are equally match'd, gain no Advantage over each other; but as soon as one of them is any ways weakned and disabled, it becomes a Prey to all the rest, each taking in a part of its Space, and at last usurping it all.[90]

In this vast and terrifying landscape "Father Mersennius and the *Old Gentleman* were diverting themselves, by Vaulting from Vortex to Vortex." [91] Was Urizen, hampered in his journey by the centrifugal force of the "Vortexes," following in their tracks?

> *Oft would he sit in a dark rift & regulate his books,*
> *Or sleep such sleep as spirits eternal, wearied in his dark*
> *Tearful & sorrowful state; then rise, look out & ponder*
> *His dismal voyage, eyeing the next sphere tho' far remote;*
> *Then darting into the Abyss of night his venturous limbs*
> *Thro' lightnings, thunders, earthquakes & concussions, fires & floods*
> *Stemming his downward fall, labouring up against futurity,*
> *Creating many a Vortex, fixing many a Science in the deep,*
> *And thence throwing his venturous limbs into the vast unknown,*
> *Swift swift from Chaos to chaos, from void to void, a road immense.*
> *For when he came to where a Vortex ceas'd to operate,*
> *Nor down nor up remain'd, then if he turn'd & look'd back*
> *From whence he came, 'twas upward all; & if he turn'd & view'd*
> *The unpass'd void, upward was still his mighty wand'ring,*
> *The midst between, an Equilibrium grey of air serene.*[92]

This giddy nightmare is an accurate description of how the vortexes would operate, driving any heavy body from center to periphery, so that when the traveler looked back, " 'twas upward all" to reach the center from which he was repelled. The passage continues:

> *But Urizen said: "Can I not leave this world of Cumbrous wheels,*
> *Circle o'er Circle, nor on high attain a void*

*Where self sustaining I may view all things beneath my feet?*
*Or sinking thro' these Elemental wonders, swift to fall,*
*I thought perhaps to find an End, a world beneath of voidness*
*Whence I might travel round the outside of this dark confusion.*
*When I bend downward, bending my head downward into the deep,*
*'Tis upward all which way soever I my course begin;*
*But when A Vortex, form'd on high by labour & sorrow & care*
*And weariness, begins on all my limbs, then sleep revives*
*My wearied spirits; waking then 'tis downward all which way*
*Soever I my spirits turn, no end I find of all*
*O what a world is here, unlike those climes of bliss.*[93]

So, on a Miltonic echo ("Is this the Region, This the Soil, the
Clime . . . That we must change for Heav'n"), Blake implies that the
Cartesian-Newtonian mechanistic universe is the true metaphysical hell.

But to return to Descartes: when a vortex begins to operate, its
repelling force drives the traveler "downward" from center to periphery, and
this is what happens to Urizen. In this world there is neither up nor down nor
end nor limit. The labor, sorrow, care, and weariness involved in the
formation of vortexes is a not inapt description of the grinding down of
matter when the Cartesian revolutions begin, the paring off of all angles by
the friction of particles. The smooth round balls so pared move toward the
circumference faster than the less mobile irregular particles, which therefore
fall toward the center, "to constitute a Mass of that extreamly fine and
powder'd Dust, that still whirl'd round, and attempted to recover the
Circumference from which the *Balls* of the *second Element* had chas'd it:
But all in vain." [94] The paring down of the first element produces, therefore,
two products: the "second matter," consisting of the little balls, perfect
spheres; and the angular residue of very fine parings, called the Third
Element. In the whirling pillar of dust and the "arrowy wedges" that cut and
bruise Orc we recognize the landscape of a forgotten scientific hypothesis;
Urizen tells the victim of this phase of thought:

*Beneath thee & around. Above, a shower of fire now beats,*
*Moulded to globes & arrowy wedges, rending thy bleeding limbs.*
*And now a whirling pillar of burning sands to overwhelm thee,*
*Steeping thy wounds in salts infernal & in bitter anguish.*[95]

The vortexes reappear in *Milton*, but here they are less Cartesian, as if
Blake is no longer describing them in the first enthusiasm of his reading the

scientific account of their operation. He is no longer at pains to give us the correct details:

> *The nature of infinity is this: That every thing has its*
> *Own Vortex, and when once a traveller thro' Eternity*
> *Has pass'd that Vortex, he percieves it roll backward behind*
> *His path, into a globe itself infolding like a sun,*
> *Or like a moon, or like a universe of starry majesty,*
> *While he keeps onwards in his wondrous journey on the earth,*
> *Or like a human form . . .*

Here Blake carries the vortexes quite beyond the world of Descartes, and transforms them into "Men Seen Afar":

> *. . . a friend with whom he liv'd benevolent.*
> *As the eye of man views both the east & west encompassing*
> *Its vortex, and the north & south with all their starry host,*
> *Also the rising sun & setting moon he views surrounding*
> *His corn-fields and his valleys of five hundred acres square,*
> *Thus is the earth one infinite plane, and not as apparent*
> *To the weak traveller confin'd beneath the moony shade.*
> *Thus is the heaven a vortex pass'd already, and the earth*
> *A vortex not yet pass'd by the traveller thro' Eternity.*[96]

The "weak traveller" is surely a reminiscence of Urizen's journey.

149 Woodcut by Blake (1821) for Vergil's first Eclogue

# CHAPTER 19

# The Children of Urizen

Blake believed that "*all* Bibles and sacred codes" have placed man under the rule of the ratio; and in Urizen we find attributes that link him with the world rulers of all the religions known to him. Miss Nanavutty's identification of the web of Brahma has already been mentioned; and the classical demiurge, Jupiter, contributes many features.

Zeus, according to the Orphic tradition, is the demiurge, a second deity, and himself the usurper of Saturn's rule. The reign of Saturn, or Uranus, is the Golden Age—Blake's Eden. The second, or silver, age is under the rule of Zeus (Urizen, too, in his unfallen state, is ruler of the silver age). Blake seems to have drawn upon the first book of Ovid's *Metamorphoses*, where the four ages are described in turn, and the silver age ascribed to Jove:

> *But when Good* Saturn, *banish'd from above,*
> *Was driven to Hell, the World was under* Jove.[1]

Urizen speaks of "The mountains of Urizen, once of silver, where the sons of wisdom dwelt." [2] He slept on a "silver bed," his horses grazed in "silver pastures," and he wore a "silver helmet." His scepter, emblem of his authority, was silver; but his crown was gold [3]—emblem of the power conferred upon him from above; [4] and his children, also, are "crowned" with gold.

The recurrent theme of Urizen exploring his dens contains elements from the story of Jupiter setting out to explore the earth after his conquest of the Titans. (Jupiter's battle with the Titans is itself the foundation of Milton's battle in heaven, and the hurled mountains are common to both.)

Ovid's Jupiter is so dismayed by what he finds on earth that he determines to destroy mankind by a flood.[5] There is a vestigial flood, so to say, in *The Book of Urizen*, suggesting that Blake had not forgotten that both Jupiter and his biblical counterpart did in fact cause a deluge — the flood of hyle:

> *. . . for his dire Contemplations*
> *Rush'd down like floods from his mountains,*
> *In torrents of mud settling thick,*
> *With Eggs of unnatural production:*
> *Forthwith hatching, some howl'd on his hills,*
> *Some in vales, some aloft flew in air.*[6]

With "Eggs of unnatural production" we are again pointed back to Ovid, whose earth, after the Flood, is peopled by spontaneous generation. Ovid's Jupiter, like other figures of the demiurge, is responsible for the creation of "earthborn" men and creatures; and indeed the whole theory of metamorphosis, the theme of Ovid's work of that name, rests upon the notion of protean matter:

> *But this by sure Experiment we know,*
> *That living Creatures from Corruption grow.*[7]

Vergil defends the same theory in his fourth *Georgic;* and Ovid's first example is the same that Vergil gives, the approved method of raising bees:

> *Hide in a hollow Pit a slaughter'd Steer,*
> *Bees from his putrid bowels will appear* [8]

Urizen's "army of horrors," his monsters "sin-bred" and "lust form'd" that "teem'd vast enormities," are generated from corruption. Ovid gives a list of proved instances; from the slaughtered horse breed "Wasps and Hornets of the Warrior Kind," and the monstrous list continues:

> *Cut from a Crab his crooked Claws, and hide*
> *The rest in Earth, a Scorpion thence will glide,*
> *And shoot his Sting, his Tail in Circles toss'd*
> *Refers the Limbs his backward Father lost:*
> *And Worms, that stretch on Leaves their filmy Loom,*
> *Crawl from their Bags, and Butterflies become.*
> *Ev'n Slime begets the Frog's loquacious Race:*
> *Short of their Feet at first, in little space*
> *With Arms and Legs endu'd, long Leaps they take*
> *Rais'd on their hinder Part, and swim the Lake* [9]

Ahania complains that her children are bred from "the dark body of corruptible death," and that man's

> *. . . corrupting members*
> *Vomit out the scaly monsters of the restless deep.*[10]

[147] So Urizen finds his earthborn children. His four elemental sons are generated from earth, air, fire, and water,

> *All his eternal sons in like manner;*
> *His daughters from green herbs & cattle,*
> *From monsters & worms of the pit.*[11]

The earthbred monsters he encounters in his dens have more than a
[1, 17] suggestion of Ovid's creatures bred from corruption:

> *Many in serpents & in worms, stretched out enormous length*
> *Over the sullen mould & slimy tracks, obstruct his way*
> *Drawn out from deep to deep, woven by ribb'd*
> *And scaled monsters or arm'd in iron shell, or shell of brass*
> *Or gold; a glittering torment shining & hissing in eternal pain;*
>
> .     .     .
>
> *Oft would he stand & question a fierce scorpion glowing with gold;*
> *In vain; the terror heard not. Then a lion he would sieze* [12]

Blake, in making Urizen's creatures the spontaneous generation of the slime of the earth, is implicitly criticizing all forms of thought, including Ovid's, which attribute the origin of life to matter; life is, as Blake believed, spiritual in origin, and "earthborn" creatures are a fantasy of Urizen's scientific universe.[13]

Odin likewise enters the composite figure of Urizen; and a connecting link between Odin and Jupiter is provided by the theme of the god exploring this world. When Urizen appears with spear and helmet, to drink the waters of a spring guarded by three terrible women, we are with Odin at Mimir's well:

> *So Urizen arose, & leaning on his spear explor'd his dens.*
> *He threw his flight thro' the dark air to where a river flow'd,*
> *And taking off his silver helmet filled it & drank;*

150 Illustration to Gray's *Descent of Odin* (early 1790's)

> *But when, unsatiated his thirst, he assay'd to gather more,*
> *Lo, three terrific women at the verge of the bright flood,*
> *Who would not suffer him to approach, but drove him back*
> *with storms.*[14]

Under the root of the world-ash Yggdrasill, which lies in the north, there is a fountain. It is guarded by the Norns—Urd, Verdandi, and Skuld—who have knowledge of past, present, and future, and determine the fates of mankind. To this well Odin traveled, disguised, to drink its waters. Among his illustrations to Gray's poems Blake made a series of drawings for *The Descent of Odin;* and it was probably at this time that he read Mallet's *Northern Antiquities.*[15] In these early designs he represented Odin fully armed and wearing the helmet appropriate to his "code of war." Urizen's unwonted appearance as an armed man prepares us for his encounter with his three "daughters," Blake's Norns or Fates.

Gray's poem tells how Odin travels, disguised, to "Hela's drear abode," and calls up a prophetess who tells him of the slaying of Balder and the end of the world. The poem takes the form of a dialogue. Odin asks:

> *What Virgins these, in speechless woe,*
> *That bend to earth their solemn brow,*
> *That their flaxen tresses tear,*
> *And snowy veils, that float in air.*
> *Tell me whence their sorrows rose.*

Who these virgins are we are not told, but we may presume them to be the Norns.

There is a thrice repeated question and the answers of the prophetess:

> *Tell me what is done below,*
> *For whom yon glitt'ring board is spread*

Odin does not know the prophetess, nor she him, until the dramatic moment of mutual recognition at the end of the poem:

[150]

> Prophetess: *Ha! No Traveller art thou,*
> *King of Men, I know thee now;*
> *Mightiest of a mighty line——*
> Odin:       *No boding Maid of skill divine*
> *Art thou, nor Prophetess of good,*
> *But mother of the giant-brood!*

This is the pattern of Urizen's encounter with his daughters. In turn he asks each of the women who and what they are, for he does not recognize them, or they him; at last

> *And Urizen rais'd his spear, but they rear'd up a wall of rocks.*
> *They gave a scream, they knew their father. Urizen knew his*
> *                                                        daughters.*
> *They shrunk into their channels, dry the rocky strand beneath*
> *                                                        his feet,*
> *Hiding themselves in rocky forms from the Eyes of Urizen.*[16]

But Blake, with his habitual syncretism, has drawn, for this episode, upon other myths as well. The Greek Fates—Atropos, Clotho, and Lachesis—are also fontal goddesses. The Orphic Hymn to the Fates opens with an attribution of their power over the waters:

> *Daughters of darkling Night, much-nam'd, draw near*
> *Infinite Fates, and listen to my pray'r;*
> *Who in the heav'nly lake (where waters white*
> *Burst from a fountain hid in depths of night,*
> *And thro' a dark and stony cavern glide,*
> *A cave profound, invisible) abide;*
> *From whence, wide coursing round the boundless earth,*
> *Your pow'r extends to those of mortal birth.*[17]

The Fates seem to be but another aspect of the Furies, who inhabit the dark cavern whence flows the holy water of Styx:

> *Tisiphone, Alecto, and Megara dire:*
> *Deep in a cavern merg'd, involved in night,*
> *Near where Styx flows impervious to the sight;*
>
> .   .   .
>
> *Furious and fierce, whom Fate's dread law delights;*
> *Revenge and sorrows dire to you belong,*
> *Hid in a savage veil, severe and strong.*
> *Terrific virgins, who for ever dwell*
> *Endu'd with various forms, in deepest hell.*[18]

There is another allusion to the Daughters of Urizen, in which Blake clearly is seeing them as the Furies:

> *Then bursting from his troubled head, with terrible visages &*
> *                                        flaming hair,*
> *His swift wing'd daughters sweep across the vast black ocean.*[19]

Their powers begin at the source of generated life, and extend wherever its waters flow.

It is not surprising that the Fates should be Urizen's daughters, since "The Father is Destiny." Past, present, and future begin with his creation of a finite time-world, and "Eternals" who enter the cave become subject to these three. Therefore, they are said to dwell at the hidden source of generation, in the depths of the world-cave. The waters issue, the Greek myth says, from night; but Blake traces their flow back to "The Eternal mind," Urizen.

> *The Eternal mind, bounded, began to roll*
> *Eddies of wrath ceaseless round & round,*
> *And the sulphureous foam, surging thick,*
> *Settled, a lake, bright & shining clear,*
> *White as the snow on the mountains cold.*[20]

This is the Stygian lake. Taylor, in a note, says that the heavenly lake named in the Hymn to the Fates is the same as the Stygian pool, and adds that Hesiod (*Theog.* V. 791) speaks of the Stygian waters "falling into the sea with silvery whirls." Blake, in creating his own vision of Alph, the Sacred River, has made these "eddies of wrath," transforming the image into a symbol of evil. The detail of whiteness belongs also to the Norse version, for the water of the Urdar fountain is so holy, says the Edda, "that everything placed in the spring becomes as white as the skin within an egg-shell." Whiteness in Blake's poetry is almost always associated with death, age, cold, snow, and sorrow; it is an attribute of Urizen's deathbound "north."

"That the waters were the first materiall principle, of which the world was made . . . the Text of *Moses* doth seem evidently to confirme"–so writes Fludd.[21] The "waters" precede creation in Genesis; and to this primary significance of the lake, as hyle, Blake has added a further meaning: Urizen's lake is Udan Adan, the "Lake of Spaces," one of the "Wonders of the Grave":

> *Eastward of Golgonooza stands the Lake of Udan Adan, In*
> *Entuthon Benithon, a Lake not of Waters but of Spaces,*
> *Perturb'd, black & deadly; on its Islands & its Margins*
> *The Mills of Satan and Beelzeboul stand round the roots of*
> *Urizen's tree.*[22]

Entuthon Benithon is Enion's "depths" of matter; and in situating the "Lake of Spaces" in the region of matter's *non-ens*, Blake is commenting upon the view, first expressed by Descartes, that extendedness in space was the primary quality of material objects. Spatiality, therefore, is the first manifestation of the scientists' world outside mind. It is logical that Urizen's journey through his own creation should begin at the source of his illusion, and that his first encounter should be with those three terrible daughters. Existence flows from the divine mind; and in Urizen's lament [23] he speaks of his "fountains": "My fountains, once the haunt of swans, now breed the scaly tortoise." Two swans are fed in the Urdar fountain of the Norns; and Urizen's allusion to his fountain with its swans is another link with this Norse myth. The swan, emblem of the winged soul, has been changed to a wingless reptile, "the scaly tortoise." Vergil called the Stygian lake "Aornus" [24] – birdless.

The Daughters of Urizen "would not suffer him to approach, and drove him back with storms." Here there may be an echo of another memorable description of the source of Styx, from Apuleius' *Cupid and Psyche*. One of the tasks imposed by Venus upon Psyche was to draw water from the source of Styx:

> Then Venus spake unto Psyches again: saying, Seest thou the toppe of yonder great hill, from whence there ronneth downe water of blacke & deadly colour, whiche nourisheth the floodes of Stix and Cocitus, I charge thee to goe thither and bring me a vessell of that water . . . Then poore Psyches went in all hast to the toppe of the mountaine, rather to ende hir life then to fetche any water, and when she was come up to the ridge of the hill, she perceaued that it was impossible to bringe it to passe: For she sawe a great rocke gushinge out moste horrible fountaines of waters, whiche ranne downe & fell by many stoppes and passages into the valley beneath, on eche side she sawe great Dragons, stretching out their longe and bloudy neckes, that never slept, but apointed to keepe the riuer there: the waters seemed to themselves likewise: saying, Away, away, what wilt thou doo? Fly, fly, or els thou wilt be slaine. Then Psyches (seeing the impossibility of this affaire) stood still as though she were transformed into a stone, and although she was present in body, yet was she absent in spirit and sense, by reason of the great perill which she saw.[25]

The source of the river involves us in an elaborate piece of Neoplatonic mythology that seems to have haunted Blake's imagination as he wrote the early Lambeth books. The soul's "descent" involves a progressive immersion in hyle. "The whole planetary system is under the dominion of Neptune," Taylor writes, and the planets are "so many streams. Hence when the soul falls into the planet Saturn, which Capella compares to a river voluminous, sluggish, and cold, she then first merges herself into fluctuating matter." [26] In the lunar orb the soul "bids adieu to everything of a celestial nature," and on the ninth day of her descent "falls into the sublunary world and becomes

united with a terrestrial nature." Saturn's "sluggish" waters are recalled in
Urizen's speech to Ahania,[27] in which he remembers a time when "river" and
"cavern" were places of beauty and repose; he calls Ahania

> *A sluggish current of dim waters on whose verdant margin*
> *A cavern shagg'd with horrid shades, dark, cool & deadly, where*
> *I laid my head in the hot noon after the broken clods*
> *Had wearied me; there I laid my plow, & there my horses fed.*[28]

The *prima materia*, says Vaughan,[29] was "*In forma confusa Aquae;*
and this Primitive *spermatic Ocean* filled all that space which we now
attribute to the *Air*, for it extended even to the lunar circle." The "binding"
of the earthborn man within the five senses Blake seems to have associated,
on the one hand, with the soul's descent into the "stream" of Neptune, and on
the other, with the Newtonian system:

> *. . . then all the eternal forests were divided*
> *Into earths rolling in circles of space, that like an ocean rush'd*
> *And overwhelmed all except this finite wall of flesh.*[30]

At this point heaven becomes "a mighty circle turning, God a tyrant
crown'd." The tyrant is of course Urizen. This passage is immediately
followed by a description of the fall of Urizen from the "sweet south" (the
place of the Eternals) into a river that flows through the northern gate into
generation; and the image of the lodestone is used to express, appropriately
enough (though of course it does not form part of Porphyry's myth), the
irresistible attraction toward generation exerted by the "north." The "caverned" brain of man is in this passage called (with an obscurity of meaning
remarkable even for Blake) "the Stone of Night," which we must suppose,
from the context, to be the lodestone that is drawn to the north:

> *Once open to the heavens, and elevated on the human neck,*
> *Now overgrown with hair & cover'd with a stony roof.*
> *Downward 'tis sunk beneath th' attractive north, that round the feet,*
> *A raging whirlpool, draws the dizzy enquirer to his grave.*[31]

We recognize Urizen as the "dizzy enquirer," and in the "mighty waters"
of the daughters, the same whirlpool that draws the fallen mind into generation through the fountain "hid in depths of night."

The three fontal goddesses of Orphic theology Blake knew from
Taylor's *Dissertation:* "there are many divine fountains contained in the

essence of the demiurgus of the world; and that among these there are three of a very distinguished rank, *viz.* the fountain of souls, or Juno, the fountain of virtues, or Minerva, and the fountain of nature, or Diana." [32] These figures have contributed some of the attributes of Urizen's daughters. We know that they were once beautiful:

> . . . *those whom I loved best,*
> *On whom I pour'd the beauties of my light, adorning them*
> *With jewels & precious ornament labour'd with art divine,*
> *Vests of the radiant colours of heaven & crowns of golden fire.*[33]

Urizen does not recognize his daughters in their fallen state; yet he addresses each according to her proper attributes, in a way that suggests that they are degraded forms of the Orphic fontal goddesses.

"Urizen knew them not, & thus addressed the spirits of darkness" (the Orphic Fates are "Daughters of darkling night"):

> *Who art thou, Eldest Woman, sitting in thy clouds?*
> *What is that name written on thy forehead? what art thou?*
> *And wherefore dost thou pour this water forth in sighs & care?*
>
> *She answer'd not, but fill'd her urn & pour'd it forth abroad.*[34]

Is this woman sitting in her clouds Juno, "Thron'd in the bosom of caerulean air"? [35] Her "urn" suggests the Cave of the Nymphs and the "bowls or urns of workmanship divine," through which the generating souls enter the world. She is the fountain of souls. Urizen next addresses his second daughter:

> *"Answerest thou not?" said Urizen. "Then thou maist answer me,*
> *Thou terrible woman, clad in blue, whose strong attractive power*
> *Draws all into a fountain at the rock of thy attraction;*
> *With frowning brow thou sittest, mistress of these mighty waters."* [36]

The rock of attraction takes us back to the dizzy whirlpool of the earlier passage, and the "mighty waters" are evidently drawn into their fountain by the magnetic power of the north. Is the second daughter the Virgin of the Zodiac? There is a passage in Fludd's *Mosaicall Philosophy* that seems to describe the activity of Blake's "terrible woman clad in blue." The magnetic pole, Fludd writes, "and the fixt constellation of *Virgo*, whose totall attractive and retentive nature is contracted in the Pole-star, as it were the whole basis of a Pyramis, into the point of the Cone; and therefore by contraction of the dilative privative vertue, the power is the stronger; as we see, that *a broad River gathered into a strait betwixt two Rocks, is the more swift and violent.*" [37] Fludd was no doubt familiar with the "river" of the Zodiac, as described by Taylor, and with that sluggish current of the planet Saturn which is the beginning of generated life. By whatever way Blake reached this complex symbol, its meaning is almost certainly related to this theme. We can of course read the lines without knowing what a complex of ideas lies behind them; but it is always well to realize that Blake did write continually from exact and objective, if recondite, sources; and that behind even his slightest symbolic figures there is likely to be a far greater pressure of meaning than is now expected of poets. In fact, it is precisely this imaginative complexity, depth, and richness of material which gives such power to everything he wrote. The Virgin of the Zodiac he perhaps equated with the Orphic fontal goddess Athena.

The third daughter, "clad in shining green," would then be the fountain of nature—Diana:

> *With labour & care thou dost divide the river into four.*
> *Queen of these dreadful rivers, speak, & let me hear thy voice.*[38]

The river dividing into four streams recalls a whole range of symbolic associations with the earthly Paradise and the Garden of Eden. We think, first of all, of the account in the second chapter of Genesis: "And a river went out of Eden to water the garden; and from thence it was parted, and became into four heads" [39]—Pison, Gihon, Hiddekel, and Euphrates. These four rivers of Paradise are to be found in Indian, Celtic, and Greek mythology. Their flow determines the directions of space, and their waters fertilize all the world. Milton describes the river that rose as a fountain on the hill of Paradise, and afterward flowed down underground

> *. . . and met the neather Flood,*
> *Which from his darksom passage now appeers,*
> *And now divided into four main Streams,*
> *Runs divers. . . .*

These,

> *Rowling on Orient Pearl and sands of Gold,*
> *With mazie error under pendant shades*
> *Ran Nectar, visiting each plant, and fed*
> *Flours worthy of Paradise.*[40]

Calypso's isle is yet another earthly paradise, where, close by a cave mouth, four springs pour out clear water to fertilize green gardens, parsley, and violets, so that the gods themselves, visiting that enchanted place, pause to admire its beauty. Spenser's Bower of Bliss [41] is such another place; and the unmistakable allusion to the four rivers of Paradise makes the terrible irony of Urizen's address to the fontal goddess of nature, as "queen of these dreadful rivers." They are now the four rivers of Hades: Styx, Acheron, Phlegethon, and Cocytus.

Ona, the youngest daughter and therefore the one clad in green, who presides over the four rivers, is the child of *A Little Girl Lost*. Here she is in her garden of nature, happy with her lover, until terrified into guilt by "her father white," who with his "holy book" and "dismal care" is clearly Urizen. It is this father who transforms the maiden in Paradise to "Ona! pale and weak." The implication clearly is that Urizen himself is responsible for the metamorphosis of all his three daughters into monsters, the "iron hearted sisters." [42]

To these daughters Urizen gives power over chained Orc, whom they feed with the "bread of Sorrow." The imagery has a Scandinavian quality about it that seems in keeping with the mythology of the Norns and the Urdar fountain, and with the "iron-sleet of arrowy shower" of Gray's *The Fatal Sisters*, whose "dreadful song" Orc must hear:

> *Rending the Rocks, Eleth & Uveth rose, & Ona rose,*
> *Terrific with their iron vessels, driving them across*
> *In the dim air; they took the book of iron & plac'd above*
> *On clouds of death, & sang their songs, kneading the bread of Orc.*
> *Orc listen'd to the song,*[43] *compell'd, hung'ring on the cold wind*
> *That swagg'd heavy with the accursed dough; the hoar frost rag'd*
> *Thro' Ona's sieve; the torrent rain poured from the iron pail*
> *Of Eleth, & the icy hands of Uveth kneaded the bread.*
> *The heavens bow with terror underneath their iron hands,*
> *Singing at their dire work the words of Urizen's book of iron*
> *While the enormous scrolls roll'd dreadful in the heavens above;* [151]
> *And still the burden of their song in tears was pour'd forth:*
> *"The bread is kneaded, let us rest, O cruel father of children!"*
>
> *But Urizen remitted not their labours upon his rock.*[44]

But the Scandinavian suggestion of all this imagery of iron, cold

151 The Lazar House: water color (1795)
The Law is here represented as a scroll in the hands of Urizen.

wind, rain, ice, and frost is misleading, for the allusion is to the Book of Exodus and the feeding of the Children of Israel in the desert. Exodus has given Blake much of the imagery of *Vala;* and here again we discover a familiar theme disguised. Urizen's book of iron "plac'd above On clouds of death" is the Mosaic law: and the bread prepared by the daughters is the "bread from heaven" sent, by that same "very cruel being" who gave the law to Moses, to his children in the desert:

> Then said the Lord unto Moses, Behold I will rain bread from heaven for you; and the people shall go out and gather a certain rate every day, that I may prove them, whether they will walk in my law, or no.   .   .   .
>
> And when the dew that lay was gone up, behold, upon the face of the wilderness there lay a small round thing, as small as the hoar frost on the ground.
>
> . . . And Moses said unto them,
>
> . . . This is the thing which the Lord hath commanded, Gather of it every man according to his eating, an omer for every man, according to the number of your persons.[45]

"One curse, one weight, one measure, / One King, one God, one Law," [46] says Urizen; but the Proverb of Hell says, "Bring out number, weight & measure in a year of dearth." Blake turns into indictment of the Lawgiver the poverty that he rains down upon the suffering children of man—type of the hardships of the poor and laborious of all ages and civilizations.

With the energy of his visualizing imagination, he has made concrete the image of raining bread from heaven, and given to the Fates the task of feeding mankind with the bread of sorrow. This is the meaning of the gathering of the "dough" while clouds rained down as rain (Gray's "arrowy shower"?) into the iron pail of Eleth, and scattered as "hoar frost"—the biblical image used to describe the manna. The thunderings of Jehovah, "that I may prove them, whether they will walk in my law, or no," are echoed in the otherwise inexplicable appearance of the book of iron in the clouds. It is according to the law written in this "book of iron"—written for the Iron Age of the world, not for the golden clime of Eden—that the people are undergoing their lifelong trial in the wilderness. The passage that follows places the guilt upon fallen reason, which permits such things:

> *But Urizen remitted not their labours upon his rock,*
> *And Urizen Read in his book of brass in sounding tones:*
>
> .    .    .
>
> *"Compell the poor to live upon a Crust of bread, by soft mild arts.*
> *Smile when they frown, frown when they smile; & when a man looks*
> > *pale*
>
> *With labour & abstinence, say he looks healthy & happy;*
> *And when his children sicken, let them die; there are enough*
> *Born, even too many, & our Earth will be overrun*
> *Without these arts. If you would make the poor live with temper,*
> *With pomp give every crust of bread you give; with gracious cunning*
> *Magnify small gifts; reduce the man to want a gift, & then give with*
> > *pomp.*
>
> *Say he smiles if you hear him sigh. If pale, say he is ruddy.*
> *Preach temperance: say he is overgorg'd & drowns his wit*
> *In strong drink, tho' you know that bread & water are all*
> *He can afford. Flatter his wife, pity his children, till we can*
> *Reduce all to our will, as spaniels are taught with art.*[47]

A later reference to the "pestilential food" as

> *. . . the fruit of the mysterious tree*
> *Kneaded in Uvith's kneading-trough. . . .*[48]

brings in another image from Exodus. The bread here is the unleavened bread of the Passover: "And the people took their dough before it was leavened, their kneadingtroughs being bound up in their clothes upon their shoulders." [49] Blake holds Urizen, and not Pharaoh, responsible for the fate of the laborers of the brick kilns, whether of Raamses and Pithom, or of London. Egypt is eternal, and so is the wilderness. Subsistence level, as Moses measured out the manna, is oppression. So for Orc, chained energy, the daughters "Measur'd his food morning & evening in cups & baskets of iron" [50] — an omer to each man. So accustomed are we to reading this story of the manna as one of merciful preservation, that to recognize its imagery in Blake's story of the serpent's meat, "Which never was made for Man to Eat," [51] is something of a shock. One might, however, say that Blake is scripturally justified by a text in St. John: "Verily, verily, I say unto you, Moses gave you not that bread from heaven; but my Father giveth you the true bread from heaven." [52]

152 Device from Bryant's *Mythology*, vol. 2 (1774), plate XVI

# Part VI

# The Zoas of Perception

Whether we approach Blake's thought through his myths or through his philosophic aphorisms, by way of his Neoplatonic and alchemical roots or his criticisms of his contemporaries, we are led to the same central affirmation: mind, and not matter, is the only substance, and the material world has its existence in mind, as maya. Matter has no independent existence apart from mind. The mistaken belief in the independent substantial existence of matter Blake recognized as the blind spot of the modern West, and he attempted to destroy it by every means in his power. Yet what he himself so plainly saw he encountered not so much as a conscious belief as an underlying assumption, a climate of opinion, a mental limitation of which the English nation, to whom he addressed himself, was hardly even aware, so self-evident is materialism to the materialist who has not yet seen that there is any metaphysical question begged in his unspoken assumptions. Even among the religious he found the same tacit assumptions about the material universe, but with the addition of "another world" where, so the pious believe,

> . . . an Eternal life awaits the worms of sixty winters
> In an allegorical abode where existence hath never come.*

To Blake, however, the immortality of the soul was a question not of afterlife, with or without a physical body, but of a true understanding of the nature of consciousness. This he attempted to illustrate in terms of current theories of perception; his answers to Bacon, Newton, and Locke were given in their own terms. To their views of the nature of the phenomena he opposed that of the *philosophia perennis*. To "reason and good sense" (those mental virtues upon whose possession men of the Enlightenment so prided themselves) Blake opposed Swedenborgian occultism and poetic enthusiasm. The philosophy of the Enlightenment is, on the contrary, extremely naïve as compared with that of Blake, Coleridge, and Shelley, or with that of Thomas Taylor, from whom these poets learned again the terms of the great philosophic tradition, so long forgotten by English (and, *a fortiori*, by Scottish) philosophers.

* *Europe*, Pl. 5, 6–7; K. 240.

CHAPTER *20*

# The Sensible World

When in 1808 Blake read and annotated Reynolds' *Discourses*, he recalled his earlier annotations of Locke, now lost; he leaves us in no doubt about what he then thought of Locke and the fact that his opinion had in no way changed:

> Burke's Treatise on the Sublime & Beautiful is founded on the Opinions of Newton & Locke; . . . I read Burke's Treatise when very Young; at the same time I read Locke on Human Understanding & Bacon's Advancement of Learning; on Every one of these Books I wrote my Opinions, & on looking them over find that my Notes on Reynolds in this Book are exactly Similar. I felt the Same Contempt & Abhorrence then that I do now. They mock Inspiration & Vision. Inspiration & Vision was then, & now is, & I hope will always Remain, my Element, my Eternal Dwelling place; how can I then hear it Contemned without returning Scorn for Scorn?[1]

Blake's tractates on Natural Religion are his considered refutation of Locke. Like the frontispiece of the series of engravings for *The Gates of Paradise* completed soon after, they might have been entitled "What is Man?", for this is the real question that they ask and answer. Blake approaches it, as philosophers had been accustomed to do from Descartes to Berkeley, in terms of an examination of the five senses as the sources of human knowledge. Under the engraving "What is Man?" Blake in 1818 added the lines: [153]

> *The Sun's Light when he unfolds it*
> *Depends on the Organ that beholds it.*[2]

The design shows, in the form of an emblem, two phases of consciousness, which we may, if we choose, see as the materialist and the immaterialist

What is Man!

153 Frontispiece to *For Children: The Gates of Paradise* (1793)

points of view. The first is represented by a caterpillar blindly devouring a leaf. On another leaf lies a pupa, within which a human infant is forming, still asleep, but soon to open its eyes and perceive the sun with human organs. The psyche, or soul, is, of course, the moth or butterfly, which is to emerge from lower modes of consciousness like a winged nymph from its pupal integuments.

Locke was the philosopher of the Newtonian cosmology, while the chief modern exponent of the immaterialist philosophy was Berkeley, who himself is rooted in the Neoplatonic and Hermetic tradition to which Blake also turned. Blake's debt to Berkeley can be traced in the details of his vocabulary and arguments, as will be shown. In his later annotations to Berkeley's *Siris* Blake names only the Bible and Jesus as the ground of his theory of the imagination, and is at pains to reject Plato and Platonism, unfairly enough if we take note that nearly every one of Blake's affirmations is essentially Platonic. "What Jesus came to Remove was the Heathen or Platonic Philosophy, which blinds the Eye of Imagination, The Real Man." [3] But from Christian sources alone Blake could never have reached his own bold realization of the nature of "Jesus the Imagination." Without the aids of Plotinus and Porphyry, the *Pymander* of Hermes, and, above all, Taylor, Blake's Christianity itself would have been a more limited and lesser matter.

The very title of the third of the tractates, however, *All Religions Are One*, declares Blake's earlier intention to build upon the foundations of the *philosophia perennis*. The term he uses in this tractate as a synonym for the Poetic Genius, "the true Man," points to Taylor as the inspiration of his earliest wrestlings with the philosophic objections to the materialist philosophy. For Taylor "the *true man*, both according to Aristotle and Plato, is intellect." [4] Indeed, it is very likely that the tractates were the first fruits of Blake's acquaintance with Taylor's work. Most of the material of his argument is to be found in that same essay *On the Restoration of the Platonic Theology* which gave Blake the myth of Porphyry's *De Antro Nympharum*. This essay, included in Volume II of Taylor's translation of Proclus' commentaries on Euclid, had been published separately some time earlier (there is no date recorded), and it may have been Taylor's first published work. In the *Dissertation on the Platonic Doctrine of Ideas* included in the first volume of Taylor's *Proclus*, there is more material on the same subject. Was this *Dissertation* the substance of the series of six lectures Taylor is known to have given at Flaxman's house? There is no way of proving this, but it seems likely that Taylor would have given his lectures from work in progress. He was a mathematician and a metaphysician engaged in works on the theory of ideas, and his formulation of the Platonic objections to Bacon and Locke, as well as the Platonic view of intellect as the substantial reality and source of form, is far more minutely stated and argued in these two essays than in Blake's aphorisms, which read rather like a summary of Taylor's work. At all events, their arguments are similar; Taylor even uses Blake's phrase "the true Man"—which, as he says, is intellect.

Taylor equals Blake in his enthusiasm for those whom he calls "the ancients" and in his contempt for "the moderns"—that is, for Locke and the mechanical and experimental scientists. He contrasts with Plato's view of ideas as "eternal and immaterial beings, the originals of all sensible forms," Locke's opinion that "ideas are formed from sensible particulars, by a kind of mechanical operation": "According to Mr. Locke, the soul is a mere *rasa tabula*, an empty recipient, a mechanical blank. According to Plato, she is an ever-written tablet, a plenitude of forms, a vital and intellectual energy. On the former system, she is on a level with the most degraded natures, the receptacle of material species, and the spectator of delusion and non-entity." [5] He joins the names of Blake's two enemies, Bacon and Locke:

The former of these is celebrated for having destroyed the jargon of the schoolmen, and brought experimental enquiries into repute; and for attempting to investigate causes through the immensity of particular effects. Hence, he fondly expected, by experiment piled on experiment, to reach the principle of the universe . . . The latter of these, Mr. Locke, is applauded for having, without assistance from the ancients, explained the nature, and exhibited the genuine theory of human understanding.

Taylor accurately describes these philosophies (for they have no basis either in tradition or in "vision") as "self-taught systems."

Blake, however, certainly had no intention, in the tractates or at any time, of rejecting Christianity; the title page of *There Is No Natural Religion* shows a Gothic door (symbol of spiritual religion), and there is no mistaking, in the last plate, the identity of the Divine Humanity with his [154] haloed head. *All Religions Are One* is, besides, spoken by the poet in the person of John the Baptist, prophet of Jesus, "The Voice of one crying in the wilderness."

Turning back to *There Is No Natural Religion* (first series)[6] we may follow the steps by which Blake arrived by hard thought at a vision so seemingly effortless. The *Argument* is a summary of the main conclusions of Locke, as given in the first book of the *Essay concerning Humane Understanding:* "Man has no notion of moral fitness but from Education. Naturally he is only a natural organ subject to Sense." (A natural organ subject to sense is a fair description of what Blake meant by the caterpillar.) Locke argues that there are no innate principles in the mind, and that our notions of moral fitness come only through education; and Blake in no way distorts or misrepresents his argument, expressed in such passages as this on children:

If we will attentively consider new-born *Children*, we shall have little Reason, to think, that they bring many *Idea's* into the World with them. For, bating, perhaps, some faint *Idea's*, of Hunger, and Thirst, and Warmth, and some Pains, which they may *have* felt in the Womb, there is *not* the least appearance of any setled *Idea's* at all in them; especially of *Idea's, answering the Terms, which make up those universal Propositions*, that are esteemed innate Principles. One may perceive how, by Degrees, afterwards *Idea's* come into their Minds; and that they get no more, nor no other, than what Experience, and the

Observation of things, that come in their way, furnish them with; which might be enough to satisfie us, that they are not Original Characters, stamped on the Mind.[7]

How far this is from Blake's own conception of the child is evident if we only consider his *Songs of Innocence;* and there is no reason to suppose that Blake thought differently in 1788 from what he wrote in the margins of *Siris* in 1820: "Jesus supposes every Thing to be Evident to the Child & to the Poor & Unlearned. Such is the Gospel"; and "the Spiritual Body or Angel as little Children always behold the Face of the Heavenly Father."[8] The child is not "a natural organ" waiting for imprints from a physical environment, but a living essence.

Yet Blake accepts, provisionally, Locke's thesis as being true of the natural man: "*Naturally* he is only a natural organ subject to Sense." He then subjects Locke's argument to a *reductio ad absurdum:* "I. Man cannot naturally Percieve but through his natural or bodily organs."[9] This is Locke's view: "Perception," says Locke, "is the first Operation of all our intellectual Faculties, and the inlet of all Knowledge into our Minds." It is "the first step and degree towards Knowledge, and the inlet of all the Materials of it."[10] Blake is thinking of Locke when he writes of "the five Senses, the chief inlets of Soul in this age."[11] (Not the only inlets even in the present age, and in other ages not even the chief inlets, so this compact sentence implies.)

Blake's second proposition is also taken from Locke: "II. Man by his reasoning power can only compare & judge of what he has already percieved." Reason, according to Locke, is what "we call *Illation,* or *Inference,* and consists in nothing but the Perception of the Connection there is between the *Ideas,* in each step of the Deduction."

Blake's third proposition takes up an argument that Locke uses with great effect, and that was later used by Berkeley as the starting point of his refutation of Locke: "III. From a perception of only 3 senses or 3 elements none could deduce a fourth or fifth." Locke argues that a blind man cannot conceive colors, or a deaf man sounds:

This is the Reason why, though we cannot believe it impossible to God, to make a Creature with other Organs, and more ways to convey into the Understanding the Notice of Corporeal things, than those five, as they are usually counted, which he has given to Man:

> Yet I think, it is *not possible*, for any one to *imagine* any other *Qualities* in Bodies, howsoever constituted, whereby they can be taken notice of, besides Sounds, Tastes, Smells, visible and tangible Qualities. And had Mankind been made with but four Senses, the Qualities then, which are the Object of the Fifth Sense, had been as far from our notice, Imagination, and Conception, as now any *belonging to a Sixth, Seventh, or Eighth Sense*, can possibly be.[12]

Perhaps Locke himself felt something of the claustrophobia that Blake experienced in a universe bounded by organs of sense; or so we might guess from the simile he employs in a famous passage:

> He that will not set himself proudly at the top of all things; but will consider the Immensity of this Fabrick, and the great variety, that is to be found in this little and inconsiderable part of it, which he has to do with, may be apt to think, that in other Mansions of it, there may be other, and different intelligent Beings, of whose Faculties, he has as little Knowledge or Apprehension, as a worm shut up in one drawer of a Cabinet, hath of the Senses or Understanding of a Man.[13]

Locke's fertile fancy attempts to enlarge the bounds of his universe by postulating new senses; his mentality was that of modern science fiction, which, in purely quantitative terms—vast spaces, new senses, and so forth—seeks to discover final imaginative satisfaction in a material universe. "Were our Senses alter'd, and made much quicker and acuter, the Appearance and outward Scheme of things would have quite another Face to us." This may be so, but would it, Blake asks, make any essential difference? Like the universe of science fiction, Locke's universe, whether it be expanded or contracted, remains "the same dull round": "V. If the many become the same as the few when possess'd, More! More! is the cry of the mistaken soul; less than All cannot satisfy Man." It is Locke who cries "More! More!"; and "the many" may be taken to mean either new senses or new sense data.

It is Berkeley's argument that Blake brings to bear upon Locke. Berkeley shows the fallacy of supposing that we can ever know more than we already do about the nature of the material universe through additional senses (or, of course, scientific aids to sense such as the microscope or telescope). Berkeley argues from the infinite divisibility of matter, which at that time was universally allowed: "There is an infinite number of parts in each particle of matter, which are not perceived by sense. The reason therefore, that any particular body seems to be of a finite magnitude, or exhibits only a finite number of parts to sense, is, not because it contains no more, since in itself it contains an infinite number of parts, but because *the sense is not acute enough to discern them.*" [14] Man, Blake says, "perceives more than sense, (tho' ever so acute) can discover."

What will happen, Berkeley asks, if the senses become infinitely acute? What will they discover in the supposed material objects before them?

> In proportion . . . as the sense is rendered more acute, it perceives a greater number of parts in the object, that is, the object appears greater, and its figure varies, those parts in its extremities which were before unperceivable, appearing now to bound it in very different lines and angles from those perceived by an obtuser sense. And at length, after various changes of size and shape, when the sense becomes infinitely acute, the body shall seem infinite. During all which there is no alteration in the body, but only in the sense.

Blake expresses this variation concisely:

> *If Perceptive Organs vary, Objects of Perception seem to vary:*
> *If the Perceptive Organs close, their Objects seem to close also.*
> "*Consider this, O mortal Man, O worm of sixty winters . . .*" [15]

But, Berkeley concludes, we shall be none the wiser about matter itself, which, "considered in it self, is infinitely extended, and consequently void of all shape or figure." It is (supposing it to exist) "infinite and shapeless, and it is the mind that frames all that variety of bodies which compose the visible world, any one whereof does not exist longer than it is perceived." This is exactly Blake's view; it is also that of Plotinus, whose "non-ens" of matter gave Blake his Enion, as we have seen.

There are, besides, many pages of Swedenborg's *Divine Love and Wisdom* that reflect something very like Berkeleyan immaterialism: the Angels live in a world of flexible and subjective time and space, in which objects vary in appearance according to their "correspondence" with states of mind. Swedenborg may have taken this from Berkeley; visionaries necessarily think in terms of the science and philosophy of their day.

This argument used by Berkeley to refute Locke is the very same that

Blake was to use in the *Marriage:* the improvement of the senses will result in the perception of an object that shall "seem infinite":

> . . . the whole creation will be consumed and appear infinite and holy, whereas it now appears finite & corrupt.
>
> This will come to pass by an improvement of sensual enjoyment.
>
> But first the notion that man has a body distinct from his soul is to be expunged; this I shall do . . . melting apparent surfaces away, and displaying the infinite which was hid.
>
> If the doors of perception were cleansed every thing would appear to man as it is, infinite.[16]

Blake, by the addition of the word "holy," transforms Berkeley's argument that senses of infinite acuteness will perceive an infinite object, from a quantitative to a qualitative concept.

On Berkeley's argument, also, Blake bases his second set of aphorisms, arising out of his conclusion that "less than All cannot satisfy Man." Having shown in the first series that no matter what senses the creature may possess, the "All" cannot be the material universe, Blake proceeds to show that the "All" is the mind itself, which perceives: "He who sees the Infinite in all things, sees God, He who sees the Ratio only, sees himself only." The natural man (who is only a natural organ subject to sense) is bounded by Locke's ratio; but the perceiving mind is "the Infinite in all things." This is "the true Man," "Poetic Genius," or "Imagination," through which man has his part in the "Infinite." "Therefore God becomes as we are, that we may be as he is." This, in the words of St. Irenaeus, is Blake's statement of what he understood by the Incarnation. God, the universal mind in which all things exist, is also the Imagination present in man, the consciousness that experiences our human world. The thought is surely also colored by Swedenborg's teaching, "that the Lord should come into the World, in order that he might glorify his Humanity, that is, unite it to the Divinity which was in Him by virtue of conception." [17] Jesus is the divine presence in, or to, every man. He "becomes as we are."

Berkeley nowhere (in his published writings, at all events) affirms that the divine mind is that in man by virtue of which he partakes of the infinite; but he does conclude the being of a God: "Things perceived by the senses are immediately perceived; and things immediately perceived are ideas; and ideas cannot exist without the mind; their existence therefore consists in being perceived; when therefore they are actually perceived, there

[154]

154 *There Is No Natural Religion* (second series, 1788), p. 9

can be no doubt of their existence. . . . it necessarily follows, there is an *omnipresent eternal Mind*, which knows and comprehends all things." [18] For Blake the life of all creatures is in the infinite mind of God.

Blake's marginal annotations to *Siris*, made about 1820, return to the same arguments that he set forth for the first time in the third tractate, *All Religions Are One*. The 1820 annotations are a clearer, more undisguised and uncompromising reaffirmation of the overwhelming realization of the nature of the Divine Humanity that Blake had already reached in 1788. In the earlier tractates Blake is a little more cautious; he writes of "the true Man" and "the Poetic Genius," and represents the figure of the Divine Humanity only as an emblem. In the later marginalia he is bolder: "Imagination is the Divine Body in Every Man," "the All in Man. The Divine Image or Imagination."

In the annotations to *Siris* Blake makes explicit what is only implicit in the tractates—that by the poetic genius he understands the divine presence in man. Berkeley writes: "God knoweth all things as pure mind or intellect;

but nothing by sense, nor in nor through a sensory. Therefore to suppose a sensory of any kind—whether space or any other—in God would be very wrong." [19] Beside this, Blake has written: "Imagination or the Human Eternal Body in Every Man." This is plain enough: what Berkeley writes of God, Blake affirms of man, or rather, of that in man which is divine by the "influx" of God. But Blake also knew the teaching from other sources. One of these is almost certainly the *Poimandres* or *Pymander* of Hermes Trismegistus, a work praised in *Siris* and perhaps first known to Blake through Berkeley. The account of the Pymander, the indwelling divinity and "shepherd of men," is unsurpassed in the religious literature of "the Ancients":

> My thoughts being once seriously busied about the things that are, and my Understanding lifted up, all my bodily Senses being exceedingly holden back, as it is with them that are heavy of sleep . . . Me-thought I saw one of an exceeding great stature, and of an infinite greatness, call me by my name, and say unto me . . . What wouldst thou understand to learn and know?
>
> Then said I, *Who art Thou?* I am, quoth he, *Poemander*, the mind of the great *Lord*, the most mighty and absolute *Emperor:* I know what thou wouldst have, and I am always present with thee.

Presently the Pymander declares himself:

> I am that Light, *the* Mind, thy God. . . .
> How is that quoth I?

> Thus, replied he, understand it: *That which in thee seeth and heareth, the Word of the Lord, and the Mind the Father, God, differ not one from the other; and the union of these is Life.*
> Trismegistus.    I thank thee.
> Poemander.    But first conceive well the Light in thy mind, and know it.

> When he had said thus, for a long time we looked steadfastly one upon the other, insomuch that I trembled at his *Idea* or *Form*.
> But when he nodded to me, I beheld in my mind the Light. . . .
> These things I understood, seeing the Word, or Pimander; and when I was mightily amazed, he said again unto me, Hast thou seen in thy mind that Archetypal Form which was before the interminated and infinite Beginning? [20]

Certainly a very far cry from Locke.

For Blake this conception of the Divine Humanity, which he surely found in traditions other than Christian, increasingly came to seem the very essence of Christianity. Jesus not only taught, but was, the divine mind incarnate; and the Hebrew tradition, with its value placed upon the Prophets and their suprarational god-inspired utterances, came, likewise, to seem to Blake the true imaginative tradition, as against the rational tradition of classical thought: "we of Israel taught that the Poetic Genius (as you now call it) was the first principle and all the others merely derivative, which was the cause of our despising the Priests & Philosophers of other countries, and prophecying that all Gods would at last be proved to originate in ours & to be the tributaries of the Poetic Genius." [21] These words are put into the mouth of Ezekiel.

The third proposition of *All Religions Are One* is Blake's answer to an argument that Locke brings against those who claim inspiration by some inner light or divine revelation: "*Principle 3d.* No man can think, write, or speak from his heart, but he must intend truth. Thus all sects of Philosophy are from the Poetic Genius adapted to the weaknesses of every individual."

The pretense to immediate revelation from God, Locke says, is a short cut of lazy minds that will not undertake "the tedious and not always successful Labour of strict Reasoning." How do such men pretend to know that their thoughts come from God? Mere conviction is no proof: "Much less is a strong Perswasion that it is true, a Perception that it is from GOD, or so much as true. But however it be called light and seeing; I suppose it is at most but Belief, and Assurance: and the Proposition taken for a Revelation is not such, as they know, to be true, but take to be true." [22] And again: "the question then here is. How do I know that GOD is the Revealer of this to me; that this Impression is made upon my Mind by his holy Spirit, and that therefore I ought to obey it? If I know not this, how great soever the Assurance is, that I am possess'd with, it is groundless; whatever Light I pretend to, it is but *Enthusiasm*." [23]

Blake thought it necessary to give Locke an answer. Locke, he would say, has failed to discover the very nature of the human mind, grounded in the divine mind itself; all that springs from "the true Man" or "Poetic Genius" must be a divine revelation, "adapted to the weaknesses of every individual." This is likewise true of religious traditions: "*Principle 5th.* The Religions of all Nations are derived from each Nation's different reception of the Poetic Genius, which is every where call'd the Spirit of Prophecy."

The guarantee of the truth of man's deepest thoughts is man's nature itself – too simple and too bold an answer for Locke's century or Blake's. But "Antiquity," Blake elsewhere says, "taught the religion of Jesus" – that is to say, all religious traditions are manifestations of the imagination, "the true Man," and not of the ratio.

To this argument with Locke, Blake presently returned with more powerful weapons in the *Marriage*. It seems likely that Isaiah and Ezekiel "dined" with Blake (on "the bread of sweet thought & the wine of delight"?) for no other purpose than to refute Locke, as two such mighty personifications of the prophetic genius and tradition were best qualified to do. Blake lost no time in putting to them Locke's objection to "Enthusiasm," which had been worrying him:

> The Prophets Isaiah and Ezekiel dined with me, and I asked them how they dared so roundly to assert that God spoke to them . . .
>
> Isaiah answer'd: "I saw no God, nor heard any, in a finite organical perception; but my senses discover'd the infinite in every thing, and as I was then perswaded, & remain confirm'd, that the voice of honest indignation is the voice of God, I cared not for consequences, but wrote." [24]

Here we find again the two themes of the tractates, the ratio of the senses (finite organical perception) and the infinite and divine nature of mind. Isaiah answers Blake's question by a reaffirmation that the voice of God speaks to man not from without but from within, because God dwells in man.

But Blake wants a specific answer to Locke's specific objection to enthusiasm – "Much less is a strong Perswasion that it is true, a Perception that it is from GOD, or so much as true," Locke challenging the view that "firmness of Perswasion is made the cause of Believing" [25] – and Isaiah gives it to him:

> Then I asked: "does a firm perswasion that a thing is so, make it so?"
>
> He replied: "All poets believe that it does, & in ages of imagination this firm perswasion removed mountains; but many are not capable of a firm perswasion of any thing."

Ezekiel now takes up the theme, and attributes to the tradition of Israel what Blake had learned in great part from Berkeley and the Hermetica: "The philosophy of the east taught the first principles of human perception: some nations held one principle for the origin, & some another: we of Israel taught that the Poetic Genius (as you now call it) was the first principle." "I heard this with some wonder," Blake tells us, "& must confess my own conviction."

However, one other objection of Locke's against visionaries still rankles: they perform irrational, not to say mad, actions at times, and attribute these to the guidance of heaven: "Their Minds being thus prepared, whatever groundless Opinion comes to settle itself strongly upon their Fancies, is an Illumination from the Spirit of GOD, and presently of divine Authority: And whatever odd Action they find in themselves a strong Inclination to do, that impulse is concluded to be a call or direction from Heaven, and must be obeyed; 'tis a Commission from above, and they cannot err in executing it." [26] But Ezekiel is more than a match for Locke: "I then asked Ezekiel why he eat dung, & lay so long on his right & left side? he answer'd, 'the desire of raising other men into a perception of the infinite . . . is he honest who resists his genius or conscience only for the sake of present ease or gratification?' "

It is clear that "the perception of the infinite" means, quite specifically, the realization that the infinite lies within man himself as the indwelling mind of God. It is this voice that he must obey, whether or not his actions seem reasonable to other men. So violent a demonstration of the authority of inner conviction as Ezekiel gave is best fitted to convince more timid souls that faith removes mountains. Both Blake and Ezekiel would have been dear to the hearts of the masters of Zen.

The choice here of Isaiah and Ezekiel suggests that Blake may have been reading Swedenborg on "the Church from the Word, represented by the Prophets." Swedenborg himself uses the Word in the sense of the Logos, and is expounding the prophetic tradition of inspiration. It is the Word—not only in "the Lord Himself as the Greatest Prophet" but in all in whom the prophetic spirit dwells—that bears the sins of the people; and the theme of Swedenborg's tract is the continual salvation and regeneration of mankind by ever-renewed manifestations of the Logos in human lives, through the prophetic vision. Types of the prophetic spirit bearing the sins of society are Isaiah, who "went naked and bare-footed three Years, for a Sign and

Wonder," and Ezekiel, "commanded to lie three hundred and ninety days on his left side, and forty days on his right side, against Jerusalem, and to eat a cake of barley made with cow's dung." [27]

What perhaps most strongly attracted Blake in Swedenborg's thought was his presentation of the prophetic tradition as the true utterance of the Logos, supremely in Jesus but also in all inspired utterance. For Blake it seems clear that Swedenborg's New Age and New Jerusalem were to be the final triumph of this inspired wisdom over the knowledge of the ratio and those who, like Locke, deny the indwelling Word, "the same . . . that was manifested by Moses, the Prophets, and the Evangelists. . . . from which is derived all the Wisdom that exists with Angels, and all spiritual Intelligence with Men." [28]

On October 19, 1801, perhaps in a hopeful mood because of the peace with France then about to be concluded, Blake wrote to Flaxman, "The Kingdoms of this World are now become the Kingdoms of God & his Christ, & we shall reign with him for ever & ever. The Reign of Literature & the Arts Commences. Blessed are those who are found studious of Literature & Humane & polite accomplishments. Such have their lamps burning & such shall shine as the stars." [29]

This is not a flight of fancy. Blake was speaking, in a language he must have presumed Flaxman as a fellow Swedenborgian would understand, [155] of the prophetic character of the New Age. Some years later (about 1807) he engraved a plate of Enoch, surrounded by emblems of the arts of painting, music, and poetry, while other studious figures approach the central group. [30] The allusion here is to Boehme, [31] who foretold that there would be seven ages, from the creation of Adam to the end, the times being named from "the line of the covenant," Adam, Seth, Enos, Cainan, Mahalaleel, Jared, Enoch:

> The *seventh* Time begins with *Enoch, viz.* with the prophetical Mouth, who declares the secret Wonders of God under all the six Times. . . . and even then the *Enochian* Prophet's Mouth does express and speak forth the great Wonders of the *Triple Cross*, that is, he speaks *no* more magically, [*viz.* in Types and Parables,] but shews the holy Trinity in the Figure, *viz.* the formed Word of God in all visible Things, and reveals all Mysteries, *within* and *without*. And even *then* is the Time when *Enoch* and the Children

155 Enoch: lithograph on brown paper (1807?)

The name Enoch is written in Hebrew characters on the open book on the knee of the patriarch.

under his Voice lead a *divine Life*, of which the first Life of *Enoch* was a Type . . . and then the *Turba* is born, which, when it shall enkindle its Fire, the *Floor shall be purged*, for it is the *End of all Time*.[32]

It is evident that Blake (and perhaps Flaxman also) understood Swedenborg's New Age as the Age of Enoch, which is to be the epiphany of the prophetic or poetic genius. "The Reign of Literature & the Arts Commences" gives expression to Blake's belief that in this age the arts are to be the chief "way" to knowledge of the divine vision.

Blake's letter to Flaxman, therefore, was written in hope and faith; and Blake saw himself not as a lonely figure but as the leader of a revival that was sure to come, a national and perhaps a world revival of the imaginative vision, which is the true religion and utterance of the Word: "Nations are Destroy'd or Flourish in proportion as Their Poetry, Painting and Music are Destroy'd or Flourish! The Primeval State of Man was Wisdom, Art and Science." [33] And again: "The Foundation of Empire is Art & Science. Remove them or Degrade them, & the Empire is No More. Empire follows Art & Not Vice Versa as Englishmen suppose." [34] All nations must at last come under subjection to "the jews' god," the poetic genius, this God being the omnipresent Logos itself. Blake could throw Locke to the winds, therefore, strong in his belief that *magna est veritas et praevalebit.*

The nature of the perceptible world is central to Blake's thought; about it his great myth revolves. Blake felt that if he could only break down the one fundamental falsehood that makes, in Berkeley's words, "visible objects to be corporeal substances," [35] and which is the root of the philosophy of modern Europe from Descartes to Locke, Albion might awaken and experience in a Last Judgment a release from the power of illusion. Nothing would be changed in the world but the way in which we experience it:

> . . . *God-appointed Berkeley that proved all things a dream,*
> *That this pragmatical, preposterous pig of a world, its farrow that*
> *so solid seem,*
> *Must vanish on the instant if the mind but change its theme.*[36]

So Yeats wrote; and Blake:

> Error, or Creation, will be Burned up, & then, & not till Then, Truth or Eternity will appear. It is Burnt up the Moment Men cease to behold it.[37]

> *He who Doubts from what he sees*
> *Will ne'er Believe, do what you Please.*
> *If the Sun & Moon should doubt,*
> *They'd immediately Go out.*[38]

This is Berkeley's argument: sensible things do really exist because they are perceived; their "*esse* is *percipi.*" Perhaps this aphorism was suggested to Blake by the third Dialogue of Hylas and Philonous, in which the former at last professes himself a convinced sceptic: man can know nothing, he says, "I know not the real nature of any one thing in the universe." To this the philosopher replies, "I am of a vulgar cast, simple enough to believe my senses, and leave things as I find them. To be plain, it is my opinion that the real things are those very things I see and feel and perceive by my senses." [39]

This is precisely Blake's point. We may doubt the existence of a material object, but we cannot doubt that we see and hear and feel. The sun and moon themselves exist in the omnipresent eternal mind, and even they would go out should "the mind but change its theme."

The opening passage of *Europe* introduces Berkeley's theme with an image that seems also to have been transferred, along with the argument, from the *Three Dialogues*. Is the streaked tulip that makes its seemingly arbitrary appearance here named for its philosophic associations—like the lily, sunflower, thistle, elm, and anemone elsewhere?

> *"Five windows light the cavern'd Man: thro' one he breathes the air;*
> *Thro' one hears music of the spheres; thro' one the eternal vine*
> *Flourishes, that he may recieve the grapes; thro' one can look*
> *And see small portions of the eternal world that ever groweth;*
> *Thro' one himself pass out what time he please; but he will not,*
> *For stolen joys are sweet & bread eaten in secret pleasant."*
>
> *So sang a Fairy, mocking, as he sat on a streak'd Tulip,*
> *Thinking none saw him: when he ceas'd I started from the trees*
> *And caught him in my hat, as boys knock down a butterfly.*
> *"How know you this," said I, "small Sir? where did you learn this*
> *song?"*
> *Seeing himself in my possession, thus he answer'd me:*
> *"My master, I am yours! command me, for I must obey."*
>
> *"Then tell me, what is the material world, and is it dead?"* [40]

The fairy promises:

> *"I'll . . . shew you all alive*
> *The world, where every particle of dust breathes forth its joy."* [41]

A fairy in this context is appropriate, because a spirit of vegetation may reasonably be expected to answer questions upon the nature of the sensible world. "Shakspeare's Fairies also are the rulers of the vegetable world, and so are Chaucer's; let them be so considered, and then the poet will be understood, and not else." [42] But this fairy, who expounds Berkeley from the very flower that Berkeley chose to illustrate his argument, is no common elf.[43] Berkeley's discussion of the relation of natural objects to the five senses leads to the conclusion that their existence is in mind:

> *Hylas:* The sensation I take to be an act of the mind perceiving; beside which, there is something perceived; and this I call the *object*. For example, there is red and yellow on that tulip. But then the act of perceiving those colours is in me only, and not in the tulip.

*Philonous:*   What tulip do you speak of? is it that which you see?
*Hylas:*        The same.
*Philonous:*   And what do you see beside colour, figure, and exten-
               sion?
*Hylas:*        Nothing.
*Philonous:*   What you would say then is, that the red and yellow are
               coexistent with the extension; is it not?
*Hylas:*        That is not all: I would say, they have a real existence
               without the mind, in some unthinking substance.
*Philonous:*   That the colours are really in the tulip which I see, is
               manifest. Neither can it be denied, that this tulip may
               exist independent of your mind or mine; but that any
               immediate object of the senses, that is, any idea, or com-
               bination of ideas, should exist in an unthinking sub-
               stance, or exterior to all minds, is in itself an evident
               contradiction. Nor can I imagine how this follows from
               what you said just now, to wit that the red and yellow
               were on the tulip *you saw*, since you do not pretend to
               *see* that unthinking substance.[44]

Berkeley goes on to extend the argument to the other senses, smell, sight,
and touch; and he concludes:

*Philonous:*   . . . In short, do but consider the point, and then con-
               fess ingenuously, whether light and colours, tastes,
               sounds, &c. are not all equally passions or sensations in
               the soul. You may indeed call them *external objects*, and
               give them in words what subsistence you please. But ex-
               amine your own thoughts, and then tell me whether it
               be not as I say?
*Hylas:*        I acknowledge, Philonous, that upon a fair observation
               of what passes in my mind, I can discover nothing else,
               but that I am a thinking being, affected with variety of
               sensations; neither is it possible to conceive how a sensa-
               tion should exist in an unperceiving substance.[45]

This, set out at length, is the substance of Blake's dialogue with the
fairy on the streaked tulip; and the answer to the question, "What is the
material world and is it dead?" is of course Berkeley's: it is not dead, for its

existence is in the perceiving mind. Everything is living, for its life is that of mind itself; and "every particle of dust breathes forth its joy." Man's folly and tragedy—for it is both these—is that he allows himself to be bounded by his finite perceptions and to become "a natural organ subject to sense." The prison is of man's own making; as the fairy tells the poet, he can "pass out what time he please; but he will not": "For man has closed himself up, till he sees all things thro' narrow chinks of his cavern." [46]

The cavern is of course Plato's world-cave, and that cave, as Blake understood it, is created by the "closing" of the infinite senses. It is none the less a tragedy for being the result of error:

> *Ah weak & wide astray! Ah shut in narrow doleful form,*
> *Creeping in reptile flesh upon the bosom of the ground!*
> *The Eye of Man a little narrow orb, clos'd up & dark,*
> *Scarcely beholding the great light, conversing with the Void;*
> *The Ear a little shell, in small volutions shutting out*
> *All melodies & comprehending only Discord and Harmony;*
> *The Tongue a little moisture fills, a little food it cloys,*
> *A little sound it utters & its cries are faintly heard,*
> *Then brings forth Moral Virtue the cruel Virgin Babylon.*
>
> *Can such an Eye judge of the stars? & looking thro' its tubes*
> *Measure the sunny rays that point their spears on Udanadan?*
> *Can such an Ear, fill'd with the vapours of the yawning pit,*
> *Judge of the pure melodious harp struck by a hand divine?* [47]
> *Can such closed Nostrils feel a joy? or tell of autumn fruits*
> *When grapes & figs burst their covering to the joyful air?*
> *Can such a Tongue boast of the living waters? or take in*
> *Ought but the Vegetable Ratio & loathe the faint delight?*
> *Can such gross Lips percieve? alas, folded within themselves*
> *They touch not ought, but pallid turn & tremble at every wind.*[48]

These are the senses when man looks not *through* but *with* the bodily organ. It is the mind that truly perceives: "I question not my Corporeal or Vegetative Eye any more than I would Question a Window concerning a Sight. I look thro' it & not with it." [49] The conviction and fire of this affirmation testifies to the reality of the experience; but Blake's aphorism stems from a continuous tradition. We find almost the same words in Swedenborg: "how sensually, that is, how much from the bodily Senses and the Darkness thereof, they think in spiritual Things, who say that Nature is from herself; they think from the Eye, and cannot think from the Understanding; Thought from the Eye shuts the Understanding, but Thought from the Understanding opens the Eye"; [50] and behind Swedenborg, Plato: "It appears to me, Socrates, that it is more proper to consider the eyes and ears as things through which, rather than as things by which, we perceive." [51] It is the one living soul that looks through all the windows of sense; and Blake may have known a passage in the *Pymander* that is very close to Berkeley (not surprisingly in view of Berkeley's great admiration of the work):

> For thou both seest, speaketh and hearest, smellest, tastest, and touchest, walkest, understandest, and breathest.
>
> And it is not one that sees, and another that heareth, and another that speaketh, and another that toucheth, and another that smelleth, and another that walketh, and another that understandeth, and another that breatheth, but one that doth all these things.[52]

Paracelsus may have been the source of Blake's vivid picture of the incarceration of immortal senses in perishing bodily organs; for he distinguishes at length between the senses, which belong to the celestial body, and the sense organs, which belong to the natural body. Paracelsus calls the bodily organs "coffers in which the senses are generated. . . . for the aforesaid senses have their proper insensible and impalpable body, even as on the contrary the other part of the body is tangible, for every man is composed of two, *viz.* of a materiall and of a spirituall body." [53]

The theme of *Europe*, introduced by the fairy of the tulip, is the overwhelming of mind by sense—the characteristically European experience:

> *. . . the five senses whelm'd*
> *In deluge o'er the earth-born man; then turn'd the fluxile eyes*
> *Into two stationary orbs, concentrating all things:*
> *The ever-varying spiral ascents to the heavens of heavens*
> *Were bended downward, and the nostrils' golden gates shut,*
> *Turn'd outward, barr'd and petrify'd against the infinite.*[54]

There is in these passages a progression from the merely conceptual thought about the senses of the tractates, and the same concept realized in terms of feeling in the *Marriage*, to a truly Blakean transformation of concept into myth. In *The Song of Los* the theme is still more mythopoeic. The ancestral Har and Heva [55] undergo this tragic metamorphosis as their senses shrink:

> *And all the vast of Nature shrunk*
> *Before their shrunken eyes.*

This shrinkage of the senses is the cause of the creation of a seemingly external world of objects separate from mind. It is so described in several passages:

> *. . . their eyes*
> *Grew small like the eyes of a man,*
> *And in reptile forms shrinking together,*
> *Of seven feet stature they remain'd.*
>
> *Six days they shrunk up from existence,*
> *And on the seventh day they rested,*
> *And they bless'd the seventh day, in sick hope,*
> *And forgot their eternal life.*[56]

Of this disaster to human consciousness Yeats has written: "The mischief began at the end of the seventeenth century when man became passive before a mechanized nature; that lasted to our own day with the exception of a brief period between Smart's *Song to David* and the death of Byron, wherein imprisoned man beat upon the door." [57] It was Blake who "Beat upon the wall / Till God obeyed his call."

The seven days make it clear that Blake is describing the creation of the world; the seven days of creation correspond to changes in man himself. For this reading of the Mosaic myth Blake has the authority of Berkeley, who so interprets it in the third Dialogue of Hylas and Philonous:

*Hylas:*  The Scripture account of the Creation, is what appears to me utterly irreconcileable with your notions. Moses tells us of a Creation: a Creation of what? Of ideas? No certainly, but of things, of real things, solid corporeal substances. . . .

*Philonous:*  Moses mentions the sun, moon, and stars, earth and sea, plants and animals: that all these do really exist, and were in the beginning created by God, I make no question. If by *ideas*, you mean fictions and fancies of the mind, then these are no ideas. If by *ideas*, you mean immediate objects of the understanding, or sensible things which cannot exist unperceived, or out of a mind, then these things are ideas. . . . The Creation therefore I allow to have been a creation of things, of *real* things . . . But as for solid corporeal substances, I desire you to shew where Moses makes any mention of them . . . I imagine that if I had been present at the Creation, I should have seen things produced into being; that is, become perceptible, in the order described by the sacred historian.[58]

The account of the binding of "the eternal mind" is three times repeated: in *The First Book of Urizen*, in *The Four Zoas*, and again in *Milton*. From this we may judge the great importance Blake attached to this account describing the seven days of creation in terms of the immaterialist philosophy. Blake's final version appears on the third page of *Milton*. The binding takes place through man's

> *. . . envy of Living Form, even of the Divine Vision,*
> *And of the sports of Wisdom in the Human Imagination,*
> *Which is the Divine Body of the Lord Jesus, blessed for ever.*

Urizen falls from an imaginative to a materialistic vision:

> *Urizen lay in darkness & solitude, in chains of the mind lock'd up*
> *Los siez'd his Hammer & tongs; he labour'd at his resolute Anvil*
> *Among indefinite Druid rocks & snows of doubt & reasoning.*
>
> *Refusing all Definite Form, the Abstract Horror roof'd, stony hard;*
> *And a first Age passed over, & a State of dismal woe.*
> *Down sunk with fright a red round Globe, hot burning, deep,*
> *Deep down into the Abyss, panting, conglobing, trembling;*
> *And a second Age passed over, & a State of dismal woe.*
>
> *Rolling round into two little Orbs, & closed in two little Caves,*
> *The Eyes beheld the Abyss, lest bones of solidness freeze over all;*
> *And a third Age passed over, & a State of dismal woe.*
>
> *From beneath his Orbs of Vision, Two Ears in close volutions*

*Shot spiring out in the deep darkness & petrified as they grew;*
*And a fourth Age passed over, & a State of dismal woe.*

*Hanging upon the wind, two nostrils bent down into the Deep;*
*And a fifth Age passed over, & a State of dismal woe.*

*In ghastly torment sick, a Tongue of hunger & thirst flamed out;*
*And a sixth Age passed over, & a State of dismal woe.*

*Enraged & stifled without & within, in terror & woe he threw his*
*Right Arm to the north, his left Arm to the south, & his Feet*
*Stamp'd the nether Abyss in trembling & howling & dismay;*
*And a seventh Age passed over, & a State of dismal woe.*[59]

In *The Book of Urizen* the account of the binding is preceded by the
formation of "a Lake bright and shining clear, white as snow." This is the
lake of Udan Adan, a "Lake of Spaces." The creation of the great ocean of
time and space (to use the image of Locke and Newton for the "soul-
shudd'ring vacuum") precedes the creation of all other attributes of nature,
since it is extendedness in space that is said by Descartes and his followers
to constitute the primary quality of bodies.[60] This earlier account of the
binding concludes with the unambiguous statement of Blake's belief that
this change in consciousness is a disaster:

*All the myriads of Eternity,*
*All the wisdom & joy of life*
*Roll like a sea around him,*
*Except what his little orbs*
*Of sight by degrees unfold.*

*And now his eternal life*
*Like a dream was obliterated.*[61]

The first appearance of some of the images fully developed in the
binding of Urizen is in a passage in *Visions of the Daughters of Albion*, and
the "binding" is an attempt to deceive Oothoon, the soul. Here we find the
theme taking shape in the context of Blake's most concentrated attack upon
the Lockean philosophy. For a moment Oothoon is imposed upon by the
falsehood of the cave:

*They told me that I had five senses to inclose me up,*
*And they inclos'd my infinite brain into a narrow circle,*

*And sunk my heart into the Abyss, a red, round globe, hot burning,*
*Till all from life I was obliterated and erased.*[62]

In the later books it is Vala or her generated form, the beautiful Tirzah, who is responsible for this disastrous binding. Albion says:

*. . . Go and Die the Death of Man for Vala the sweet wanderer.*
*I will turn the volutions of your ears outward, and bend your nostrils*
*Downward, and your fluxile eyes englob'd roll round in fear;*
*Your with'ring lips and tongue shrink up into a narrow circle.*[63]

And in a very similar passage Tirzah says to Albion:

*These fibres of thine eyes that used to wander in distant heavens*
*Away from me, I have bound down with a hot iron.*
*These nostrils that Expanded with delight in morning skies*
*I have bent downward . . .*[64]

The theme was one that never lost its importance for Blake, or seemed to him less tragic.

The conflict of materialist and immaterialist philosophies upon the nature of the sensible world inspires the eloquent debate of Oothoon with Bromion, in *Visions of the Daughters of Albion*. Oothoon, speaking in the name of the soul, is opposed by Bromion, whose argument is that of Locke. Locke sees all experience as determined and limited by material objects, and his fancies on the theme of other and more numerous senses are all entirely quantitative. Far different is the imagination that is able:

*To see a World in a Grain of Sand*
*And a Heaven in a Wild Flower* [65]

Locke speculates upon the possible perceptions of spirits other than man:

imagine, that Spirits can assume to themselves Bodies of different Bulk, Figure, and Conformation of Parts. Whether one great advantage some of them have over us, may not lie in this, that they can so frame, and shape to themselves Organs of Sensation or Perception, as to suit them to their present Design, and the Circumstances of the

Object they would consider. For how much would that Man exceed all others in Knowledge, who had but the Faculty so to alter the Structure of his Eyes, that one Sense, as to make it capable of all the several degrees of Vision, which the assistance of Glasses. . . . has taught us to conceive? [66]

Size is a special case of these possible worlds, vividly brought to the notice of philosophy by the use of the microscope:

Nay, if that most instructive of our Senses, Seeing, were in any Man 1000, or 100000 [times] more acute than it is now by the best Microscope, things several millions of Times less than the smallest Object of his Sight now, would then be visible to his naked Eyes . . . But then he would be in a quite different World from other People: Nothing would appear the same to him, and others: the visible *Ideas* of everything would be different. [67]

But Blake saw in this "More! More!" the cry of the "mistaken soul."

Bromion's very fine speech in *Visions of the Daughters of Albion* seems to have been inspired by this or similar passages in Locke and probably also in Berkeley: [68]

*Thou knowest that the ancient trees seen by thine eyes have fruit,*
*But knowest thou that trees and fruits flourish upon the earth*
*To gratify senses unknown? trees, beasts and birds unknown;*
*Unknown, not unperciev'd, spread in the infinite microscope,*
*In places yet unvisited by the voyager, and in worlds*
*Over another kind of seas, and in atmospheres unknown* [69]

But Bromion's possible worlds remain within the Mill or "infinite microscope." His speech concludes with the affirmation that the same law governs all things, the philosophy of the mechanist who conceives the world as a single machine which, whether it be perceived by few senses or by many, remains unalterable in its operations:

*And is there not one law for both the lion and the ox?*  [156]
*And is there not eternal fire and eternal chains*
*To bind the phantoms of existence from eternal life?* [70]

Oothoon proclaims the doctrine of the imagination: every living creature is a different expression of the divine mind. Creatures differ in their

156 "One Law for the Lion & Ox is Oppression": *The Marriage of Heaven and Hell* (1790–93?), plate 24 Nebuchadnezzar. Cf. [152, 185].

imaginative essence, not in the structure of their sense organs; and as each creature imagines, so its world will be:

> *With what sense is it that the chicken shuns the ravenous hawk?*
> *With what sense does the tame pigeon measure out the expanse?*
> *With what sense does the bee form cells? have not the mouse & frog*
> *Eyes and ears and sense of touch? yet are their habitations*
> *And their pursuits as different as their forms and as their joys.*
> *Ask the wild ass why he refuses burdens, and the meek camel*
> *Why he loves man: is it because of eye, ear, mouth or skin,*
> *Or breathing nostrils? No, for these the wolf and tyger have.*
> *Ask the blind worm the secrets of the grave, and why her spires*
> *Love to curl round the bones of death; and ask the rav'nous snake*
> *Where she gets poison, & the wing'd eagle why he loves the sun;*
> *And then tell me the thoughts of man, that have been hid of old.*[71]

It is not Locke's hypothetical "sixth seventh or eighth sense" that makes these differences, but the living *esse* of each creature. Berkeley is the background against which we ought to read Oothoon's speech or those visionary lines:

> *How do you know but ev'ry Bird that cuts the airy way,*
> *Is an immense world of delight, clos'd by your senses five?* [72]

Locke thinks in terms only of new senses, Berkeley in terms of "spirits of different orders and capacities":

> That there are a great variety of spirits of different orders and capacities, whose faculties, both in number and extent, are far exceeding those the Author of my being has bestowed upon me, I see no reason to deny. And for me to pretend to determine by my own few, stinted, narrow inlets of perception, what ideas the inexhaustible power of the Supreme Spirit may imprint upon them, were certainly the utmost folly and presumption.[73]

In every creature is evoked a different world by the power of imagination alone. Swedenborg took a similar view—himself possibly influenced by Berkeley; and again, we must not underrate his importance as an influence on Blake's thought. Indeed, one might read all this eloquent doctrine of the senses as Blake's inspired interpretation of the Swedenborgian concept of "influx" and "correspondence," foreshadowing Teilhard de Chardin's theory of the "within" of the world, which is the constant counterpart of the "without." A long passage (the same from which Blake seems to have taken the figure of his "Clod of Clay") is even nearer than Berkeley to the animism of Blake's poetic vision:

> That there is in every Thing an Internal and an External, and that the External dependeth on the Internal, as the Body does on its Soul, must be evident to any one that considers attentively the particular parts of Creation. In Man this Truth is very manifest. . . . There is an Internal and an External also in every Bird and Beast, nay, in every Insect and Worm; also in every Tree, Plant and Shrub, nay, in every Stone and smallest Particle of Dust. For the Illustration of this Truth it may suffice to consider a few Particulars respecting a Silkworm, the Bee, and a Particle of Dust. The Internal of the Silkworm is that, by Virtue whereof its External is impelled to spin its silken Web, and afterwards to assume Wings like a Butterfly and fly abroad. The Internal of a Bee is that, by Virtue whereof its External is impelled to suck Honey out of Flowers, and to construct waxen Cells after a wonderful Form. . . . The Case is the same in Things of an opposite Nature, as for Instance, in a Spider, which hath both an Internal and an External, and its Internal, by which its External is impelled, is an Inclination and a Faculty thence

derived, to weave a most curious Web, in the Centre whereof it may watch.[74]

The forms of bodies are the "correspondence" or "signature" of the soul.

From this difference in nature, Oothoon pleads for the recognition of the freedom of every creature to follow its innate impulse of life:

*Does the whale worship at thy footsteps as the hungry dog;*
*Or does he scent the mountain prey because his nostrils wide*
*Draw in the ocean? does his eye discern the flying cloud*
*As the raven's eye? or does he measure the expanse like the vulture?*
*Does the still spider view the cliffs where eagles hide their young;*
*Or does the fly rejoice because the harvest is brought in?*
*Does not the eagle scorn the earth & despise the treasures beneath?*
*But the mole knoweth what is there, & the worm shall tell it thee.*
*Does not the worm erect a pillar in the mouldering church yard*
*And a palace of eternity in the jaws of the hungry grave?*
*Over his porch these words are written: "Take thy bliss, O Man!*
*And sweet shall be thy taste, & sweet thy infant joys renew!"* [75]

This is Blake's conception of "nature" — not a mechanistic system subject to the Newtonian "laws" but a manifestation of the ever-various energy of the divine mind that is always and everywhere its own law. These manifestations Blake calls "the sports of Wisdom," the "play," as Vedanta says, of God. "Every thing that lives is holy" not because the poet chooses to think so, but because all consciousness and all impulse is from the living divine spirit. Nature has no other "laws." "Take thy bliss, O Man!" is the law of life; for the living spirit is reality itself, and its impulses divinely implanted:

*Does the sun walk in glorious raiment on the secret floor*
*Where the cold miser spreads his gold; or does the bright cloud drop*
*On his stone threshold? does his eye behold the beam that brings*
*Expansion to the eye of pity? or will he bind himself*
*Beside the ox to thy hard furrow? does not that mind beam blot*
*The bat, the owl, the glowing tyger, and the king of night?*
*The sea fowl takes the wintry blast for a cov'ring to her limbs,*
*And the wild snake the pestilence to adorn him with gems & gold;*
*And trees & birds & beasts & men behold their eternal joy.*
*Arise, you little glancing wings, and sing your infant joy!*
*Arise, and drink your bliss, for every thing that lives is holy!* [76]

It is but just to add that Oothoon's "One Law for the Lion and Ox is Oppression" might also stand as the summing up of Rousseau's theory of education. All creatures, he too argued, are different; and to attempt to impose on all alike the same education is oppression: true education should allow the innate talent of every child to develop organically. No doubt Blake was indebted, directly or indirectly, to Rousseau for such notions, which he adopted with the more fervor, perhaps, because they came to him through Mary Wollstonecraft. Rousseau, writing of the folly of molding children by education, says: "Infancy has a manner of perceiving, thinking, and feeling peculiar to itself." Premature instruction is

> without regard to the peculiar genius of each. For, besides the constitution common to its species, every child at its birth possesses a peculiar temperament, which determines its genius and character; and which it is improper either to pervert or restrain; the business of education being only to model and bring it to perfection. All these characters are . . . good in themselves: for nature makes no mistakes. All the vices imputed to malignity of disposition are only the effect of the bad form it had received . . . there is not a villain upon earth, whose natural propensity, well directed, might not have been productive of great virtues.[77]

The education that produced Tiriel was of the oppressive kind that "formed the infant head" according to external rules; Tiriel might be the answer to Rousseau's question, "What must be the consequence then of an education begun in the cradle, and carried on always in the same manner, without regard to the vast diversity of temperaments and genius in mankind?" Tiriel's view that the "infant head" must be "formed" is, of course, Locke's; but "Every man's genius is peculiar to his individuality," says Blake.

Tiriel, in his last protest, asks: "Why is one law given to the lion & the patient Ox?" [78] A deleted passage continued the argument much as it is later given to Oothoon:

> *Dost thou not see that men cannot be formed all alike,*
> *Some nostril'd wide, breathing out blood. Some close shut up*
> *In silent deceit, poisons inhaling from the morning rose,*
> *With daggers hid beneath their lips & poison in their tongue;*
> *Or eyed with little sparks of Hell . . .*[79]

Tiriel has been made what he is, a blind tyrant, because he was "Compell'd to pray repugnant & to humble the immortal spirit." [80] The spirit is "humbled" when it is required to subject itself to laws external to itself. It is in the name of this spirit, not in the name of any class or nation, sex or party, that Blake demands freedom. Freedom is the birthright of all the living, because nothing is more holy than life itself. The poem *Infant Joy*, in appearance so simple, is in truth the fine flower of this philosophy. "Joy is my name" does not so much describe as define a child. Joy is not an attribute of life: life is joy, *ananda;* and all lives delight in the play of their own existence in the divine Being.

157 Woodcut by Blake (1821) for Vergil's first Eclogue

CHAPTER *21*

# Visionary Time and Space

In the figures and mythology of Los and Enitharmon, Blake carries his attack upon eighteenth-century philosophy to the most fundamental issue of all, the nature of time, space, and material bodies. Descartes himself held that there is a distinction between the primary and the secondary qualities of objects, and allowing that color, sound, and the rest exist only in the perceiving mind, claimed that the nature of body consists in extension alone: "the nature of matter or body in its universal aspect, does not consist in its being hard, or heavy, or coloured, or one that affects our senses in some other way, but solely in the fact that it is a substance extended in length, breadth and depth." [1] Berkeley breaks down Descartes' distinction between primary and secondary qualities and affirms that "*all* (place or) *extension exists only in the mind*." He believes that every sensible body "is nothing but a complexion of such qualities or ideas, as have no existence distinct from being perceived by a mind," whether these properties be primary or secondary; and concludes, of absolute space,

> that phantom of the mechanic and geometrical philosophers, it may suffice to observe that it is neither perceived by any sense, nor proved by any reason, and was accordingly treated by the greatest of the ancients as a thing merely visionary. From the notion of absolute space springs that of absolute motion, and in these are ultimately founded the notions of external existence, independence, necessity, and fate. [2]

Since, according to Descartes, extension constitutes body, Berkeley's refutation of the notion that time and space have an existence apart from mind applies equally to body: "But . . . though we should grant this unknown substance [matter] may possibly exist, *yet where can it be supposed*

131

*to be?* That it exists not in the mind is agreed, and that it exists not in place is no less certain: since all (place or) extension exists only in the mind, as hath already been proved. It remains therefore that it exists no where at all." [3] Blake is but repeating, with feeling, Berkeley's argument when he writes: "Mental Things are alone Real: what is call'd Corporeal, Nobody Knows of its Dwelling Place: it is in Fallacy, & its Existence an Imposture. Where is the Existence Out of Mind or Thought? Where is it but in the Mind of a Fool?" [4] Berkeley particularizes: "It is indeed an opinion strangely prevailing amongst men, that houses, mountains, rivers, and in a word all sensible objects have an existence natural or real, distinct from their being perceived by the understanding." [5] And Blake uses the same images:

> *For all are Men in Eternity, Rivers, Mountains, Cities, Villages,*
> *All are Human, & when you enter into their Bosoms you walk*
> *In Heavens & Earths, as in your own Bosom you bear your Heaven*
> *And Earth & all you behold; tho' it appears Without, it is Within,*
> *In your Imagination, of which this World of Mortality is but a*
> > *Shadow.* [6]

Blake had certainly direct access to at least some of the "ancients" here mentioned by Berkeley: "it is observed in the *Asclepian Dialogue* that the word *space* or *place* hath by itself no meaning; and again, that it is impossible to understand what space alone or pure space is. And Plotinus acknowledgeth no place but soul or mind, expressly affirming that the soul is not in the world, but the world in the soul. And farther, the place of the soul, saith he, is not body, but soul is in mind, and body in soul." [7] The passage in the Asclepian Dialogue to which Berkeley refers is:

| | |
|---|---|
| *Asclepius:* | What shall we call the place in which the whole Universe is moved? |
| *Hermes:* | Call it incorporeal, O *Asclepius.* |
| *Asclepius:* | What is that, incorporeal or unbodily? |
| *Hermes:* | The Mind and Reason, the whole, wholly comprehending itself, free from all Body, undeceivable, invisible, impassible from a Body itself, standing fast in itself, capable of all things. . . . [8] |

Again, in Book X: "All things are in God, not as lying in a place, for Place is both a body and unmoveable, and those things that are placed, have no motion. For they lie otherwise in that which is unbodily, than in the fantasie, or to appearance. Consider him that contains all things, and understand that nothing is more capacious, than that which is incorporeal." [9]

"God," Locke writes, "every one easily allows, fills Eternity; and 'tis hard to find a reason, why anyone should doubt, that he likewise fills Immensity." [10] To this Blake might seem to assent in the aphorism "One thought fills immensity." But Locke and Blake are in truth at opposite poles, for Locke conceives God filling space and time, whereas the Platonic tradition in its various forms speaks, more correctly, of space and time in God or mind; immensity is but a single thought in the divine mind.

Proclus' commentaries on Euclid, one of Taylor's earliest publications, contain a most subtle discussion of the mental nature of space. It is even likely that Blake first became familiar with the notion of the mental nature of space and place through Proclus and through Taylor's own brilliant essay *On the Restoration of the Platonic Theology*. Taylor argues: "For what place could there be prior to the existence of the world? But the parts of the world are reduced to the universe, and are placed in its comprehensive bond. And soul is not in the world, but rather the world is in soul; for neither is body the place of soul, but soul is in intellect, and body in soul. . . . the highest principle is contained in no other, and is on this account said to be no where." [11]

Once more it is important to remember Swedenborg. We are constantly reminded, when we read his many pages upon the subjective nature of space and time, that he was a man of science and a man of his age: "in the spiritual World, where Spirits and Angels are, there appear Spaces like the Spaces upon Earth, nevertheless they are not Spaces but Appearances; for they are not fixed, and stationary, as in the Earth; they can be lengthened and contracted, changed and varied; and therefore because they cannot be determined by Measure, they cannot in that World be comprehended by any natural Idea, but only by a spiritual Idea." [12]

Swedenborg concludes that "the Divine Love and the Divine Wisdom in themselves are a Substance and Form: for they are Essence and Existence itself." Love, he says, is space, and wisdom time—the evident origin of Blake's Los and Enitharmon. Swedenborg considered that in man's present state the flexibility of mind (love and wisdom in the human imagination) which knows all times, spaces, and objects to be subject to it has been lost, and that, as a consequence, things appear to be—and in that sense are—fixed and, as he says, dead. Time and space, the ground of the Cartesian view of material nature, Swedenborg saw for what they are, a mode of apprehension by which modern man realizes what the scientists call "nature." "The Divine," he wrote, "is not in Space . . . ," and though He is omnipresent, "cannot be comprehended by any natural Idea," because in that idea is space.[13] In the margin Blake wrote, beside these words, "What a natural Idea is"[14]—that is, thought confined to the terms of time and space as conceived by science. What must seem surprising to the modern mind accustomed to a more subtle psychology is the apparent difficulty with which philosophers of the scientific school were able to comprehend any nonspatial idea. For Blake, as for Berkeley, Swedenborg, and the ancients, time and space are mental concepts—"visionary." This is not mysticism but mere philosophy. When a Last Judgment has removed from men the illusion of the temporal, men converse like Swedenborg's angels:

> . . . in Visions
> In new Expanses, creating exemplars of Memory and of Intellect,
> Creating Space, Creating Time, according to the wonders Divine
> Of Human Imagination throughout all the Three Regions immense
> Of Childhood, Manhood & Old Age . . .
>
>            .        .        .
>
> . . . & every Word & Every Character
> Was Human according to the Expansion or Contraction, the
>                                              Translucence or
> Opakeness of Nervous fibres: such was the variation of Time & Space
> Which vary according as the Organs of Perception vary . . .[15]

In the two figures of Los and Enitharmon we see the Locke-Berkeley dispute on the nature of time and space transposed into myth. This fixed external space-time is the "fathomless void," the "soul-shudd'ring vacuum" into which the mind falls when it is "rent from eternity"—that is, from the "I am" of consciousness:

> . . . the space, undivided by existence,
> Struck horror into his soul.[16]

That same "boundless invariable Ocean of duration and expansion"[17]—literally a "Lake of Spaces"—Locke describes in terms that suggest Joyce's Jesuit sermon on the endless duration of hell:

> When we would think of infinite Space or Duration, we at first step usually make some very large Idea, as, perhaps, of Millions of Ages, or Miles, which possibly we double and multiply several

times. . . . But what still remains beyond this, we have no more a positive distinct notion of, than a Mariner has of the depth of the Sea; where having let down a large portion of his Sounding-Line, he reaches no bottom, whereby he knows the depth to be so many fathoms, and more . . . And could he always supply new Line, and find the Plummet always sink without ever stopping, he would be something in the posture of the Mind reaching after a compleat and positive *Idea* of Infinity. . . . So much as the Mind comprehends of any Space, it has a positive *Idea* of; but in this thought of Infinity, it being always enlarging, always advancing, the *Idea* is still imperfect and incompleat.[18]

This is but a fragment of a theme on which Locke wrote at great length, building up a landscape of vertiginous dark voidness, which Blake has recreated in poetic terms, translated from concept to imaginative experience, in *The First Book of Urizen*. Several of the designs show "Those in Eternity" as they look into this horrible abyss of space and time:

158 Eternals (The Four Zoas?) gazing into the abyss: *Urizen* (1794), plate 8, detail
Cf. [144, 146].

*The Abyss of Los stretch'd immense;*
*And now seen, now obscur'd, to the eyes*
*Of Eternals the visions remote*
*Of the dark seperation appear'd:*
*As glasses discover Worlds*
*In the endless Abyss of space,*
*So the expanding eyes of Immortals*
*Beheld the dark visions of Los* [19]

Within this infinite void—outside mind, explored by the glasses of microscope and telescope—within this "soul-shudd'ring vacuum," science sets its
bounds and limits, what Locke calls "Landmarks." Without these arbitrary
known points, fixed by man himself in the boundless distances of space-time,
science would be unable to build its universe:

> *Time* in general is to *Duration*, as *Place* to *Expansion*. They are so
> much of those boundless Oceans of Eternity and Immensity, as is
> set out and distinguished from the rest, as it were by Landmarks;
> and so are made use of, to denote the Position of finite real Beings,
> in respect to one another, in those uniform infinite Oceans of Duration
> and Space. These rightly considered, are nothing but *Ideas* of
> determinate Distances, from certain known points fixed in distin-
> guishable sensible things. [20]

159 Newton on the sea
floor: color print (1795)
Note the white cloth
("the woof of Locke"?)
issuing from behind the
head of the scientist.

Blake turns Locke into myth. "Marks and known Boundaries" become the biblical "Tent" and "cords & stakes" of the universe. When Enitharmon and Los fall into the "abyss," the Eternals say:

> *"Spread a Tent with strong curtains around them.*
> *Let cords & stakes bind in the Void,*
> *That Eternals may no more behold them."*
>
> *They began to weave curtains of darkness,*
> *They erected large pillars round the Void,*
> *With golden hooks fasten'd in the pillars;*
> *With infinite labour the Eternals*
> *A woof wove, and called it Science.*[21]

The image is developed in *Vala*, Night II:

> *Beneath the Caverns roll the weights of lead & spindles of iron,*
> *The enormous warp & woof rage direful in the affrighted deep.*
>
> *While far into the vast unknown the strong wing'd Eagles bend*
> *Their venturous flight in Human forms distinct; thro' darkness deep*
> *They bear the woven draperies; on golden hooks they hang abroad*
> *The universal curtains & spread out from Sun to Sun*
> *The vehicles of light . . .*[22]

This is the woof woven on "the loom of Locke"; and Blake's depiction of Newton shows the same white woof spreading from a point of origin behind or within the thinking head of the scientist, as he bends over his mathematical diagrams spread on the floor of "the Sea of Time & Space." On the loom of Locke is woven the immense expanse of time and space, ever extending into "the vast Inane." [159]

With these fixed points established in the abyss as "scaffolding," Urizen can create his world:

> *Then rose the Builders. First the Architect divine his plan*
> *Unfolds. The wondrous scaffold rear'd all round the infinite,*
> *Quadrangular the building rose, the heavens squared by a line,*
> *Trigons & cubes divide the elements in finite bonds.*[23]

Science creates a universe of compelling beauty, although it is in truth but Satan's Pandemonium, built in outer darkness outside mind:

*A wondrous golden Building, many a window, many a door.*
*And many a division let in & out the vast unknown.*
*Circled in infinite orb immoveable, within its walls & cielings*
*The heavens were clos'd, and spirits mourn'd their bondage night &*
                                                            *day* [24]

This is "the Mundane Shell builded by Urizen's strong power," whose magnificence seems to justify Urizen's claim:

*"Am I not God?" said Urizen, "Who is Equal to me?*
*Do I not stretch the heavens abroad, or fold them up like a*
                                                            *garment?"* [25]

But these "stupendous works" of Urizen, continually created, Los can destroy by "altering the ratio." Here again Locke has put into Blake's hands the concept of the changes in the apparent world brought about by a mere change of scale, as in the microscope or telescope. Vastness is only relative; the Spectre (the figure who in *Jerusalem* takes the place of Urizen) takes "the Starry Heavens / Like to a curtain & folding them according to his will."

*. . . Los beheld undaunted, furious,*
*His heav'd Hammer; he swung it round & at one blow*
*In unpitying ruin driving down the pyramids of pride,*
*Smiting the Spectre on his Anvil & the integuments of his Eye*
*And Ear unbinding in dire pain, with many blows*
*Of strict severity self-subduing, & with many tears labouring.*

*Then he sent forth the Spectre: all his pyramids were grains*
*Of sand, & his pillars dust on the fly's wing, & his starry*
*Heavens a moth of gold & silver, mocking his anxious grasp.*
*Thus Los alter'd his Spectre, & every Ratio of his Reason*
*He alter'd time after time with dire pain & many tears*
*Till he had completely divided him into a separate space.* [26]

By continually altering the ratio, Los can at last convince the reasoner of the unreality of the great edifices that he takes to be substantial, thus bringing him back to a perception of the "infinite in all things," the living mind that builds them. The heavens are an adornment on the wings of the soul—the moth, Psyche, the figure so beautifully depicted on the title page of *Jerusalem*. The lovely image reveals its strength only when we have trained ourselves in the symbolic language that Blake employs.

We may now follow Blake's original conception of the myth of Los and Enitharmon as it was planned in the original *Vala*. With the fall of man, Los and Enitharmon, as the living agents of perception, fall with him; and from the imaginative flexibility of the Swedenborgian angelic state, time and space become fixed and rigid, while at the same time their original unity and harmony is destroyed.

Time and Space are born together; they are the twin children of Enion, who is matter:

> *His head beam'd light & in his vigorous voice was prophecy.*
> *He could controll the times & seasons & the days & years;*
> *She could controll the spaces, regions, desart, flood & forest* [27]

Blake constantly uses "desart" to describe Newton's world of physical "particles" or "atoms," which he likens to grains of sand: "flood" is the hylic flux of matter, and the "forest" is nature. Enitharmon's powers, therefore, are defined with precision. Her name suggests that she is "in harmony" with Los (ἐν—in; ἁρμωνία—harmony).

> *"Thy name is Enitharmon," said the fierce prophetic boy.*
> *"While thy mild voice fills all these caverns with sweet harmony"* [28]

"Caverns," again, locates this cosmic scene: the two are in the cave of this world. Without the harmonious cooperation of Space, Time can accomplish nothing; she is the medium of Los's artistry; but fallen, Enitharmon refuses to obey Los and calls down Urizen the demiurge, whom she now accepts as her god. At the wedding feast of now fallen Time and Space, a "terrible" song celebrates the fall of all things into Urizen's power—that is, into his world created outside the eternity of mind or imagination. The fallen Zoas celebrate the beginning of this new universe, in which "Man shall be no more" because material objects have been declared to exist as such and apart from the perceiving mind.

Before their fall into the inflexible external Cartesian mode, Time and Space were flexible, imaginative; and Blake is doubtless following Swedenborg's account of the state of the angels, in whose world love determines space, wisdom time. "Time makes one with thought grounded in affection; for hence is derived the quality of a man's state." As in dreams, times and spaces are only apparent; they still appear progressive, because angels and spirits are finite. Only in God times and spaces are not progressive, "because

He is infinite, and infinite things in Him are one. . . . the Divine is in all time without time."

But behind Swedenborg there lies a long tradition; and Blake probably knew several versions of the Hermetic teaching on the expansive nature of thought. There is an often-copied passage in the tenth book of the *Pymander:*

> Consider him that contains all things, and understand that nothing is more capacious, than that which is incorporeal, nothing more swift, nothing more powerful, but it is most capacious, most swift, and most strong.
>
> And judge of this by thyself, command thy Soul to go into *India*, and sooner than thou canst bid it, it will be there. Bid it likewise pass over the *Ocean*, and suddenly it will be there; not as passing from place to place, but suddenly it will be there.
>
> Command it to fly into Heaven, and it will need no wings, neither shall anything hinder it, not the fire of the Sun, not the *Aether*, not the turning of the Spheres, not the bodies of any other Stars, but cutting through all, it will fly up to the last and farthest Body.
>
> . . . Increase thy self unto an immeasureable greatness, leaping beyond every Body, and transcending all Time, become Eternity, and thou shalt understand God . . . Become higher than all height, lower than all depths, comprehend in thy-self the qualities of all the Creatures, of the Fire, the Water, the Dry and Moist; and conceive likewise, that thou canst be everywhere, in the Sea, in the Earth.
>
> Thou shalt at once understand thy self, not yet begotten in the Womb, young, old, to be dead, the things after death, and all these together, as also times, places, deeds, qualities, quantities, or else thou canst not yet understand God.
>
> But if thou shut up thy Soul in the Body, and abuse it, and say, I understand nothing, I can do nothing, I am afraid of the Sea, I cannot climb up to Heaven, I know not who I am, I cannot tell what I shall be; What hast thou to do with God? [29]

Los and Enitharmon in their imaginatively expansive state possess these faculties of expansion and contraction; and the images used in the Hermetica reappear in Blake's account of their powers:

*For Los & Enitharmon walk'd forth on the dewy Earth*

> *Contracting or expanding their all flexible senses*
> *At will to murmur in the flowers small as the honey bee,*
> *At will to stretch across the heavens & step from star to star,*
> *Or standing on the Earth erect, or on the stormy waves*
> *Driving the storms before them, or delighting in sunny beams,*
> *While round their heads the Elemental Gods kept harmony.*[30]

Therefore, Blake admonishes,

> *Let the Human Organs be kept in their perfect Integrity,*
> *At will Contracting into Worms or Expanding into Gods,*
>
> .    .    .
>
> *. . . for tho' we sit down within*
> *The plowed furrow, list'ning to the weeping clods till we*
> *Contract or Expand Space at will, or if we raise ourselves*
> *Upon the chariots of the morning, Contracting or Expanding Time,*
> *Every one knows we are One Family, One Man blessed for ever.*[31]

In "Night the Fifth" we find that a change has taken place in Los and Enitharmon as a result of the fall of man. Time and Space are now fixed and dead:

> *Now fix'd into one stedfast bulk his features stonify,*
> *. . . Enitharmon stretched on the dreary earth.*
> *Felt her immortal limbs freeze, stiffening, pale, inflexible.*
> *His feet shrink with'ring from the deep, shrinking & withering,*
> *And Enitharmon shrunk up, all their fibres with'ring beneath,*
> *As plants wither'd by winter, leaves & stems & roots decaying*
> *Melt into thin air, while the seed, driv'n by the furious wind,*
> *Rests on the distant Mountain's top. So Los & Enitharmon,*
> *Shrunk into fixed space, stood trembling on a Rocky cliff,*
> *Yet mighty bulk & majesty & beauty remain'd, but unexpansive.*
> *As far as highest Zenith from the lowest Nadir, so far shrunk*
> *Los from the furnaces, a space immense . . .*
>
> .    .    .
>
> *Their senses unexpansive in one stedfast bulk remain.*[32]

Los and Enitharmon are dead and dehumanized, for their appearances no longer correspond to thoughts. This image is pre-eminently Swedenborgian:

Forasmuch as the lowest Substances of Nature which constitute Earths are dead, and are not mutable and various according to the State of the Affections and Thoughts, as in the spiritual World, but immutable and fixed, therefore there are Spaces there and Distances of Spaces; Such Things are in Consequence of Creation closing there, and subsisting in it's Rest: hence it is evident that Spaces are proper to Nature; and forasmuch as Spaces in Nature are not Appearances of Spaces according to States of Life, as in the spiritual World, they also may be called dead.[33]

The same idea is stated even more plainly in *Milton;* imaginative vision is "frozen" into unexpansive space and time:

> *How are the Beasts & Birds & Fishes & Plants & Minerals*
> *Here fix'd into a frozen bulk subject to decay & death?*
> *Those Visions of Human Life & Shadows of Wisdom & Knowledge*
> *Are here frozen to unexpansive deadly destroying terrors* [34]

Los laments the death-change of Enitharmon. The spaces of nature that, when animated by "her spirit," are so beautiful, emptied of imaginative life are withered and dead:

> *Los saw her stretch'd, the image of death, upon his wither'd valleys;*
> *Her shadow went forth & return'd. Now she was pale as snow*
> *When the mountains & hills are cover'd over & the paths of Men*
> > *shut up,*
> *But when her spirit return'd, as ruddy as a morning when*
> *The ripe fruit blushes into joy in heaven's eternal halls.*[34a]

In another passage the fall of Enitharmon is described as, first, a fall from the bosom of the "eternal" Urthona; then she is a corpse guarded by Tharmas and Enion in their world of hyle:

> *. . . Tharmas took her in, pitying. Then Enion in jealous fear*
> *Murder'd her & hid her in her bosom, embalming her for fear*
> *She should arise again to life. . . .*[35]

This "embalming" of space by matter, as a "corse," is another way of expressing, in symbolic terms, the same event.

Blake's grasp of the idea of space and time and all appearances as creations of mind itself finds its most splendid expression in a long passage in *Milton*, pages 28–29. Here Blake's power as a poet matches his grasp as a philosopher; and in lines of unsurpassed strength and eloquence he describes the labors of Los, who may here be defined in the words in which Coleridge describes the primary imagination, "the living Power and prime Agent of all human Perception, and as a repetition in the finite mind of the eternal act of creation in the infinite I AM." Blake describes the creation of visible objects and appearances by the "sons of Ozoth," [36] who are the living agents of the faculty of sight; they are of the family of Los:

> *The Sons of Ozoth within the Optic Nerve stand fiery glowing,*
> *And the number of his Sons is eight millions & eight.*
> *They give delights to the man unknown; artificial riches*
> *They give to scorn, & their possessors to trouble & sorrow & care,*
> *Shutting the sun & moon & stars & trees & clouds & waters*
> *And hills out from the Optic Nerve, & hardening it into a bone*
> *Opake and like the black pebble on the enraged beach,*
> *While the poor indigent is like the diamond which, tho' cloth'd*
> *In rugged covering in the mine, is open all within*
> *And in his hallow'd center holds the heavens of bright eternity.*[37]

The passage continues with a magnificent account of the imaginative creation of time:

> *But others of the Sons of Los build Moments & Minutes & Hours*
> *And Days & Months & Years & Ages & Periods, wondrous buildings;*
> *And every Moment has a Couch of gold for soft repose,*
> *(A Moment equals a pulsation of the artery),*
> *And between every two Moments stands a Daughter of Beulah*
> *To feed the Sleepers on their Couches with maternal care.*
> *And every Minute has an azure Tent with silken Veils:*
> *And every Hour has a bright golden Gate carved with skill:*
> *And every Day & Night has Walls of brass & Gates of adamant,*
> *Shining like precious Stones & ornamented with appropriate signs:*
> *And every Month a silver paved Terrace builded high:*
> *And every Year invulnerable Barriers with high Towers:*
> *And every Age is Moated deep with Bridges of silver & gold:*
> *And every Seven Ages is Incircled with a Flaming Fire.*
> *Now Seven Ages is amounting to Two Hundred Years.*
> *Each has its Guard, each Moment, Minute, Hour, Day, Month &*
>          *Year.*
>
> *All are the work of Fairy hands of the Four Elements:*
> *The Guard are Angels of Providence on duty evermore.*

*Every Time less than a pulsation of the artery*
*Is equal in its period & value to Six Thousand Years,*
*For in this Period the Poet's Work is Done, and all the Great*
*Events of Time start forth & are conciev'd in such a Period,*
*Within a Moment, a Pulsation of the Artery.*[38]

But the arguments of Newton, Locke, and Berkeley also are all held clearly in mind. Locke uses the *moment* as his unit of time; he defines it as such "a small Part in Duration, may be called a *Moment*, and is the time of one *Idea* in our Minds, in the train of their ordinary succession there." [39] Newton distinguishes between "Absolute time" and "Relative, Apparent, and Common Time," which is "the measure of Duration by the means of motion, which is commonly used instead of time; such as an Hour, a Day, a Month, a Year"—and makes the same distinction between relative and absolute space. Berkeley answers Locke and Newton in terms that accord with the Platonic and Hermetic traditional view of the nature of times and spaces. He urges that any attempt to distinguish between "*Absolute* and *relative*, *true*, and *apparent* . . . doth suppose these qualities to have an existence without the mind." But, Berkeley argues, there is only time for the mind. "Time therefore being nothing, *abstracted from the succession of ideas in our minds*, it follows that the duration of any finite spirit must be estimated by the number of *ideas or actions* succeeding each other in that same spirit or mind. Hence it is a plain consequence that the soul always thinks." [40]

Blake had probably read in Sir William Jones's essay *On the Chronology of the Hindoos* what the translator calls a "wild stanza," but which to Blake would have seemed the mere truth: " 'A *thousand* Great Ages are a day of BRAHMA; a *thousand* such days are an *Indian* hour of VISHNU, *six hundred thousand* such hours make a period of RUDRA; and a million of *Rudra's* . . . are but a *second* to the Supreme Being.' The *Hindu* theologians deny the conclusion of the stanza to be orthodox: *Time*, they say, *exists not at all with GOD;* and they advise the astronomers to mind their own business without meddling with theology." [41]

Blake sums up the philosophy that sees the whole sensible world as summoned into being by mind, and by mind continuously created. Berkeley writes:

It is thought strangely absurd that upon closing my eyelids, all the visible objects round me should be reduced to nothing; and yet is not this what philosophers commonly acknowledge, when they agree on all hands, that light and colours . . . exist no longer than they are perceived? Again, it may to some perhaps seem very incredible, that things should be every moment creating, yet this very notion is commonly taught in the Schools. For the Schoolmen, though they acknowledge the existence of matter . . . are nevertheless of opinion that it cannot subsist without the divine conservation, which by them is expounded to be a continual creation.[42]

Blake underlined one of Lavater's aphorisms which states, in simpler terms, this Berkeleyan conception: "As in looking upward each beholder thinks himself the centre of the sky; so Nature formed her individuals, that each must see himself the centre of being." [43] It is by virtue of this centrality that each man inherits a unique paradise, his own "garden on a mount."

> *The Sky is an immortal Tent built by the Sons of Los:*
> *And every Space that a Man views around his dwelling-place*
> *Standing on his own roof or in his garden on a mount*
> *Of twenty-five cubits in height, such space is his Universe:*
> *And on its verge the Sun rises & sets, the Clouds bow*
> *To meet the flat Earth & the Sea in such an order'd Space:*
> *The Starry heavens reach no farther, but here bend and set*
> *On all sides, & the two Poles turn on their valves of gold;*
> *And if he move his dwelling-place, his heavens also move*
> *Where'er he goes, & all his neighbourhood bewail his loss.*
> *Such are the Spaces called Earth & such its dimension.*
> *As to that false appearance which appears to the reasoner*
> *As of a Globe rolling thro' Voidness, it is a delusion of Ulro.*
> *The Microscope knows not of this nor the Telescope: they alter*
> *The ratio of the Spectator's Organs, but leave Objects untouch'd.*
> *For every Space larger than a red Globule of Man's blood*
> *Is visionary, and is created by the Hammer of Los:*
> *And every Space smaller than a Globule of Man's blood opens*
> *Into Eternity of which this vegetable Earth is but a shadow.*
> *The red Globule is the unwearied Sun by Los created*
> *To measure Time and Space to mortal Men every morning.*[44]

Los is the imagination that creates times and spaces and all that appears within them; [45] his labors are imaginative in the highest sense, for he imagines the world into being and lays upon it the outlines of all forms and appearances. "Sense," Blake wrote in the margin of his *Siris*, is "the Eye of Imagination"; [46] for what the imagination summons into being is not some fancy but the real world itself. The "heathen or Platonic Philosophy" blinds the eye of imagination, so Blake perceived, because Plato "considered God as abstracted or distinct from the natural world." [47] Los imagines into being all that we see, hear, and experience with our five senses; he creates "the unwearied Sun"; he is the magician of perception, making our world perpetually, causing things to appear thus and not otherwise to our consciousness. "All that we See is Vision, from Generated Organs gone as soon as come, Permanent in The Imagination, Consider'd as Nothing by the Natural Man." [48]

There is a passage in Newton's *Principia Mathematica* in which Blake's very phrases about the *moving* of places seem to originate. Newton held the opinion that time, space, and motion are fixed and absolute:

> As the order of the parts of Time is immutable, so also is the order of the parts of Space. Suppose those parts to be mov'd out of their places, and they will be moved (if the expression may be allowed) out of themselves. For times and spaces are, as it were, the Places as well of themselves as of all other things. All things are placed in Time as to order of Succession; and in Space as to order of Situation. It is from their essence or nature that they are Places; and that the primary places of things should be moveable, is absurd. These are therefore the absolute places; and translations out of those places, are the only Absolute Motions . . . *If a place is mov'd, whatever is placed therein moves along with it; and therefore a body, which is mov'd from a place in motion, partakes also of the motion of its place.*[49]

From these definitions Newton proceeds to define "immoveable space," and uses the phrase "such is the dimension . . ." a few lines below the passage quoted; but Blake replies that "the soul is its own place":

> *And if he move his dwelling-place, his heavens also move*
> *Where'er he goes . . .*
> *Such are the Spaces called Earth, & such its dimension*

Berkeley refutes Newton's argument that "the *place* being moved, that which is placed therein is also moved." "Sensible body rightly considered," says Berkeley, "is nothing but a complexion of such qualities or ideas, as have no existence as distinct from being perceived by a mind."

Taylor's *Timaeus* was published in 1793; and we may be near the truth if we see, in the double aspect of Los-Urthona, Blake's attempt at a mythical statement of Plato's conception of time as the "moving image of eternity." Los makes manifest in series what in eternity exists without progression. Urthona is the eternal paradigm, and Los is eternity in process of becoming—that is, time. The Father, Timaeus tells Socrates, creates the world according to an eternal exemplar:

> Hence he determined by a dianoetic energy to produce a certain movable image of eternity; and thus, while he was adorning and distributing the universe, he at the same time formed an image flowing according to number, of eternity abiding in one; and which receives from us the appellation of time. But besides this he fabricated the generation of days and nights, and months and years, which had no subsistence prior to the universe, but which together with it rose into existence. And all these, indeed, are the proper parts of time. But the terms *it was* and *it will be*, which express the species of generated time, are transfigured by us to an eternal essence, through oblivion of the truth. For we assert of such an essence that it *was*, *is*, and *will be;* while according to truth the term *it is* is alone accommodated to its nature. But we should affirm, that *to have been* and *to be hereafter* are expressions alone accommodated to generation, proceeding according to the flux of time.[50]

Plato's fabrication of "days and nights, and months and years" may also be echoed in the building, by the sons of Los, of

> . . . *Moments & Minutes & Hours*
> *And Days & Months & Years & Ages & Periods* . . .[51]

the great edifice of time, equal to the eternal Now, which is "less than a pulsation of the artery." It is in every way likely that Plato's magnificent thought on the nature of time inspired Blake's no less magnificent poetry. But here again we may be misled by the unanimity of tradition; for Swedenborg writes that the angels "have not Days, Weeks, Months, Years and Ages; but instead of them States of Life. . . . The Angels do not know what Time is."[52]

Following the *Timaeus*, the Hermetica is full of a subtle realization of the relative nature of ideas of past, present, and future:

For while the whole world is together, it is unchangeable, O Son, but all the parts thereof are changeable.

Yet nothing is corrupted or destroyed, and quite abolished but the names trouble men.

For Generation is not life, but Sense, neither is Change Death, but Forgetfulness, or rather Occultation, and lying hid.

Or better thus: —

*For Generation is not a Creation of Life, but a production of things to Sense, and making them manifest. Neither is Change Death, but an Occultation or hiding of that which was.*

These things being so, all things are Immortal, Matter, Life, Spirit, Soul, Mind, whereof every living thing consisteth.[53]

Death destroys nothing, because "all things exist in their eternal forms in the human imagination." Blake followed the Hermetic teaching: "But the people say, That changing is Death, because the Body is dissolved, and the Life goeth into that which appeareth not . . . I affirm That the World is changed, because every day part thereof becomes invisible, but that it is never dissolved." [54]

> *I am that Shadowy Prophet who Six Thousand Years ago*
> *Fell from my station in the Eternal bosom. Six Thousand Years*
> *Are finish'd. I return! both Time & Space obey my will.*
> *I in Six Thousand Years walk up and down; for not one Moment*
> *Of Time is lost, nor one Event of Space unpermanent,*
> *But all remain: every fabric of Six Thousand Years*
> *Remains permanent, tho' on the Earth where Satan*
> *Fell and was cut off, all things vanish & are seen no more,*
> *They vanish not from me & mine, we guard them first & last.*
> *The generations of men run on in the tide of Time,*
> *But leave their destin'd lineaments permanent for ever & ever.*[55]

Time, like a great sculptor, carves in his "halls" every human story and situation possible to be imagined; and these works of time are history:

> *All things acted on Earth are seen in the bright Sculptures of*
> *Los's Halls, & every Age renews its powers from these Works*

*With every pathetic story possible to happen from Hate or*
*Wayward Love; & every sorrow & distress is carved here,*
*Every Affinity of Parents, Marriages & Friendships are here*
*In all their various combinations wrought with wondrous Art,*
*All that can happen to Man in his pilgrimage of seventy years.*[56]

But in eternity, history is the eternal Now: and Los becomes "earth-owner":

*For every thing exists & not one sigh nor smile nor tear,*
*One hair nor particle of dust, not one can pass away.*[57]

This philosophy of the relativity of time and death Blake attempted to express in *The Four Zoas*, in the triple relationship of Urthona, Los, and the Spectre of Urthona, who is a figure distinct from both; yet in the final understanding all these three are but aspects of time (or of eternity). When eternity is manifested in progression, there is time present and time past; and time past is a specter that perpetually swallows up the brief duration of the present: "The Greeks represent Chronos or Time as a very Aged Man; this is Fable, but the Real Vision of Time is in Eternal Youth. . . . But Time & Space are Real Beings, a Male & a Female. Time is a Man, Space is a Woman, & her Masculine Portion is Death." [58]

It is impossible not to recognize in the figures of Time and Space, Los and Enitharmon:

*Los is by mortals nam'd Time, Enitharmon is nam'd Space:*
*But they depict him bald & aged who is in eternal youth*
*All powerful and his locks flourish like the brows of morning:*

.    .    .

*Time is the mercy of Eternity; without Time's swiftness,*
*Which is the swiftest of all things, all were eternal torment.*[59]

Who, then, can be the "masculine portion" of Space, whom Blake calls Death, if not the "dark" Spectre of Urthona? When we examine the accounts of this specter, we discover that the identification illuminates many obscurities. A passage in *Jerusalem* [60] describes the relationship of Los, Enitharmon, and the Spectre in very similar terms, and the "masculine portion" is here named not Death but Urthona:

*And the Two that escaped were the Emanation of Los & his*
*Spectre; for where ever the Emanation goes, the Spectre*

*Attends her as her Guard, & Los's Emanation is named*
*Enitharmon, & his Spectre is named Urthona . . .*

When eternity is experienced in the mode of progression, there is time present and time past. Time past is Blake's "Spectre of Urthona" (that is, death), who forever separates "from Los's back." [61] The back of time must be the past, and this is the more likely when we consider the proverb about "taking time by the forelock," which Blake has suggested in the figure of Los, "whose locks flourish like the brows of morning," which is to say, "time present is given generously and it is always young." But the Spectre follows like a shadow, "devouring" all that Los creates, and forever seeking to possess Enitharmon, whom he claims as really his. This strange triangle explains itself when we realize that Enitharmon is the bride of Urthona in eternity; in this world she is perpetually torn between Los, who possesses the present, and the Spectre, who consumes the past. Death is simply that which is past, occluded, whose claim upon the spaces of earth is continually opposed to that of Los—time present.

Blake, in *Milton*, succeeded in giving expression to his vision of the nature of time without the cumbrous mythological vehicle of the triple figure of Urthona, Los, and the Spectre. Allusions to Urthona and the "Spectre of Urthona" in *Milton* and *Jerusalem* are merely vestigial. Blake had constructed a myth he did not need. Just as he abandoned the Spectre of Tharmas, so he abandoned the Spectre of Urthona, giving some of his lesser attributes to Satan (as the "Miller of Eternity," who is responsible for the revolutions of Newtonian time), and leaving the figure of Los in single splendor as the immortal agent of time and of all sensible appearances.

160 Woodcut by Blake (1821) for Vergil's first Eclogue

# CHAPTER 22

# The Opening of Centers

Enitharmon is space, and spaces belong specifically to her and to the "daughters of Beulah" associated with her:

> There is from Great Eternity a mild & pleasant rest
> Nam'd Beulah, a soft Moony Universe, feminine, lovely,
> Pure, mild & Gentle, given in Mercy to those who sleep,
> Eternally created by the Lamb of God around,
> On all sides, within & without the Universal Man.
> The daughters of Beulah follow sleepers in all their Dreams,
> Creating spaces, lest they fall into Eternal Death.
> The Circle of Destiny complete, they gave to it a space,
> And nam'd the space Ulro, & brooded over it in care & love.[1]

The spaces of earth are dream spaces, apparent to those who fall into the sleep or death from eternity, which we call life; and the time world is likened to a great dream-edifice, built about the sleepers by the Daughters of Beulah.[2]

Enitharmon's world is, in the symbolic sense, necessarily "moony" and nocturnal, since it is "the night of time," the period of the soul's earthly phase, its sleep or death from the world of light:

> She Creates at her will a little moony night & silence
> With Spaces of sweet gardens & a tent of elegant beauty,
> Closed in by a sandy desert & a night of stars shining
> And a little tender moon & hovering angels on the wing;
> And the Male gives a Time & Revolution to her Space
>
>          .     .     .
>
> For All Things Exist in the Human Imagination,
> And thence in Beulah they are stolen by secret amorous theft.[3]

Beulah is marriage, following Isaiah 62:4: "thy land [shall be called] Beulah: for the Lord delighteth in thee, and thy land shall be married." Why marriage should have to do with the creation of space must remain for ever obscure if we look at Blake's symbol from this side of creation; but it becomes clear if we consider that souls descending from eternity enter the space-time universe through the gates of birth. Blake's Daughters of Beulah are nymphs of marriage. His name for them is, one may say, a translation of Porphyry's naiads into a biblical equivalent. They are nymphs of the cave, guardians of the "Urns" in which the "dead" repose, and of the golden "looms" of generation.

But Porphyry has no part in the beautiful image of the Daughters of Beulah in the very act of creating the spaces and times of this world from a "moment of time" and an "atom of space."

Time and space are vital, not material; therefore their units are vital—a blood drop and a heartbeat. They have no existence outside of mind, which is itself without dimension. The most fitting symbol of eternity is the timeless moment and the nonspatial point, the "moment without duration." The Platonic and Aristotelian "atom" is without magnitude, and is not, as modern science conceives the atom, a small division of matter. Plato in the *Timaeus* speaks of the elements not as "atomic" but as existing in particles "so very small as to be invisible." Blake's moment of time and atom of space are, on the contrary, the true Platonic "atoms," without magnitude.

According to tradition, the atom or punctum is the point of intersection of time and the timeless. It is Dante's "punto dello stelo a cui la prima rota va dintorno"; "da quel punto depende il cielo e tutta la natura." [4] Blake's imagery of the nontemporal and the nonspatial becomes clear when we have understood the philosophy upon which it rests. Taylor's *Proclus* [5] may have given Blake insight into the mathematical philosophy of the point. Proclus in his first definition, "A Point is that which has no Parts," says that the point, being indivisible, contains "infinity occultly." [6] "A point presides over this whole series [that is, spatiality], unites and contains all partible natures, terminates their progressions, produces them all by its infinite power, and comprehends them in its indivisible bound." [7] Proclus quotes Plato, who in the tenth book of the *Republic* writes of center-points as uniting by "adamantine power" both the axes and bounding surfaces of spheres:

161 The timeless moment of inspiration (the youthful poet's dream): illustration (after 1818) for *L'Allegro*

The female figures within the sphere which represents the mental spaces of the soul are perhaps the muses or Daughters of Inspiration. See also [144].

He adds too, that the whole spindle of the Fates, is turned about these, and leaps round their coercive union. But other more recondite and abstruse discourses affirm, that the demiurge presides over the world, seated in the poles, and, by his divine love, converting the Universe to himself. But the Pythagoreans thought that the pole should be called the Seal of Rhea; because the zoogonic, or vivific goddess, pours through these into the universe, an inexplicable and efficacious power. And the centre they called the prison of Jupiter; because, since Jupiter has placed a demiurgical guard in the bosom of the world, he has firmly established it in the midst.[8]

Centers possess "an essence, and perfect power which pervades through all partible natures."

Such passages as this may have given Blake his beautiful figures of the Daughters of Beulah, who, like Rhea (goddess of flux) and the Fates, open spatiality from the point, multitude from unity, by giving birth—their "zoogonic" power. Blake's imagination was often fired by pure metaphysics to the creation of myth, as we have already seen in the figure of Enion; and so it is with those Daughters of Beulah, who stand between the generated and the eternal world:

> *Then Eno, a daughter of Beulah, took a Moment of Time*
> *And drew it out to seven thousand years with much care & affliction*
> *And many tears, & in every year made windows into Eden.*
> *She also took an atom of space & opened its centre*
> *Into Infinitude & ornamented it with wondrous art.*
>
> .     .     .
>
> *But Los & Enitharmon delighted in the Moony spaces of Eno.*[9]

In *Milton* the Daughters of Beulah are said to stand "between every two Moments," [10] for every moment of time originates from eternity. (Berkeley, it will be remembered, writes that things are "every moment creating" [11]):

> *There is a Moment in each Day that Satan cannot find,*
> *Nor can his Watch Fiends find it; but the Industrious find*
> *This Moment & it multiply, & when it once is found*
> *It renovates every Moment of the Day if rightly placed.*[12]

This is the ever-present door into eternity, unknown to the ratio (since, by definition, the punctum cannot be measured) but discoverable to the imagination; and so with spaces:

> *There is a Grain of Sand in Lambeth that Satan cannot find,*
> *Nor can his Watch Fiends find it; 'tis translucent & has many Angles,*
> *But he who finds it will find Oothoon's palace; for within*
> *Opening into Beulah, every angle is a lovely heaven.*[13]

In *Jerusalem* the figure of Eno is replaced by Erin,[14] who is, also, a daughter of Beulah. The Emanations

> *Concenter in one Female form, an Aged pensive Woman,*
>
> . . .
>
> *. . . With awful hands she took*
> *A Moment of Time, drawing it out with many tears & afflictions*
> *And many sorrows, oblique across the Atlantic Vale,*
>
> . . .
>
> *Into a Rainbow of jewels and gold, a mild Reflection from*
> *Albion's dread Tomb: Eight thousand and five hundred years*
> *In its extension. Every two hundred years has a door to Eden.*
> *She also took an Atom of Space, with dire pain opening it a Center*
> *Into Beulah . . .*[15]

The "opening of centers" Blake has taken from Boehme, employing, as he so often does, a symbol that cannot be fully understood unless we turn to its original author. In common with the Hermetic and Platonic traditions, that of the alchemists assumes as a matter of course that the material world originates from a nonspatial spiritual world; and by way of the alchemists, no doubt, the tradition reached Boehme, who in his turn added to it the quality of his own imagination:

> For the Stars and four Elements, and all whatever is bred and engendered out of them, and live therein, hang [or belong] to one *Punctum*, where the divine Power has manifested itself from itself in a *Form* . . . Nothing can live in this World without this *Punctum;* it is the only Cause of the Life and Motion of all the Powers; and without it, all would be in the *Stillness*, without Motion.[16]

This birth from the punctum is the *magia* of manifested being—as Blake says, "the work of fairy hands of the four elements": "The Being of all

Beings is only a magical Birth [deriving itself] out of one only into an Infinity; the *One* is God, the *Infinite* is Time and Eternity, and a Manifestation of the One; where each Thing may be reduced out of one into many, and again out of many into one." [17] To illustrate this abstract concept, Boehme uses, as an image of manifestation, the tree that issues from a seed; and a similar fine use of the image Blake doubtless found in Paracelsus:

> If the Cypres tree can spring out of a little graine, surely it may be brought into as small a quantity as that little kernell was at first. A grain and the beryll are alike. As it begins in a grain, so it ends in a beryll. Now when the separation is thus made, and every thing *reduc'd* to its nature, or first principle, to wit, into *nothing*: then is there nothing within the skie but is endlesse and eternall. For that by which it is for ever will there flourish much more largly than it did before the creation, it having no frailty or mortality in it.[18]

Manifested being expands like a tree or a cloud of smoke from a little grain or seed, and to such a dimensionless point it returns again. Proclus' point, Boehme's "punctum," Paracelsus' "grain," and Blake's "atom of space" are all akin; and Blake is but elaborating this traditional concept in all his characteristic images of minute centers in which there is eternity. His term "the opening of centres" is itself traceable to the *Three Principles of the Divine Essence*. Boehme is here writing of Lucifer: "at the Time of his Creation he stood (in the Kingdom of Heaven) in the Point, *Locus*, or Place, (where the Holy Ghost in the Birth of the Heart of God, in Paradise, did open infinite and innumerable Centres) in the eternal Birth; in this Seat or Place, he was corporified, and has his Beginning in the Opening of the Centers in the eternal Nature." [19]

Blake is never more precise than when he is most cryptic—one of the most disconcerting characteristics of his particular kind of obscurity. Nothing is vague: we find ourselves not lost in a mist, but coming with full force against a hard and stony sphinx that refuses to dissolve and will yield only to precise knowledge. Blake writes of these esoteric concepts of the mystical tradition with the tacit assumption that his readers will understand him, the same assumption we expect to find in a contemporary physicist writing of neutrons and protons and the like. His obscurity in such cases arises from his reader's ignorance of this special language. It is not always possible to defend Blake; but there are many examples—the opening of the centers is one of them—where he is employing the only existing language in which it is possible to discuss concepts of this kind, concepts which must, besides, necessarily remain incomprehensible to positivists and others who deny the vertical scale of mental reality of which the maya of sensible appearances is only one plane, in which mankind is, by our specific constitution, located.

Nevertheless, his poetic genius has, in many passages, transmuted metaphysical thought into a form that may be directly and intuitively apprehended, as in the following four lines, which might be considered the very essence of Blake:

> *To see a World in a Grain of Sand*
> *And a Heaven in a Wild Flower,*
> *Hold Infinity in the palm of your hand*
> *And Eternity in an hour.*[20]

We can understand these lines without previous knowledge of their metaphysical background; we learn of the philosophy as we read the poetry; and yet in the light of Blake's extensive use of Boehme's symbol of the opening of the centers, we may surmise that they were written in a state of imaginative delight occasioned by his reading of the *Three Principles*, perhaps this very passage: "The Eternal Center, and the Birth of Life, and the Substantiality, are every where. If you make a small Circle, as small as a little Grain, [or Kernel of Seed,] there is the whole Birth of the Eternal Nature."[21] The obscurity of such lines as

> *What is Above is Within, for every-thing in Eternity is translucent:*
> *The Circumference is Within, Without is formed the Selfish Center,*
> *And the Circumference still expands going forward to Eternity,*
> *And the Center has Eternal States; these States we now explore.*[22]

disappears when we realize that these are a paraphrase of Boehme: "The Angelical World is called *above*, and the formed outward is called *below;* in like Manner as we say, when a Fire is kindled, then the Light is *above*, and the Substance [or Matter] *below;* when we speak of God's [being] *above*, then we mean and understand *within*, for the [being] within, without the Substance, is the [being] above; for, without the Substance [or Matter] there is all *above*, no below; that which is under the Substance is also above."[23] So Blake restates Boehme's gloss upon the Gospel teaching that the Kingdom of Heaven is within:

> *The Vegetative Universe opens like a flower from the Earth's center*
> *In which is Eternity. It expands in Stars to the Mundane Shell*
> *And there it meets Eternity again, both within and without.*[24]

"Thus," says Boehme, "the starry Heaven, *viz.*, the *Third Principle* of this world, was created also as a Total Body, having a Circumscription, and standeth just like the Center of Nature; whatsoever thou seest in this Great Circumference, the same is also in the *smallest* Circle: and the whole Principle of this world outwardly, is only a manifestation and discovery of the Eternity in God." [25] The definition of God as a circle whose center is everywhere and whose circumference is nowhere belongs to this traditional thought on the nature of the nonspatial. It is noteworthy that Blake, as well as Boehme, prefers the image of the punctum, the dimensionless point,[26] to the image (equally valid *as* an image) of unbounded vastness, perhaps because it is more difficult to think of the unbounded without bringing in notions of material extension, and certainly because of the great beauty and poetic precision of the images of minuteness—the flower, the grain of sand, the "little winged fly." The poem *Milton* is full of images of the nature of inspiration, given to the poet by the Daughters of Beulah, who stand "between every two Moments." Above all, Blake attempts, in this poem, to describe all manifestation as proceeding from the atemporal moment—"smaller than a Globule of Man's blood" and "less than a pulsation of the artery"—which opens into eternity.[27] The poet must find this moment:

> *For in this Period the Poet's Work is Done, and all the Great Events of Time start forth & are conciev'd in such a Period, Within a Moment, a Pulsation of the Artery.*[28]

The moment of eternity cannot be found by Satan, who is, by definition, "the soul of the natural frame." He knows only the atoms of space and moments of time. When we consider that Boehme makes Satan's coming into existence take place at the "Opening of the Centers," Blake's meaning of Satan and Adam as the "limits" of opacity and contraction will also be understood. Satan's center is not infinity but "a white Dot." [29] This idea of the zero again links Satan with Newtonian thought and the laws of attraction to a center, rather than an expansion from a center, which dominate the world of matter as described by the Newtonian physics.[30] The "whiteness" of the dot seems to suggest that Blake was here thinking of Newton's *Opticks.* Newton observed that at the focus of the spectrum of color there is a white spot. The rainbow for Blake and Boehme, on the other hand, is the symbol of the "Opening" of the eternal world into manifestation, and therefore of the Last Judgment.[31] Newton's image would appear, in this context, as yet another symbolic expression of the metaphysical vacuity of a philosophy of natural cause. Here, at all events, is Newton's description: "The Colours of these Rain-bows succeeded one another from the Center outwards. . . . first, there was in their common center a white round spot of faint Light, which beam sometimes fell upon the middle of the Spot, and sometimes by a little inclination of the Speculum receded from the middle and left the Spot white to the center." [32] Erin, who in Blake's myth opens the "Centers," is also, we remember, accompanied always by a "Rainbow of jewels and gold"; but her atoms of space and moments of time open from eternity, and her rainbow has its "doors" and "windows" into Eden. This comparison might seem farfetched; but when we remember that Blake's entire work may in a sense be seen as his answer to Newton, the possibility remains strong. We know from Blake's letter to Butts in which is the poem on his "First vision of Light" that he had read Newton's *Opticks* with some care and considerable delight, his disagreement notwithstanding. (Newton is admitted into eternity after all, on almost the last page of *Jerusalem*.) [33] The eternal moment, unknown to Satan, is known to the poet; and in *Milton* Blake rises to heights of inspired insight and eloquence upon this theme.

With this gateway of eternity Blake beautifully associates two images, the lark and the wild thyme. From the hidden moment there springs a fountain and there grows the wild thyme, and there the lark of inspiration builds his nest. It is here that eternity flows into time. The fountain, in all traditions, bears this meaning. Plato's poet draws his inspiration from the "fountains" of the Muses; and, above all, "is the Holy Ghost any other than an Intellectual Fountain?" [34] Blake doubtless also recalled that according to Proclus, the goddess Rhea is the fontal goddess through whose punctum existence flows from nonbeing into being—a theme developed by Taylor both in his *Dissertation* and in his notes to the *Hymns of Orpheus:*

> *Just in this Moment, when the morning odours rise abroad*
> *And first from the Wild Thyme, stands a Fountain in a rock*
> *Of crystal flowing into two Streams . . .*
>
> .     .     .
>
> *The Wild Thyme is Los's Messenger to Eden, a mighty Demon,*
> *Terrible, deadly & poisonous his presence in Ulro dark;*
> *Therefore he appears only a small Root creeping in grass*
> *Covering over the Rock of Odours his bright purple mantle*
> *Beside the Fount above the Lark's nest in Golgonooza.*[35]

162 The lark: illustration (after 1818) for *L'Allegro*

The "Wild Thyme" is perhaps a pun; it is the wild *time*, the secret moment, that Blake means—the inspired, "wild" moment "that Satan cannot find." This moment that mediates between time and eternity is dreaded as a "mighty Demon" in Ulro (the world of generation), where the infinite power of imaginative influx is feared as inimical to the world of the ratio. And yet, says Blake, that moment, so mighty,[36] fraught with eternal significance, is hidden and small, like the tiniest of flowers, passed over unnoticed, easily missed if we are not "industrious" in the life of the spirit. Perhaps Blake chose the thyme as the smallest and yet sweetest of flowers, and therefore the fittest symbol of the "dimensionless point." Fragrance, too, is an apt symbol of a quality neither spatial nor temporal. It is certain that the "terrible" power of the thyme comes from its center open to eternity. In a passage of rare beauty Blake describes all flowers as possessing this power of opening the unmanifest into manifestation, by virtue of their "opening" from a dimensionless "eternal" center:

> *Thou percievest the Flowers put forth their precious Odours,*
> *And none can tell how from so small a center comes such sweets,*
> *Forgetting that within that Center Eternity expands*
> *Its ever during doors that Og & Anak* [37] *fiercely guard.*
> *First, e'er the morning breaks, joy opens in the flowery bosoms,*
> *Joy even to tears, which the Sun rising dries; first the Wild Thyme*
> *And Meadow-sweet, downy & soft waving among the reeds,*
> *Light springing on the air, lead the sweet Dance: they wake*
> *The Honeysuckle sleeping on the Oak; the flaunting beauty*
> *Revels along upon the wind; the White-thorn, lovely May,*
> *Opens her many lovely eyes listening; the Rose still sleeps,*
> *None dare to wake her; soon she bursts her crimson curtain'd bed*
> *And comes forth in the majesty of beauty; every Flower,*
> *The Pink, the Jessamine, the Wall-flower, the Carnation,*
> *The Jonquil, the mild Lilly, opes her heavens . . .*[38]

The lark, whose nest is "at the eastern Gate of wide Golgonooza," is "Los's Messenger." Blake associated the lark with Milton; and the singing lark is one of his most beautifully conceived illustrations for *L'Allegro*:

> *To hear the Lark begin his flight,* [162]
> *And singing startle the dull night*
> *From his watch-towre in the skies,*
> *Till the dappled dawn doth rise.*[39]

No doubt Blake also thought of Shakespeare's lark, which sings at "heaven's gate": "The Lark is a mighty Angel." It is not said that the lark, this little bird, like the thyme with which he is associated, is a minute center in which eternity expands, but this is implied. Implicit also is the comparison of the lark's song with the poet's. All is integral, relevant to the theme of the miracle of inspiration. The poet brings into existence works of time from the world of eternity, through the moment "less than a pulsation of the artery" with the effortlessness of a bird's song. So Blake himself claims to have written *Milton:* "the Time it has taken in writing was thus render'd Non Existent, & an immense Poem Exists which seems to be the Labour of a long Life, all produc'd without Labour or Study." [40]

This is an experience known to all imaginative poets, whose best work, like bird song, seems rather "given" than "made." Blake describes a state in which inspiration comes with such power that the poet can scarcely keep pace with the influx. Such a poet is his Milton, "the inspired man," whose utterance expresses the essence and eternal form of the human soul as bird song does the innate soul of the bird species. As all nightingales sing the one song, so he sings for the Divine Humanity in all men:

> *The Lark sitting upon his earthy bed, just as the morn*
> *Appears, listens silent; then springing from the waving Cornfield,*
> > *loud*
>
> *He leads the Choir of Day: trill, trill, trill, trill,*
> *Mounting upon the wings of light into the Great Expanse,*
> *Reechoing against the lovely blue & shining heavenly Shell,*
> *His little throat labours with inspiration; every feather*
> *On throat & breast & wings vibrates with the effluence Divine.*
> *All Nature listens silent to him, & the awful Sun*
> *Stands still upon the Mountain looking on this little Bird*
> *With eyes of soft humility & wonder, love & awe.*
> *Then loud from their green covert all the Birds begin their Song.*[41]

"I may praise it," Blake wrote of *Milton,* "since I dare not pretend to be any other than the Secretary; the Authors are in Eternity." [42]


The vastness of Newton's "soul-shudd'ring vacuum" oppressed, like black melancholy, the imagination of the eighteenth century. Man, reduced to insignificance in a universe of dizzying immensity, traveling forever in a hell of space, on a planet that was itself but a speck of dust in endless night, scanned the night sky, which had become a mathematician's nightmare. Young's *Night Thoughts* reflect the mind's wrestling with this sense of insignificance in a void; Blake's continuous use of images of the punctum as the most fit symbol of eternity is in striking contrast with the imagery of the eighteenth-century "Enlightenment." Blake's *The Fly* is a significant reversal of a commonplace image of the minuteness and insignificance of men, used by Gray in a poem that Blake had illustrated in the early 1790s. Gray compares the human race to a dance-the-hay of flies:

> *To Contemplation's sober eye*
> *Such is the race of man:*
> *And they that creep, and they that fly,*
> *Shall end where they began.*
> *Alike the busy and the gay*
> *But flutter thro' life's little day,*
> *In Fortune's varying colours drest:*
> *Brush'd by the hand of rough Mischance,*
> *Or chill'd by Age, their airy dance*
> *They leave in dust to rest.*[43]

[163]

Blake chose to illustrate the two figures of "Age" and "rough Mischance," at whose touch the little human winged figures perish. He did not, however, illustrate "Contemplation," thinking perhaps that this printer's-devil personification was less of a philosopher than Gray supposed. Blake's *The Fly*[44] is at once a compliment to Gray's fancy and an answer to his facile mood of philosophic melancholy, the reflection of the Newtonian picture of man's insignificance in the immensity of space.

The deleted first verse of the poem as Blake wrote it in his notebook is exactly in the mood in which he sketched the figure of rough Mischance:

> *Woe, alas! my guilty hand*
> *Brush'd across thy summer joy;*
> *All thy gilded, painted pride*
> *Shatter'd, fled . . .*[45]

There is an echo here of Gray's:

> *Some lightly o'er the current skim,*
> *Some shew their gaily-gilded trim*

The text within the illustration reads:

ODE ON THE SPRING.  45

And float amid the liquid noon:
Some lightly o'er the current ſkim,
Some ſhew their gaily-gilded trim
Quick-glancing to the ſun.

To Contemplation's ſober eye
Such is the race of man:
And they that creep, and they that fly,
Shall end where they began,
Alike the buſy and the gay
But flutter thro' life's little day,
In Fortune's varying colours dreſt:
Bruſh'd by the hand of rough Miſchance,
Or chill'd by Age, their airy dance
They leave in duſt to reſt.

Methinks I hear, in accents low,
The ſportive kind reply:
Poor Moraliſt! and what art thou?
A ſolitary fly!

D 2                    Thy

163 "Rough Mischance" and "Age": illustration (early 1790's) to Gray's *Ode on the Spring*

The final draft is still close to Gray, although "gilded, painted pride" has gone:

> *Little Fly,*
> *Thy summer play*
> *My thoughtless hand*
> *Has brush'd away.*

Blake's second verse is a paraphrase of Gray's

> *To Contemplation's sober eye*
> *Such is the race of man*

Blake sees that the argument works both ways: if man is like a fly (insignificant), is not a fly like man (significant)?

> *Am not I*
> *A fly like thee?*
> *Or art not thou*
> *A man like me?*

It is always to illustrate the nonspatial nature of existence that Blake returns in his later writings to Gray's images of the worm and the fly. Like the grain of sand and the minutest flower, worm and fly illustrate the nonspatial punctum of eternity. He is still talking to Gray, one may feel, in the passage in *Milton:*

> *Seest thou the little winged fly, smaller than a grain of sand?*
> *It has a heart like thee, a brain open to heaven & hell,*
> *Withinside wondrous & expansive: its gates are not clos'd:*
> *I hope thine are not; hence it clothes itself in rich array:*
> *Hence thou art cloth'd with human beauty, O thou mortal man.*
> *Seek not thy heavenly father then beyond the skies,*
> *There Chaos dwells & ancient Night & Og & Anak old.*[46]

Gray's error about the flies arose precisely because, obedient to the fashion of his time, he did see God in terms of Newton's Pantocrator, in terms of the "mathematic holiness" of vastness. (Og and Anak are giants and therefore symbols of the quantitative eternity of Locke and Newton.) There is much point in Blake's selection of the image of the fly as a point of attack on the Enlightenment.

Gray's worm, like his fly, remains associated with this idea of the nonspatial nature of the spiritual universe:

> *He wither'd up the Human Form*
> *By laws of sacrifice for sin,*
> *Till it became a Mortal Worm,*
> *But O! translucent all within.*[47]

Blake is here, as in the phrase "a brain open to heaven and hell," using one of Swedenborg's most finely imagined themes, the heavens and hells as states and places within the mind, the "interior" worlds.

For Blake flowers, worm, and fly are symbols both of the significance of even the smallest living creature and of the punctum itself, alike present in the least and in the greatest. The Newtonian-Lockean visions of magnitude, with all their implications of power and intimidation, meant nothing to Blake; neither is there, in his imagery of the minute, any trace of the sentimentalism of false humility, which is but the other side of the exaltation of vastness and power. The punctum is neither great nor small, but infinite; and the dignity it implies in every living essence is not relative but absolute. The divine life is in all, not partially but totally.

In a passage quoted above (page 156) Boehme describes the seat of Lucifer as being in the place of the opening of the centers. Here, Boehme says, he is "corporified." It is in the seventh or nature spirit that Lucifer, according to Boehme, especially reigns: "His Kingdom is the created Heaven and this World." Such was the nature of Lucifer, unfallen; he is accident, not substance. With his fall, accident becomes substance; and manifestation, nature, externality, is no longer realized as upheld by the "influx" of spirit. The "Creator also, in his wrath . . . imprisoned the Devil therein, and made an eternal lodging therein for him."

> Now the third Birth or Geniture, is the Comprehensibility or Palpability of Nature, which was rarified and transparent, lovely, pleasant and bright, *before* the time of God's Wrath, so that the qualifying or fountain Spirits could see *through* and *through* all.
>
> There was neither Stone nor Earth therein, neither had it Need of any such created or contracted Light as now; but the Light generated itself *everywhere* in the Center, and all stood in the Light.
>
> But when King *Lucifer* was created, then he excited or awakened the Wrath of God in this *third* Birth or Geniture; for the Bodies of the Angels came to be *Creatures* in this third Birth.[48]

Blake has followed Boehme closely in his understanding of Satan as the world of "accident formed into substance" by, as he says, "the cruelties of demonstration"; the ratio is "cruel" because it destroys the life in all phenomena by whose virtue they exist. The spirits can no longer see "through and through all," and Satan becomes the "limit of opacity." Thus Satan is defined at the outset as Lord of the external universe; as such Los addresses him:

*O Satan, my youngest born, art thou not Prince of the Starry Hosts*

*And of the Wheels of Heaven, to turn the Mills day & night?*
*Art thou not Newton's Pantocrator, weaving the Woof of Locke?*
*To Mortals thy Mills seem every thing . . .*[49]

These are "the dark Satanic mills"; and we are back in Locke's universe of the tractates, "a mill with complicated wheels":

*I turn my eyes to the Schools & Universities of Europe*
*And there behold the Loom of Locke, whose Woof rages dire,*
*Wash'd by the Water-wheels of Newton: black the cloth*
*In heavy wreathes folds over every Nation: cruel Works*
*Of many Wheels I view, wheel without wheel, with cogs tyrannic*
*Moving by compulsion each other, not as those in Eden, which,*
*Wheel within Wheel, in freedom revolve in harmony & peace.*[50]   [164]

The "wheels" are the causal interlocking presumed in a mechanistic universe, "wheel without wheel," because the material impulsion of one body by another is imparted from without. These presumed mechanistic causes turn "the Satanic mills" of Newton's universe. In contrast, there is the perennial philosophy of the "wheels within wheels" of Ezekiel's vision, spiritual essences that operate the causes of things in a manner quite other than that conceived by the mechanistic philosophy. According to tradition in all its various forms, the phenomenal world is the outermost and apparent product of spiritual agencies of a nonmaterial kind, springing from the "eternal centers of the birth of life," whence existence issues from a divine source. In Satan's universe there is only "void and solid":

164 Mechanistic causality contrasted with the wings of cherubim: *Jerusalem* (1804–1820), plate 22, detail

*. . . Shapeless Rocks*
*Retaining only Satan's Mathematic Holiness, Length, Bredth &*
*Highth,*
*Calling the Human Imagination, which is the Divine Vision &*
*Fruition*
*In which Man liveth eternally, madness & blasphemy against*
*Its own Qualities, which are Servants of Humanity, not Gods or*
*Lords.*[51]

Newton's Pantocrator is called the god of "Mathematic Holiness," for his divine powers and glories are all defined in terms of magnitude:

> This Being governs all things, not as the soul of the world, but as Lord over all: And on account of his dominion he is wont to be called *Lord God* Παντοκράτωρ, or *Universal Ruler*. For *God* is a relative word, and has a respect to servants; and *Deity* is the dominion of God, not over his own body, as those imagine who fancy God to be the soul of the world, but over servants. The supreme God is a Being eternal, infinite, absolutely perfect; but a being, however perfect, without dominion, cannot be said to be Lord God; for we say, my God, your God, the God of *Israel*, the God of Gods, and Lord of Lords; but we do not say, my Eternal, your Eternal, the Eternal of *Israel*, the Eternal of Gods; we do not say, my Infinite, or my Perfect; These are titles which have no respect to servants. . . . It is the dominion of a spiritual being which constitutes a God.[52]

Satan's "Mathematic Holiness, Length, Bredth & Highth" [53] is a perfectly just comment upon the Newtonian universe of phenomena. The Pantocrator we are to admire because of the vastness of his spaces and the duration of his times, "a Being eternal, infinite, absolutely perfect," known only by his attributes and by "his most wise and excellent contrivances of things, and final causes." Thus the "Holiness" of this universal ruler of a phenomenal universe is not unjustly called "Mathematic"; it is quantitative in its nature. Eternity is qualitative and nonspatial. "I know too well," Blake wrote to Cumberland a few months before the end of his life,[54] "that a great majority of Englishmen are fond of The Indefinite which they Measure by Newton's Doctrine of the Fluxions of an Atom, A Thing that does not Exist." "God keep me," he concludes (the prayer "God keep us from" is ever uppermost in his mind when he thinks of Newton), "from supposing Up and Down to be the same Thing as all Experimentalists must suppose." Certainly they must, because there is no qualitative difference between upward and downward in the directions of space, only a quantitative difference. In spiritual terms "up" and "down" are by no means the same: the phenomenal manifestation (below) is the result of a spiritual cause (above), in "order that the progression of things may form an entire whole, suspended like the golden chain of Homer from the summit of Olympus"—a Platonic image, which Blake echoes in the lines:

> *Thus were the stars of heaven created like a. golden chain*
> *To bind the Body of Man to heaven from falling into the Abyss.*[55]

Thus Blake was not venting mere emotion when he described Bacon, Newton, and Locke as "the three great leaders of Atheism, or Satan's doctrine"; for to Satan, by definition, belongs the world of the ratio; and as Blake said to Crabb Robinson, "Every Thing is Atheism which assumes the reality of the natural and unspiritual world." And just as Satan is inevitably bound up with the world of space and quantity, so is "the Body of Jesus" nonspatial, and the universe within the mind of the Divine Humanity one of essence and quality, not of quantity. In the Body of Jesus, "Length, Bredth, Highth again Obey the Divine Vision." [56]
Thus the Newtonian universe becomes

> *. . . the Void Outside of Existence, which if enter'd into*
> *Becomes a Womb. . . .*[57]

Satanic or spectral existence is a birth into this "womb" of externality. For Blake the only hell is this prison house of the soul cut off from the divine influx.

The "Space" of Satan is first described in "Night the Eighth" of *The Four Zoas*. Here for the first time is told the story of Satan later expanded into the theme of *Milton*. Newtonian space and time are defined: they are the hell into which Satan and his angels fall.

> *. . . a World of deeper Ulro was open'd in the midst*
> *Of the Assembly. In Satan's bosom, a vast unfathomable Abyss.*
>
> .    .    .
>
> *His Spectre raging furious descended into its Space.*[58]

They are also called a "lie," the lie that Gwendolen and the Daughters of Albion bring into actuality as they weave the mortal garments of mankind. The "lie" is that men live in a physical universe of the kind that they believe to be real; but the lie takes on the relative existence of "allegory," and "Became a Space & an Allegory around the Winding Worm" (the "Worm" is generated man). But above all, space and time become "an act of mercy"—the mercy of Enitharmon, who "Created a New Space to protect Satan from punishment," [59] and the Divine Assembly

> . . . ratify'd
> *The kind decision of Enitharmon & gave a Time to the Space,*
> *Even Six Thousand Years.*[60]

A limit is set to the fall, the time traditionally assigned to the duration of the created world, from calculations made from the Bible chronology.

Enitharmon's space is called a "merciful refuge" for Satan and his companions. It is created in pity, "lest they should fall into eternal death." Enitharmon

> . . . *wept, she trembled, she kissed Satan, she wept over Michael:*
> *She form'd a Space for Satan & Michael & for the poor infected.*
> *Trembling she wept over the Space & clos'd it with a tender Moon.*[61]

The "Space" is the earth as conceived by the materialistic philosophy, and the "poor infected" are the positivists, mechanists, materialists, and all those who by reason of their mistaken thought live in such a world:

> . . . *Enitharmon in Tears*
> *Wept over him, Created him a Space clos'd with a tender moon*
> *And he roll'd down beneath the fires of Orc, a Globe immense*
> *Crested with snow in a dim void.*[62]

The space is called "moony" because it is nocturnal (in the spiritual sense), being remote from the divine light, and also because it is illusory—a dream. Already in *Europe*, where she first appears, Enitharmon is the creator of "moony spaces" or "female dreams"; European history is described as such a dream:

> *Enitharmon slept*
> *Eighteen hundred years. Man was a Dream!*
> *The night of Nature and their harps unstrung!*
> *She slept in middle of her nightly song*
> *Eighteen hundred years, a female dream.*[63]

All her spaces are dreams, as "the lost Traveller's dream" or those "deadly dreams the soul falls into when it leaves Eden following the Serpent." But finally all these separate dreams are comprised in the one dream-space of Canaan, the "six thousand years" of the duration of the world:

> *Oft Enitharmon enter'd weeping into the Space, there appearing*
> *An aged Woman raving along the Streets (the Space is named*
> *Canaan): then she returned to Los, weary, frighted as from dreams.*[64]

The strange name Canaan takes us back once more to Swedenborg. The meanings he gives to the name are apparently contradictory—"external worship separate from internal," "religious corruption," but also "The Lord's Kingdom" and the Church. Canaan is the world into which Jesus is born—"the state of heaven before the coming of the Lord, and afterwards"; and it is also "in the supreme sense, the Lord's divine Humanity." It is therefore comprehensible that Blake so names the whole temporal world. It is not an eternal hell cut off forever from God but the space and time in which man's redemption will take place.

165 Woodcut by Blake (1821) for Vergil's first Eclogue

CHAPTER *23*

# The Shadowy Female

Here we must return, yet again, to the figure of Vala. We have seen her mythological antecedents as the soul, Psyche; and we have seen how in *Jerusalem* she became an independent figure, the material shadow of the soul who has become "animated" with a life of her own. This animation of "nature" as an externalized shadow of the soul we can now more perfectly understand in its relation to Blake's philosophy of the sensible world. Blake, in entitling his poem on the fall of man *Vala*, was indicating his central theme: man's lapse into a mistaken belief in the substantiality of the phenomena.

Nature as defined by Boehme is, if we but convert his symbolic terms into conceptual language, remarkably close to Berkeley's system of sensible appearances upheld by mind. Nature is the seventh fountain-spirit, "wherein Apprehensibility and Comprehensibility consists, and wherein all Creatures are formed in Heaven and on Earth. Yea, *Heaven* itself is therein formed; and all *Naturality* in the whole God consists in *this* Spirit." [1] But, says Boehme, nature is not a cause but a manifestation only: "Nature generates Nothing, be it what it will in this World, and though perhaps it should stand or continue but scarce a Minute, yet it is all generated in the Ternary, or according to the Similitude of God." [2]

This is the nature that Blake says "the Protestant" considers as "incapable of bearing a Child"; [3] and he is thinking not only of Boehme but also, no doubt, of Swedenborg, whose "influx" from the spiritual world into the natural is the only true cause of birth into this world. (He is himself speaking as a Protestant, and objected, quite mistakenly, that the Catholic Virgin Mary is the same as "nature.")

Boehme's seventh fountain-spirit is strongly personified in the *Aurora;* and in her we recognize many traits of Vala herself. Like Vala, her world is a "garden of delight":

For it is the proper House and Habitation of the six Spirits, which they continually build according to their Pleasure, or as a Garden of Delight, into which the Master of it *sows* all manner of Seeds, according to his Pleasure, and then enjoys the Fruit of it. Thus the other six Spirits continually erect this Garden of Delight and Pleasure, and *sow* their Fruits into it, and feed upon it to strengthen their Might and Joy.[4]

This is "Vala's garden," often so named, and described by Tharmas in Boehme's very words:

> . . . *O Vala, once I liv'd in a garden of delight;*
> *I waken'd Enion in the morning, & she turn'd away*
> *Among the apple trees; & all the garden of delight*
> *Swam like a dream before my eyes* . . .[5]

After the fall of Lucifer, according to Boehme, the fallen angels corrupted the nature-spirit: "they moved themselves so hard, and strongly, that the Spirit which they generated was very fiery, and *climbed up in the Fountain of the Heart, like a proud Damsel or Virgin.* . . . Here now stood the kindled Bride in the seventh Nature-spirit, like a *proud Beast;* now she supposed she was beyond or above God, nothing was like her now."[6]

Blake several times repeats this episode as part of the story of the fall of the Eternal Man:

> *The Fallen Man takes his repose, Urizen sleeps in the porch,*
> *Luvah and Vala wake & fly up from the Human Heart*
> *Into the brain from thence; upon the pillow Vala slumber'd.*[7]

This is Boehme's spirit who "climbed up in the Fountain of the Heart, like a proud Damsel or Virgin," the "kindled Bride"; and in *Jerusalem* Vala is called Albion's wife, always with a more or less strong suggestion that she has seduced him, as described in *Vala* VII:

> *Among the Flowers of Beulah walk'd the Eternal Man & saw*
> *Vala, the lilly of the desart melting in high noon;*
> *Upon her bosom in sweet bliss he fainted. Wonder siez'd*
> *All heaven; they saw him dark* . . .[8]

166 Vala drawing out the "veil" of Nature from the body of Albion: *Jerusalem* (1804–1820), plate 85, detail

[166]   Vala's veil [9] is derived from several sources. The veiled goddess Nature was known to Blake in many versions and in images of great beauty. Psyche went weeping to her marriage, and "the maid that should be married did wipe her eyes with her veile"—an image perhaps echoed in Blake's "Why dost thou weep as Vala & wet thy veil with dewy tears." [10] Psyche at her marriage was veiled. The Shulamite in the Song of Solomon also has a veil—"the keepers of the walls took away my veil from me." [11] Vaughan's Thalia has [12] a veil that does not only "look like," but in fact is, "lilies in a field of grass." Persephone was occupied in weaving a veil for Demeter herself when she fell into the power of Hades; and according to Taylor, "the web in which Proserpine had displayed all the fair variety of the material world, beautifully represents the commencement of the phantastic energies through which the soul becomes ensnared with the beauty of imaginative forms." [13]

    She was, at the time of her rape, herself wearing a garment embroidered with the sun and moon—as was the nameless woman in Revelation,[14] who is perhaps the same symbolic figure. Blake's soul on the frontispiece of *Jerusalem* is given, instead of a veil, Psyche's moth-wings, with sun and moon and stars upon them. But the prototype of all the veiled nature-goddesses of Europe is Isis; and Blake had read Apuleius' splendid description of his vision of the great goddess herself, in the eleventh book of his [167] *Metamorphoses:*

> I fortuned to fall asleepe, and by and by appeared unto me a divine and venerable face, worshipped even of the Gods themselves. Then by little and little I seemed to see the whole figure of her body,

mounting out of the sea and standing before mee, wherefore I purpose to describe her divine semblance, if the poverty of my humane speech will suffer me, or her divine power give me eloquence thereto. First, shee had a great abundance of haire, dispersed and scattered about her neck, on the crowne of her head she bare many garlands enterlaced with floures, in the middle of her forehead was a compasse in fashion of a glasse, or resembling the light of the Moone, in one of her hands she bare serpents, in the other, blades of corne, her vestiment was of fine silke yeelding divers colours, sometime yellow, sometime rosie, sometime flamy, and sometime (which troubled my spirit sore) darke and obscure, covered with a blacke robe in manner of a shield, and pleated in most subtill fashion at the skirts of her garments, the welts appeared comely, whereas here and there the starres glimpsed, and in the middle of them was placed the Moone, which shone like a flame of fire, round about the robe was a coronet or garland made with flowres and fruits. In her right hand she had a timbrell of brasse, which gave a pleasant sound, in her left hand shee bare a cup of gold, out of the mouth whereof the serpent Aspis lifted up his head, with a swelling throat, her odoriferous feete were covered with shoes interlaced and wrought with victorious palme. Thus

167 The "veiled" Goddess, Juno Samia Selenitis: engraving from Bryant's *Mythology*, vol. 2 (1774), plate VII

the divine shape breathing out the pleasant spice of fertill Arabia, disdained not with her divine voyce to utter these words unto me: Behold Lucius I am come . . . I am she that is the natural mother of all things, mistresse and governesse of all the Elements, the initiall progeny of worlds, chiefe of powers divine, Queene of heaven, the principall of the Gods celestiall, the light of the goddesses: at my will the planets of the ayre, the wholesome winds of the Seas, and the silences of hell be disposed; my name, my divinity is adored throughout all the world in divers manners, in variable customes and in many names, for the Phrygians call me the mother of the Gods: the Athenians, Minerva: the Cyprians, Venus: the Candians, Diana: the Sicilians, Proserpina: the Eleusians, Ceres: some Juno, others Bellona, others Hecate: and principally the Aethiopians which dwell in the Orient, and the Aegyptians which are excellent in all kinds of ancient doctrine, and by their proper ceremonies accustome to worship mee, doe call mee Queene Isis.[15]

Plutarch explains the multicolored garments of the goddess: "The robes . . . of *Isis* are dyed with a great variety of colours, her power being wholly conversant about *Matter*, which becomes all things and admits all things, light and darkness, day and night, fire and water, life and death, beginning and end; whereas *those* of *Osiris* are of one uniform shining colour." [16] She is the goddess of phenomenal nature; and Plutarch records an inscription upon the base of the statue of Minerva at Saïs: "I am every thing that has been, that is, and that shall be: nor has any mortal ever yet been able to discover what is under my veil." [17]

There is a passage in *Jerusalem* in which it is clear that Blake was thinking of Apuleius' Isis when he described Vala as a moon goddess, wife of the sun (Osiris) and mother of the stars:

> Is not that Sun thy husband & that Moon thy glimmering Veil?
> Are not the Stars of heaven thy Children? art thou not Babylon?
> Art thou Nature, Mother of all? . . .[18]

Minerva—so Apuleius says, and so also does Plutarch—is yet another manifestation of the veiled goddess, and from Taylor's *Orphic Hymns*, also, Blake would have known that Minerva "fabricated the variegated veil of nature, from that wisdom and virtue of which she is the presiding deity." Her web is described in Ovid's *Metamorphoses*, in the story of Arachne changed into a spider.

Blake could not but have also recalled Spenser's fine description of "great dame Nature":

*Then forth issewed (great goddesse) great dame* Nature,
*With goodly port and gracious Maiesty;*
*Being far greater and more tall of stature*
*Then any of the gods or Powers on hie:*
*Yet certes by her face and physnomy,*
*Whether she man or woman inly were,*
*That could not any creature well descry:*
*For, with a veile that wimpled euery where,*
*Her head and face was hid, that mote to none appeare.*[19]

Here again we find the strange hermaphrodite quality of the figure of Nature that seems to haunt Blake's Vala.

The nature goddesses of Europe, splendid and powerful and beautiful, all have their veils that have never been lifted. Only in the venerable metaphysical tradition of the Vedas do we see Isis unveiled. If Blake knew something more of this tradition [20] than can be traced to Wilkins' *Geeta*, and had read some of the works of Sir William Jones, we may find there a link between Blake's philosophical studies of Berkeley and the mythology of the veiled goddess.

Blake could have seen for himself the similarity of Berkeley's thought with that of Vedanta; but Jones has underlined the resemblance in his presentation of the Indian philosophy:

The fundamental tenet of the *Vedanti* school . . . consisted, not in denying the existence of matter, that is, of solidity, impenetrability, and extended figure (to deny which would be lunacy), but, in correcting the popular notion of it, and in contending, that it has no essence independent of mental perception, that existence and perceptibility are convertible terms, that external appearances and sensations are illusory, and would vanish into nothing, if the divine energy, which alone sustains them, were suspended but for a moment; an opinion, which *Epicharmus* and *Plato* seem to have adopted, and which has been maintained in the present century with great elegance, but with little publick applause.[21]

Jones wrote of the concept of maya:

> the inextricable difficulties attending the *vulgar notion* of *material substances*, concerning which "We know this only, that we nothing know," induced many of the wisest among the Ancients, and some of the most enlightened among the Moderns, to believe that the whole Creation was rather an *energy* than a work, by which the Infinite Being, who is present at all times in all places, exhibits to the minds of his creatures a set of perceptions, like a wonderful picture or piece of musick, always varied, yet always uniform; so that all bodies and their qualities exist, indeed, to every wise and useful purpose, but exist only as far as they are *perceived;* a theory no less pious than sublime, and as different from any principle of Atheism, as the brightest sunshine differs from the blackest midnight. This *illusive operation* of the Deity the *Hindu* philosophers call, MAYA, or Deception.[22]

The Hindu Maya is described as the mother of universal nature:

> *Maya*, or, as the word is explained by some Hindu scholars, "the first inclination of the Godhead to diversify himself (such is their phrase) by creating worlds," is feigned to be the mother of universal nature, and of all the inferiour Gods. . . . but the word MAYA, or *delusion*, has a more subtle and recondite sense in the *Vedanta* philosophy, where it signifies the system of *perceptions*, whether of secondary or of primary qualities, which the Deity was believed by *Epicharmus*, *Plato*, and many truly pious men, to raise by his omnipresent spirit in the minds of his creatures, but which had not, in their opinion, any existence independent of mind.[23]

In the *Marriage* Blake wrote that "the philosophy of the East taught the first principles of human perception": was he referring to the Hindu metaphysics?

Sir William Jones might have written expressly for Blake his remarks upon the Hymn to Narayena, which he translated; for he applies its metaphysical distinctions to the Descartes-Locke-Berkeley theme of primary and secondary sensible qualities. In the same way as Berkeley, the Hindu philosophy sees all alike as maya: "the *sixth* stanza ascribes the perception of *secondary* qualities by our *senses* to the immediate influence of MAYA: and the *seventh* imputes to her operation the *primary* qualities of *extension* and *solidity*."

The Hymn itself opens by telling how Maya becomes the object of the love of her divine Father in terms that strongly suggest the account given by Boehme of the Nature spirit:

> *Brahm his own mind survey'd*
> *As mortal eyes (thus finite we compare*
> *With infinite) in smoothest mirrors gaze:* [24]
> *Swift, at his look, a shape supremely fair*
> *Leap'd into being with a boundless blaze,*
> *That fifty suns might daze.*
> *Primeval MAYA was the Goddess nam'd,*
> *Who to her sire, with Love divine inflam'd,*
> *A casket gave with rich Ideas fill'd,*
> *From which this gorgeous Universe he fram'd*

The Vedantic hymn of creation is precisely such an account as Blake himself attempts in the binding of Urizen (the parallel, however, is only general, and not in detail)—a creation not in terms of a substantial material world but in terms of the building of a system of appearances:

> *For, when th' Almighty will'd,*
> *Unnumber'd worlds to build,*

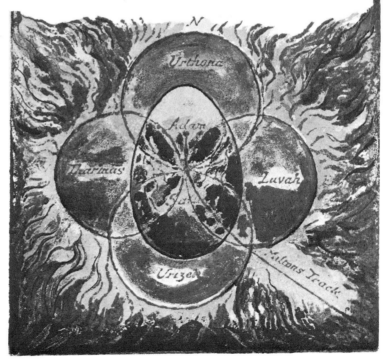

168 Diagram of mundane egg and four "worlds" in fire, with "Miltons Track": *Milton* (1804–1808), plate 36, detail

Cf. [131].

169 The Orphic world egg: from Bryant's *Mythology*, vol. 2 (1774), plate IV

[168, 169]

*From Unity diversified he sprang,*
*While gay Creation laugh'd, and procreant Nature rang.*

First the waters (matter) are created, and from them rises an egg, from which bursts the demiurge, Brahma, seated on a lotus. Thus Brahma is posterior to Maya, and dependent on her.[25] Like Blake's Eternal Man he is in the power of the veiled goddess:

*Full-gifted BRAHMA! Rapt in solemn thought*
  *He stood, and round his eyes fire-darting threw;*
  *But, whilst his viewless origin he sought,*
  *One plain he saw of living waters blue,*
*Their spring nor saw nor knew.*
*Then, in his parent stalk again retir'd,*
  *With restless pain for ages he inquir'd*
  *What were his pow'rs, by whom, and why conferr'd.*
*With doubts perplex'd, with keen impatience fir'd*
  *He rose, and rising heard*
  *Th' unknown all-knowing Word,*
  *"BRAHMA! no more in vain research persist:*
*My veil thou canst not move—Go; bid all worlds exist"*

These are the very words of Isis, "no man has yet been able to discover what is under my veil." But the Hymn ends with the conquering of Maya and the discovery that the source of all her wonders is the one indivisible spirit—a conclusion that Berkeley again reached some thousands of years later:

*Blue crystal vault, and elemental fires,*
  *That in th' ethereal fluid blaze and breathe;*
  *Thou, tossing main, whose snaky branches wreathe*
  *This pensile orb with intertwisted gyres;*
*Mountains, whose radiant spires*
*Presumptuous rear their summits to the skies,*
  *And blend their em'rald hue with sapphire light;*
  *Smooth meads and lawns, that glow with varying dyes*
  *Of dew-bespangled leaves and blossoms bright,*
*Hence! vanish from my sight:*
*Delusive Pictures! unsubstantial shows!*
  *My soul absorb'd One only Being knows,*
  *Of all perceptions One abundant source,*
  *Whence ev'ry object ev'ry moment flows:*
*Suns hence derive their force,*
*Hence planets learn their course;*
  *But suns and fading worlds I view no more:*
*God only I perceive; God only I adore.*

Vala becomes, likewise, the object of the love of the Eternal Man
when he sinks into the sleep, or death, from eternity. He falls in love with
phenomenal appearances, the "delusions of Vala," [26] and from this follows
every evil of the Fall and Urizen's immense and fruitless labors to order a
world that is essentially unreal. The terrors of war and every form of moral
tyranny follow from this fundamental error when

*The Dark'ning Man walk'd on the steps of fire before his halls,*
*And Vala walk'd with him in dreams of soft deluding slumber* [27]

The evidence that Blake knew this Hymn is presumptive only; and we must
always beware of regarding a resemblance as a proof of any actual link. Yet
the resemblance is noteworthy; and the account of Vala's veil given in *Jerusalem* is no less consistent with the metaphysical thought of the Vedas than
with the philosophy of Berkeley:

*According as they weave the little embryon nerves & veins,*
*The Eye, the little Nostrils & the delicate Tongue, & Ears*
*Of labyrinthine intricacy, so shall they fold the World,*
*That whatever is seen upon the Mundane Shell, the same*

> *Be seen upon the Fluctuating Earth woven by the Sisters.*
> *And sometimes the Earth shall roll in the Abyss & sometimes*
> *Stand in the Center & sometimes stretch flat in the Expanse,*
> *According to the will of the lovely Daughters of Albion;*
> *Sometimes it shall assimilate with mighty Golgonooza,*
> *Touching its summits, & sometimes divided roll apart.*
> *As a beautiful Veil, so these Females shall fold & unfold,*
> *According to their will, the outside surface of the Earth,*
> *An outside shadowy Surface superadded to the real Surface*
> *Which is unchangeable for ever & ever. . . .*

[170]  Does "the Mundane Shell" derive in part from the "egg" of Brahma as well as from the Orphic egg (known to Blake from various early writings of Thomas Taylor), from which Time hatches as the two halves of the shell fall apart to become heaven and earth? [28]

Man's world and its appearances are not the same for all times, civilizations, or individuals, varying not only according to our beliefs about them but according to the selectiveness of our kind and degree of consciousness: [29]

> This World Is a World of imagination & Vision. I see Every thing I paint In This World, but Every body does not see alike. . . . But to the Eyes of the Man of Imagination, Nature is Imagination itself. As a man is, So he Sees. As the Eye is formed, such are its Powers. You certainly Mistake, when you say that the Visions of Fancy are not to be found in This World. To Me This World is all One continued Vision of Fancy or Imagination. [30]

The essence of this philosophy Blake has summed up in a single line, "Thus Nature is a Vision of the Science of the Elohim." [31] (The Elohim are the seven creative spirits of God, and Los is "of the Elohim.") The deadly effect of illusion Blake describes in terms that are, again, suggestive of the Vedantic teaching on maya, but whether by chance or in part through knowledge it is impossible to say:

> *. . . What seems to Be, Is, To those to whom*
> *It seems to Be, & is productive of the most dreadful*
> *Consequences to those to whom it seems to Be, even of*
> *Torments, Despair, Eternal Death; but the Divine Mercy*
> *Steps beyond and Redeems Man in the Body of Jesus. Amen.*[32]

At length for hatching ripe
he breaks the shell
6
Published by WBlake 17 May 1793

170 *For Children: The Gates of Paradise* (1793), plate 6
Phanes, or Time, according to the Orphic theology, hatches from a world egg whose two halves are heaven and earth.

The liberation comes, as in the Vedantic hymn Maya is banished, by the vision of the divine being (the Body of Jesus) as the source "Whence ev'ry object ev'ry moment flows." With what forceful relevance, therefore, Blake implicitly compares the prevailing philosophy of Europe—which makes of maya a veil of stifling and "black" materialism—with the philosophy of Vedanta:

> *I turn my eyes to the Schools & Universities of Europe*
> *And there behold the Loom of Locke, whose Woof rages dire,*
> *Wash'd by the Water-wheels of Newton: black the cloth*
> *In heavy wreathes folds over every Nation. . . .*[33]

Blake might have seen the same looms weaving much the same cloth to this day. Rightly and precisely, he points to Locke as the weaver of this stifling cloth, Vala's veil, which becomes for deluded mankind "a Law, a Terror & a Curse!"[34] As its power over deluded Albion grows,

> *Thund'ring the Veil rushes from his hand, Vegetating Knot by*
> *Knot, Day by Day, Night by Night. . . .*[35]

As the veil deludes the fallen man, so he takes a hand in the weaving of it, realizing the horrible nightmare in what he creates—profane cities:

*Till Norwood & Finchley & Blackheath & Hounslow cover'd the
                                                    whole Earth.
This is the Net & Veil of Vala among the Souls of the Dead.*[36]

Horrible in peace, the veil is also a cause of war, a "scarlet Veil woven in
pestilence & war." [37] Vala weaves the veil "With the iron shuttle of War
among the rooted Oaks of Albion." [38] We are reminded of Gray's Fatal
Sisters and their weaving of the loom of war with the "grisly entrails" of
slain warriors. The veil of Vala also not only ensnares, but is composed of,
[171] the specters of the dead.

The veil is also a net that catches the souls who have sunk into the
waters of materialism; for it is these who are ensnared by the seeming
substantiality of appearances:

*For the Veil of Vala, which Albion cast into the Atlantic Deep
To catch the Souls of the Dead, began to Vegetate & Petrify
Around the Earth of Albion among the Roots of his Tree.*

We are here reminded of the genesis of the veil in Enion's "filmy woof" in
the sea of matter; but this passage continues:

*Thus in process of time it became the beautiful Mundane Shell,
The Habitation of the Spectres of the Dead, & the Place
Of Redemption & of awaking again into Eternity.*[39]

Perhaps Wordsworth's poetry of nature Blake might have placed here as the
veil or Mundane Shell on the way to becoming the place of redemption and
"awaking again into Eternity" through the contemplation of its beauty. Be
that as it may, the rending of the veil "where the dead dwell" is, sooner or
later, necessary; and this is the task of Jesus or Imagination. When we
recollect Boehme's Satan and the part he played in distorting men's vision of
reality by corrupting the "nature-spirit," we can without difficulty understand why Blake speaks of "that Veil which Satan puts between Eve &
Adam." The meaning is precise: Satan's veil is "apprehensibility and
comprehensibility" elevated into the reality itself; and it is Jesus the Imagination alone who can rend that veil. Los prays, "Arise O Lord, & rend the
Veil!" [40] Maya is "a veil the Saviour born & dying rends." [41]

In *The Gates of Paradise* a Vala-like figure appears:

*Round her snowy Whirlwinds roar'd,
Freezing* [42] *her Veil, the Mundane Shell.*

171 "And the Veil of Vala is composed of the Spectres of the Dead": *Jerusalem* (1804–1820), plate 47, detail

Frozen, the "fluctuating" veil of appearances becomes solid and substantial, until release comes when "I rent the Veil where the Dead dwell." The dead dwell in the "Veil," because they dwell in the illusory world of phenomenal appearances. This rending has something of the awful significance of the rending of the veil of the Temple on the day of the Crucifixion, when Mystery was at an end in the triumph of Christ.

When Albion is overcome by Vala's enchantment, he "swoons" or "sleeps" upon her bosom; but in his unfallen state he loves the beauty of nature, while also penetrating her mystery. Jerusalem reminds Vala of the happy time when soul and nature were one and indivisible, when the "Veil shone with thy brightness," and Albion in his love "rent" the veil: "Albion lov'd thee: he rent thy Veil: he embrac'd thee: he lov'd thee!" [43]

This symbol signifies that act of sublime imagination by which man may penetrate the mystery of the things of nature, and discover the reality behind the veil of the goddess whose face is forever hidden from all but those few who have attained enlightenment. In this enlightened state nature is not rejected, but seen for what it is, "One Continued Vision of Fancy or Imagination."

172 Emblem of Isis: Bryant's *Mythology*, vol. 2 (1774), plate XII

# Part VII

# What Is Man?

In the sections that follow we shall examine Blake's understanding of three figures: the Divine Humanity, or universal logos; Satan the Selfhood; and the figure of Albion, or mankind, in whom the whole cosmic myth of the Fall and the redemption is enacted. In these sections literary considerations are remote—necessarily so, since the sources of Blake's thought are not literary in their purpose, nor was Blake's interest in these ideas of a literary kind. Those who can realize that if Blake had not been more than a poet he would not have been a poet at all (since his entire symbolic expression is informed by the metaphysical vision that underlies it) may read with patience the sections that follow. These metaphysical ideas have, nevertheless, inspired some of Blake's finest passages, which cannot be experienced as "poetry" if we refuse to consider them as a formulation of essential reality.

CHAPTER *24*

# Jesus the Imagination

In the foregoing chapters we have examined the structure of Blake's impassioned affirmation—in the face of the materialist philosophy which already dominated English thought—that "mental things are alone real." We have seen how firmly laid were the foundations of ancient wisdom and modern example upon which he built, how minutely and strongly articulated were the parts within the whole of his thought. We are now brought to the central realization of Blake's vision, the figure of "Jesus the Imagination," the Logos of St. John's Gospel, the manifestation of the divine mind in human form. For Blake, Jesus was not a human person who was or is a god, but the only Person of all transient human "spectral" lives. "In him was life; and the life was the light of men." In this figure, present in all Blake's works from the early tractates to the last page of *Jerusalem*, Blake re-expressed in a living and dynamic way an idea that appears in one form or another in all the traditional doctrines, and which is the very essence of Christianity (of all traditions the most centred upon man and the human predicament), but very far from the notion of Jesus Christ held by official exponents of the Christian religion in Blake's time and place.

Such a conception, as we must conclude from Blake's insistence upon the mental nature of the real, is incompatible with materialism as such; if matter possesses a substantial existence outside of, and apart from, mind, the doctrine of the Logos can have no meaning. If, on the contrary, there is a "heavenly" or universal mind, then that mind must be and is, as Blake says of the imagination, "the Human Existence Itself."

Modern mankind is accustomed to think of the human individuality, the "worm of sixty winters," as substantially real, and of any such concept as a collective or universal mind as an abstraction, a mere concept. The traditional teaching, on the contrary, supposes the universal man (the Logos of the Platonists, the Adam Kadmon of the Cabala, the Divine Humanity of Swedenborg and Blake) to be the only life and light of individual "spectral" mankind. "All beams from him, & as he himself has said, All dwells in him"—so Blake writes of the Divine Humanity. Plato and Plotinus taught that the intelligible world alone has substantial reality and that this world is but a shadow or reflection, a *non-ens*.[1] It is the relative existence of the creatures that has, according to this philosophy, only an "abstract" or "conceptual" existence, relative to the divine reality that alone "is." Blake's Jesus the Imagination is at once the mind that knows, and, since there is no existence outside that mind, the object of all knowledge. It is as the latter that He hovers, as it were, before the face of fallen man, now near, now far. *Jerusalem*, plate 76, best shows this relationship between the human and the divine, the natural man contemplating and aspiring toward the Divine Humanity, who is, and is not, himself. Blake speaks in his own person when he writes:

[173]        *. . . I see the Saviour over me*
             *Spreading his beams of love & dictating the words of this mild song.*

             *"Awake! awake O sleeper of the land of shadows, wake! expand!*
             *I am in you and you in me, mutual in love divine"* [2]

By union with the universal man, man's soul is united with God, according to the degree of his transparency to the divine light. This imagery is identical with Blake's own account of the "darkening" and "opacity" of fallen man as he is separated from the Divine Vision, which becomes at first like a dim sun behind a mist and at last disappears entirely. Less clearly seen, Albion addresses Jesus as

             *Phantom of the over heated brain! shadow of immortality!*
             *Seeking to keep my soul a victim to thy Love! which binds*
             *Man, the enemy of man, into deceitful friendships* [3]

The "dead" can perceive the divine vision only dimly:

             *The Lamb of God is seen thro' mists & shadows, hov'ring*
             *Over the sepulchers in clouds of Jehovah & winds of Elohim,*
             *A disk of blood distant, & heav'ns and earths roll dark between.*[4]

But repentant Albion says:

             *O Human Imagination, O Divine Body I have Crucified,*
             *I have turned my back upon thee into the Wastes of Moral Law* [5]

173 Jesus on the Tree and
Albion: *Jerusalem* (1804–
1820), plate 76

Tragically and splendidly ominous is Blake's image of the setting sun of
divine light within Albion's soul:

> *Then the Divine Vision like a silent Sun appear'd above*
> *Albion's dark rocks, setting behind the Gardens of Kensington*
> *On Tyburn's River in clouds of blood, where was mild Zion Hill's*
> *Most ancient promontory; and in the Sun a Human Form appear'd.*[6]

Last of all,

> . . . the Divine Vision appear'd with Los
> Following Albion into his Central Void among his Oaks.[7]

The body of Jesus, however, lies even in the "Sepulcher" of man spiritually dead, awaiting resurrection:

> Dost thou appear before me, who liest dead in Luvah's Sepulcher?
> Dost thou forgive me, thou who wast Dead & art Alive?
> Look not so merciful upon me, O thou Slain Lamb of God!
> I die! I die in thy arms, tho' Hope is banish'd from me.[8]

It is fallen reason which seeks to destroy imagination:

> Abstract Philosophy warring in enmity against Imagination
> (Which is the Divine Body of the Lord Jesus, blessed for ever).[9]

"Inspiration deny'd, Genius forbidden by laws of punishment, / I saw terrified," says Los.[10] This denial is nothing less than the blotting out of the vision of God:

> Displaying the Eternal Vision, the Divine Similitude,
> In loves and tears of brothers, sisters, sons, fathers and friends [11]

Thus Imagination may become infinitely remote, "dead" and "buried" in the sepulcher of the natural man; but it is eternal, and on the last day will be the judge of the temporal man:

> But as the Will must not be bended but in the day of Divine
> Power, silent calm & motionless in the mid-air sublime
> The Family Divine hover around the darken'd Albion.[12]

Thus does the intelligible world of essence remain, eternal and unchangeable, looking down upon the flux of the shadow-world.

Sometimes the vanishing of the Divine Vision is described as the fading of the object of knowledge. This is only another way of seeing the same event, since knower and known are identical. It happens through the "shrinking" of man's organs of perception:

> And as their eye & ear shrunk, the heavens shrunk away:
> The Divine Vision became First a burning flame, then a column

174 The rout of the Rebel Angels: water-color design (1808) for *Paradise Lost*

Blake's "Jesus the Imagination" is en-sphered in the eternal world, which triumphs over Satan's "spectrous chaos" of separate self-hoods. The "bow of burning gold" also suggests the form of the rainbow round the spiritual sun.

*Of fire, then an awful fiery wheel surrounding earth & heaven,*
*And then a globe of blood wandering distant in an unknown night.*
*Afar into the unknown night the mountains fled away.*[13]

The Last Judgment is the illuminating moment of revelation of that eternal [174]
world, in whose presence "Error, or Creation, will be Burned up."[14] To
Blake this Judgment is infinitely to be desired, as the final epiphany and
shining forth of the real, which banishes the clouds of maya.

The idea of the universal or heavenly man, and especially the doctrine of Christ as the Logos, existing eternally in heaven, as creator of the cosmos, is an integral part of the orthodox Christian teaching. It is clearly stated, for example, in the Nicene Creed: Jesus Christ is "Begotten of his Father before all worlds. . . . By whom all things were made. Who for us men and for our salvation, came down from heaven."

Blake's understanding of Jesus the Imagination was attained through his knowledge both of this tradition and of the original sources of the Christian Logos. Blake's Jesus the Imagination is at once a person and a world of ideas that has its existence in a living mind. When he wrote that the "Gods of Greece & Egypt were Mathematical Diagrams—See Plato's Works," [15] he referred to the difference between Plato's world of abstract "ideas," conceived in terms of number and geometric form, as in the *Timaeus*, and that same world as conceived in the Christian tradition, within the *living* and *human* person of the Son. Nevertheless, it is precisely in the conception of the Logos that the confluence of Greek philosophy and Hebrew prophecy took place, to emerge in a new vision different from either. The Alexandrian Jew Philo is the first philosopher who personified the Platonic concept of the Logos. Blake no doubt knew his thought through Priestley's *Early Opinions concerning Jesus Christ*, where he would have found long quotations from Philo and a summary of his teaching on the Logos. The Logos is *in the likeness of a man*, and Philo also uses the image of the Shepherd, dear to Blake, and found also in the Hermetica. Philo's Logos is "that by which he both made the world, and also conversed with the patriarchs of the Old Testament"; thus the Logos is both the Platonic world of ideas and the Hebrew spirit of prophecy. The Platonists' ideal world, Philo says, "is no other than the logos of God, who makes the world" [16]—and the physical world is a copy of this divine archetype.

Blake also said that Plato and Aristotle "considered God as abstracted or distinct from the Imaginative World, but Jesus, as also Abraham & David, consider'd God as a Man in the Spiritual or Imaginative Vision." [17] But this ancient conception of Christ as the universal man, *Makroanthropos*, so splendidly portrayed in Byzantine iconography, was, if not lost, at least very much obscured by later Latin (Roman) and Protestant theology; and especially from the time of the Renaissance, the idea of Christ as the eternal Logos or divine Intellect gave place increasingly to a concentration on the merely human or historical figure of Jesus. Man, at the same time, came to be conceived of as merely a creature, and not (as for the Hindu and other traditions) containing the divine essence as his inmost self. In Protestant countries the traditional concept survived,[18] or was revived, only in an esoteric tradition.

There can be no doubt that Blake's understanding of "Jesus the Imagination" had been renewed by a return to the original sources of the idea of the Logos in Greek philosophy. The works of the English Pagan thus served to illuminate, for Blake, the essence of Christianity:

> The Treasures of Heaven are not Negations of Passion, but Realities of Intellect, from which all the Passions Emanate Uncurbed in their Eternal Glory. . . .[19]

Blake uses the Platonic word Intellect. Heaven, or the human imagination, is the world of eternal forms. Such passages as ". . . Imagination, the real & eternal World of which this Vegetable Universe is but a faint shadow, & in which we shall live in our Eternal or Imaginative Bodies when these Vegetable Mortal Bodies are no more"[20] seem to echo Plotinus so closely that it is impossible to doubt that Blake had in mind this or some like passage:

> Intellect indeed is beautiful, and the most beautiful of all things, being situated in a pure light and in a pure splendor, and comprehending in itself the nature of beings, of which indeed this our beautiful material world is but the shadow and image; but intellect, that true intelligible world, is situated in universal splendor, living in itself a blessed life, and containing nothing unintelligible, nothing dark, nothing without measure; which divine world whoever perceives, will be immediately astonished, if, as is requisite, he profoundly and intimately merges himself into its inmost recesses, and becomes one, with its all-beauteous nature.[21]

Like Plotinus, Blake speaks of the joys of contemplating these visionary realities: "If the Spectator could Enter into these Images in his Imagination, approaching them on the Fiery Chariot of his Contemplative Thought . . . or could make a Friend & Companion of one of these Images of wonder, which always intreats him to leave mortal things (as he must know), then would he arise from his Grave, then would he meet the Lord in the Air & then he would be happy."[22]

The Lord is the Imagination itself, whom the Spectator approaches through access to the visionary image, or idea. Plotinus himself occasionally personifies his intellect, and even calls this figure the Son of God: "he who beholds and admires the intelligible world, should diligently inquire after its author, investigating who he is, where he resides, and how he produced such an offspring as intellect; a son beautiful and pure, and full of his ineffable fire. But his father is neither intellect nor a son, but superior to both." [23]

It should by now be clear that to call imagination man's "Eternal Body," "the Divine Body in Every Man," is no figurative expression. "The Eternal Body of Man is The Imagination, that is, God himself," [24] and "Imagination or the Human Eternal Body in Every Man," and "Imagination is the Divine Body in Every Man" [25] summarize the doctrine as Blake found it in these authors. "The true Man" is intellect, the Logos, who is, and contains, the intelligible world. This universal divine "body" is eloquently evoked by Boehme:

> O dear Christians, leave off your Contentions about the Body of Jesus Christ; he is every where in all Places, yet in the Heaven: and the Heaven (wherein God dwells) is also every where. God dwells in the body of Jesus Christ, and in all holy Souls of Men, even when they depart from this outward Body; and if they be regenerated, then they are in the Body of Jesus Christ, even while they are in this earthly Body. A Soul here in our Body upon Earth has not the Body of Christ in a palpable Substance, but in the Word of Power which comprehends all Things.[26]

It may well be that his use of the word imagination in this sense Blake learned from Boehme: ". . . the Father's second Will, which is the Looking-Glass of Wisdom he sharpens to his Heart's Center [Boehme's term for God the Son, who is Blake's Imagination, or Jesus], becomes impregnated with the substantiality of the Father's *Imagination* . . . in the . . . Substantiality, all Powers, Colours and Virtues, lie in the Imagination; moreover, all *Wonders*." [27] Or again,

> God himself in the Abyss would not be manifest to himself, but his Wisdom is from Eternity *become* his Ground or Byss. After which therefore the Eternal Willing of the Abyss of the Deity has *pleased* to long, from whence the *divine Imagination* has existed, so that the Abyssal will of the Deity has thus from Eternity, in the Imagination, with the power of the Aspect, or from the Looking-Glass of Wonders, impregnated itself.[28]

The Son as "the substantiality of the Father's Imagination" is precisely Blake's own meaning of Jesus the Imagination; for the imagination in man is not humanly constructed but divinely implanted. By different ways Blake reached a definition of the imagination practically identical (but for the name of Jesus) with Coleridge's definition of the primary imagination as "the living power and prime agent of all human perception, and as a repetition in the finite mind of the eternal act of creation in the infinite I AM." [29] Had Coleridge perceived, as Blake did, that this living power and prime agent is indeed the eternal Jesus, the lifelong conflict between the poet and the Christian in Coleridge might have found, as in Blake, a perfect resolution and harmony.

In his proud and courageous affirmation that the divine imagination is present in and to every soul, Blake is affirming an aspect of the traditional doctrine that had been strongly reaffirmed by early Protestantism. Protestantism need never have come into existence as a separate sect had not the Roman [30] Church tended for a time to present the objects of faith more and more as external and objective persons and events; but given this decline, the writings of Boehme [31] and others are a necessary reaffirmation of something that had been forgotten:

> therefore though we speak of the Creation of the World, as if we had been by as present, and had seen it, none ought to marvel at it, nor hold it for impossible. For the Spirit that is in us, which one Man inherits from the other, that was breathed out of Eternity into *Adam*, that same Spirit has seen it all, and in the Light of God it sees it still; and there is nothing that is far off, or unsearcheable: For the eternal Birth, which stands hidden in the Center of Man, that does nothing new, it knows, works and does even the same that ever it did from Eternity. [32]

This is the Spirit upon whom Milton called to inspire his song:

> . . . *Thou O Spirit, that dost prefer*
> *Before all Temples th' upright heart and pure,*
> *Instruct me, for Thou know'st; Thou from the first*
> *Wast present, and with mighty wings outspread*
> *Dove-like satst brooding on the vast Abyss*
> *And mad'st it pregnant; What in me is dark*
> *Illumine. . . .* [33]

Blake's great love of *Paradise Regained*, which he illustrated with such visionary insight, may in part be attributed to his reading of the poem—rightly, perhaps—as the triumph of Jesus in his own sense, as the Imagination overcoming Satan the Selfhood. Satan's temptations are the various aspects of the world of the ratio, and last of all he offers human wisdom, the learning that belongs to the Daughters of Memory, who preside over the "Myrtle Grove of Academe." Milton's argument [34] is very close to Boehme's and to Blake's own: there is no wisdom preserved by history and culture that the imagination may not draw from the fountain itself:

> *Think not but that I know these things, or think*
> *I know them not: not therefore am I short*
> *Of knowing what I aught: he who receives*
> *Light from above, from the fountain of light,*
> *No other doctrine needs, though granted true.*[35]

True knowledge is an influx from the eternal wisdom.

Milton further argues that the Greeks' human wisdom is ignorant of the things of God, citing Socrates. In Blake's words, "how can a lesser kind be called knowing?"

> *The first and wisest of them all profess'd*
> *To know this only, that he nothing knew;*
>
>                    .      .      .
>
> *Alas what can they teach, and not mislead;*
> *Ignorant of themselves, of God much more,*
> *And how the world began, and how man fell*
> *Degraded by himself, on grace depending?* [36]

Milton's Jesus goes on to praise, rather, the Hebrew scriptures, which he opposes to the Greek literature (as does Blake in the *Marriage*), on the ground that the Hebrew tradition relies upon divine inspiration rather than on human knowledge and the art of rhetoric:

> *Remove their swelling Epithetes thick laid*
> *As varnish on a Harlots cheek, the rest,*
> *Thin sown with aught of profit or delight*
> *Will far be found unworthy to compare*
> *With* Sion's *songs, to all true tasts excelling,*
> *Where God is prais'd aright, and Godlike men,*

> *The Holiest of Holies, and his Saints;*
> *Such are from God inspir'd, not such from thee.*[37]

In the margins of Reynolds' *Discourses* [38] Blake wrote that "Plato was in Earnest: Milton was in Earnest" when "They believ'd that God did Visit Man Really & Truly & not as Reynolds pretends," and that the "Ancients did not mean to Impose when they affirm'd their belief in Vision & Revelation." So we often find that Plato is, after all, on the side of the angels, and that Blake knew it. But the Prophetic tradition, which turns solely to the higher source of knowledge, the divine mind, is undoubtedly more fully expressed in the Hebrew literature, and Blake is justified in calling imagination "the jews' god":

> The philosophy of the east taught the first principles of human perception: some nations held one principle for the origin, & some another: we of Israel taught that the Poetic Genius (as you now call it) was the first principle and all the others merely derivative, which was the cause of our despising the Priests & Philosophers of other countries, and prophecying that all Gods would at last be proved to originate in ours & to be the tributaries of the Poetic Genius.[39]

Milton's Jesus makes another point that Blake followed up—that the Greeks derived their arts from the older, more authentic tradition of the Hebrews:

> *Or if I would delight my private hours*
> *With Music or with Poem, where so soon*
> *As in our native Language can I find*
> *That solace? All our Law and Story strew'd*
> *With Hymns, our Psalms with artful terms inscrib'd,*
> *Our Hebrew Songs and Harps in* Babylon,
> *That pleas'd so well our Victors ear, declare*
> *That rather* Greece *from us these Arts deriv'd;*
> *Ill imitated. . . .*[40]

This theory that the Greek myths were copies of the Hebrew legends was held by Bryant. But to Blake the meaning lay deeper than Bryant's naïve euhemerism, in the nature of the theory of inspiration held by the two races. The "jews' god" is the primary imagination from whom all the gods of the world derive:

No man can . . . believe, that the Greek statues, as they are called, were the invention of Greek Artists; perhaps the Torso is the only original work remaining; all the rest are evidently copies, though fine ones, from greater works of the Asiatic Patriarchs. The Greek Muses are daughters of Mnemosyne, or Memory, and not of Inspiration or Imagination, therefore not authors of such sublime conceptions.[41]

According to the tradition of cabalism (as with other Gnostic systems), there were two creations: an eternal and a temporal world. The first, eternal creation is called by the Jewish cabalists, as it is by Blake, Eden. This name Blake could not have learned from the Christian cabalists Fludd and Agrippa, for they do not use it in their writings. He may have learned this venerable tradition from conversation with some rabbi. Boehme uses the name Eden and it is therefore likely that he is Blake's source; but so interwoven are the strands of tradition, from the time of the common origin of cabalism and other forms of Gnosticism in the Platonic and other philosophies of the ancient world, that it is not always possible—nor is it necessary—to know at what point Blake picked up the threads that appear and disappear in the ever-growing pattern of European thought.

Characteristic of the cabalistic Eden is what Scholem calls "the original coexistence and correlation of things." This is of course also characteristic of Plato's intelligible world, and it is difficult to say upon which tradition he is drawing, for his Eden is likewise characterized by this unity, in

> . . . *mild fields of happy Eternity*
> *Where thou & I in undivided Essence walk'd about.*[42]

Plotinus says that "the supreme intellect is itself all things, dwells ever with itself," and is "in want of nothing"; and elsewhere,

> . . . the nature of intellect, and of being, is the true and primary world, not distant from itself, neither debile by any divisible condition . . . since no part is there separate from the whole, but the whole of its life, and the whole of its intellect, ever living in *one*, and at the same time ever intelligent, renders a part as the whole, and the whole amicable to itself; where one thing is not separated from another, nor any thing solitary or destitute of the rest; and on this account one thing is not detrimental nor contrary to another.[43]

In the created world—here again the Platonic and cabalistic philosophies are at one—this unity gives place to diversity. Plotinus' discourse continues: "From this true intelligible world therefore, completely one, this intellect itself, our world depends, which is not truly one, it is diversified therefore and distributed into multitude, in which one thing becomes foreign and distant from another; so that friendship alone no longer flourishes here, but discord arises." [44] The one becomes the many, "because it does not contemplate that which is one; for when it speculates *the one*, it does not behold it as one," Plotinus says; and this process of alternation of perception, Blake, as is his custom when his imagination takes fire, has beautifully brought to life as a fragment of myth:

> *Then those in Great Eternity met in the Council of God*
> *As one Man, for contracting their Exalted Senses*
> *They behold Multitude, or Expanding they behold as one,*
> *As One Man all the Universal family; & that One Man*
> *They call Jesus the Christ, & they in him & he in them*
> *Live in Perfect harmony, in Eden the land of life,*
> *Consulting as One Man above the Mountain of Snowdon Sublime.*[45]

"All these things are written in Eden," Blake says of his visions. "The artist is an inhabitant of that happy country; and if every thing goes on as it has begun, the world of vegetation and generation may expect to be opened again to Heaven, through Eden, as it was in the beginning." [46]

Eden, it is here clearly implied, is not the supreme heaven. Blake has been by some praised and by others blamed for a "humanism" that was not his; his view of the divine transcendence was entirely orthodox: as the Son, or Logos, the unknowable Father becomes knowable. Blake was indeed the prophet of the Son, of the Divine Humanity, only as such an epiphany; of natural man he has little good to say, as has been sufficiently shown.

According to the symbolism of the cabalistic Tree of God, the Supreme Deity is unknowable in the highest essence (Kether) and only made known in the second Name or numeration, Hochmah, who corresponds to the Son or Logos, and is equated by Fludd and the other Christian cabalists with Jesus. The *Ensof*, or supreme Godhead, is "the fountain or root of infinity," and Christ is compared to a tree springing from that root. The third name or numeration is the "Workman," who, with the seven Elohim, creates the temporal world. But the eternal world is in Christ, whom Fludd calls "the trunk before the boughs, twigs, leaves or fruit." Blake's fondness for the image of "the true Vine" [47] reflects this vision of Jesus as the life in all. All eternal worlds, angelical or human, are, according to Fludd, included in "their body *Christ Jesus*": "And for this reason it is said, that, *He is the image of the invisible God, the first begotten of all creatures, for in him are made all things, both in heaven and earth, as well visible as invisible. . . . And he is before all, and all consist in him.*" [48] So Blake writes of Jesus: "Around the Throne Heaven is open'd and the Nature of Eternal Things Display'd, All Springing from the Divine Humanity. All beams from him & as he himself has said, All dwells in him." [49] The "Throne" is the highest and most divine place; and it is here that, through Jesus, the unknowable is "opened" into the knowable. In Jesus eternal things are made knowable—"displayed"; but that there is a divine darkness above and beyond the "opened" heaven, this Blake states plainly. What Blake found endlessly adorable in his Jesus the Imagination was precisely that in him alone is the divine made knowable to mankind: "No man cometh to the Father but through me."

Imagination, or Eden, may be conceived as a place but also as a person, because the place has no existence apart from the mind in which it abides. An identification of the place and the person occurs in the introduction to *Milton* (1804): "our own Imaginations, those Worlds of Eternity in which we shall live for ever in Jesus our Lord." [50] In the address *To the Christians*, which prefaces the fourth book of *Jerusalem*, Imagination and the imaginative body are used in a sense that makes no distinction between place, state, or person. Nevertheless, if for "Imagination" we read "intellect," the Platonism of many such passages is obvious:

> The world of Imagination is the world of Eternity . . . This World of Imagination is Infinite & Eternal, whereas the world of Generation, or Vegetation, is Finite & Temporal. There Exist in that Eternal World the Permanent Realities of Every Thing which we see reflected in this Vegetable Glass of Nature. All Things are comprehended in their Eternal Forms in the divine body of the Saviour, the True Vine of Eternity, The Human Imagination. [51]

To the supreme God, who became incarnate as Jesus the Imagination, Blake gives the name of Jehovah (the name usually given by Swedenborg to the supreme Godhead). Jehovah becomes knowable only as Jesus:

175 The Nativity, with the descent of Peace: water color (1809) for Milton's *Hymn on the Morning of Christ's Nativity*

*And Jehovah stood in the Gates of the Victim, & he appeared*
*A weeping Infant in the Gates of Birth in the midst of Heaven.*  [175]

This beautiful image captures the very moment of manifestation of the unmanifest. Satan is wrongly "worshipped by the names divine / Of Jesus and *Jehovah*"; and some verses in Wordsworth's *Excursion* troubled Blake so much as to make him ill, so the story goes:

> *Jehovah with his Thunder and the choir*
> *Of shouting Angels and the Empyreal Throne*
> *I pass them unalarmed.*

"Does Mr. W. think his mind can *surpass* Jehovah?"[52] Blake asked, and his question shows that he venerated the divine name.[53]

The vision of the Divine Humanity as the one-in-many is also characteristically Swedenborgian. In his time and place Swedenborg realized and expressed—as if for the first time, and recapturing the original depth of meaning of the symbol—the doctrine of the Logos. Upon this insight, new to him and to his world, though in its origins old, he based his claim as prophet of a new Church and a new age, the church and age of the Divine Humanity, of the Redeemer incarnate not only in one man but universally, as the divine spirit within every soul. Perhaps one might say he had an intuitive apprehension of a new revelation or sensibility beginning to awaken in mankind, described more recently in other terms by Teilhard de Chardin—that of the Logos working toward some collective epiphany or Second Coming, through and throughout the human race. This aspect of Swedenborg's teaching Blake took over absolutely, indeed re-created in a form more enduring and more potent than could Swedenborg himself. But there can be no doubt that Blake first found the Heavenly Man in the writings of Swedenborg; and to him we must look for Blake's earliest idea of his figure of Jesus. "In all the Heavens there is no other Idea of God than that of a Man; the Reason is, because Heaven in the Whole, and in Part, is in Form as a Man, and the Divine, which is with the Angels, constitutes Heaven; and Thought proceedeth according to the Form of Heaven."[54] The form of heaven "in it's greatest and least Parts is like itself."

Swedenborg's Heavenly Man is a composite figure in whom is contained every minute particular of life: "The universal Heaven, which Consisteth of Myriads of Myriads of Angels, in it's universal Form is as a man; so also is every Society in Heaven, as well great as small."[55] Swedenborg's "Angels" are human souls, and these subsidiary group souls are comprehended in the body of the universal Divine Humanity.

In *Jerusalem* we find an essentially Swedenborgian vision of the omnipresent Divine Humanity in Jesus, who is incarnated in every human life:

176 The Last Judgment: pencil drawing (1809?)
The various groups of figures are described by Blake in his Notebook for the year 1810
(K. 604–617).

*The Divine Vision still was seen,*
*Still was the Human Form Divine,*
*Weeping in weak & mortal clay,*
*O Jesus, still the Form was thine.*

*And thine the Human Face, & thine*
*The Human Hands & Feet & Breath,*
*Entering thro' the Gates of Birth*
*And passing thro' the Gates of Death.*[56]

Jesus is conceived in multitude:

*And the Divine voice came from the Furnaces, as multitudes without*
*Number, the voices of the innumerable multitudes of Eternity!*
*And the appearance of a Man was seen in the Furnaces*
*Saving those who have sinned from the punishment of the Law*
*(In pity of the punisher whose state is eternal death)*
*And keeping them from Sin by the mild counsels of his love:*

*"Albion goes to Eternal Death. In Me all Eternity*
*Must pass thro' condemnation and awake beyond the Grave."* [57]

Swedenborgian still is the fine collective image that sums up the wisdom of
Los:

*He who would see the Divinity must see him in his Children,*
*One first, in friendship & love, then a Divine Family, & in the midst*
*Jesus will appear; so he who wishes to see a Vision, a perfect Whole,*
*Must see it in its Minute Particulars, Organized . . .*

*                .    .    .*

*. . . General Forms have their vitality in Particulars, & every*
*Particular is a Man, a Divine Member of the Divine Jesus.*[58]

The divine, Swedenborg taught, is the same in all men: "Man is a Recipient,
and Recipients or Receptacles are various; a wise Man is more adequately,
and therefore more fully, a Recipient of the Divine Love and Divine
Wisdom, than a simple Man . . . but nevertheless the Divine is the same
in the one that it is in the other." [59] In the greatest and least things the divine
being is one and the same. So Swedenborg taught and so Blake ever
believed, from the time of the tractates, when he wrote of "an universal
Poetic Genius" who is "the true Man." Whatever Thomas Taylor did

toward Platonizing Blake's thought, he never, apparently, shook his allegiance to Swedenborg's teaching of the Divine Humanity.

Blake's "brotherhood" is the relationship of human souls within the Divine Humanity. This is a truer union than natural "love," an invention of Vala in the world of generation, where man is by nature the enemy of man: [60]

> *. . . Man subsists by Brotherhood & Universal Love.*
> *We fall on one another's necks, more closely we embrace.*
> *Not for ourselves, but for the Eternal family we live.*
> *Man liveth not by Self alone, but in his brother's face*
> *Each shall behold the Eternal Father & love & joy abound.*[61]

This collective life of the many-in-one and the one-in-many is expressed in a composition for which several drawings and two long descriptions remain, *A Vision of the Last Judgment*. The pencil drawings of this subject convey an astonishing sense of the collective life of the innumerable small figures who seem to flow and circulate within the divine unity: "when distant they appear as One Man, but as you approach they appear Multitudes of Nations." [62] This is Swedenborgian not only in thought but in the terminology of "distance" and "approach," so common in Swedenborg's accounts of the spiritual communities of the heavens and hells.

[176]

At first sight it must seem surprising that Blake, in his description of the great composition of the Last Judgment, whose theme for him was of central and supreme significance, seems to be concerned more with questions of art than with those of morality. But this is for reasons far more fundamental than the natural bias of a craftsman, who sees all in terms of his own craft; it rests, rather, upon Blake's insight into the nature of imagination as the divine essence. As compared with, for example, the metaphysics of Hinduism, it may seem that Christian theology has tended to overlook the Light of which the first chapter of St. John's Gospel speaks, considering only the individual soul and not the universal *atman* in mankind. This emphasis Blake, taking as his foundation the best elements of the Protestant reaffirmation of the Spirit, labored to change. Whatever act or work springs from the imagination, the divine indwelling spirit, is "Christianity," because Jesus is Imagination itself. "Jesus & his Apostles & Disciples were all Artists. Their Works were destroy'd by the Seven Angels of the Seven Churches in Asia, Antichrist Science." [63] Under the term "art" Blake plainly includes imaginative actions as well as poems, paintings, buildings, and other embodiments of imaginative ideas. He saw no difference in kind, and doubtless he would have agreed with David Jones, who underlines a Platonic meaning in the words of the Mass, "Do this in anamnesis of me," and adds: "Calvary itself (if less obviously than the Supper) involves *poiesis*. For what was accomplished on the Tree of the Cross presupposes the sign-world." [64] Life itself, seen thus, can be called art (*poiesis*) insofar as it is imaginatively informed. This Yeats also understood when he wrote that it is all one, "those hard symbolic bones under the skin," whether we write a poem or "live our thought."

It is needless at this point to say that Blake's view of the supremacy of art is at the opposite pole from a kind of humanism often met at the present time, which seeks to make a religion of art, replacing spiritual knowledge by aestheticism. For Blake art was never an end, only a means, a language of imaginative knowledge. There were for him two kinds of art and two kinds of life: the art and life of the imagination, informed by intellectual vision; and the art of the ratio, of the human spectral selfhood, based upon the copying of nature; and if the terms seem strange, the underlying thought is powerful, consistent, and fundamental to an understanding of the nature of imaginative art. It is in this sense that he writes:

> A Poet, a Painter, a Musician, an Architect: the Man Or Woman who is not one of these is not a Christian.
> You must leave Fathers & Mothers & Houses & Lands if they stand in the way of Art.
> Prayer is the Study of Art.
> Praise is the Practise of Art.
> Fasting &c., all relate to Art.
> The outward Ceremony is Antichrist.
> The Eternal Body of Man is The Imagination, that is,
> God himself
>           } יֵשׁוּעַ, Jesus: we are his Members.
> The Divine Body
> It manifests itself in his Works of Art (In Eternity All is Vision). [65]

Christianity is "Art" because Jesus is the Imagination:

> I know of no other Christianity and of no other Gospel than the liberty both of body & mind to exercise the Divine Arts of Imagination, Imagination, the real & eternal World of which this Vegetable

Universe is but a faint shadow, & in which we shall live in our Eternal or Imaginative Bodies when these Vegetable Mortal Bodies are no more. The Apostles knew of no other Gospel. What were all their spiritual gifts? What is the Divine Spirit? is the Holy Ghost any other than an Intellectual Fountain? What is the Harvest of the Gospel & its Labours? What is that Talent which it is a curse to hide? What are the Treasures of Heaven which we are to lay up for ourselves, are they any other than Mental Studies & Performances? What are all the Gifts of the Gospel, are they not all Mental Gifts? Is God a Spirit who must be worshipped in Spirit & in Truth, and are not the Gifts of the Spirit Every-thing to Man? O ye Religious, discountenance every one among you who shall pretend to despise Art & Science! I call upon you in the Name of Jesus! What is the Life of Man but Art & Science? is it Meat & Drink? is not the Body more than Raiment? What is Mortality but the things relating to the Body which Dies? What is Immortality but the things relating to the Spirit which Lives Eternally? What is the Joy of Heaven but Improvement in the things of the Spirit? What are the Pains of Hell but Ignorance, Bodily Lust, Idleness & devastation of the things of the Spirit? Answer this to yourselves, & expel from among you those who pretend to despise the labours of Art & Science, which alone are the labours of the Gospel.[66]

All art (or action) that imitates appearances and not essences is what Blake calls "bad art"; and since "Mental Things are alone Real," it follows that the "Last Judgment is an Overwhelming of Bad Art and Science." "Some People flatter themselves that there will be No Last Judgment & that Bad Art will be adopted & mixed with Good Art, That Error or Experiment will make a Part of Truth, & they Boast that it is its Foundation; these People flatter themselves: I will not Flatter them. Error is Created. Truth is Eternal." [67]

The Last Judgment conceived as an overwhelming of "Bad Art" may in part take its unexpected form from Boehme's prophecy of the Age of Enoch. At the end of Enoch's reign of the prophetic genius (see above, p. 114 *passim*) comes the fire of the Last Judgment, and the line of the "Wonders" (that is, of the created world) comes to an end:

And when *Enoch's* Line shall be at the *End* . . . then comes the greatest Grief and Sorrow of all upon the Nature of the Wonders, that *it* is at the End, and there is no more any *Remedy* for it; even then comes the *last* Motion with the *Turba* in the first Principle of the eternal Nature, and swallows up the outward Nature in the *Fire:* Even then the formed Word shall be *wholly freed* from Vanity, and gives by its *last REPENTANCE the holy Spiritual World. AMEN.*[68]

In similar terms Blake writes that when "Imagination, Art & Science & all Intellectual Gifts, all the Gifts of the Holy Ghost, are look'd upon as of no use & only Contention remains to Man, then the Last Judgment begins, & its Vision is seen by the Imaginative Eye of Every one according to the situation he holds." [69] Thus the Last Judgment (which is the end not of the world but only of the created illusion) can truly be described as an overwhelming of bad art and science by the triumph of the imaginative vision. This is why for Blake the Last Judgment is the event supremely to be desired.

## *Appendix*

Two obscure passages clearly relate the figure of Jesus to some form of Christian cabalism. The "Seven Eyes of God" appear to be the seven lower Sefiroth, the Elohim. The "Family Divine"

[177]
> . . . *Elected Seven, called the Seven*
> *Eyes of God & the Seven Lamps of the Almighty.*
> *The Seven are one within the other; the Seventh is named Jesus* [70]

A fuller passage, in "Night the Eighth," names the seven:

> . . . *And those in Eden sent Lucifer for their Guard.*
> *Lucifer refus'd to die for Satan & in pride he forsook his charge.*
> *Then they sent Molech. Molech was impatient. They sent*
> *Molech impatient. They sent Elohim, who created Adam*
> *To die for Satan. Adam refus'd, but was compell'd to die*
> *By Satan's arts. Then the Eternals sent Shaddai.*
> *Shaddai was angry. Pachad descended. Pachad was terrified.*
> *And then they sent Jehovah, who leprous stretch'd his hand to*
> > *Eternity.*
> *Then Jesus came & Died willing beneath Tirzah & Rahab.*[71]

177 The Four and Twenty Elders: water color (1805?)
The seven spirits are here represented with flames on their heads as the "Seven Lamps of the Almighty." See also [193].

The fall of the seven lower Sefiroth was a much-debated theme of Jewish mysticism during the seventeenth century; [72] and here, if anywhere, we have evidence that Blake may have had access to the learning of some Jewish rabbi or maybe some Christian cabalistic group (possibly that of Barrett, as suggested by Miss Nanavutty). I have found no written source in English that describes this strange event of the fall of the seven. Blake evidently attached importance to it, for it is described again, more fully, in *Milton*. In the *Milton* version the fall is still more closely identified with the duration of the created world. A time and a space is given to this creation:

*Even Six Thousand years, and sent Lucifer for its Guard.*
*But Lucifer refus'd to die & in pride he forsook his charge:*
*And they elected Molech, and when Molech was impatient*
*The Divine hand found the Two Limits, first of Opacity, then of*
                                                          *Contraction.*
*Opacity was named Satan, Contraction was named Adam.*
*Triple Elohim came: Elohim wearied fainted: they elected Shaddai:*
*Shaddai angry, Pahad descended: Pahad terrified, they sent Jehovah,*
*And Jehovah was leprous; loud he call'd, stretching his hand to*
                                                          *Eternity,*
*For then the Body of Death was perfected in hypocritic holiness,*
*Around the Lamb, a Female Tabernacle woven in Cathedron's*
                                                          *Looms.*[73]

This is Blake at his worst, incorporating unintegrated fragments of a system extraneous to his own myth, without any attempt to recreate its figures or even in terms of the action of his own spiritual drama. There are all too many uninspired passages of this kind scattered throughout the Prophetic Books, obscure not because Blake is recording visions too personal for communication, but because he could never resist introducing all the variants of some myth that he could lay hands on. Possibly he believed that he was providing his readers with an invaluable key—the Tree of God deserves to be no less well known than the pantheons of the Gentiles—but if so, his treatment of so complex and deep a theme is too perfunctory. Yet we must not overlook the importance that Blake attached to this fragment of myth, for it again reappears in *Jerusalem:*

*Lucifer, Molech, Elohim, Shaddai, Pahad, Jehovah, Jesus.*
*They nam'd the Eighth: he came not, he hid in Albion's forests.*[74]

The eighth appears to be man himself.

Blake could have found these names in Agrippa or in Fludd, though not precisely as he uses or spells them—which suggests that he had some other source also. Agrippa gives: "Elohim (Understanding), El (Goodness and Mercy), Elohim Gibor, or Pachad (Might, Judgment and Punishment), Eloha (Beauty and Glory), Jehova Sabaoth (Victory, Triumph), Elohim Sabaoth (God of Hosts, Peace and Honour), Sadai (Redemption) and Adonai Melech, who is the Messiah of the Cabala." [75] Blake's "Triple Elohim" might be explained by the three numerations that bear the name

Elohim, but even when these allowances are made, there are discrepancies. Agrippa, moreover, says nothing of the successive fall of these potencies, which is the significant point of Blake's use of them, and neither does Fludd. That Blake had some other, unwritten, source of cabalistic knowledge remains a distinct possibility.

178 World egg with lunar crown: Bryant's *Mythology*, vol. 1 (1774), plate IV

CHAPTER *25*

# Satan the Selfhood

Satan is the sum of those "dead" from eternity, the specters: "These they nam'd Satans, & in the Aggregate they nam'd them Satan." [1] These dead have fallen "Beyond the Limit of Translucence" into the night of darkness of Boehme's "outmost birth or Geniture of this World," which will never comprehend the light. Formerly this phenomenal world was "rarified and transparent, lovely, pleasant and bright," but the kindling of the "bodies" of the devils in this outermost world has rendered it opaque and dark to the influx of divine light. Satan is the selfhood or, as Swedenborg says, the proprium, which, when so cut off, considers itself as a self-sustained and independent person.

There is a good deal of Swedenborg in Blake's selfhood Satan. All creatures, so Swedenborg taught, exist only by divine influx: "Man is an Organ of Life, and God alone is Life, God infuses his Life into the Organ and all its Parts, as the Sun infuses its Heat into a Tree and all its Parts, and God granteth Man to perceive that Life in himself as his own, and is desirous that he should have such a Perception of it, to the Intent that he might live, as of himself." [2]

Urthona tells this to his temporal agent Los in Swedenborg's very words:

> . . . *if thou dost refuse, Another body will be prepared*
> *For me, & thou, annihilate, evaporate & be no more.*
> *For thou art but a form & organ of life, & of thyself*
> *Art nothing, being Created Continually by Mercy & Love divine.* [3]

But even angels are attracted toward their proprium. Swedenborg taught that

> self love is a property inherent in angels as well as men; that this is
> contrary to the laws of heaven, and that the angels excel in love and

214

wisdom only so far as they are kept from it by the Lord; and as otherwise, they would be carried away by this propensity, therefore these vicissitudes of states are appointed for good to them. . . . the Lord does not produce these changes in their states . . . the hindrance is in themselves, by giving way to that principle of self, which renders them unreceptive of those blessings.[4]

Love of self rules in Swedenborg's hells, and his Satan is the sum or aggregate of all self-loving spirits, a composite figure.

Satan is in the state of Swedenborg's evil spirits, who "are indignant, yea, express their aversion at hearing it said, that they do not live from themselves; it is self-love which causes such indignation and aversion . . . they imagine, that if they lived from another, and not from themselves, all the delight of their life would perish, not aware that it is directly the reverse." [5]

Writing of Adam, Swedenborg says that there are

some who imagine, that Adam was in such a State of Freedom or of Free-will, that from himself he was able to love God and be wise, and that this Free-will was lost in his Posterity; but this is a Mistake; for Man is not Life but a Recipient of Life. . . . and he . . . cannot, from any Thing of his own, love and be wise; wherefore also Adam, when he was desirous from that which was his own to be wise and to love, fell from Wisdom and Love, and was cast out of Paradise.[6]

This is the condition of original sin, shared by all the sons of Adam; and this is Blake's answer to those who teach a natural morality and a natural religion: "Man is born a Spectre or Satan & is altogether an Evil, & requires a New Selfhood continually, & must continually be changed into his direct Contrary. But your Greek Philosophy . . . teaches that Man is Righteous in his Vegetated Spectre: an Opinion of fatal & accursed consequence to Man, as the Ancients saw plainly by Revelation" [7] — an allusion, surely, to the Swedenborgian interpretation of Adam's fall.

"The Angels are not Angels from their own Propriety," Swedenborg writes; and "in Proportion as it is removed, they receive Love and Wisdom, that is, the Lord in themselves." [8] When they are in their proprium they are sad: "I have conversed with some of them in this state . . . but they told me, that they hoped to be soon restored to their heavenly state; for it is heaven to them to be delivered from propriety or self love." [9] Swedenborg's propriety and Blake's Satan the Selfhood is what is now called the ego.

Selfhood, in this sense, has nothing to do with "selfishness," as commonly understood. On the contrary, the ego often appears as altruistic and moral, and the spontaneity of the spirit's "Life delights in life" is "selfish" by spectral standards.[10] It represents, rather, a philosophic position, with implications in every aspect of life. The belief in the substantial existence of the human individuality and the denial of the divine influx has as its consequence the supposition that the world perceived by the senses is all. We come back to a familiar point, Blake's rejection of positivism and the philosophy of Locke. Satan is the realization of Locke's view of the human personality: a realization of an unreality, of "States that are not, but ah! Seem to be." [11] The state called Satan is built up in that empty recipient, mechanical blank, and receptacle of material species which, as Taylor says, is Locke's notion of the soul. For Locke experience is the only teacher; whereas for Blake the world of Experience is the true hell, cut off from "the divine bosom," imagination. Some writers have so far mistaken Blake as to suppose he believed the worlds of Innocence and Experience to be of equal, though opposite, value; but this is in every way untrue: Experience is the created error—Satan's kingdom of illusion and nonentity—which obscures the eternal truth. Satan denies the divine order in the best arguments of modern positivism:

> "I am your Rational Power, O Albion, & that Human Form
> You call Divine is but a Worm seventy inches long
> That creeps forth in a night & is dried in the morning sun,
> In fortuitous concourse of memorys accumulated & lost.
> It plows the Earth in its own conceit, it overwhelms the Hills
> Beneath its winding labyrinths, till a stone of the brook
> Stops it in midst of its pride among its hills & rivers.
> Battersea & Chelsea mourn, London & Canterbury tremble:
> Their place shall not be found as the wind passes over.
> The ancient Cities of the Earth remove as a traveller,
> And shall Albion's Cities remain when I pass over them
> With my deluge of forgotten remembrances over the tablet?"
>
> So spoke the Spectre to Albion: he is the Great Selfhood,
> Satan, Worship'd as God by the Mighty Ones of the Earth[12]

Blake observes, with great perceptiveness, that the specter can only build itself up with the help of memory; and in this he does no violence to Locke's theories. Locke's theory of perception is, in fact, this view, set out at length, together with an explicit denial of innate ideas. Blake's specter Satan is "a ratio of the five Senses," and "a ratio of memory," since sense-data alone are available to consciousness cut off from imaginative influx.

A newborn child has no selfhood because he has no memory; yet he has being, "the human existence itself," and is a fit symbol of the imagination—such as Blake's child on the cloud and babes in his *Vision of the Last Judgment*, which signify "births of intellect." The selfhood, on the contrary, has no real existence, and must continually construct for itself a "false body" with the help of memory and the ratio. The imagination has innate knowledge; the specter is the product of education and "experience," and dies, like Tiriel, who was all specter, cursing the educator. Children in the world of Innocence play; in the world of Experience they are sent to school. When Satan is cast off, it is "the rotten rags of memory" that are discarded; for these have but served to obscure the innate knowledge of imagination, which has "nothing to do with memory."

Here again Swedenborg may have given Blake a cue, for he writes of learned spirits in the hells, who "speak only from the memory; therefore, in the other life, when the things of the natural memory are no longer permitted to be reproduced, they are more stupid than others, because their knowledge was all hearsay, and devoid of true intellectuality." Goethe's Mephistopheles, who is not omniscient but claims to know a great many things, is the type of this spectral knowledge, whereas one might say of the imagination that it knows nothing yet is omniscient. That the memory of imagination is an anamnesis of the innate order of the intellect Plato believed when he sought to demonstrate that we can teach a child only what he already knows, whereas the memory of the selfhood is a "Spectrous Chaos" of arbitrary impressions devoid of any ordering principle:

> *Turning his back to the Divine Vision, his Spectrous*
> *Chaos before his face appear'd, an Unformed Memory*

The Spectrous Chaos is Satan's world, as Eden is the world of the Imagination; and as the Imagination is both a world (Eden) and the person of Jesus, so the Spectrous Chaos is both the world and the person of Satan. It is this Spectrous Chaos who, in the name of the rational power, addresses to Albion the denial (quoted above, p. 216) of "that Human Form You call Divine." Satan's world is a chaos because it lacks the ordering principle of the imagination, Coleridge's "esemplastic power." If Locke were right, the whole knowledge of any individual could only be, as the Spectre says, "a fortuitous concourse of memorys accumulated and lost," a "deluge of forgotten remembrances" imprinted upon the "tablet" of the mind, that *tabula rasa* which Taylor in his criticism of Locke contrasts with the "plenitude of forms" of the intelligible world.

Blake's Daughters of Memory bear to his Daughters of Inspiration the same relation as does Coleridge's Fancy to his Imagination. The Greek Muses, Blake writes, "are not Inspiration as the Bible is. Reality was Forgot, & the Vanities of Time & Space only Remember'd & call'd Reality. Such is the Mighty difference between Allegoric Fable & Spiritual Mystery." [13] Coleridge also points out that, apart from imagination, memory is the only source of knowledge. "Fancy . . . has no other counters to play with, but fixities and definites. The Fancy is indeed no other than a mode of Memory emancipated from the order of time and space; while it is blended with, and modified by that empirical phenomenon of the will, which we express by the word CHOICE. But equally with the ordinary memory the Fancy must receive all its materials ready made from the law of association." [14]

Again and again Blake returns to this difference, not in degree but in kind, between the art and poetry of the imagination and of fancy, or *allegory*, as he calls it. "Allegory & Vision ought to be known as Two Distinct Things, & so call'd for the Sake of Eternal Life." [15] This is so since eternal life is, precisely, the Logos or Imagination.

Just as for Locke "Error or Experiment" must seem to be the foundation of truth because his philosophy denies the imaginative principle by virtue of which "Truth is Eternal," [16] so for Newton the phenomenal universe is all; Satan is "Newton's Pantocrator":

> *And Satan vibrated in the immensity of the Space, Limited*
> *To those without, but Infinite to those within* [17]

Like the "spider" Brahma, who spins a universe from his own entrails, the spider Satan sits in his web. "Those without" are all those who, having access to the world of imagination, see the phenomenal universe for what it is, a maya or system of appearances or aspect presented by the senses, "the chief inlets of Soul in this age." Those "within" are the materialists for whom this aspect is all. Satan is indeed the materialist mentality itself, and, as Blake describes him in *Milton*, sets out upon his predestined course of destruction in the firm conviction of the rightness of his beliefs, with the "extreme mildness" of the Enlightenment: it is the Immortals who rage.

   Many of the themes and arguments against Locke which in the earlier Lambeth books Blake had expressed in the mythology of Urizen, he transfers, in *Milton*, to the more fully developed figure of Satan, who is the mind of the *ratio:* "Satan is Urizen, / Drawn down by Orc & the Shadowy Female into Generation." [18] The myth of Satan and Palamabron is therefore prefaced by the account of the binding of Urizen, taken more or less unchanged from the earlier *Book of Urizen*.

   But *Milton* is also Blake's answer to Calvin or rather to Milton's Calvinism, which he saw as the satanic or natural morality. In this poem a new complication is added by the Calvinist terminology of the Elect, the Redeemed, and the Reprobate. Blake introduces these terms because Calvin's [19] theology of predestination is that of Milton, at all events of those passages in *Paradise Lost*, Book III, that concern the redemption and the atonement. Blake's three classes are represented by Satan, Rintrah, and Palamabron:

> . . . *the Class of Satan shall be call'd the Elect, & those*
> *Of Rintrah the Reprobate, & those of Palamabron the Redeem'd:*
> *For he is redeem'd from Satan's Law . . .* [20]

Again, we are told:

> *The first, The Elect from before the foundation of the World:*
> *The second, The Redeem'd: The Third, The Reprobate & form'd*
> *To destruction from the mother's womb:*
>
> .     .     .
>
> *Of the first class was Satan . . .* [21]

That Satan is the type of the Elect is at first sight surprising; but when we consider his nature as the selfhood or proprium, we see that Blake is not being simply paradoxical. Calvin defined the Elect as those who live by the will and grace of God at every moment; and this is the very nature of the proprium, as defined by Swedenborg:

> *Satan is fall'n from his station & never can be redeem'd,*
> *But must be new Created continually moment by moment.*
> *And therefore the Class of Satan shall be call'd the Elect . . .* [22]

The selfhood or proprium, insofar as it exists, is "new Created continually" by "influx" as a "form and organ of life."

Blake called the specter a "Negation," in contrast to the "Contraries." This
distinction occurs first in *Milton*:

> *For the Elect cannot be Redeem'd, but Created continually*
> *By Offering & Atonement in the cruelties of Moral Law.*
> *Hence the Three Classes of Men take their fix'd destinations.*
> *They are the Two Contraries & the Reasoning Negative.*[23]

And again:

> *There is a Negation, & there is a Contrary:*
> *The Negation must be destroy'd to redeem the Contraries.*
> *The Negation is the Spectre, the Reasoning Power in Man:*
> *This is a false Body, an Incrustation over my Immortal*
> *Spirit, a Selfhood which must be put off & annihilated alway.*[24]

The contraries—"married" by Blake in his heaven and hell—are good and
evil, equally necessary to the progression of things:

> *They take the Two Contraries which are call'd Qualities, with which*
> *Every Substance is clothed: they name them Good & Evil;*
> *From them they make an Abstract, which is a Negation*
> *Not only of the Substance from which it is derived,*
> *A murderer of its own Body, but also a murderer*
> *Of every Divine Member: it is the Reasoning Power,*
> *An Abstract objecting power that Negatives every thing.*[25]

The difference between the contraries and the negation is that the
former have essential existence, and the latter not; Los says to his Spectre:

> *Negations are not Contraries: Contraries mutually Exist;*
> *But Negations Exist Not. Exceptions & Objections & Unbeliefs*
> *Exist not, nor shall they ever be Organized for ever & ever.*[26]

Existence and nonentity: here we have a distinction far different from the
conventional distinction between good and evil. Jesus the Imagination is
"the human existence itself," and Satan is nonentity itself. Plotinus in his
discourse *On the Nature and Origin of Evil* defines evil as that which is in
the last instance nonexistent; and the good itself, Plotinus says,

> is in want of nothing, but is perfectly sufficient to itself, independent
> of desire; it is the measure and bound of all things, from itself
> producing intellect, essence, soul, life, and intellectual energy; all of

which are beautiful; but intellect, which is the beautiful itself, reigns over all that is best in the intelligible world; an intellect not such as we possess, conversant with propositions, and perceiving what reason collects; inferring one thing from another, and beholding things through their consequences, as if void before its perception. . . . The supreme intellect of which we are now speaking is not of this kind, but is itself all things, dwells ever with itself, is perfectly united to itself, and, without possession, possesses all things.

Plotinus goes on to argue that evil "cannot be found in beings, and much less in that which is superior to being, for all these are good. It remains, therefore, that if evil any where subsists, it must be found among non-entities, must be itself a certain species of non-entity." [27]

In the same way Blake's specter is a nonentity, a negation. He told Crabb Robinson that "there is error, mistake, &c. And if these be evil – then there is evil but these are only negations." [28] Thus it is that Satan's empire is "the empire of nothing." The nature of the specter is negation itself:

> . . . *Life lives on my*
> *Consuming, & the Almighty hath made me his Contrary*
> *To be all evil, all reversed & for ever dead: knowing*
> *And seeing life, yet living not . . .*[29]

Evil, therefore, for Blake, as for Plotinus, is ultimately a nonentity, with no part in the divine reality. Satan, Blake says, "is the State of Death & not a human existence." Whatever is outside being is spectral, unreal; Satan is a philosophical nonentity, for there are no evil essences. "Everything is Atheism which assumes the reality of the natural and unspiritual world." [30]

The spectral man is therefore said to be "a false body":

> . . . *a false Body, an Incrustation over my Immortal*
> *Spirit, a Selfhood which must be put off & annihilated alway.*

Satan then has only the existence of the mask, the puppet, animated by the divine influx; and the Elect cannot be "redeem'd," but are "Created continually": [31]

> *And the Elect shall say to the Redeem'd: "We behold it is of Divine*
> *Mercy alone, of Free Gift and Election that we live"* [32]

When Satan assumes autonomous existence, he falls from the Divine

179 Satan in his original glory: water color

Lucifer's realm is "the starry floor" of nature upon which he walks. He is the demiurge, "prince of the starry wheels" of Destiny. Note the elemental spirits of Nature which surround him.

Humanity, and his real existence is lost at the very moment he claims it. This truth about Satan's nature explains Los's "Trouble me no more; thou canst not have Eternal Life." [33] Los is not being unkind, but is stating a truth about the nature of the phenomena, as such. The painting of Lucifer before the Fall shows a Satan whose masklike beauty suggests his nature as the proprium: he is surrounded by elemental "fairies." These express his nature and his reign, for they are the Paracelsian "elementals"; and another passage of *Milton* identifies Satan explicitly with the world of the four elements, [179] outer nature:

> And all the Living Creatures of the Four Elements wail'd
> With bitter wailing; these in the aggregate are named Satan
> And Rahab: they know not of Regeneration, but only of Generation:
> The Fairies, Nymphs, Gnomes & Genii of the Four Elements,
> Unforgiving & unalterable, these cannot be Regenerated
> But must be Created, for they know only of Generation:
> These are the Gods of the Kingdoms of the Earth, in contrarious
> And cruel opposition, Element against Element, opposed in War.[34]

To Crabb Robinson, also, Blake said that "Nature is the work of the Devil. The Devil is in us, as far as we are in Nature." [35]

These references to the Elect, the Redeemed, and the Reprobate refer to Milton's three classes of men, as described by his God the Father,[36] who here speaks with the voice of Calvin:

> Some I have chosen of peculiar grace
> Elect above the rest; so is my will

The second class is the Redeemed:

> The rest shall hear me call, and oft be warnd
> Thir sinful state, and to appease betimes
> Th' incensed Deitie, while offerd grace
> Invites; for I will cleer thir senses dark,
> What may suffice, and soft'n stonie hearts
> To pray, repent, and bring obedience due.

The Reprobate are those sinners upon whom falls that condemnation of the fierce doctrine of the Atonement, which many besides Blake have found repellent in Milton's God the Father; fallen man, he says,

> To expiate his Treason hath naught left,
> But to destruction sacred and devote,
> He with his whole posteritie must dye,
> Dye hee or Justice must; unless for him
> Som other able, and as willing, pay
> The rigid satisfaction, death for death.[37]

In *Milton* we see repeated, with maturer mastery and deeper insight, the theme of *The Book of Urizen*—the fall of the Miltonic "Messiah," who is Blake's Satan, and like Urizen, a usurper:

> *. . . under pretence to benevolence the Elect Subdu'd All*
> *From the Foundation of the World. The Elect is one Class: You*
> *Shall bind them separate: they cannot Believe in Eternal Life*
> *Except by Miracle & a New Birth. The other two Classes,*
> *The Reprobate who never cease to Believe, and the Redeem'd*
> *Who live in doubts & fears perpetually tormented by the Elect* [38]

The Elect are the once-born, the children of this world. Only a second birth
can give them knowledge of eternity. The other two classes are the
Redeemed and the Reprobate, represented by Palamabron and Rintrah.
Jesus is of the Reprobate: "He died as a Reprobate, he was Punish'd as a
Transgressor." [39] Here Blake is following Scripture; for the death of Jesus
was taken by the authors of the Gospels [40] as a fulfillment of the Old
Testament prophecy that the Messiah would be punished as a transgressor.
The law transgressed by the living Logos is, of course, the law of the fallen
selfhood. Satan declares himself God:

> *There is no other! let all obey my principles of moral individuality.*
> *I have brought them from the uppermost innermost recesses*
> *Of my Eternal Mind: transgressors I will rend off for ever*
> *As now I rend this accursed Family from my covering.* [41]

The "accursed Family" are the Redeemed and the Reprobate; and we
recognize, as in the earlier Urizen, "Unknown, abstracted, brooding secret,"
the devil's account of Milton's God the Father's "High Decree, Unchangeable, Eternal."

Blake locates for us Satan's "Starry Mills," the Newtonian universe,
as belonging to Plato's cave, "beneath the earth," the world of generation:

> *Beneath the Plow of Rintrah & the Harrow of the Almighty*
> *In the hands of Palamabron, Where the Starry Mills of Satan*
> *Are built beneath the Earth & Waters of the Mundane Shell:*
> *Here the Three Classes of Men take their Sexual texture, Woven* [42]

Thus we are told that the plow and the harrow are *above* Satan's world of the
"Mills," the cave, and the waters of hyle. Rintrah and Palamabron are
figures more mysterious, and the myth of the exchange of tasks between
Satan and Palamabron is one of the strangest of Blake's themes. We may
guess that the laws that guide the harrow of redemption are the laws of
energy, of life, of spirit, irrational and mysterious. What these laws may be,

Satan in his very nature cannot know. His task, as "Newton's Pantocrator," is "saving the appearances," as Los implies when he contemptuously replies to Satan's request to be allowed to guide the harrow:

> *"O Satan, my youngest born, art thou not Prince of the Starry Hosts*
> *And of the Wheels of Heaven, to turn the Mills day & night?*
> *Art thou not Newton's Pantocrator, weaving the Woof of Locke?*
> *To Mortals thy Mills seem every thing, & the Harrow of Shaddai*
> *A Scheme of Human conduct invisible & incomprehensible.*
> *Get to thy Labours at the Mills & leave me to my wrath."*
>
> *Satan was going to reply, but Los roll'd his loud thunders.*
>
> *"Anger me not! thou canst not drive the Harrow in pity's paths:*
> *Thy Work is Eternal Death with Mills & Ovens & Cauldrons.*
> *Trouble me no more; thou canst not have Eternal Life."* [43]

But Satan continually pleads with Los to allow him to guide the harrow, while Palamabron guides the "Mills" as "the easier task." Nature, Satan supposes, being a simpler mechanism than the human mind, must be "easier" to guide and safely left to the irrational; to control human conduct, only he himself, the principle of reason, is, so he thinks, fitted. There seems also to be a suggestion that Satan's motives are humanitarian: he pleads "pity," blaming the incomprehensible order of things that decrees much undeserved suffering and what seems, to human understanding, much injustice; and Los speaks of "wrath," in contrast with the "extreme mildness" of reason. All this his rational morality would set right.

To Satan's request, unwillingly and against his better judgment, Los accedes. When Satan guides the harrow, reason becomes the supreme law of human conduct.

But who is Palamabron? We know that he is of the Redeemed; and turning again to *Paradise Lost*, we learn that the guiding principle of the Redeemed is not reason but the innate divine light:

> *And I will place within them as a guide*
> *My Umpire Conscience, whom if they will hear,*
> *Light after light well us'd they shall attain,*
> *And to the end persisting, safe arrive.* [44]

This divinely implanted conscience, and not the laws of the ratio, is the principle by which Palamabron conducts the world; and when this is

exchanged for natural morality, disaster follows. The divine name "Shaddai," according to cabalistic tradition,[45] means the "Redeemer"; and it is
[180]  therefore evident why Palamabron guides the harrow of Shaddai, he being of the Redeemed. The motives of conscience are above and beyond the ratio, and conscience is the Redeemer, the divine Imagination working in man.

The strange episode of the exchanging of tasks points to another source of the Palamabron myth in some verses in Job, which describe the drawing of the plow and the harrow by the unicorn:

> Will the unicorn be willing to serve thee, or abide by thy crib?
> Canst thou bind the unicorn with his band in the furrow? or will he harrow the valleys after thee?
> Wilt thou trust him, because his strength is great? or wilt thou leave thy labour to him?
> Wilt thou believe him, that he will bring home thy seed, and gather it into thy barn? [46]

These verses seem to warn against leaving human labor (which is rational) to the unicorn, whose nature is mysterious and irrational, a type of the incomprehensible divine mystery that God reveals to Job in Behemoth and Leviathan and in all his creatures. If we remember that "in the Book of Job, Miltons Messiah is call'd Satan," and that in this book Blake found the supreme expression of his own belief in the spirit above and beyond reason, we may begin to see that Palamabron is the mysterious principle of living energy. Whether or not Palamabron is the unicorn, the episode of the exchange of labor ("wilt thou leave thy labour to him? Wilt thou believe him, that he will bring home thy seed. . . ?") is quite plainly based upon this episode in Job.

[181]  There is in *Jerusalem* a representation of "the Plow of Jehovah and the Harrow of Shaddai" [47]—one or the other or both. The entire plow or harrow (mentioned in the text) is not shown in the design, but only the fore part, like some form of chariot, serpent-wheeled and dragged by two man-headed horse-hoofed powerful creatures. Each has upon his head a single horn, coiled ramlike; [48] they are unicorns of a sort. Each horn mysteriously terminates in a hand. The hand of the horn on the right is directed backward

180 Plow with the horses of Palamabron: *Jerusalem* (1804–1820), plate 33, detail

181 The plow of Jehovah: *Jerusalem* (1804–1820), plate 46, detail Note Palamabron's horse-hoofed "unicorns" and the "gnomes." Cf. [152, 185].

to receive a pen from one of two small bird-headed, winged figures who ride the great beasts. Are these the "horses" of Palamabron and are the small figures his "gnomes"? Are the two man-headed creatures themselves Rintrah and Palamabron, the contraries of good and evil? The whole plow is shown in another design, drawn by similar man-headed horses.

The grave powerful mysterious faces of the two "unicorns" strongly suggest the grandeur of the "invisible and incomprehensible" scheme of human conduct ordained by God, as higher than Satan's laws of reason. They are akin to the Zoas themselves, of whom it is said:

> *What are the Natures of those Living Creatures the Heav'nly Father*
> *only*
> *Knoweth. No Individual knoweth, nor can know in all Eternity.*[49]

It is to replace the guidance of the unknowable spiritual law that Satan falls and sets up his unreal kingdom of the selfhood, governed by the humanly formulated laws of nature. Into this natural universe he lures mankind:

> *. . . Rome, Babylon & Tyre.*
> *His Spectre raging furious descended into its Space.*[50]

The space is of course Canaan, the space-time world of "six thousand years."

Satan's first overtures toward power are made by him in perfect good faith: he really believes that he can conduct the world according to the only laws he knows:

> . . . *with incomparable mildness,*
> *His primitive tyrannical attempts on Los, with most endearing love*
> *He soft intreated Los to give to him Palamabron's station,*
> *For Palamabron return'd with labour wearied every evening.*
> *Palamabron oft refus'd, and as often Satan offer'd*
> *His service, till by repeated offers and repeated intreaties*
> *Los gave to him the Harrow of the Almighty; alas, blamable,*
> *Palamabron fear'd to be angry lest Satan should accuse him of*
> *Ingratitude & Los believe the accusation thro' Satan's extreme*
> *Mildness. Satan labour'd all day: it was a thousand years:*
> *In the evening returning terrified, overlabour'd & astonish'd,*
> *Embrac'd soft with a brother's tears Palamabron, who also wept.*[51]

When reason guides what should be guided by a higher principle, the energies of life are enraged: we have seen Blake making this statement in the *Marriage*, in *The Book of Urizen*, and in the myth of Orc; and again, in the myth of Palamabron, he returns to the same theme:

> *Next morning Palamabron rose: the horses of the Harrow*
> *Were madden'd with tormenting fury, & the servants of the Harrow,*
> *The Gnomes, accus'd Satan with indignation, fury and fire.*
> *Then Palamabron, reddening like the Moon in an eclipse,*
> *Spoke, saying : "You know Satan's mildness and his self-imposition,*
> *Seeming a brother, being a tyrant, even thinking himself a brother*
> *While he is murdering the just: prophetic I behold*
> *His future course thro' darkness and despair to eternal death."*[52]

Satan cannot believe that it is through his fault, and declares that "the Gnomes, being Palamabron's friends, / Were leagued together against Satan thro' ancient enmity." He regards the irrational as primitive barbarism, which it is his task to subdue. Meanwhile,

> . . . *the strongest of Demons trembled,*
> *Curbing his living creatures; many of the strongest Gnomes*
> *They bit in their wild fury, who also madden'd like wildest beasts.*[53]

This rebellion of the reason-curbed forces of life Blake contrasts with the joyous disorder that Palamabron has introduced into the mills in his "day" of guidance:

> *. . . Los beheld*
> *The servants of the Mills drunken with wine and dancing wild*
> *With shouts and Palamabron's songs, rending the forests green*
> *With ecchoing confusion . . .*[54]

The fall of Satan, as Blake reinterprets the myth, comes about through no splendid gesture of rebellion. His sense of injured merit is sincere; for he believes in his own laws. He offers to conduct the harrow by reason instead of by the inner light, with the best of intentions, like Swedenborg's Adam, who, "when he was desirous to be wise and to love from that which was his own, fell from wisdom and love, and was cast out of Paradise." Palamabron's prophetic judgment seems hard on so well-meaning a Satan, if we fail to grasp the essential point about his nature and the innate fallacy of supposing that the selfhood can be good or wise, or indeed, that it has any existence at all in itself. Even so, his seeming virtue deceives even Los:

> *What could Los do? how could he judge, when Satan's self believ'd*
> *That he had not oppres'd the horses of the Harrow nor the*
> *servants.*[55]

But Satan, cut off in Enitharmon's moony space of Canaan, the Newtonian "void outside existence, which if enter'd into becomes a womb," deteriorates from this initial mildness of his "youth and beauty" to ever-increasing cruelty, tyranny, and blasphemy against the Divine Humanity. This appears in the unfolding of the action of *Milton*. A "Great Solemn Assembly" of the immortals is called,

> *That he who will not defend Truth, may be compelled to*
> *Defend a Lie, that he may be snared & caught & taken.*[56]

The "Lie" that Satan has to defend is Locke's view of the nature of the selfhood and the law of the ratio.

Satan's first step is to invent a moral code based upon the false belief that individuals can of themselves be good or evil. This is in direct contradiction to the real nature of things, by which the proprium is merely the recipient of

the divine influx. The morally "good" specter is as satanic in every way as
the morally "evil," since what is alike in both is their negation of the
Imagination. Both alike "blaspheme," as Blake constantly reiterates, against
the divine vision. Such "goodness" may be socially expedient, but that is an
entirely different matter. What is more, "Every body naturally hates a
perfect character because they are all greater Villains than the imperfect, as
Eneas is here shewn a worse man than Achilles in leaving Dido"; and "If
Homer's merit was only in . . . Moral sentiments he would be no better
than Clarissa." [57] Richardson's "good" characters are monsters of moral
virtue, almost to the point of caricature. But "the grandest Poetry is
Immoral, the Grandest characters Wicked" [58]—or will seem so, because
their conduct originates in essence. Satan, then, begins his work of evil by
setting up a code of righteousness. The "four iron pillars of Satan's Throne"
are the classical virtues of "Temperance, Prudence, Justice, Fortitude." [59]
This is but an extension of "One Law for Lion and Ox":

> *He created Seven deadly Sins, drawing out his infernal scroll*
> *Of Moral laws and cruel punishments upon the clouds of Jehovah,*
> *To pervert the Divine voice in its entrance to the earth*
> *With thunder of war & trumpet's sound, with armies of disease,*
> *Punishments & deaths muster'd & number'd, Saying: "I am God*
> *alone:*
> *There is no other! let all obey my principles of moral individuality."* [60]

"Martyrdoms and wars" are an inevitable accompaniment of Satan's moral
religion; and the bloodstained history of Christendom (the "Spectral
Churches") arises from precisely this heresy of supposing individuals to be
good or evil. If individuals can be evil, then the good will feel justified in
burning them or making war upon them—quite logically, by spectral logic,
but according to the real nature of things, a blasphemy against the Divine
Humanity in all men. Blake shows that Jesus broke all the commandments;
this is the theme of *The Everlasting Gospel*—"Was Jesus humble," "Was
Jesus chaste," etc.—and also of one of the *Memorable Fancies* of the
*Marriage:*

> hear how he has given his sanction to the law of ten commandments:
> did he not mock at the sabbath, and so mock the sabbath's God?
> murder those who were murder'd because of him? turn away the law
> from the woman taken in adultery? steal the labor of others to sup-

port him? bear false witness when he omitted making a defence before Pilate? covet when he pray'd for his disciples, and when he bid them shake off the dust of their feet against such as refused to lodge them? I tell you, no virtue can exist without breaking these ten commandments. Jesus was all virtue, and acted from impulse, not from rules.[61]

It is not from his wickedness but from his code of "selfish virtue" that Satan becomes the cause of martyrdoms and wars:

*Striving to Create a Heaven in which all shall be pure & holy*
*In their Own Selfhoods: in Natural Selfish Chastity to banish Pity*
*And dear Mutual Forgiveness, & to become One Great Satan*
*Inslav'd to the most powerful Selfhood: to murder the Divine*
*Humanity*
*In whose sight all are as the dust & who chargeth his Angels with*
*folly!* [62]

Satan is the Accuser:

*For Moral Virtues all begin*
*In the Accusations of Sin,*
*And all the Heroic Virtues End*
*In destroying the Sinner's Friend.*[63]

Blake no more spares the morality of the Enlightenment than that of the spectral twenty-seven Churches of Christendom.[64] The Satan of the Churches accuses the spectral humanity of sin, and persecutes; the Enlightenment imputes to the same spectral humanity righteousness. The error is equal and the result is the same:

*Rahab created Voltaire, Tirzah created Rousseau,*
*Asserting the Self-righteousness against the Universal Saviour,*
*Mocking the Confessors & Martyrs, claiming Self-righteousness,*
*With cruel Virtue making War upon the Lamb's Redeemed*
*To perpetuate War & Glory, to perpetuate the Laws of Sin.*[65]

The prose passage addressed "To the Deists," [66] which prefaces the fourth book of *Jerusalem*, identifies the error of believing man to be "Righteous in his Vegetated Spectre." The morality of Satan is individualistic, creating a world in which "man is by nature the enemy of man," competitive, warlike, given to persecution, and whose unions are those of

182 The hypocrites with Caiaphas: illustration no. 44 (1826) for Dante's *Inferno*

self-interest only. This is a different kind of unity from that of the Divine Humanity. Satan "compels into form" by external compulsion; such are the Synagogues of Satan:

> *But the Divine Humanity & Mercy gave us a Human Form*
> *Because we were combin'd in Freedom & holy Brotherhood,*
> *While those combin'd by Satan's Tyranny, first in the blood of War*
> *And Sacrifice & next in Chains of imprisonment, are Shapeless*
> *Rocks* [67]

Masses, armies, nations, parties, crowds, these are Satanic aggregates, in every way unlike the spiritual conception of the union of all souls in the body of Jesus, the Augustinian *Civitas Dei*. Thus it is that the spectral individualism of "myself alone" has, as its outcome, its apparent opposite, the crowd.

[182]  The worship of the natural person of Jesus is Satan's travesty of Christianity. Caiaphas, symbol of natural religion, is depicted in Blake's *Dante* illustration Number 44 as the object of the worship of hypocrites. This spectral Christianity is clearly challenged in a passage of *Jerusalem;* the

human *persona* cannot in its nature be divine, is indeed by definition satanic, and this truth applies no less to the historical Jesus than to any other man:

> *Los cries: "No individual ought to appropriate to Himself*
> *Or to his Emanation any of the Universal Characteristics*
> *Of David or of Eve, of the Woman or of the Lord,*
> *Of Reuben or of Benjamin, of Joseph or Judah or Levi.*
> *Those who dare appropriate to themselves Universal Attributes*
> *Are the Blasphemous Selfhoods, & must be broken asunder.*
> *A Vegetated Christ & a Virgin Eve are the Hermaphroditic*
> *Blasphemy; by his Maternal Birth he is that Evil-One*
> *And his Maternal Humanity must be put off Eternally,*
> *Lest the Sexual Generation swallow up Regeneration.*
> *Come Lord Jesus, take on thee the Satanic Body of Holiness!"* [68]

In *The Everlasting Gospel* Blake again returns to this theme of the worship of the spectral—that is, the satanic—humanity of Jesus. Of the Divine Humanity he writes:

> *And thus with wrath he did subdue*
> *The Serpent Bulk of Nature's dross,*
> *Till He had nail'd it to the Cross.*
> *He took on Sin in the Virgin's Womb,*
> *And put it off on the Cross & Tomb*
> *To be Worship'd by the Church of Rome.*[69]

Doctrinally, this is an unjust imputation, but in practice the whole of the Christian Church in the West has been deeply permeated by this form of idolatry.

The relationship between the Divine Humanity and Satan the Selfhood was, for Blake, of the most intimate possible; that is to say, the two were, and are, eternally united in man. Jesus "descends" into generation and dies on the Cross, both to overcome and to "save" Satan, and in his human selfhood is that Satan whom he overcomes. It is in his own human nature that Jesus meets Satan, and he is himself the battlefield. He "takes on" human sin in precisely this sense:

> *If he intended to take on Sin*
> *The Mother should an Harlot been* [70]

for he must take on the whole burden, the worst. In his own humanity are all
the figures of temptation:

> *He scourg'd the Merchant Canaanite*
> *From out the Temple of his Mind,*
> *And in his Body tight does bind*
> *Satan & all his Hellish Crew;* [71]

Perhaps by the Merchant Canaanite Blake intended the natural racial bent
of the Jews toward commerce that Jesus, as a Jew, had to overcome.

In his view of the Crucifixion, Blake is again basing his theology on
that of Swedenborg, for whom also it is through the "mother" that Jesus
inherited all the evils of human nature. At the Crucifixion,

> the Lord put off the Human from the mother, which, in itself, was
> like the human of another man, and thus material, and put on the
> Human from the Father, which, in itself, was like His Divine, and
> thus substantial; from which the Human also was made Divine . . .
> Now, as the Lord had from the beginning a Human from the mother
> and put this off successively, therefore, while He was in the world,
> He had two states . . . He was in the state of humiliation so far as,
> and when, He was in the Human from the mother; and He was in the
> state of glorification so far as, and when, He was in the Human from
> the Father. In the state of humiliation He prayed to the Father, as to a
> being distinct from Himself. In this latter state He said that the
> Father was in Him, and He in the Father, and that the Father and He
> were One; but in the state of humiliation He underwent temptations,
> and suffered on the cross, and prayed to the Father not to forsake
> Him; for the Divine could not be tempted, still less could it suffer
> on the cross. From these considerations it is now evident that, by
> temptations, and by continual victories in them, and by the passion of
> the cross, which was the last of the temptations, He fully conquered
> the hells, and fully glorified the Human. [72]

This is also Blake's view of the Crucifixion; the human selfhood of Jesus is
the Satan which on the Cross was finally and absolutely overcome. Satan is
the spectral "shadowy Man":

> *Then Roll'd the shadowy Man away*
> *From the Limbs of Jesus, to make them his prey,*

> *An Ever devouring appetite*
> *Glittering with festering Venoms bright*
>
> .    .    .
>
> *But, when Jesus was Crucified,*
> *Then was perfected his glitt'ring pride:*
> *In three Nights he devour'd his prey,*
> *And still he devours the Body of Clay.*[73]

For Swedenborg, as for Blake, there is no reconciliation possible between the natural man and the spiritual man. Both saw the victory of Christ as the triumph of the spiritual over the natural, Jesus over Satan. The Last Judgment is the final banishing of the spectral or satanic illusion by the Divine Humanity; its "terrors" are for the specters alone. That is why Blake writes:

> *God's Mercy & Long Suffering*
> *Is but the Sinner to Judgment to bring.*
> *Thou on the Cross for them shalt pray*
> *And take Revenge at the Last Day.*[74]

The "Revenge" is upon Satan's illusory kingdom. The passage concludes with the destruction of that "error or creation," Satan's world:

> *Jesus replied & thunders hurl'd:*
> *"I never will Pray for the World.*
> *Once I did so when I pray'd in the Garden;*
> *I wish'd to take with me a Bodily Pardon."* [75]

The passage concludes with a verbless sentence that states once again Blake's case against positivism, in the now familiar terms of those theories of perception he had so closely examined when as a young man he first did battle against Locke:

> *Can that which was of woman born* [Swedenborg's "Human from
> the mother"]
>
> *In the absence of the Morn,*
> *When the Soul fell into Sleep*
> *And Archangels round it weep,*
> *Shooting out against the Light*
> *Fibres of a deadly night* [the polypus of natural generation],
> *Reasoning upon its own dark Fiction,*

*In doubt which is Self Contradiction?*
*Humility is only doubt,*
*And does the Sun & Moon blot out,*
*Rooting over with thorns & stems*
*The buried Soul & all its Gems.*
*This Life's dim Windows of the Soul* [the five senses, the "chief
                                          inlets in this age"]
*Distorts the Heavens from Pole to Pole*
*And leads you to Believe a Lie*
*When you see with, not thro', the Eye*
*That was born in a night to perish in a night,*
*When the Soul slept in the beams of Light.*[76]

So Blake concludes with a return to the Platonic doctrine of the death or sleep of the soul in the world of generation.

In his vivid and unambiguous depiction of the serpent with his glittering venoms nailed to the Cross and put off in the tomb (for it is plainly said that it is "the Serpent Bulk of Nature's dross" that was nailed to the Cross by Jesus), Blake is less unorthodox than he may seem, for he has here the authority of the Gospel of St. John, "And as Moses lifted up the Serpent in the wilderness, even so must the Son of man be lifted up." [77] And besides Swedenborg, Blake probably drew upon Stukeley when writing on the union of the divine and the satanic natures in Jesus. We know that Blake knew Stukeley well. Ruthven Todd [78] pointed out that *Jerusalem*, plate 100, is based upon Stukeley's reconstruction of the "serpent-temple" of Avebury; and Blake follows him in calling the "Druid" stone circles "serpent-temples." There are other traces of Blake's debt to Stukeley, some of which have already been noted. For Stukeley the snake is a prophylactic symbol, of double aspect. On the one hand, it is the type of sin and of the human nature that Jesus "took on" in order to carry human sin. It is for this reason that the brazen serpent of Moses has always been considered as the type of Christ crucified. Stukeley writes of "the union of the divine and human nature in our blessed saviour. The venomous serpent is his human nature, sinful, infected by the devil's treachery; *he was made sin for us*, tho' not contaminated himself. Tho' not venomous, he cures the venom of our nature." [79] But Stukeley goes further; the serpent becomes the very type of Jesus:

our saviour himself was not fearful in comparing himself to it, and the rather on that account, took it for a very express type of his crucifixion, and of his being accursed for our sakes. . . . So our christian writers explain the type between our saviour and the brazen serpent in the wilderness. . . . And here we see the nature of types, where a man that undergoes the curse and punishment of the law, becomes in reality a type of the messiah. . . . Assuredly Moses, by the holy Spirit, meant it to regard christ's crucifixion.

Sir Anthony Blunt, in a note on "Blake's Brazen Serpent," [80] reaches a similar conclusion by a different route. He points out that the iconography of "The Brazen Serpent," one of Blake's Bible illustrations,[81] is traditional. The serpent is shown on a T-shaped cross, and Blake certainly knew examples of this tradition in older paintings, together with its implicit parallel with the Crucifixion. However, Blake also had his written authority in Stukeley, who says that Moses' miracle is made "more illustrious and divine, that God should direct a snake to cure those bitten by snakes."

There is another quality of the serpent mentioned by Stukeley, by which it also becomes a fit emblem of the divinity of Christ: "thro' that remarkable quality of their throwing off old age with their skin, and returning to youth again. . . . A fit emblem of his resurrection from the dead, and of returning to an immortal life." [82]

This sloughing of the serpent-skin seems to be strongly suggested in Blake's description of Jesus on the Cross:

> *Then Roll'd the shadowy Man away*
> *From the Limbs of Jesus, to make them his prey,*
> *An Ever devouring appetite*
> *Glittering with festering Venoms bright* [83]

The "shadowy Man" is the natural body sloughed by the Divine Humanity.

With the glittering "festering Venoms" we are back once again in the context of the Orc-serpent symbolism and its association with Boehme's "poison-apples" and the tree of life. The passage continues:

> *But, when Jesus was Crucified,*
> *Then was perfected his glitt'ring pride:*
> *In three Nights he devour'd his prey,*
> *And still he devours the Body of Clay;*

*For dust & Clay is the Serpent's meat,*
*Which never was made for Man to Eat.*[84]

It will be remembered that Boehme said the same of the "Wrath Apples," which man should not have eaten with his bodily mouth, feeding on material food, but inwardly, on the food of the spirit. It was the serpent who first ate the apple and was condemned to eat the "dust" of the earth. The symbolic implications of this passage are many, and some of them have been discussed earlier.[85]

The serpent as a symbol of matter—"Nature's dross"—Blake might have discovered from many sources. Vaughan, for example, describes matter as a serpent, and the emblem that accompanies *Lumen de Lumine* shows hyle as a cockatrice with its tail in its mouth. Blake's use of the phrase the "prester serpent" suggests his knowledge of Vaughan's account of the prester in this work. But nature as a serpent Blake seems to have owed chiefly to Bryant, who records that "in the ritual of Zoroaster, the great expanse of the heavens, and even nature itself, was described under the symbol of a serpent."[86] Hence, in all likelihood, Blake wrote that "thought chang'd the infinite to a serpent," and described the consequent building of the serpent-temple:

[1, 50, 52, 53]

> *Then was the serpent temple form'd, image of infinite*
> *Shut up in finite revolutions, and man became an Angel,*
> *Heaven a mighty circle turning . . .*[87]

The account of the fall of Luvah and Vala in the "Paradise" of the heart of the Eternal Man describes their first condition, when "the vast form of Nature like a Serpent play'd before them," and the fallen state, when, after their "descent," "the vast form of Nature, like a Serpent, roll'd between."[88] Nature, the jeweled serpent, beautiful and deadly, is redeemed at "the time of the End":

> *And the all wondrous Serpent clothed in gems & rich array, Humanize*
> *In the Forgiveness of Sins according to thy Covenant,*
> *Jehovah. . . .*[89]

# CHAPTER 26

# States

If, as the satanic philosophy maintains, "the Spectre is the Man," it necessarily follows that the man can only be good or evil in his spectral selfhood. If "the Spectre is the Man" (the first heresy), and "eternal life awaits the worm of sixty winters" (the necessary consequence of the first, and the teaching of the spectral Churches), eternal hell must be the reward of the wicked, and heaven the reward of the good. This belief in the immortality of "spectral" man is perhaps the most serious deviation within Christendom from the norm of traditional doctrine,[1] and again we find Blake following Swedenborg in his rejection of it; for both of them the real and substantial "body" of man, raised in the Resurrection, is a spiritual body. Blake returns to something much nearer to the normal teaching in his distinction between states and individuals. Individuals are eternal essences; states belong to the changes undergone by the spectral selfhood in the phenomenal world:

> *Judge then of thy Own Self: thy Eternal Lineaments explore,*
> *What is Eternal & what Changeable, & what Annihilable.*
> *The Imagination is not a State: it is the Human Existence itself.*
> *Affection or Love becomes a State when divided from Imagination.*
> *The Memory is a State always, & the Reason is a State*
> *Created to be Annihilated & a new Ratio Created.*
> *Whatever can be Created can be Annihilated: Forms cannot:*
> *The Oak is cut down by the Ax, the Lamb falls by the Knife,*
> *But their Forms Eternal Exist For-ever. Amen. Hallelujah!* [2]

The conception of the states, as well as the word itself, derives from Swedenborg, who speaks of the "states" of love and wisdom, or their opposites; and he relates the states to the selfhood or proprium: "the angels excel in love and wisdom only so far as they are kept from [self love] by the

Lord; and as, otherwise, they would be carried away by this propensity, therefore these vicissitudes of states are appointed for good to them." [3] These changes of state in the angelic spirits Swedenborg likens to a wheel or cycle: "they return . . . from one degree to another by various successions, like to the changes in the world between day-light and twilight, heat and cold, morning, noon, and night; and also according to the various seasons of the year." [4]

Swedenborg's spiritual communities are aggregates of souls in the same spiritual state; hell, "taken as a whole, is what is called the Devil and Satan"; and of heaven he writes:

> The Lord governs the universal heaven . . . as if they were all but one angel, and consequently those in every particular society; whence it sometimes follows, that a whole society is represented under the appearance of a single angel, which the Lord has vouchsafed to grant me the sight of. When it pleases the Lord to manifest his personal appearance in the midst of the angels, he does not appear under the particular distinction of being surrounded by many of them, but as one of them in an angelical form . . . Michael, Gabriel, and Raphael, signify so many angelical societies, deriving those names from their different functions.[5]

These are states, eternal as possibilities, but not eternally binding upon those who enter and leave them.

Blake adopts from Swedenborg the concept of the composite life of states:

> It ought to be understood that the Persons, Moses & Abraham, are not here meant, but the States Signified by those Names, the Individuals being representatives or Visions of those States as they were reveal'd to Mortal Man in the Series of Divine Revelations as they are written in the Bible . . . when distant they appear as One Man, but as you approach they appear Multitudes of Nations. . . . I have seen, when at a distance, Multitudes of Men in Harmony appear like a single Infant, sometimes in the Arms of a Female; this represented the Church.[6]

And again: "in like manner The figures of Seth & his wife comprehend the Fathers before the flood & their Generations; when seen remote they appear as One Man." [7] Blake here falls into Swedenborg's very style ("I· have seen . . .") and into his distinction between "near" and "distant," a mode of expression that Swedenborg continually uses to describe these spiritual societies.

Jesus is not, Blake says, a state. He is the divine Self in all humanity, perpetually entering, suffering, passing through, and "stepping beyond" the states:

> *For God himself enters Death's Door always with those that enter*
> *And lays down in the Grave with them, in Visions of Eternity,*
> *Till they awake & see Jesus & the Linen Clothes lying*
> *That the Females had Woven for them, & the Gates of their Father's*
> House.[8]

This universality of Jesus is stated again and again:

> *And the Divine voice came from the Furnaces, as multitudes without*
> *Number, the voices of the innumerable multitudes of Eternity!*
> *And the appearance of a Man was seen in the Furnaces*
> *Saving those who have sinned from the punishment of the Law*
> *(In pity of the punisher whose state is eternal death)*
> *And keeping them from Sin by the mild counsels of his love:*

> *"Albion goes to Eternal Death. In Me all Eternity*
> *Must pass thro' condemnation and awake beyond the Grave.*
> *No individual can keep these Laws, for they are death*
> *To every energy of man and forbid the springs of life.*
> *Albion hath enter'd the State Satan! Be permanent, O State!*
> *And be thou for ever accursed! that Albion may arise again.*
> *And be thou created into a State! I go forth to Create*
> *States, to deliver Individuals evermore! Amen."* [9]

"Distinguish therefore," Blake says,

> *Distinguish therefore States from Individuals in those States.*
> *States Change, but Individual Identities never change nor cease.*
> *You cannot go to Eternal Death in that which can never Die.*
> *Satan & Adam are States Created into Twenty-seven Churches,*
> *And thou, O Milton, art a State about to be Created,*
> *Called Eternal Annihilation, that none but the Living shall*
> *Dare to enter, & they shall enter triumphant over Death*
> *And Hell & the Grave: States that are not, but ah! Seem to be.*[10]

Satan cannot understand this; he fears annihilation because there is nothing deathless in him; he knows only of specters and nothing of the living essence, which is in its very nature incorruptible:

> *Truly, My Satan, thou art but a Dunce,*
> *And dost not know the Garment from the Man.*
> *Every Harlot was a Virgin once,*
> *Nor can'st thou ever change Kate into Nan.*
>
> *Tho' thou art Worship'd by the Names Divine*
> *Of Jesus & Jehovah, thou art still*
> *The Son of Morn in weary Night's decline,*
> *The lost Traveller's Dream under the Hill.*[11]

Kate and Nan are essences; harlot or virgin are states; for "each man in his life plays many parts": infant, schoolboy, lover, soldier, pantaloon, all these are states; and the man, like a traveler, passes through them:[12]

> *. . . Man in the Resurrection changes his Sexual Garments at will.*
> *Every Harlot was once a Virgin: every Criminal an Infant Love.*[13]

The conception of states underlies Blake's critical essay on Chaucer's Canterbury Pilgrims:

> The characters of Chaucer's Pilgrims are the characters which compose all ages and nations: as one age falls, another rises, different to mortal sight, but to immortals only the same; for we see the same characters repeated again and again, in animals, vegetables, minerals, and in men; nothing new occurs in identical existence; Accident ever varies, Substance can never suffer change nor decay.
>
> Of Chaucer's characters, as described in his Canterbury Tales, some of the names or titles are altered by time, but the characters themselves for ever remain unaltered, and consequently they are the physiognomies or lineaments of universal human life, beyond which Nature never steps. Names alter, things never alter. I have known multitudes of those who would have been monks in the age of monkery, who in this deistical age are deists. As Newton numbered the stars, and as Linneus numbered the plants, so Chaucer numbered the classes of men.[14]

This view of human character may give a rude shock to the widely accepted conception of the personality, the conviction of individual uniqueness that is so marked an attribute of the specter. To Blake it seemed, rather, that we are all manifestations of the one humanity, as all starlings or blackbirds live the life, over and over again, of the group soul. Every life is a more or less partial and imperfect realization of the one human essence.[15] An art of "self-expression" is spectral; supreme art expresses the universal human essence and therefore speaks for, and to, all.

Buddhist doctrine teaches that nothing binds man to the Wheel but his own illusion of being bound; and Blake's view is almost identical. Souls are held prisoner in the hells and the heavens only by their own proprium, and can at any moment find release in entering the Divine Humanity. If this were not so, it would be mere hypocrisy to speak of forgiveness of sins: Satan can accuse or punish; and according to his philosophy, forgiveness could mean nothing more than condoning evil. He has no power to release from sin, because, according to his philosophy, "The Spectre is the Man." But as Blake understood forgiveness, it is a dynamic process, a true redemption; for insofar as the soul is released from the prisoning states, it is truly absolved; it is no longer the sinner it was, but restored to its place within the Divine Humanity, freed from long confinement in some hell or heaven. Every state of "Death And Hell & the Grave" has been transcended by this Saviour, who harrows hell perpetually, regenerating souls, releasing from death, and restoring to eternal life.

Rahab, the temporal name for Vala, "Satan's Wife" Nature, is an active agent in the specter's morality:

> *Imputing Sin & Righteousness to Individuals, Rahab*
> *Sat, deep within him hid . . .*[16]

But from her, Imagination is the Saviour, able to

> *. . . take away the imputation of Sin*
> *By the Creation of States & the deliverance of Individuals Evermore.*
> *Amen.*

> .   .   .

> *But many doubted & despair'd & imputed Sin & Righteousness*
> *To Individuals & not to States . . .*[17]

Blake resolves the apparent irreconcilability of Satan's eternal exclusion from the divine kingdom with the divine love and omnipotence and the eternal being of all things in God, by saying that there is no *being* called Satan, but only a *state* so named, the "false body." His is an "empire of nothing,"[18] and he is "Satan this Body of Doubt that seems but Is Not":[19]

*There is a State nam'd Satan; learn distinct to know, O Rahab!*
*The difference between States & Individuals of those States.*
*The State nam'd Satan never can be redeem'd in all Eternity;*
*But when Luvah in Orc became a Serpent, he descended into*
*That State call'd Satan. . . .*[20]

We know also that Urizen became satanic ("Satan is Urizen, / Drawn down by Orc & the Shadowy Female into Generation"); [21] but Imagination is "the remover of limits," who perpetually seeks to open the closed selfhood to the influx of the divine. The "limits" must be perpetually "removed" by the Divine Humanity, who thus releases man from his spectral selfhood:

*Each Man is in his Spectre's power*
*Untill the arrival of that hour*
*When his Humanity awake*
*And cast his Spectre into the Lake* [22]

(presumably Udan Adan, the lake of Newtonian-Lockean space-time, where spectral existence rightly belongs).

Those who have no faith in this essential humanity can have no hope of being other than, or in any way free from, the sum of their human actions, thoughts, and memories in this lifetime; in other words, the states are the man, who has no existence apart from them. This is the true metaphysical hell. This is the picture of man depicted by Sartre and other French existentialists, for whom there is no *esse* apart from *existere*. As we might expect, this philosophy lends itself to a symbolism of hell, as in Sartre's *Huis Clos*. In contrast to these, Blake affirms that "the Imagination is not a state: it is the Human Existence itself":

*Voltaire insinuates that these Limits are the cruel work of God,*
*Mocking the Remover of Limits & the Resurrection of the Dead* [23]

The deists, believing that "the Spectre is the Man," may still have had a God to blame. Modern existentialists have no God to blame, but the limits are still there; and their philosophy gives no hope of a resurrection of the dead.

When all the heavens and hells have been harrowed by the Saviour, there will perhaps be no one left in "that State call'd Satan," which is "Eternal Death." Hell, when the souls have been redeemed, remains empty. The state is reprobate, "doomed to destruction"; but the release of the souls is a release *from* and, in that sense, also *of* Satan. It is thus possible to say—as

Blake does – that Jesus died to "save Satan." To speak of Satan's reclamation and his destruction is the same thing, since, reclaimed, he is no longer a selfhood and a specter; the "false body," open to the influx of the Imagination, ceases to exist, as a "complex" may be said to cease to exist when the psychological energies operating within it are restored to the human personality from which they had become divided. States exist only so long as they are, as it were, occupied; and between the state called Christ and the state called Satan lie every possible kind of human personality, in the circles of hells and heavens: "these States Exist now. Man Passes on, but States remain for Ever; he passes thro' them like a traveller who may as well suppose that the places he has passed thro' exist no more, as a Man may suppose that the States he has pass'd thro' Exist no more. Every thing is Eternal." [24]

Satan is the "lost Traveller," and his "Dream under the Hill" is maya, "States that are not, but ah! Seem to be." The hill is, one must suppose, the mountain of purgatory, a symbol taken from Dante, whose hells are "under the Hill." Dante and Vergil emerge from Satan's realms into the sweet light to find themselves at the foot of the mountain of purgatory, and all the hells reversed beneath them. The Traveller who "hasteth in the Evening" [25] is the    [183]

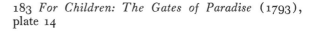
The Traveller hasteth in the Evening

183 *For Children: The Gates of Paradise* (1793), plate 14

man who has seen eternity, and hastens to end his journey through the states. It is in the nature of hell that its states are, or seem, binding, whereas in purgatory the souls are free to progress. Blake made it clear in his illustration of Dante's Hell Gate that the hells are this world, for Satan is there represented as the "God of this world."

That the states are in themselves perpetual, Blake, however, insists. In this sense one may say that he is an orthodox Christian,[26] accepting the permanence of hell in the total pattern of existence: "The Spiritual States of the Soul are all Eternal. Distinguish between the Man & his present State." [27] They are, at the same time, all illusory, as Satan is, since they all partake, more or less, of the selfhood, except the supreme state called Christ, who is "not a state" but life itself: "I do not consider either the Just or the Wicked to be in a Supreme State, but to be every one of them States of the Sleep which the Soul may fall into in its deadly dreams of Good & Evil when it leaves Paradise following the Serpent." [28]

William Empson first pointed out to me the resemblance of Blake's states to the Buddhist Wheel of hells and heavens. It is conceivable that Blake knew something of those hells and heavens from the volumes of the *Proceedings of the Calcutta Society.* They are in every way as horrible as the Christian hells (inevitably so, since the human experience of anguish is everywhere the same), but without the doctrine that souls are prisoners in these states for all eternity. For the Eastern religions "Man passes on"—a doctrine made less difficult by the concept of rebirth; but that which has distorted Christian (and especially Protestant) thought in this respect is not the Christian exclusion of the concept of reincarnation so much as the error that Blake diagnosed, the illusion that "the Spectre is the Man" and that "eternal life awaits the worm of sixty winters." Yet in spite of this resemblance, it remains a fact that Blake reached this doctrine of the soul's journey through the states not by way of the East but by way of Swedenborg and, of course, Dante.

Swedenborg himself never fully realized the implication of his own vision of ever-changing states, for there is no passing for him (nor indeed for Dante) from the hells to the heavens, and it is above all on this ground that Blake reproaches him:

> *O Swedenborg! strongest of men, the Samson shorn by the Churches,*
> *Shewing the Transgressors in Hell, the proud Warriors in Heaven,*
> *Heaven as a Punisher, & Hell as One under Punishment* [29]

Dante, too, "saw devils" where Blake "saw none." Blake, who makes no essential difference between the heavens and the hells, is again strangely close to the Indian religions and remote from the Christian. To the Indian religions both the heavens of bliss and the hells of torment are, in the final instance, illusory. Nirvana is a state beyond anything conceived as "heaven"; for heaven belongs, still, to the human personality. Christians who, by and large, fail to conceive anything higher in man than his personality can therefore conceive of nothing higher than these heavens. It is because Jesus harrows both the hells and the heavens that the Imagination is called the Saviour:

> *Remove from Albion, far remove these terrible surfaces;*
> *They are beginning to form Heavens & Hells in immense*
> *Circles, the Hells for food to the Heavens, food of torment,*
> *Food of despair: they drink the condemn'd Soul & rejoice*
> *In cruel holiness in their Heavens of Chastity & Uncircumcision;*
> *Yet they are blameless, & Iniquity must be imputed only*
> *To the State they are enter'd into, that they may be deliver'd.*
> *Satan is the State of Death & not a Human existence;*
> *But Luvah is named Satan because he has enter'd that State:*
> *A World where Man is by Nature the enemy of Man,*
> *Because the Evil is Created into a State, that Men*
> *May be deliver'd time after time, evermore. Amen.*
> *Learn therefore, O Sisters, to distinguish the Eternal Human*
> *That walks about among the stones of fire in bliss & woe*
> *Alternate, from those States or Worlds in which the Spirit travels.*
> *This is the only means to Forgiveness of Enemies.*[30]

There is one state to which Blake attaches a special importance: this he calls "Self-annihilation." It is not yet the perfect attainment of the "supreme State" beyond the states, but it represents the last human condition before this release from Satan's kingdom. This state is symbolized for Blake not, as might have been the case in former ages or in other civilizations, by the monk or the ascetic but by the inspired poet, who transcends, in the moment of inspiration, his human individuality; for true poetry begins where human personality ends.

> *And thou, O Milton, art a State about to be Created,*
> *Called Eternal Annihilation, that none but the Living shall*

*Dare to enter, & they shall enter triumphant over Death*
*And Hell & the Grave: States that are not, but ah! Seem to be.*[31]

Only the living—the spiritually living, that is—can dare to "annihilate" the spectral selfhood; for to the specters the human personality is all. To the spiritually dead the claims of imagination are meaningless, as they were to Locke. True and inspired poetry begins where the human personality ends, upon those altar steps of the gods to which the dying Keats with such pain raised himself in a supreme imaginative act of "Self-annihilation," whose reward is the true poetic apotheosis.

[184]        Blake's Milton speaks as the inspired poet:

*To bathe in the Waters of Life, to wash off the Not Human,*
*I come in Self-annihilation & the grandeur of Inspiration,*
*To cast off Rational Demonstration by Faith in the Saviour,*
*To cast off the rotten rags of Memory by Inspiration,*
*To cast off Bacon, Locke & Newton from Albion's covering,*
*To take off his filthy garments & clothe him with Imagination,*
*To cast aside from Poetry all that is not Inspiration,*
*That it no longer shall dare to mock with the aspersion of Madness*
*Cast on the Inspired by the tame high finisher of Paltry Blots*
*Indefinite, or paltry Rhymes, or paltry Harmonies,*
*Who creeps into State Government like a catterpiller to destroy;*
*To cast off the idiot Questioner who is always questioning*
*But never capable of answering, who sits with a sly grin*
*Silent plotting when to question, like a thief in a cave,*
*Who publishes doubt & calls it knowledge, whose Science is Despair,*
*Whose pretence to knowledge is envy, whose whole Science is*
*To destroy the wisdom of ages to gratify ravenous Envy*
*That rages round him like a Wolf day & night without rest;*
*He smiles with condescension, he talks of Benevolence & Virtue,*
*And those who act with Benevolence & Virtue they murder time on*
                                                            *time.*
*These are the destroyers of Jerusalem, these are the murderers*
*Of Jesus, who deny the Faith & mock at Eternal Life,*
*Who pretend to Poetry that they may destroy Imagination*
*By imitation of Nature's Images drawn from Remembrance.*
*These are the Sexual Garments, the Abomination of Desolation,*

> *Hiding the Human Lineaments as with an Ark & Curtains*
> *Which Jesus rent & now shall wholly purge away with Fire*
> *Till Generation is swallow'd up in Regeneration.*[32]

It may seem strange that Blake's Christianity is so closely bound up with his view of poetry, but it is not strange when we have understood that to him poetry means the utterance not of the poet but of the Divine Humanity himself:

> *"Let the Bard himself witness. Where hadst thou this terrible Song?"*

> *The Bard replied: "I am Inspired! I know it is Truth! for I Sing*
> *According to the inspiration of the Poetic Genius*
> *Who is the eternal all-protecting Divine Humanity."* [33]

It is, in Plato's words, "the god himself speaking, and through these men publishing his mind to us." The poem *Milton* was written in order to demonstrate the redeeming power of the imagination; and it is from the

184 Milton, the inspired man: *Milton* (1804–1808), plate 13

"states" that man is redeemed, both the terrible and the blissful. Milton is chosen as the type of inspired self-annihilation because he, of all English poets, is—both in his stature and in his own belief in the divinely inspired nature of true poetry—most apt as type and symbol of Blake's conception of the poet as prophet.

In his pictorial representation of Milton, Blake has expressed, in the poet's gesture, the spiritual state of self-annihilation. In contrast with that commanding gesture of so many Renaissance depictions of Apollo bringing the world under the rule of his ordering harmony, Blake has been at pains to show the poet as one who is casting away everything he possesses. His inspired face looks upward, intent upon some vision invisible; his attitude suggests that of some self-denying saint, some St. Francis whose poverty is all of the spirit—a renunciation not only of possessions and power but of the selfhood as such.

185 Device from Bryant's *Mythology*, vol. 2 (1774), plate XVI

# CHAPTER 27

# The Sickness of Albion

There remains still one figure of Blake's myth: Albion, the universal man. In a sense all that has been written of the Zoas is about Albion, for in him is enacted the Fall and the redemption; Satan is Albion's selfhood, and Jesus the Imagination the divine presence revealed in, and to, man; Jerusalem, the soul, is Albion's "daughter" and the bride of Jesus, and the Zoas are his vehicles, or energies.

Blake had several models for his figure of the cosmic man. He knew the Jewish tradition of Adam Kadmon (whether through Fludd or through some more immediate source we do not know), for in his address *To the Jews* that prefaces *Jerusalem*, II, he wrote: "You [the Jews] have a tradition, that Man anciently contain'd in his mighty limbs all things in Heaven & Earth: this you recieved from the Druids. . . . Albion was the Parent of the Druids, & in his Chaotic State of Sleep, Satan & Adam & the whole World was Created by the Elohim." [1]

Man as a microcosm of the universe was an idea current throughout the Middle Ages; and Boehme, inheriting this tradition, gives a fine description of the microcosmic man:

> Take *Man* for a Similitude or Example, *who is made after the Image or Similitude of God*, as it is written.
>
> The *Interior, or Hollowness in the Body of Man*, is, and signifies the Deep betwixt the Stars and the Earth.
>
> *The whole Body with all its Parts* signifies Heaven and Earth.
>
> *The Flesh* signifies the Earth.
>
> *The Blood* signifies the Water, and is from the Water.
>
> *The Breath* signifies the Air, and is also Air.
>
> *The Wind-pipe and Arteries*, wherein the Air qualifies or operates, signify the Deep betwixt the Stars and the Earth. . . .

[186]

*The Veins* signify the powerful Flowings out from the Stars, and are also the powerful Egressions of the Stars; for the Stars with their Powers reign in the Veins, and give Form and Shape to Men.

*The Entrails* or *Guts* signify the Operation of the Stars, or their consuming all that which is proceeded from their Power, for whatsoever *themselves* have made, that they consume again.[2]

This enumeration continues, identifying the heart with the element of fire, the lungs with the earth, the head with heaven and the sphere of the stars, and so on. What Boehme is describing is not resemblance but cosmic analogy, correspondence. Blake was no doubt also familiar with the macrocosmic figure of Zeus, as described in the Orphic Hymn to Zeus:

> *For in Jove's royal body all things lie,*
> *Fire, night and day, earth, water, and the sky;*
>
> .    .    .
>
> *See how his beauteous head and aspect bright*
> *Illumine heav'n, and scatter boundless light!*
> *Round which his pendent golden tresses shine,*
> *Form'd from the starry beams, with light divine,*
>
> .    .    .
>
> *His eyes the Sun and Moon with borrow'd ray;*
> *His mind is truth, unconscious of decay,*
> *Royal, etherial; and his ear refin'd*
> *Hears ev'ry voice and sounds of ev'ry kind.*
> *Thus are his head and mind immortal bright,*
> *His body boundless, stable, full of light* [3]

The line that is repeated like a refrain in *Milton* [4] and *Jerusalem*,[5] "But now the Starry Heavens are fled from the mighty limbs of Albion," is

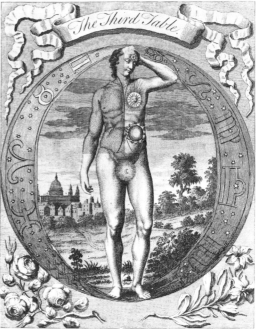

186 "The Third Table," by Freher, illustrating Law's Boehme (1764)

The figure at left represents Man as a microcosm containing within himself both the light and the fire-principles of the divine essence. His feet are in the dark fire-world of the abyss, peopled by monsters; the smoke of generated nature ascends from the fires; sun, moon, and stars are contained within Man's body. Cf. Blake's depiction of Albion [187]. (In these diagrams from Law's Boehme, hinged flaps of paper are lifted to reveal other pictures beneath. "The Third Table" with flaps closed is shown at right.)

like the writing on the tomb of man under the dominion of the Cartesian-Lockean philosophy; for "the Sickness of Albion" is the loss of his world through the belief that the phenomena possess a substantial existence independent of mind. Thus he has lost part of his soul; and conversely, the phenomenal world, emptied of spiritual life, has become a desert, a "soul-shudd'ring vacuum" of space and time, filled with "rocks and solids."

Blake again and again describes this disease of man. It may be conceived in two ways: as the "shrinking" of man's senses or as the "wandering away" of the creatures. Blake employs both symbols with great power. In the binding of Urizen and related .myths, Blake describes the separation as a shrinking of man himself from "giant" to "worm." The same event, seen as a "wandering away" of the creatures from man, is to be found in many passages.

The flight of the creatures is described in *Jerusalem*, page 66:

*They send the Dove & Raven & in vain the Serpent over the*
*mountains*
*And in vain the Eagle & Lion over the four-fold wilderness:*
*They return not, but generate in rocky places desolate:*
*They return not, but build a habitation separate from Man.*
*The Sun forgets his course like a drunken man; he hesitates*
*Upon the Cheselden hills, thinking to sleep on the Severn.*
*In vain: he is hurried afar into an unknown Night:*
*He bleeds in torrents of blood as he rolls thro' heaven above.*
*He chokes up the paths of the sky; the Moon is leprous as snow,*
*Trembling & descending down, seeking to rest on high Mona,*
*Scattering her leprous snows in flakes of disease over Albion.*
*The Stars flee remote; the heaven is iron, the earth is sulphur,*
*And all the mountains & hills shrink up like a withering gourd*
*As the Senses of Men shrink together under the Knife of flint*
*In the hands of Albion's Daughters . . .*[6]

[187]  This is the episode illustrated on page 25 of *Jerusalem*, where Albion—sun, moon, and stars in his limbs—is sacrificed by the cruel female powers of generation. The separation of sun, moon, and stars from Albion's body is described in an earlier plate as a "flight":

*. . . the Blue*
*Of our immortal Veins & all their Hosts fled from our Limbs*

187 Female powers sacrificing Albion: *Jerusalem* (1804–1820), plate 25 (Coll. Kerrison Preston)

Note the "fibres of life" or "soft sinewy threads" drawn out from the fingers of the woman with arms outstretched over Albion, and the sun, moon, and stars in his limbs.

> *And wander'd distant in a dismal Night clouded & dark.*
> *The Sun fled from the Briton's forehead, the Moon from his mighty*
> *loins* [7]

(Blake is here using Boehme's identification of the veins with the stars and their influences.) It is this process

> *Which separated the stars from the mountains, the mountains from*
> *Man*
> *And left Man, a little grovelling Root outside of Himself.*[8]

From an early stage Blake seems to have identified the sickness of Albion with the sickness of Job. In *Vala* we find man afflicted with Job's boils:

> *. . . left prostrate upon the crystal pavement,*
> *Cover'd with boils from head to foot, the terrible smitings of Luvah* [9]

and Job's loss of his children:

> *. . . [man] wander'd in mount Ephraim seeking a Sepulcher,*
> *His inward eyes closing from the Divine vision, & all*
> *His children wandering outside, from his bosom fleeing away.*[10]

In *Jerusalem* the god who takes away Albion's children is Satan:

> *. . . God takes vengeance on me: from my clay-cold bosom*
> *My children wander, trembling victims of his Moral Justice* [11]

Blake implies that Albion loses his children and his possessions because he "forgets" eternity (Albion's "flocks & herds & tents" recall the nomadic Job):

> *. . . Many sons*
> *And many daughters flourish'd round the holy Tent of Man*
> *Till he forgot Eternity, delighted in his sweet joy*
> *Among his family, his flocks & herds & tents & pastures.*
> *But Luvah close conferr'd with Urizen in darksom night*
> *To bind the father & enslave the brethren. Nought he knew*
> *Of sweet Eternity . . .*[12]

Externalized, nature becomes dead, and humanity alien:

*O weakness & O weariness! O war within my members!*
*My sons, exiled from my breast, pass to & fro before me.*
*My birds are silent on my hills, flocks die beneath my branches.*
*My tents are fallen, my trumpets & the sweet sound of my harps*
*Is silent on my clouded hills that belch forth storms & fire.*
*My milk of cows & honey of bees & fruit of golden harvest*
*Are gather'd in the scorching heat & in the driving rain.*
*My robe is turned to confusion, & my bright gold to stone.*
*Where once I sat, I weary walk in misery and pain,*
*For from within my wither'd breast grown narrow with my woes*
*The Corn is turned to thistles & the apples into poison,*
*The birds of song to murderous crows, My joys to bitter groans,*
*The voices of children in my tents to cries of helpless infants,*
*And all exiled from the face of light & shine of morning*
*In this dark world, a narrow house, I wander up & down.*[13]

In *Jerusalem*, plates 18 and 19, this passage is expanded in a way that leaves no doubt that Blake was working from the story of Job. First he describes, in retrospect, Albion happy with his children around him. He has lost these through "natural religion." The work of Blake's Satan the Selfhood is the destruction of the world of Jesus the Imagination, in which man, his children, and his world are one in the Divine Humanity. But the satanic morality looks upon the pity and forgiveness of Eden as "Our Father Albion's sin and shame":

*. . . But father now no more,*
*Nor sons, nor hateful peace & love, nor soft complacencies,*
*With transgressors meeting in brotherhood around the table*
*Or in the porch or garden. No more the sinful delights*
*Of age and youth, and boy and girl, and animal and herb,*
*And river and mountain, and city & village, and house & family,*

188 Nature externalized by sacrifice: *Jerusalem* (1804–20), plate 91, detail

Externalization of his universe from fallen man. The emblem on the right appears to be an ear of corn, emblem of vegetation; on the left the seal of Solomon which "stamps with solid form." See cosmological diagrams for Law's Boehme [126].

*Beneath the Oak & Palm, beneath the Vine and Fig-tree,*
*In self-denial!—But War and deadly contention Between*
*Father and Son, and light and love! All bold asperities*
*Of Haters met in deadly strife, rending the house & garden,*
*The unforgiving porches, the tables of enmity, and beds*
*And chambers of trembling & suspition, hatreds of age & youth,*
*And boy & girl, & animal & herb, & river & mountain,*
*And city & village, and house & family . . .*[14]

There follows the account first written in *Vala* (quoted above) of the externalization of nature; and the Job parallel is continued in the description of Albion's loss of his sons by their becoming external to himself:

[188]
*All his Affections now appear withoutside: all his Sons,*
*Hand, Hyle &c. . . .*[15]

He then becomes, like Job, diseased:

*. . . the seven diseases of the Soul*
*Settled around Albion . . .*

And Blake gives his own reason for this:

*. . . withoutside all*
*Appear'd a rocky form against the Divine Humanity.*[16]

Albion's lament, which presently follows, is again based upon the story of Job:

*The disease of Shame covers me from head to feet. I have no hope.*
*Every boil upon my body is a separate & deadly Sin.*
*Doubt first assail'd me, then Shame took possession of me.*

.        .        .

*First fled my Sons & then my Daughters, then my Wild Animations,*
*My Cattle next, last ev'n the Dog of my Gate; the Forests fled,*
*The Corn-fields & the breathing Gardens outside separated,*
*The Sea, the Stars, the Sun, the Moon, driv'n forth by my disease.*
*All is Eternal Death . . .*[17]

For Blake the only death is spiritual death—alienation from eternity.

There can therefore be no doubt that when later Blake made his twenty-two illustrations of the Book of Job, he conceived Job's sufferings in

these terms. As the Eternal Man fell from the Divine Bosom, so Job loses the
vision of God through the agency of Satan the Selfhood; Satan afflicts Job, as
he afflicted Albion, first with the externalization of his world, then with the
"boils" of "deadly sin," the torments of the morality that follows upon this
externalization. Thus externalized, his children are "dead" to him and his
pastoral riches lost, for possession of riches in the world is the imaginative
power to enjoy, not the material power to purchase. As Albion's soul,
Jerusalem, suffers with him, so does Job's wife. Job's three friends who give
him evil counsel correspond to the three fallen Zoas—Urizen, Tharmas, and
Luvah. It seems that Blake had, in *Jerusalem*, already identified the Zoas
with the friends of Job, for he calls them "The Friends of Albion," and
describes them as "visiting" Albion at his house in a way not otherwise
characteristic of the appearances of the Zoas, but reminiscent of the Bible
story:

> *Los shudder'd at beholding Albion, for his disease*
> *Arose upon him pale and ghastly, and he call'd around*
> *The Friends of Albion; trembling at the sight of Eternal Death*
> *The four appear'd . . .*
>
> .   .   .
>
> *. . . weeping every one*
> *Descended and fell down upon their knees round Albion's knees,*
> *Swearing the Oath of God with awful voice of thunders round*
> *Upon the hills & valleys, and the cloudy Oath roll'd far and wide.*
>
> *"Albion is sick!" said every Valley, every mournful Hill*
> *And every River: "our brother Albion is sick to death.*
> *He hath leagued himself with robbers: he hath studied the arts*
> *Of unbelief. Envy hovers over him: his Friends are his abhorrence:"*
>
> .   .   .
>
> *. . . the Living Creatures wept aloud, as they*
> *Went along Albion's roads, till they arriv'd at Albion's House.*[18]

It is easy to identify the Zoas in the pictorial characterization of the three
friends in the Job series,

> *Urizen cold & scientific, Luvah pitying & weeping,*
> *Tharmas indolent & sullen . . .*[19]

Los, who tells Albion, "Three thou hast slain. I am the Fourth: thou canst [189]
not destroy me,"[20] is perhaps Elihu, who appears to Job, in Blake's

189 Job with Elihu: engraving (1826) for *Job*, plate 12

imagination of the scene, as a beautiful youth, a bringer of hope to Job, who, while Elihu approaches, raises his eyes for the first time; for he is the unfallen Zoa who "kept the divine vision in time of trouble," and who never ceased to tell Albion of eternal things. In the reconciling vision Job again sees the creation as living—a human-formed living sun and moon, and the stars of the morning singing together; his children are restored to him, as one with him in the "Divine Family"; and this, of course, is also the story of Albion.

Abstract philosophy kills; far from exalting nature, the idolatrous worship of phenomena as substantial entities empties them of that which alone gives them meaning and beauty. Conversely, far from degrading the body and the natural world, its realization as a "portion of soul" regenerates, resurrects, both body and nature:

> . . . & all the tremendous unfathomable Non Ens
> Of Death was seen in regenerations terrific or complacent, varying
>
> .   .   .
>
> . . . according to the Expansion or Contraction, the Translucence or
> Opakeness of Nervous fibres: such was the variation of Time & Space
> Which vary according as the Organs of Perception vary . . .[21]

There seems no doubt that the Job series is Blake's final and most perfect statement of the myth of Albion: the satanic philosophy, in externalizing the phenomena, deprives man of the living enjoyment of his own kind (his children), of his possessions, of nature, and even of his own body. Blake's visions of Job are the direct outcome of the thought first expressed in the tractates. His diagnosis of the sickness of English civilization (Albion) is precisely that rift between mind and phenomena which separates the soul from its world; and it was a prophetic urgency to preach to the English a return to spiritual vision that dictated Blake's choice of the theme of his last and greatest completed work.

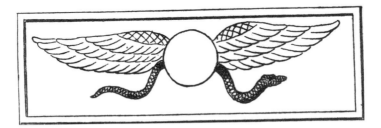

190 Winged disk and serpent: Bryant's *Mythology*, vol. 1 (1774), plate VIII

In Bryant's *Mythology* there is a group of drawings showing various versions of the emblem of the winged disk and serpent, engraved, it may be, [190] by Blake himself in his apprenticeship to Basire. The series is taken from Stukeley's *Abury*,[22] and perhaps Blake became acquainted with Stukeley while working on Bryant. In any case, Blake remembered this "sacred heirogram," as Stukeley calls it. Plate 37 of *Jerusalem* contains two draw- [191] ings, separated by a few lines of text. The upper section shows Albion sinking into "sleep," but upheld by Jesus. Albion is under an oak–the druid tree; and behind Jesus is a palm. A winged disk appears to support the whole. Below is Albion, now "sunk in deadly sleep" on the "oozy rock" in the Atlantic, upon which he "vegetates" into long weedy strands. He is no longer upheld by Jesus, and instead of the supporting winged disk, there is a hovering specter with bony skeleton and batlike wings. Stukeley describes the emblem of the winged disk and serpent as signifying, in ancient Egypt, the Trinity. The Father is the circle, the Son is the serpent, and the wings are the Holy Ghost. Therefore, it seems likely that in showing Albion's world upheld by the Father and the Holy Ghost, while the head of the man

191 Albion woven into the
filmy    woof:   *Jerusalem*
(1804–1820), plate 37

reclines in the bosom of Jesus, Blake is following Stukeley in a symbolic
depiction of the world upheld by God, in contrast with the death-sleep of
fallen man in the sea of hyle.

Several of the engraved emblems strongly express the contrasting
opposites of good and evil in the eagle-wings and the serpent; and a
comparison with Blake's eagle and serpent depicted in plate 15 of the

*Marriage* suggests that they may have been a source of this design and its underlying meaning. The wholeness of man expressed in the disk is a reconciliation of the contraries. [i, 56; ii, 134]

The fallen man is surrounded by symbols of the indefinite. Albion sleeps his death-sleep upon a "rock" (the solid substance which forms the basis of materialist philosophy),

> . . . *a Rocky fragment from Eternity hurl'd*
> *By his own Spectre, who is the Reasoning Power in every Man,*
> *Into his own Chaos, which is the Memory between Man & Man.*[23]

Individual memory is a "Chaos" because it is without intelligible meaning or order, whereas the recollection of the eternal world is of the archetypal, intelligible order of the mind itself. The temporal personality is a "fortuitous concourse of memorys accumulated & lost" by the "Worm seventy inches long." [24] The "fragmentary" rock is washed by the tides of hyle, overgrown with "vegetated" life; the Specter overshadows him:

> *The sea encompasses him & monsters of the deep are his companions.*
> *Dreamer of furious oceans, cold sleeper of weeds & shells* [25]

With slight variations this imagery is repeated. The rock is "beyond the remotest Pole"; it is "Beneath the Furnaces & the starry Wheels"; or it is the "Rock of Ages"—of unending time and space:

> . . . *Albion upon the Rock of Ages,*
> *Deadly pale outstretch'd and snowy cold, storm cover'd,*
> *A Giant form of perfect beauty outstretch'd on the rock*
> *In solemn death: the Sea of Time & Space thunder'd aloud*
> *Against the rock, which was inwrapped with the weeds of death.*[26]

In contrast with the amorphous imagery of the sleeping man, the regenerate Albion is described in the typical imagery of the mandala,[27] characteristic of all subjective representations of the soul—sphere and quaternity apprehended as symbols of indescribable power and glory. Buddhist art is rich in such representations, of which Ezekiel and the Apocalypse provide examples.

Blake's Four Zoas are the four faces or faculties of the human soul:

> *Four Mighty Ones are in every Man; a Perfect Unity*

> *Cannot Exist but from the Universal Brotherhood of Eden,*
> *The Universal Man. . . .*[28]

In "the Brain of Man we live & in his circling Nerves."[29] This fourfold humanity Blake has based upon the visions in St. John and Ezekiel—more especially the latter—of the "four living creatures": "And this was their appearance; they had the likeness of a man. And every one had four faces, and every one had four wings." They have each the faces of lion, man, ox, and eagle: "And they went every one straight forward: whither the spirit was to go, they went."[30] Blake describes them in like terms:

> *The Four Living Creatures, Chariots of Humanity Divine*
> *Incomprehensible,*
> *In beautiful Paradises expand. These are the Four Rivers of Paradise*
> *And the Four Faces of Humanity, fronting the Four Cardinal Points*
> *Of Heaven, going forward, forward irresistible from Eternity to*
> *Eternity.*[31]

As with the universal man, so with every individual: ". . . every Man stood Fourfold; each Four Faces had."[32]

The soul is, according to the Platonic tradition, a sphere. Blake's Albion is also a sphere, with center and circumference, a perfect, bounded form; the boundless ocean of hyle is replaced by the circumscribed *temenos.* The circle is at the same time fourfold:

[192]
> *And the Four Points are thus beheld in Great Eternity:*
> *West, the Circumference: South, the Zenith: North,*
> *The Nadir: East, the Center, unapproachable for ever.*
> *These are the four Faces towards the Four Worlds of Humanity*
> *In every Man. Ezekiel saw them by Chebar's flood.*[33]

The east is the place of the rising sun, where the divine Being is always seen by Swedenborg's angels—"unapproachable for ever," the "dayspring from on high" in every man. The symbolism of the western circumference we shall presently examine.

Albion in his immortal glory is four-faced, like Indian Brahma, like the man seen in Ezekiel's vision, and like Jung's more recent symbolic representations of the Self. In *Jerusalem* Blake develops the symbolism of the fourfold City of Golgonooza.[34] Golgonooza is Blake's "Mansoul."[35] It bears the same relation to the holy fourfold city (Jerusalem) as Albion

192 The Vision of Ezekiel—the eyes of God and four-headed human figure: water color (engraved 1794)

(generated man) to the Divine Humanity; it is the city, one might say, of "work in progress," the "Spiritual Fourfold London."

Blake must certainly have known Swedenborg's vision of a spiritual fourfold London—for Swedenborg, also, had his vision of the mandala symbol, which he describes in characteristically pedestrian style. He saw, in fact, two cities, one of the good, the other of the evil, spirits: "The Middle of [one city] answers to that Part of London, where the Merchants meet, called the Exchange, and there the Moderators dwell; above that Middle Part is the East, Below it is the West; on the right Side is the South, on the left Side is the North." (This insistence on the four cardinal points is not altogether mere pedantry; it is a common feature of all accounts of this strange archetype.) "The Eastern Quarter is inhabited by those who have been particularly distinguished for leading Lives of Charity, and in that Quarter there are magnificent Palaces; the Southern Quarter is inhabited by such as have been distinguished for Wisdom . . . the Northern Quarter is inhabited by those who have been particularly delighted with the Liberty of speaking and writing; and in the Western Quarter are they who maintain the Doctrine of Justification by Faith alone."[36] Blake's Golgonooza is likewise fourfold in its whole and in its parts:

> . . . fourfold
> The great City of Golgonooza: fourfold toward the north,
> And toward the south fourfold, & fourfold toward the east & west,
> Each within other toward the four points: that toward
> Eden, and that toward the World of Generation,
> And that toward Beulah, and that toward Ulro.
> Ulro is the space of the terrible starry wheels of Albion's sons,
> But that toward Eden is walled up till time of renovation,
> Yet it is perfect in its building, ornaments & perfection.[37]

With this, we should remember the four universes of the Zoas:

> One to the North, Urthona: One to the South, Urizen:
> One to the East, Luvah: One to the West, Tharmas.
> They are the Four Zoas that stood around the Throne Divine.[38]

There is virtually no difference between the four-faced man, Albion, and the fourfold city; they are one and the same. The city is human-faced; man is diagrammatic.

Albion's western gate is "toward Eden." And we must now consider a strange feature of Blake's city, the closed western gate. The folklore of Europe has ever located the Islands of the Blessed in the Western Sea. There lies St. Brandan's Isle, Avalon, the Celtic Land-under-Wave. This western paradise was a favorite theme of the early mythologists. On a phrase in Ossian, "The gates of the west are closed on the sun's eagle eye," the learned Stukeley commented: "these *gates* are often mention'd by Homer, and by our poet [Macpherson]. The former means Brittain . . . tho' he knew not the name." [39] Captain Wilford thought he had discovered a Hindu tradition according to which Eden was Britain.[40] In Edward Davies' *Celtic Researches* (1804), a work Blake took very seriously, he would have read: "as the whole of Europe lay directly west of Asia, it was overshadowed by the darkness of the night, when the morning arose upon the Eastern habitations of the Noachidae: and the evening sun would appear to descend, in its progress toward the *western continent*, as to a *lower* sphere. Hence the portion of Japheth, or of Dis, obtained the description of a *lower* Region, *the land of Shades and of Night*." [41] Thus the west is the country of the Fortunate Isles of classical mythology, of lost Paradise, and of the dead. Taylor also writes that the west is assigned to Pluto, "who governs the earth, because the west is allied to earth on account of its dark and nocturnal nature." [42] Annwn, the Welsh Hades, is in the west; and this, too, Blake would find in Davies. It is also identified with Britain or Ireland:

> As *Annwn*, or the *west*, was the peculiar land of the dead, we find sepulchral monuments most frequent in the *western* extremities of those countries, where *Druidism* was professed, as in *Britany*, *Cornwall*, and *Mona*.[43] There was perhaps a time, when these *Druids* regarded *Ireland* as the *land of spirits*. The *Mabinogion*, or *institutional* tales, represent *Annwn* as lying off *Dyved*, or *Pembrokeshire;* and the *Irish* acknowledge *Annan*, or *Annun*, as an old name of their country.[44]

Whence, I suggest, Blake's *Annandale*—a name for the west of Britain, considered as Hades, a country of the dead. "Annandale" is "the valley of the dead." A "valley" is his constant symbol of the natural world, and this symbol, combined with a root meaning Hades, forms an anglicized name appropriate to the old myth that this country is Hades. Again, we think

of Joyce, who would have understood Blake's pleasure in this sort of play
with names:

> *Jehovah stood among the Druids in the valley of Annandale*
> *When the Four Zoas of Albion, the Four Living Creatures, the*
> *Cherubim*
> *Of Albion tremble before the Spectre in the starry Harness of the*
> *Plow*
> *Of Nations. . . .*[45]

A second use of the name, prefacing an eloquent indictment of the mechanization of life in England that resulted from the mechanization of philosophy,
seems to confirm that Annandale is associated with spiritual death:

> *They forg'd the sword on Cheviot, the chariot of war & the battle-ax,*
> *The trumpet fitted to mortal battle, & the Flute of summer in*
> *Annandale;*
> *And all the Arts of Life they chang'd into the Arts of Death in*
> *Albion.*[46]

The lost western Eden is sometimes America, sometimes Atlantis.[47] In
either case, "those infinite mountains of light, now barr'd out by the Atlantic
sea" lie beyond the closed western gate: "Albion clos'd the Western Gate, &
shut America out by the Atlantic, for a curse, and hidden horror, and an
altar of victims to Sin and Repentance." [48] The closing of Albion's western
gate marks the onset of his death: "Albion's Western Gate is clos'd: his
death is coming apace." [49] Sometimes the lost Eden is associated with Erin,
again because of her western nature:

> *. . . With awful hands she took*
> *A Moment of Time, drawing it out with many tears & afflictions*
> *And many sorrows, oblique across the Atlantic Vale,*
> *Which is the Vale of Rephaim dreadful from East to West.*[50]

In all the accounts, which vary a little from the early to the late books,
one feature remains constant: the western gate is closed, and a western Eden
lost, because of the flood of "the Sea of Time & Space," which submerges or
cuts off the lost country. Of this the Atlantic Ocean is a symbol.

The biblical story of the expulsion from Eden and the closing of the
gate, and that of the Deluge, are, of course, quite distinct; but to Blake they
are, in symbolic terms, the same story, and he therefore does not scruple to

combine them. Albion's western gate is closed; and a western ocean bars out Paradise by "the flood of the five senses." By the same logic of the symbol, the lost Paradise becomes a Hades of the dead.

The western gate is the gate of Tharmas, the Zoa of sensory life. Tharmas is the "parent power, dark'ning in the west," the "rough demon of the waters" that have drowned the Western world, the "cold expanse where wat'ry Tharmas mourns." The other three gates in man—reason, feeling, and poetic vision—are open gates. This is not to say that these faculties cannot often mislead man; but they are alike in this, that we take them to be of mental nature; our thoughts, feelings, and intuitions we naturally assume to be part of ourselves, whereas the world revealed to us by the senses we take to be exterior to ourselves—that is, excluded, as by a closed gate. We take this for granted; we do not even see in so obvious an assumption a problem at all. So, one imagines, to primitive people [51] certain intuitions and imaginings, which to us seem to come from our own minds, come as if from outside, as spirits, ghosts, fairies, gods, and the rest. But Albion—that is to say, ourselves—is no less living in superstition and darkness, in supposing the world revealed by the senses to be other than within consciousness itself, "barred out by the Atlantic sea." It is very difficult for most Western peoples even to conceive a state of consciousness in which the sensible world might seem a part of our subjectivity.[52] It is precisely this almost constitutional inability, this blockage of consciousness, that Blake has represented in his mandala with the closed gate. Materialist Western philosophy destroys for man precisely the material world, which it externalizes, banishing the phenomena into "the far remote." This handicap is, as it were, innate in the people of Golgonooza: "The Western Gate fourfold is clos'd."[53] Albion, washed by the Atlantic Ocean, on his rock, is the dead awaiting resurrection; and the "resurrection of the body" means, according to this symbolism, precisely the restoration of the physical universe to the imaginative whole of man:

> But the gate of the tongue, the western gate, in them is clos'd,
> Having a wall builded against it . . .
>
> .    .    .
>
> And the North is Breadth, the South is Heighth & Depth,
> The East is Inwards, & the West is Outwards every way.[54]

The west is man's outer world, his "circumference," his physical environment; "although it appears without, it is within, in your Imagination." In this respect, the English race as a whole thinks, feels, experiences as one; it is only by an extreme effort that a few individuals can come to see the world otherwise than as Albion sees it.

The western gate of Golgonooza is guarded by cherubim:

*The Western Gate fourfold is clos'd, having four Cherubim*
*Its guards, living, the work of elemental hands, laborious task,*
*Like Men hermaphroditic, each winged with eight wings.*

.     .     .

*But all clos'd up till the last day, when the graves shall yield their*
*dead.*[55]

The image of the cherub leads us back to the *Marriage:* "the notion that man has a body distinct from his soul is to be expunged." This will happen when the cherub leaves his guard over Eden's western gate. (See Chap. Thirteen, Appendix II: Vol. I, p. 330.)

Everything in the world has a fourfold nature; it is apprehensible— that is to say, it exists—in terms of reason, feeling, vision, and sense; but in all Golgonooza the fourth gate is closed:

*And every part of the City is fourfold; & every inhabitant, fourfold.*
*And every pot & vessel & garment & utensil of the houses,*
*And every house, fourfold; but the third Gate in every one*
*Is clos'd as with a threefold curtain of ivory & fine linen & ermine.*[56]

The curtain of ivory bones, woven flesh, and ermine skin is the body. It is the "little curtain of flesh on the bed of our desire" that Thel saw, and recoiled from generation. Blake writes of a great world of delight "clos'd" by our senses five. In the regenerate Albion all of man's four senses open to him their proper worlds:

*South stood the Nerves of the Eye; East, in Rivers of bliss, the Nerves*
*of the*
*Expansive Nostrils; West flow'd the Parent Sense, the Tongue;*
*North stood*
*The labyrinthine Ear: Circumscribing & Circumcising the*
*excrementitious*
*Husk & Covering, into Vacuum evaporating, revealing the*
*lineaments of Man,*

> *Driving outward the Body of Death in an Eternal Death &*
> *Resurrection,*
> *Awaking it to Life among the Flowers of Beulah, rejoicing in Unity*
> *In the Four Senses, in the Outline, the Circumference & Form, for*
> *ever* [57]

This is the destruction only of an illusion; the supposed "Body of Death" has no substantial existence, such as is supposed by the materialist philosophies: "I assert for My Self that I do not behold the outward Creation & that to me it is hindrance & not Action; it is as the Dirt upon my feet, No part of Me." [58] From what immediately precedes, it is perfectly obvious that Blake does not behold the outward creation only because he has realized that such a thing does not exist ("Where is it but in the Mind of a Fool?"), because "To Me This World is all One continued Vision of Fancy or Imagination." [59]

Even in Albion's land there are some who have passed through this Last Judgment, and whose consciousness has been regenerated:

> *So spoke, unheard by Albion, the merciful Son of Heaven*
> *To those whose Western Gates were open, as they stood weeping*
> *Around Albion; but Albion heard him not; obdurate, hard,*
> *He frown'd on all his Friends, counting them enemies in his sorrow.* [60]

Blake himself was one of these:

> *To find the Western path*
> *Right thro' the Gates of Wrath*
> *I urge my way.* [61]

The way leads to Eden, man's native country, and "in Paradise they have no Corporeal & Mortal Body—that originated with the Fall & was call'd Death & cannot be removed but by a Last Judgment . . . The Whole Creation Groans to be deliver'd." [62] There are no "Corporeal" or "Mortal" bodies except to man's fallen consciousness. The transformation of consciousness by which the outer world comes to be experienced as within the soul has often been described, and those who have experienced this all bear witness to the ecstatic joy of the illumination of nature that it brings. This is a return "to paradise," man's original perfection, lost with the Fall. The phenomenal world is seen as "infinite and holy," whereas now it is "finite and corrupt." This resurrection of nature is not the vision of the supreme heaven, but it makes that further vision possible. "The artist is an inhabitant of that happy country; and . . . the world of vegetation and generation may expect to be opened again to Heaven, through Eden, as it was in the beginning." [63] We must clearly realize, therefore, that Blake's mandala of Albion is not a "subjective" projection of his own spiritual state; it is, on the contrary, yet another symbol in which he has attempted to illustrate the defect of his age. He himself had experienced an opening of the gates:

> *. . . Even I already feel a World within*
> *Opening its gates, & in it all the real substances*
> *Of which these in the outward World are shadows which pass*
> *away.*[64]

It is interesting to know what image occupies the center of a mandala, this being the most significant statement of the symbol. Blake places in the center a symbol of divine generative power from which manifested being opens:

> *And Luban stands in middle of the City; a moat of fire*
> *Surrounds Luban, Los's Palace & the golden Looms of Cathedron.*[65]

The holy of holies, where stand the golden looms of the female and the "furnace of beryll" of the male, must be considered as the center in which eternity expands and issues into time. Cathedron means seat or throne; and "There is a Throne in every Man, it is the Throne of God." [66] It is upon this throne that Jesus sits to reign and judge: "Around the Throne Heaven is open'd & the Nature of Eternal Things Display'd." [67] Cathedron is the place in which the Son, the Divine Humanity, is generated in the soul of man, from the Father's "principle," to use Boehme's term.[68] Blake's mandala thus resembles very closely the classical Tibetan Buddhist pattern, at whose center there is, in many examples, a generative symbol, often a *dorje* or thunderbolt, surrounded by fire, and in others the God and his *shakti* or (in Blake's terms) emanation, in sacred sexual union. This is the meaning of Blake's looms and furnaces, the generative center of this emblem of divine manifestation.

The name Albion already appears in the later passages and alterations of *The Four Zoas*, and in *Milton* the collective being of the English nation has replaced the earlier more generalized "eternal man." Albion's giant limbs are the regions of England, and his dreams are her history. Joyce must have appreciated this forerunner of his own Finnegan:

> . . . *London & Bath & Legions & Edinburgh*
> *Are the four pillars of his Throne: his left foot near London*
> *Covers the shades of Tyburn: his instep from Windsor*
> *To Primrose Hill stretching to Highgate & Holloway.*
> *London is between his knees, its basements fourfold;*
> *His right foot stretches to the sea on Dover cliffs, his heel*
> *On Canterbury's ruins; his right hand covers lofty Wales,*
> *His left Scotland; his bosom girt with gold involves*
> *York, Edinburgh, Durham & Carlisle, & on the front*
> *Bath, Oxford, Cambridge, Norwich; his right elbow*
> *Leans on the Rocks of Erin's Land, Ireland, ancient nation.*
> *His head bends over London . . .*[69]

One may compare such poetry with Joyce's wedding of Dublin and Irish history to the myth of *Finnegans Wake*. If Ireland is called "holy," is it not precisely because since pre-Christian times saints and poets have never ceased to wed, as Yeats says, the imagination to the land? "Have not all races had their first unity from a mythology, that marries them to rock and hill?"[70] This is Blake's "reign of Literature and the Arts," an imperialism of the imagination that brings a nation within the order of some myth until every familiar landmark serves also as a symbol.

Both Joyce and Yeats looked to Blake as a master; and we may think also of George Russell (AE) and his attempt to make the "politics of time" correspond with the "politics of eternity." Every poem and ballad, in some measure, accomplishes this wedding of the imagination to place and history. It is one of the most alarming features of the modern mechanistic civilization that it destroys all traces of the work of human imagination upon place, and creates instead a landscape entirely profane. Ireland retained her old mythology alongside her Catholic Christianity, while England all but lost hers under successive waves of invasion and conversion, to become at last completely demythologized under Protestantism. Only the Arthurian legends to this day retain some slight hold upon the national imagination; the "deeds of Arthur are the acts of Albion," even though Milton himself rejected the theme to write a poem which, for all its greatness, does nothing to wed the English imagination to the land. Inheriting, therefore, no native mythology, and living at a time when the old landmarks of pre-industrial

England were already beginning to be obliterated by mills and furnaces, Blake attempted to bring back the gods to a country from which they were being driven even as he wrote the verses whose poignancy has found its echo in our own profane century:

> *And did those feet in ancient time*
> *Walk upon England's mountains green?* [71]

Blake found neither local saints nor local deities; yet he set about to repeople the rivers and mountains and cities of England with spiritual forms and energies. He was not merely perpetuating historical associations when he wrote of "Tyburn's deathful shades" or the "golden builders" of London; he was giving to hell and heaven "a name and a habitation." Jesus and the Council of God hover over "Snowdon sublime." The terrible sea of hyle, where Albion sleeps upon his rocky sepulcher, is the Atlantic Ocean, which has drowned the fields of Eden. The gate of Los, by which the souls of the dead "ascend," crosses Oxford Street. Los and Enitharmon, regents of the sun and moon, reign in Avebury. St. Paul's is the temple of Newton's natural philosophy, and the Gothic architecture of Westminster Abbey, the temple of the true religion of the imagination.

In *Jerusalem* this localization of the myth "in England's green and pleasant land" seems to have been one of the chief intentions of the poem. It is a pity that Blake attempted to place the centers of England under the governance of the twelve tribes of Israel, introducing biblical place-names and persons emptied of all their original connotation. But when Los keeps watch over the Isle of Dogs, or Vala weeps among the brick kilns and furnaces of nineteenth-century industry, the myth comes to life. One may think of:

> *I behold London, a Human awful wonder of God!*
> *He says: "Return, Albion, return! I give myself for thee.*
> *My Streets are my Ideas of Imagination.*
> *Awake Albion, awake! and let us awake up together.*
> *My Houses are Thoughts: my Inhabitants, Affections,*
> *The children of my thoughts walking within my blood-vessels"* [72]

Or:

> *. . . I heard in Lambeth's shades.*
> *In Felpham I heard and saw the Visions of Albion.*

> *I write in South Molton Street what I both see and hear*
> *In regions of Humanity, in London's opening streets.*[73]

Or:

> *What are those golden builders doing? where was the burying-place*
> *Of soft Ethinthus? near Tyburn's fatal Tree? is that*
> *Mild Zion's hill's most ancient promontory, near mournful*
> *Ever weeping Paddington? is that Calvary and Golgotha*
> *Becoming a building of pity and compassion? Lo!*
> *The stones are pity, and the bricks, well wrought affections*
> *Enamel'd with love & kindness, & the tiles engraven gold,*
> *Labour of merciful hands . . .*[74]

Here London is not described; it is defined in terms of its mythological correspondence; it is created. London's "opening streets" lead into the world of imagination like the "Grain of Sand" in Lambeth, which is

> *. . . translucent & has many Angles,*
> *But he who finds it will find Oothoon's palace; for within*
> *Opening into Beulah, every angle is a lovely heaven.*[75]

Blake gives to every place a visionary interior landscape, a qualitative value.

A mechanistic philosophy brings after it a mechanistic world. The machines of the dark satanic mills of Albion's towns are the visible and tangible reflection of the philosophy of Newton and Locke; and the mentality that sets men and women to tend such machines is the mentality (also satanic) that is the necessary and logical result of such a philosophy. Blake hated tyranny—civil, military, and ecclesiastical; he hated it because he believed in the divine nature of man and therefore in his divine rights: "it is a part of our duty to God & man to take due care of his Gifts; & tho' we ought not to think *more* highly of ourselves, yet we ought to think *As* highly of ourselves as immortals ought to think."[76] So Blake answers the false philosophy that teaches humility to "mortal worms." Such humility, also, belongs to Satan's kingdom. Jesus "acted with open, honest pride," and so should every man who knows himself to be a son of God.

But to Blake the worst tyranny of all is that false system of thought he identifies as satanic: natural religion, mechanistic philosophy. To suggest that Blake could ever have been a supporter of Marxist materialism or any of the other forms of materialism that are all but world-wide today is either foolish or dishonest. "I am really sorry to see my Countrymen trouble themselves about Politics. If Men were Wise, the Most arbitrary Princes could not hurt them. If they are not wise, the Freest Government is compell'd to be a Tyranny." [77] The enslavement of mankind to the machine and to the philosophy of a mechanistic universe, he not only would have condemned, but did condemn. He accused Albion of idolatrous worship of the machine, [164] "Attracted by the revolutions of those Wheels." [78] Spirits of the imaginative world attempt continually to carry Albion back into his native country, Eden:

> *With one accord in love sublime, &, as on Cherubs' wings,*
> *They Albion surround with kindest violence to bear him back*
> *Against his will thro' Los's Gate to Eden. Four-fold, loud,*
> *Their Wings waving over the bottomless Immense, to bear*
> *Their awful charge back to his native home; but Albion dark,*
> *Repugnant, roll'd his Wheels backward into Non-Entity.*
> *Loud roll the Starry Wheels of Albion into the World of Death* [79]

Blake, accusing Albion of idolatrous worship of the machine universe, compares this false religion to the (supposed) idolatry of the ignorant African worshipers of stocks and stones, but shows it to be even worse: [80]

> *Albion's Western Gate is clos'd: his death is coming apace.*
> *Jesus alone can save him; for alas, we none can know*
> *How soon his lot may be our own. When Africa in sleep*
> *Rose in the night of Beulah and bound down the Sun & Moon,*
> *His friends cut his strong chains & overwhelm'd his dark*
> *Machines in fury & destruction, and the Man reviving repented:*
>
> .      .      .
>
> *. . . But Albion's sleep is not*
> *Like Africa's, and his machines are woven with his life.* [81]

Not only has Albion's philosophy become bound up with the worship of the machine, but his way of life as well. Blake's picture of the good life was pastoral; shepherd and plowman and the craftsman who uses the skill of his hands are living imaginatively, as poet and painter and musician live imaginatively. England's mechanistic philosophy he indicted because it destroyed a way of life better than the one it brought into being:

> *Then left the Sons of Urizen the plow & harrow, the loom,*
> *The hammer & the chisel & the rule & compasses; from London*
>                                                             *fleeing,*

*They forg'd the sword on Cheviot, the chariot of war & the battle-ax,*
*The trumpet fitted to mortal battle, & the Flute of summer in*
*Annandale;*
*And all the Arts of Life they chang'd into the Arts of Death in*
*Albion.*
*The hour-glass contemn'd because its simple workmanship*
*Was like the workmanship of the plowman, & the water wheel*
*That raises water into cisterns, broken & burn'd with fire*
*Because its workmanship was like the workmanship of the shepherd;*
*And in their stead, intricate wheels invented, wheel without wheel,*
*To perplex youth in their outgoings & to bind to labours in Albion*
*Of day & night the myriads of eternity: that they may grind*
*And polish brass & iron hour after hour, laborious task,*
*Kept ignorant of its use: that they might spend the days of wisdom*
*In sorrowful drudgery to obtain a scanty pittance of bread,*
*In ignorance to view a small portion & think that All,*
*And call it Demonstration, blind to all the simple rules of life.*[82]

It is not the mere insufficiency of the wages in quantitative terms that
Blake condemns: even the highest wages would still be a "scanty pittance"
and a poor price for the loss of life and joy, for man does not live by bread
alone. In his illustrations to *Paradise Regained* Blake represents Satan
suggesting to Jesus that he turn the stones to bread. Satan points down to a    [1, 20b]
rock; and Jesus points up to heaven. He is rejecting the temptation of all
Welfare States, to feed man on bread made of stone (that is, of matter,
"calling rocks the atomic origins of existence"). The good life is a life in
harmony with a world experienced in its full spiritual reality—an impossi-
bility, given a mechanistic philosophy:

*. . . A Rock, a Cloud, a Mountain,*
*Were not now Vocal as in Climes of happy Eternity*
*Where the lamb replies to the infant voice, & the lion to the man of*
*years*
*Giving them sweet instructions; where the Cloud, the River & the*
*Field*
*Talk with the husbandman & shepherd. . . .*[83]

It is possible to argue that the vision of innocence, even in a factory of
machines, may see the divine order. It is argued that man's cities and
machines are just as much "part of nature" as trees. But Blake is defending

nothing on these grounds: "The devil is the Mind of the Natural Frame." [84]
Such machines are evil precisely insofar as they are the expressions of nature
worship, of the failure of the imaginative vision. They are the visible
expression of a lie, an idolatry, an atheism; and they wound and destroy the
human souls they enslave, both those who conceive them and those who toil
beneath them. Gilchrist recalls in his *Life of William Blake* a story of
Blake's having been shown, for his admiration, a copy of the *Mechanic's
Magazine*, by some progressive acquaintance. "Ah, Sir," he said, "these
things we artists hate." He wrote: "Art is the Tree of Life. . . . Science is
the Tree of Death." [85] Blake was the champion of man but not of a
civilization, whether capitalist or socialist, serving a religion of materialism.
He condemned the beginnings of industrialization; he would not have
applauded its ends. "In politics a Platonist," as Samuel Palmer recalled him
in his later years, "he put no trust in demagogues." A society must be
founded on abiding first principles, "the simple rules of life." He stands with
all those who condemn a civilization that destroys in man precisely what is
most human in him—the expression, in all he does and makes, of his
craftsman's skill, his artist's imagination.

Blake was not a poet who was against the natural world, in contrast
with Wordsworth who "loved" nature. It is true that Wordsworth writes
more about man in a natural setting than does Blake, and that much of
Blake's most characteristic imagery is taken from the city, from philosophy,
and from myth. But the contrast is not between a poet who loved nature and
a poet who did not; rather it is between one view of nature and another.
Wordsworth, Blake thought, was at times (though not always, or at his
best) inclined to nature worship; when Blake writes about nature, it is
invariably as "vision," alive with the spirit. He is invariably
animistic—closer to Shakespeare than to Wordsworth. He never sees the
objects of nature *as* objects; they are the "sons of Los," the children of
imaginative vision:

> *Thou seest the Constellations in the deep & wondrous Night:*
> *They rise in order and continue their immortal courses*
> *Upon the mountain & in vales with harp & heavenly song,*
> *With flute & clarion, with cups & measures fill'd with foaming wine.*
> *Glitt'ring the streams reflect the Vision of beatitude,*
> *And the calm Ocean joys beneath & smooths his awful waves:*

*These are the Sons of Los, & these the Labourers of the Vintage.*
*Thou seest the gorgeous clothed Flies that dance & sport in summer*
*Upon the sunny brooks & meadows: every one the dance*
*Knows in its intricate mazes of delight artful to weave:*
*Each one to sound his instruments of music in the dance,*
*To touch each other & recede, to cross & change & return:*
*These are the Children of Los; thou seest the Trees on mountains,*
*The wind blows heavy, loud they thunder thro' the darksom sky,*
*Uttering prophecies & speaking instructive words to the sons*
*Of men: These are the Sons of Los: These the Visions of Eternity,*
*But we see only as it were the hem of their garments*
*When with our vegetable eyes we view these wondrous Visions.*[86]

The quintessence of Blake's pastoral vision is to be found in his woodcuts for Thornton's *Virgil*. The pastoral vision for Blake is, precisely, human life in an environment of nature experienced imaginatively, a world one and the same with man himself, whose "Sky is an immortal tent built by the sons of Los." Nothing is external, nothing is lifeless matter. "I see Every Thing I paint In This World . . . to the eyes of the Man of Imagination, Nature is Imagination itself. As a man is, So he Sees." [87] Such is nature to the innocent world of childhood; such it is to primitive peoples and to poets. Such was the vision of nature that he transmitted, for a while, to Palmer and Calvert. When man begins to conceive his world as separate from his spiritual life, all its creatures "wander away." A meadow or a pasture or a mountain or a flock of sheep is then no more beautiful to him than a machine.

Life in harmony with a living nature, as the Chinese landscape painters supremely conceived it, is also Blake's pattern of the good life. This oneness of man and his world is conveyed in every line of the illustrations to Vergil's Pastorals, whose human figures, houses, and animals belong to their landscape as do those sages, fishermen, villages, and bridges in the middle distance of Chinese landscape paintings, those figures entirely occupied with their coming or going or standing still, merged with their surroundings. The sage looks at the tree, and the tree looks at the sage, in the same way as Blake's cloud, mountain, and rock are "vocal." So in Blake's woodcuts the line of the house-roof repeats the line of the hill, or the rays of the sun are repeated in the bright horns of the oxen and shafts of the plow, smoothed by the hands of the plowman. The sheep repeat the forms of woods and

thickets; the energy of a shepherd and his dog running on a hill seems part of
the flood of sunlight behind him; all are animated with one and the same life.
Every shepherd seems to be imaginatively at one with his world, to possess
it, as no mere purchaser of land can ever possess; for possession is vision,
and every man is the possessor of his own Eden, his "garden on a
mount." [88]

193 Thenot and Colinet: woodcut designed and engraved by Blake
(1821) as frontispiece for Vergil's first Eclogue

# Notes: Chapters 16–27

*with Abbreviations and Bibliographical Note*

# Abbreviations and Bibliographical Note

QUOTATIONS from Blake's writings, except for certain of those from *The Four Zoas*, are taken from *The Complete Writings of William Blake*, ed. Geoffrey Keynes (London: Nonesuch Press, and New York: Random House, 1957). References are indicated by number of plate (in the case of an engraved poem), book, or part (when the poem is so divided), and the letter "K," followed by Keynes's page and line numbers. When *The Four Zoas* is quoted or cited in the edition of H. M. Margoliouth (*Blake's Vala*, London: Oxford University Press, 1956), the title *Vala* is used, followed by the recto or verso numbering; line and page references to Keynes are also given for these citations. For Blake's Notebook (the Rossetti Manuscript) references are to the manuscript pages as given by Keynes.

For the convenience of scholars I have used the same abbreviations for the titles of Blake's works as Northrop Frye's in *Fearful Symmetry* (Princeton University Press, 1947).

| | | | |
|---|---|---|---|
| A.R.O. | *All Religions Are One* | M.H.H. | *The Marriage of Heaven and Hell* |
| B.A. | *The Book of Ahania* | | |
| B.L. | *The Book of Los* | N.N.R. | *There is No Natural Religion* |
| B.T. | *The Book of Thel* | | |
| B.U. | *The Book of Urizen* | P.A. | *Public Address* (Notebook) |
| D.C. | *A Descriptive Catalogue* | | |
| E.G. | *The Everlasting Gospel* | P.S. | *Poetical Sketches* |
| F.R. | *The French Revolution* | S.E. | *Songs of Experience* |
| F.Z. | *The Four Zoas* | S.I. | *Songs of Innocence* |
| G.P. | *The Gates of Paradise* | S.L. | *The Song of Los* |
| I.M. | *An Island in the Moon* | S.Lib. | *A Song of Liberty* |
| J. | *Jerusalem* | V.D.A. | *Visions of the Daughters of Albion* |
| M. | *Milton* | V.L.J. | *A Vision of the Last Judgment* (Notebook) |

[continued]

The following abbreviations for works other than Blake's have been used (full particulars of which are given in the Bibliography, below, pp. 323 ff.).

| | | | |
|---|---|---|---|
| A.C. | Swedenborg, *Arcana Coelestia* | O.H. | Taylor, *The Mystical Initiations, or, Hymns of Orpheus* |
| D.E. | Taylor, *A Dissertation on the Eleusinian and Bacchic Mysteries* | P.C.B. | Taylor [Plotinus], *Concerning the Beautiful* |
| D.L.W. | Swedenborg, *The Wisdom of Angels concerning Divine Love and Divine Wisdom* | P.F.B. | Taylor, *Five Books of Plotinus* |
| | | P.L. | Milton, *Paradise Lost* |
| | | P.R. | Milton, *Paradise Regained* |
| E.P.T. | Taylor, *An Essay on the Restoration of the Platonic Theology* | Pym. | [Hermes], *Divine Pymander of Hermes Mercurius Trismegistus* |
| F.Q. | Spenser, *The Faerie Queene* | T.C.R. | Swedenborg, *True Christian Religion* |
| H.H. | Swedenborg, *A Treatise concerning Heaven and Hell* | | |

References to the writings of Jacob Boehme are to *The Works of Jacob Behmen*, ed. Ward and Langcake (4 vols., London, 1764–81), known as "Law's Boehme." For the writings of Thomas Vaughan, references are given both to the original editions and to the A. E. Waite edition (London, 1919).

# Notes

## 16.  *The Tyger*

1.  *M.H.H.* 8; K. 151.
2.  *F.Z.* I; K. 275, 402–403.
3.  *F.Z.* VIII; K. 344, 116–22.
4.  Mr. K. D. Sethna, who kindly allowed me to read his unpublished essay on *The Tyger*, also sees the "fires" of the Tyger as a manifestation of the Divine Essence, and his conclusion is in accord with what we know of Blake's indebtedness to Boehme and the alchemists. I cannot accept all Mr. Sethna's conclusions, but many of them, reached by lines of thought different from those followed in this work, strikingly confirm what had been the inevitable outcome of a retracing of Blake's reading. After becoming acquainted with Mr. Sethna's essay I found myself obliged to rewrite some pages of this study, not so much in order to adopt his conclusions as, in one or two particulars, to strengthen my reasons for not doing so. I must therefore thank Mr. Sethna for what I have learned from him through a correspondence that has, apart from its particular application to this poem, confirmed me in the belief that a knowledge of tradition, such as he possesses (though in a form unknown to Blake), is of more value in giving insight into his work than the profane "learning" of academic critics, who are ignorant of the order of reality that Blake is at all times attempting to communicate.
5.  *S.I.;* K. 115, 13–18.
6.  *F.Z.* VI; K. 314, 102–103.
7.  *Europe* 2; K. 238, 6.
8.  *Tiriel* 7; K. 109, 15–18.
9.  Paracelsus, *Mysteries of Creation*, Bk. III, text 3, p. 58.
10. Ibid., Bk. I, text 22, p. 22.
11. *F.Z.* VII; K. 320, 9–10. See also *F.Z.* VIIb; K. 335, 110.
12. *F.Z.* IX; K. 366, 361. See our I, pp. 274–75.
13. *F.Z.* IX; K. 359, 67–70.
14. Notebook 80–81; K. 609. Italics mine.
15. *Europe* 2; K. 238, 1–9.
16. *Europe* 1; K. 238, 10.
17. Yeats, *Vacillation* II.

18.  *Siris*, § 190; *Works*, v, 196.

19.  *Aurora*, Chap. 15, §§ 93–100; *Works*, I, 155.

20.  Plowman, in his otherwise admirable introduction to the facsimile edition of the *Marriage*, writes of Blake's *Songs of Experience*, expressing "the bitterness and resentment we all experience in our first discovery of evil and its works."

21.  It was brought from Ethiopia by James Bruce, traveler and explorer of the sources of the Nile, in 1730–94. He also brought back the Book of Enoch, which appeared in English translation in 1821 and was illustrated by Blake at the end of his life.

22.  Tr. Archibald Maclaine, 1765.

23.  Morley, *Blake, Coleridge, etc.*, p. 23.

24.  *J.* 27; K. 649.

25.  *Ecclesiastical History*, Vol. I, Bk. I, Pt. II, Chap. 1, §§ 8–9, pp. 39–40.

26.  *F.Z.* I; K. 273, 318–19.

27.  Mosheim, Vol. I, Bk. I, Pt. II, Chap. 5, § 16, p. 69.

28.  *Mysteries of Creation*, Bk. II, text 1, p. 27.

28a. *F.Z.* VI; K. 314, 94.

29.  Notebook 25; K. 172, 16–17.

30.  *Pym.* v.23; p. 33.

31.  Notebook 25; K. 172, 18–20.

32.  *J.* 53; K. 684, 28.

33.  *S.E.;* K. 220.

34.  *F.Z.* VI; K. 315, 124–25.

35.  Notebook 26; K. 173.

36.  K. 214.

37.  *Magia Adamica*, p. 70; *Works*, p. 183.

38.  *Introduction;* K. 210.

39.  *Of the Chymical Transmutation*, p. 44 ("Of the Genealogy of Minerals").

40.  *Archidoxes* x.viii; p. 154.

41.  The "generating father" "determined by a dianoetic energy to produce a certain movable image of eternity: and thus while he was adorning and distributing the Universe, at the same time formed an eternal image flowing according to number, of eternity abiding in one" (*Works*, II, 290–91).

42.  *Pym.* II.13–15; pp. 9–10.

43.  *Republic* x.

44.  See below, Appendix, pp. 210 ff.

45.  Five planets only were known to antiquity (the earth was not counted as a planet) —Saturn, Jupiter, Mars, Venus, and Mercury. The number seven included the sun and moon.

46.  Blake's furnaces also owe much to Boehme's seven creative spirits, which are also said to revolve each within the other like the living spirits of Ezekiel's wheels.

47.  *F.Z.* IV; K. 302, 175–76.

48.  *F.Z.* IV; K. 304, 275–78. Boehme's seventh spirit is nature; it is in the seventh furnace, therefore, that Jesus is born as man. See our II, pp. 172 f.

49.  *F.Z.* IV; K. 301, 165–67.

50.  *Of the Chymical Transmutation*, Chap. 4, p. 18.

51.  See our II, p. 12.

52.  *Of the Chymical Transmutation*, Chap. 4, p. 17.

53. The word "beryll" suggests Paracelsus, though he nowhere describes the "athanor" as made of beryl. Beryl is the stone that is the end-process of the consuming away of nature, which begins in a seed and ends in a beryl.

54. Los as the blacksmith-god suggests perhaps Thor but, more especially, Vulcan. We may be sure that Vulcan entered into the composition of Los, for after the Last Judgment, Urthona "rose from the Golden feast . . . limping from his fall, on Tharmas lean'd, / In his right hand his hammer. . . ." (*F.Z.* IX; K. 377, 774–76).

The Homeric allusion to the golden feast of the gods and Hephaestus limping from his fall from heaven is unmistakable:

> . . . *lame* Ephaistus *fil'd*
> *Nectar to all the other Gods. A laughter never left,*
> *Shook all the blessed deities, to see the lame so deft.*
> [*Iliad* 1.577–79; p. 13]

But Blake no doubt knew also the occult significance of Vulcan, the principle of fire, from the Orphic Hymn to Vulcan:

> *Strong, mighty Vulcan, bearing splendid light,*
> *Unweary'd fire, with flaming torrents bright:*
> *Strong-handed, deathless, and of art divine,*
> *Pure element, a portion of the world is thine:*
> *All-taming artist, all-diffusive pow'r,*
> *'Tis thine supreme, all substance to devour:*
> *Aether, Sun, Moon, and Stars, light pure and clear,*
> *For these thy lucid parts to men appear.*
> *To thee, all dwellings, cities, tribes belong,*
> *Diffus'd thro' mortal bodies bright and strong.*
> [*O.H.* (1792 edn.) LXV, pp. 197–98]

It is needless to point out how many of these attributes of the god belong also to Los, the unwearied blacksmith-artist, who is also the builder of Golgonooza, the edifice of human civilization: "This deity according to Proclus, adorns by his artifice the sensible machine of the universe. . . . But he requires the assistance of Venus that he may invest sensible effects with beauty" (note to *O.H.*)—as Los requires the cooperation of Enitharmon and her golden looms in all his works.

The human body is in a sense the furnace of Los and its organs, the hammers and bellows:

> *Translucent the Furnaces, of Beryll & Emerald immortal*
> *And Seven-fold each within other, incomprehensible*
> *To the Vegetated Mortal Eye's perverted & single vision.*
> *The Bellows are the Animal Lungs, the Hammers the Animal Heart,*
> *The Furnaces the Stomach for Digestion; terrible their fury*
> *Like seven burning heavens rang'd from South to North.*
> [*J.* 53; K. 684, 9–14]

55. *J.* 96; K. 744, 36–37.
56. *F.Z.* I; K. 264, 14.
57. *Aurora*, Chap. 3, §§ 14–19; *Works*, I, 33.

58.  See below, pp. 110–11.
59.  K. 210.
60.  Morley, *Blake, Coleridge, etc.*, p. 3.
61.  *Pym.* II.8–9; pp. 8–9.
62.  *J.* 42; K. 669, 6–8.
63.  *F.Z.* V; K. 311, 222–27.
64.  *P.L.* VI.838–40.
65.  Ibid. 850–52.
66.  *Mysterium Magnum*, Chap. 8, § 24; *Works*, III, 33.

## 17.   The Ancient Trees

1.  *S.E.;* K. 218.
2.  Notebook 114; K. 165.
3.  *S.E.;* K. 217.
4.  Notebook 107; K. 174.
5.  So defined by the Buddha himself. See W. Y. Evans-Wentz, *The Tibetan Book of the Great Liberation*, p. 2.
6.  *Mysteries of Creation*, Bk. II, text 9, p. 36.
7.  See also our II, pp. 8 f.
8.  *Europe* 1, Praeludium; K. 238, 8–10. See our II, p. 201–202, Jesus as the Tree and True Vine.
9.  In Taylor, *O.H.* (1792 edn.), p. 129 n.
10.  Fludd's description of the Tree of God that springs from the Ensoph as its root and the Messiah or Logos as its trunk is as follows:

> so the divine emanation in like manner proceedeth directly from *Ensoph* or the fountain or root of infinity, by way of emanation not divided or separated from his eternall Originall: and by reason of this emanation, the Spirit is said, *to be the first created before all things*, as the trunck before the boughs, twigs, leaves or fruit. So that in respect of his essentiall existence he is eternall; but in regard of his emanation into the world, he is said to be aeviall, that is, to have a beginning without end, and therefore becometh the head and Prince of all the aeviall world, I mean the Angelicall creatures. We proceed therefore in the progression and multiplication of this universall emanation, thus: From the trunck of the tree issueth the generall, speciall, and individuall branches, where the most strongest (after the trunck) are all armes of the body, the next boughs, then twigs, and lastly the leavs, &c. To this we compare, in our Angelicall or aeviall world, the divers stations of the Angells, assigned unto them according to their dignity and riches, in the divine influences, which they receive from the root or fountain of light, by the mediation of their body Christ Jesus. [*Mosaicall Philosophy*, Sec. II, Bk. II, Chap. 2, p. 171]

This tree is certainly an image of the manifestation of being; but—apart from its not being, as described by Fludd, an inverted tree—it is extremely unlikely that Blake's lamenting Shadowy Female, who compares herself to a tree, could have been based upon this tree, in which the divine life pulses in every branch, twig, and leaf, from the highest source to the lowest manifested particle.

At the time of going to press the author has read Miss Désirée Hirst's admirable book, *Hidden Riches: Traditional Symbolism from the Renaissance to Blake* (London, 1964). Besides giving the best account to be found anywhere of Blake's association with the Swedenborgians (and other Protestant sects) Miss Hirst has discovered a very great deal in the literature of Christian cabalism which the interested reader will find of great value. She has taken the trouble to look up Fludd's Latin texts, and there in his *Philosophia Sacra* (Frankfurt, 1626) has found a depiction of the inverted Tree of God (reproduced in her own book opposite p. 177) which Blake could very well have seen. This merely confirms that the symbol was certainly familiar to him, in several forms and from several sources; certainly including Wilkins' *Geeta*, a book he is known to have read.

*11.*  *Bhagvat-Geeta*, tr. Wilkins, Bk. xv, p. 111.
*12.*  Notebook 2–3; K. 417. A variant verse reads:

> *Till I turn from Female Love,*
> *And root up the Infernal Grove,*
> *I shall never worthy be*
> *To Step into Eternity.*

*13.*  *F.Z.* vii; K. 321, 28–39.
*14.*  *P.L.* ix. 1099–1107.
*15.*  There is a deleted passage in a poem in the Rossetti manuscript attributing the same enrooting to a tree said to grow in Java, which suggests that Blake had also read some traveler's account of the banyan tree. Here it is the Queen of France who is compared to the banyan, and with obvious reference to Milton's "mother tree":

> *The Queen of France just touched this Globe,*
> *And the Pestilence darted from her robe;*
>
> .   .   .
>
> *There is just such a tree at Java found.*
> *And a great many suckers grow all around.*
> [Notebook 99–98; K. 185]

*16.*  *Mysterium Magnum*, Chap. 35, § 3; *Works*, iii, 187–88.
*17.*  *Three Principles*, Chap. 11, § 39; *Works*, i, 81. Cf. the passage of Paracelsus quoted above, p. 6.
*18.*  See below, Vol. II, pp. 201–202, Jesus as the Tree and True Vine.
*19.*  It is also a Buddhist teaching that the *samsara* and *nirvana* are really one and not two. Proclus' symbol of the nature of this relationship is that of the real and the reflected tree.
*20.*  *Mysterium Magnum*, Chap. 17, §§ 10–14; *Works*, iii, 69. The "middlemost kingdom" is the world of the Son or Logos, the eternal world of which the "outermost," temporal world is a shadow or copy.
*21.*  Ibid., § 16; *Works*, iii, 69–70.
*22.*  *Aurora*, Chap. 21, § 23; *Works*, i, 207.
*23.*  Notebook 105; K. 178.
*24.*  *Three Principles*, Chap. 20, § 41; *Works*, i, 203.
*25.*  Ibid., Chap. 10, § 29; *Works*, i, 70.

26.  Ibid., Chap. 11, § 10; *Works*, I, 76.
27.  *Aurora*, Chap. 17, §§ 23–24; *Works*, I, 170.
28.  *F.Z.* VII; K. 325, 212–19.
29.  *To My Mirtle*, Notebook 106; K. 176.
30.  *Metamorphoses*, Bk. x; ed. Garth, tr. Dryden, p. 357. Evidence that Blake had read the *Metamorphoses* before he wrote the poems in the Rossetti manuscript is a pencil drawing illustrating another tree-metamorphosis, *Daphne Changed into a Laurel* (Notebook 2).
31.  *F.Z.* VIII; K. 342–43, 67–85.
32.  *S.E.;* K. 217.
33.  See our II, p. 50.
34.  The wingless mind of the caterpillar of scientific materialism feeds on "nature"; but the "raven" of "natural religion" has also made its nest in the "deepest shade" of the tree of maya.
35.  Notebook 103; K. 180. Why is Sparta introduced here? Is this fragment an imitation of a Socratic dialogue?
36.  *B.U.* 25; K. 235, 15–22.
37.  *T.C.R.*, Vol. I, 72, pp. 96–97.
38.  See our II, pp. 51 f.
39.  I.e. Vala.
40.  *F.Z.* VIII; K. 345, 171–81.
41.  *J.* 98; K. 746, 46–50.
42.  *V.L.J.* 85; K. 613.
43.  *V.L.J.* 90–91; K. 613.
44.  *B.A.* 3–4; K. 252, 55–67, 2–4.
45.  *A.C.*, Vol. II, § 1266, p. 67.
46.  Ibid., Vol. VI, § 4950, p. 507.
47.  "William Blake and Hindu Creation Myths," in V. Pinto, ed., *The Divine Vision*.
48.  *A Comparison of the Institutions of Moses with Those of the Hindoos*, p. 50.
49.  *B.U.* 25; K. 235, 7–11.
50.  *F.Z.* VI; K. 318, 243–45.

## *18.  Governor of the Unwilling*

1.  *To Winter;* K. 3.
2.  The Felpham thistle appears in a verse-letter to Thomas Butts, Nov. 22, 1802:

> *With my inward Eye 'tis an old Man grey;*
> *With my outward, a Thistle across my way.*

The thistle offers Blake counsels of despair:

> *"If thou goest back," the thistle said,*
> *"Thou art to endless woe betray'd;"*
>                                        [K. 817, 29–32]

and lists the temporal ills that will result from a return to London. No doubt Blake found real thistles at Felpham; but I very much doubt whether "The old man weltering upon my path" (K. 818, 54) would have attracted Blake's notice if the thistle had not already possessed symbolic associations. Certainly the white-bearded thistle is an obvious symbol for an old man, but Blake did not invent it; the thistle is a druid: "There the flower of the mountain grows, and shakes its white head in the breeze. The thistle is there alone, and sheds its aged beard. Two stones, half sunk in the ground, shew their heads of moss. The deer of the mountain avoids the place, for he beholds the gray ghost that guards it" (Ossian, *Carthon; Works*, I, 180). The double vision of thistle and "gray ghost" comes from Ossian. The ghost of an old man is no uncommon apparition in Ossian's world: "the gray mist rises, slowly, from the lake. It came, in the figure of an aged man, along the silent plain. Its large limbs did not move in steps; for a ghost supported it in mid air. It came towards Selma's halls, and dissolved in a shower of blood" (*Carthon; Works*, I, 187–88). I believe that this fine Urizen-like ghost was in Blake's mind when he encountered his thistle; for a few lines on, "The heavens drop with human gore" (82) — like Macpherson's ghost dissolving in a shower of blood.

3. Pl. 15.
4. *G.P.;* K. 771.
5. *E.G.;* K. 752, 35–39.
6. *M.H.H.* 6; K. 150.
7. Dorothy Plowman, facsimile edition of *B.U.*, p. 17 n.
8. *P.L.* VII.224–31.
9. *B.U.* 22; K. 234, 39–41.
10. *B.U.* 2; K. 222, 5–7.
11. *B.U.* 2; K. 222, 1–4.
12. *M.H.H.* 17–20; K. 156–57.
13. *P.L.* III.556–57.
14. Ibid. II.892–94.
15. Ibid. III.446, 451–52.
16. Ibid. III.474–75.
17. Ibid. 493–96.
18. *V.L.J.* 91–92; K. 614.
19. *B.U.* 3; K. 223, 36–39.
20. *B.U.* 14; K. 230, 28–34.
21. *B.U.* 27; K. 236, 31–38.
22. *B.U.* 3; K. 222, 1–9.
23. *P.L.* III.372–77.
24. Notebook 109; K. 171.
25. *B.U.* 4; K. 224, 6–8.
26. *B.U.* 3; K. 223, 21–26.
27. Thornton, *Lord's Prayer;* K. 788.
28. *P.L.* I.45–49.
29. *B.U.* 3; K. 223, 28–31.
30. *P.L.* VI.829–39.
31. See our I, p. 51, Fig. 17.
32. *P.L.* II. 891–92.
33. Ibid. 624–28.
34. *B.U.* 3; K. 222, 13–17.

35. *B.U.* 23; K. 234, 11–18.
36. *B.U.* 23; K. 235, 24–26.
37. *B.L.* 3; K. 256, 7–26.
38. *B.U.* 4; K. 224, 14–20. Cf.:

> *. . . this wilde Abyss,*
> *The Womb of nature and perhaps her Grave,*
> *Of neither Sea, nor Shore, nor Air, nor Fire,*
> *But all these in thir pregnant causes mixt*
> *Confus'dly, and which thus must ever fight,*
> *Unless th' Almighty Maker them ordain*
> *His dark materials to create more Worlds.*
> [*P.L.* ii.910–16]

39. *B.U.* 4; K. 224, 24–25.
40. *P.L.* vi.817–20.
41. *B.U.* 4; K. 224, 38–40.
42. *V.D.A.* 3; K. 191, 5–6.
43. "All the seven deadly sins of the soul" are "fallen fiends of heavenly birth" become violent through the tyranny of Urizen, who has dragged them down into the "hell" of his world cut off from life. "Eno, aged Mother" remembers their unfallen beauty:

> *O Times remote!*
> *When Love & Joy were adoration,*
> *And none impure were deem'd:*
> *Not Eyeless Covet,*
> *Nor Thin-lip'd Envy,*
> *Nor Bristled Wrath,*
> *Nor Curled Wantonness;*
>
> *But Covet was poured full,*
> *Envy fed with fat of lambs,*
> *Wrath with lion's gore,*
> *Wantonness lull'd to sleep*
> *With the virgin's lute*
> *Or sated with her love;*
>
> *Till Covet broke his locks & bars*
> *And slept with open doors;*
> *Envy sung at the rich man's feast;*
> *Wrath was follow'd up and down*
> *By a little ewe lamb,*
> *And Wantonness on his own true love*
> *Begot a giant race.*
> [*B.L.* 3; K. 256, 7–26]

44. *B.U.* 4; K. 224–25, 44–49, 1–2. Blake further summarizes the battle in heaven, in which the angels, threatened by the artillery of hell, hurl mountains upon the rebel hosts:

*Light as the Lightning glimps they ran, they flew,*
*From thir foundations loosning to and fro*
*They pluckt the seated Hills with all thir load,*
*Rocks, Waters, Woods, and by the shaggie tops*
*Up lifting bore them in thir hands. . . .*

> .   .   .

*Till on those cursed Engins triple-row*
*They saw them whelmd, and all thir confidence*
*Under the weight of Mountains buried deep,*
*Themselves invaded next, and on thir heads*
*Main Promontories flung. . . .*

*[P.L.* VI.642–54]

So Urizen "ran raging" from the flames of his adversaries, until at last he quenched them with mountains:

*In fierce anguish & quenchless flames*
*To the desarts and rocks he ran raging*
*To hide; but he could not; combining,*
*He dug mountains & hills in vast strength,*
*He piled them in incessant labour,*
*In howlings & pangs & fierce madness,*
*Long periods in burning fires labouring.*

*[B.U.* 5; K. 225, 19–25]

45. *B.U.* 5; K. 225, 3–8.
46. *P.L.* VI.858–68.
47. See Margoliouth's text, *Blake's Vala*.
48. *F.Z.* II; K. 280, 3–6. See *Vala*, 12^R, 1–3.
49. See Barfield, *Saving the Appearances*.
50. *F.Z.* I; K. 272, 302–304.
51. *F.Z.* I; K. 273, 319, 336.
52. *V.L.J.* 69–70; K. 605.
53. *F.Z.* I; K. 273, 337–41.
54. *Blake and Modern Thought*.
55. *F.Z.* II; K. 287, 258–68.
56. *P.L.* I.710–15. Milton's impressive account of the metallurgy of Hell,

*. . . veins of liquid fire*
*Sluc'd from the Lake, a second multitude*
*With wondrous Art founded the massie Ore,*

> .   .   .

*A third as soon had form'd within the ground*
*A various mould, and from the boyling cells*
*By strange conveyance fill'd each hollow nook*
*[P.L.* I.701–707]

becomes in Blake a fine image of modern industry; Milton's lofty "strange convey-ance" becomes "spades, & pickaxes" and the earthy plow:

*Then were the furnaces unseal'd with spades, & pickaxes*
*Roaring let out the fluid: the molten metal ran in channels*
*Cut by the plow of ages . . .*

[*F.Z.* II; K. 283, 117–19]

This suggestion of the industrial revolution haunts the lines "Heated red hot they, hizzing, rend their way," the "weights of lead & spindles of iron," and "The enormous warp & woof," on which, a few lines below, the "atmospheres" are woven.

57. *F.Z.* II; K. 286, 240–54. See also *Vala* 16ᵛ, 7, and 17ᴿ, 4.
58. *F.Z.* II; K. 287, 292–94.
59. *F.Z.* II; K. 280, 19–24.
60. *P.L.* I.242–45.
61. *F.Z.* V; K. 310, 190–91.
62. *P.L.* I.84–87.
63. *F.Z.* VI; K. 311, 229–33.
64. *F.Z.* V; K. 310, 216–17.
65. Job 26:7.
66. *B.U.* 3; K. 223, 32–33.
67. *Aurora*, Chap. 13, §§ 66–68; *Works*, I, 124.
68. *D.L.W.*, § 160, p. 129.
69. *Mos. Phil.*, Sec. I, Bk. V, § 1, Chap. 2, p. 87.
70. Ibid., Bk. III, § 1, Chap. 6, p. 54.
71. Ibid.
72. I must thank Mr. Rupert Gleadow for this information.
73. *B.U.* 4; K. 224, 21–23.
74. This strange impressive image of the frozen waves recalls a landscape described in *Songs of Ossian* (*Temora*, Bk. VIII; *Works*, II, 181–82): "As when the wintry winds have seized the waves of the mountain-lake, have seized them, in stormy night, and cloathed them over with ice; white, to the hunter's early eye, the billows still seem to roll. He turns his ear to the sound of each unequal ridge. But each is silent, gleaming." It is possible that Blake had read Fludd when he wrote *Earth's Answer*, the first poem in which this action of freezing is attributed to Urizen:

> *Break this heavy chain*
> *That does freeze my bones around.*
> [K. 211]

However, the image is not specific, as in the later passages, in attributing the creation of the world to the action of cold.

75. *F.Z.* VI; K. 313, 49–54.
76. *F.Z.* IV; K. 302, 170–72.
77. *F.Z.* VI; K. 318, 239–41.
78. *F.Z.* VII; K. 322, 72–86.
79. *Mos. Phil.*, Sec. II, Bk. II, § 2, Chap. 2, p. 205.
80. *F.Z.* VIII; K. 352, 448–53.
81. *M.* 34–35; K. 525, 53–55, 1.
82. *J.* 73; K. 713, 17–24.
83. Fludd, *Mos. Phil.*, Sec. I, Bk. III, § 1, Chap. 6, p. 54.

*84.* *F.Z.* IV; K. 304, 269–73.

*85.* *Mos. Phil.*, Sec. II, Bk. II, Chap. 2, p. 204.

*86.* See our II, pp. 158 ff.

*87.* *Mathematical Principles*, Bk. I, def. VIII, Vol. I, p. 7.

*88.* *F.Z.* IX; K. 363, 225–31.

*89.* P. 213.

*90.* P. 223.

*91.* P. 221.

*92.* *F.Z.* VI; K. 316, 180–94.

*93.* *F.Z.* VI; K. 316–17, 196–208.

*94.* *Cartesius*, p. 215.

*95.* *F.Z.* VII; K. 321, 51–54.

*96.* *M.* 15; K. 497, 21–35.

## *19.* *The Children of Urizen*

*1.* *Metamorphoses*, Bk. I; ed. Garth, tr. Dryden, p. 6.

*2.* *F.Z.* V; K. 310, 192.

*3.* Kether, the Crown, is the first and highest of the *Sefiroth*.

*4.* *F.Z.* V; K. 311, 220.

*5.* There is icononographic confirmation of Blake's identification of Urizen with *Jupiter pluvius*, described by Sir Anthony Blunt in the *Warburg Journal*, VI (1943), 212. The figure of Urizen with outstretched arms, as he first appears in an engraving—after Fuseli in Darwin's *Botanic Garden*—entitled "The Nile," is clearly taken from an illustration from Montfaucon in *L'Antiquité expliquée*, I, pl. XIII. The beard and garments of the god stream with water; and the streaming beard of Urizen perpetuates this ancient theme of Jupiter and his deluge.

*6.* *B.A.* 3; K. 250, 7–12.

*7.* *Metamorphoses*, Bk. XV; ed. Garth, tr. Dryden, p. 526.

*8.* Ibid.

*9.* Ibid.

*10.* *F.Z.* VIII; K. 354, 510–11.

*11.* *B.U.* 23; K. 234, 19–21.

*12.* *F.Z.* VI; K. 314–15, 117–32.

*13.* Swedenborg's fantasy, also, has some part in peopling the caves and dens of Urizen: "Some of the hells appeared like caverns in rocks . . . Some resembled the dens of wild beasts in the woods; others the subterraneous works in mines, with different chambers and descents to still lower floors" (*H.H.*, § § 585–86, pp. 400–401). In these hells every spirit appears as "an image of his evil," so that all are deformed. "With some, no face appears, but in its stead something hairy or bony; and with some, teeth only are seen." Elsewhere he writes of "horrible deformed faces . . . running to and fro like mad persons, so monstrous that it would be impossible to describe them." Such "dishumaniz'd" creatures are shown in some of the drawings that accompany the text of *The Four Zoas;* and Blake writes:

> *And his world teem'd vast enormities,*
> *Fright'ning, faithless, fawning*

*Portions of life, similitudes*
*Of a foot, or a hand, or a head,*
*Or a heart, or an eye; they swam mischevous,*
*Dread terrors, delighting in blood.*

[*B.U.* 23; K. 234, 2–7]

and:

*The shapes screaming flutter'd vain:*
*Some combin'd into muscles & glands,*
*Some organs for craving and lust;*
*Most remain'd on the tormented void,*
*Urizen's army of horrors.*

[*B.A.* 4; K. 253, 31–35]

*14.*   *F.Z.* VI; K. 311, 1–6.
*15.*   Mallet, *Northern Antiquities* II, 35 ff.
*16.*   *F.Z.* VI; K. 312, 20–23.
*17.*   Taylor, *O.H.* (1792 edn.) LVIII, pp. 100–101.
*18.*   Ibid. LXVIII, p. 200.
*19.*   *F.Z.* VII; K. 320, 25–26.
*20.*   *B.U.* 10; K. 227, 19–23.
*21.*   *Mos. Phil.*, Sec. I, Bk. III, Chap. 3, p. 47. The "fontal" character of Urizen has links with cabalism as well as with Neoplatonism. The identity of Urizen with the third numeration of the Tree of God (Binah) has been established elsewhere (see Chap. 16) and Binah is associated with the flow of the "waters" of life which descend, river-like, from "Eden" (the second numeration, "Wisdom," the Christian Logos) into manifestation, ending in the "garden of Eden," the Shekhinah, Malkuth. Blake makes the issuing flow sinister, in keeping with his indictment of the creator (the demiurgic "second creator") as "a very cruel being." See our II, Chap. 23, p. 310, n. 4.
*22.*   *F.Z.* VIII; K. 346, 224–27.
*23.*   *F.Z.* V; K. 310, 194.
*24.*   Taylor writes at length of this symbol in his *Dissertation*. Milton O. Percival (*William Blake's Circle of Destiny*, p. 68) identifies Udan Adan with Vergil's Stygian lake, interpreted by Taylor as an emblem of corporeal nature.
*25.*   *The Golden Asse*, tr. Adlington, p. 60. Cf. the alchemical source of "Nilus" described by Vaughan. See our I, pp. 114 f.
*26.*   *D.E.*, pp. 115–16.
*27.*   See our I, p. 159.
*28.*   *F.Z.* III; K. 295, 121–24.
*29.*   *Euphrates*, p. 32; *Works*, p. 401.
*30.*   *Europe* 10; K. 241, 18–20.
*31.*   *Europe* 10; K. 242, 28–31.
*32.*   P. 73.
*33.*   *Vala* VI, 34$^v$, 6–9; K. 312, 25–28.
*34.*   *F.Z.* VI; K. 312, 8–11.
*35.*   *O.H.* (1792 edn.) X, p. 140.
*36.*   *F.Z.* VI; K. 312, 12–15.

*37.*    *Mos. Phil.*, Sec. ɪɪ, Bk. ɪɪ, Chap. 2, p. 205. Italics mine.

*38.*    *F.Z.* vɪ; K. 312, 18–19.

*39.*    Gen. 2:10.

*40.*    *P.L.* ɪv.231–34, 238–41.

*41.*    *F.Q.* ɪɪ.xii.

*42.*    At some time later than the *Vala* text, Blake added a passage to Night II describing the building by the Architect Divine (Urizen) of his city or palace; the world-city, with its twelve halls and central temples, is evidently based upon Plato's plan of the ideal city, given in *The Laws*. Plato's city, Blake at once perceived, was essentially Urizenic, a work of reason, so much so that it must be added forthwith to Urizen's world, where it may be recognized as Platonic by its topography: "it should be divided into twelve parts, the temple of Vesta, Jupiter and Minerva being first of all raised under the appellation of the Acropolis, or tower of the city. This temple should be circularly enclosed, and from this enclosure, the city and all the region should be divided into twelve parts" (*Laws*, 745B; *Works*, ɪɪ, 139). It is from this work that Blake took his symbolism of The Mental Traveller, a fact which strengthens the argument that Urizen's palace is based upon Plato's city. Blake was quick to grasp the essential fact about this city—that it is built upon a symbolic structure. The twelve parts of it seem to correspond (like the gates of the New Jerusalem) to the house of the Zodiac, so that no structure could be more appropriate to Urizen as the Starry King of the firmament. The Golden Hall of Zeus is a Homeric image and, as such, well known to Blake:

> *Twelve halls after the names of his twelve sons compos'd*
> *The wondrous building, & three Central Domes after the Names*
> *Of his three daughters were encompass'd by the twelve bright halls.*
> *Every hall surrounded by bright Paradises of Delight*
> *In which were towns & Cities, Nations, Seas, Mountains & Rivers.*
> *Each Dome open'd toward four halls, & the Three Domes Encompass'd*
> *The Golden Hall of Urizen . . .*
>
>                      [*F.Z.* ɪɪ; K. 284, 173–79]

*43.*    Was their "song" suggested by Gray's *Fatal Sisters*, who "sang the following dreadful song" as they wove the web of war and death in their cave:

> *Now the storm begins to lower,*
> *(Haste, the loom of Hell prepare,)*
> *Iron-sleet of arrowy shower*
> *Hurtles in the darken'd air.*

These Fatal Sisters are likewise the Fates, and their song of "Orkney's woe and Randver's bane" is all of death and slaughter. May we supply Gray's text—or something very like it—as the missing "song" of Urizen's daughters?

*44.*    *F.Z.* vɪɪ; K. 322, 95–108.

*45.*    Exod. 16:4, 14–16.

*46.*    *B.U.* 4; K. 224, 39–40.

*47.*    *F.Z.* vɪɪ; K. 322–23, 108–29. Dr. Bronowski suggests that this passage may have been suggested to Blake by his reading of Malthus.

*48.*    *F.Z.* vɪɪɪ; K. 343, 76–77.

*49.*    Exod. 12:34.

50.  *F.Z.* VIII; K. 343, 81. See above, Chap. 18, n. 43.
51.  *E.G.* 48–52; K. 755, 96. Cf. "Upon thy belly shalt thou go, and dust shalt thou eat all the days of thy life" (Gen. 3:14).
52.  6:32.

## 20.  *The Sensible World*

1.   *Annotations to Reynolds* 244; K. 476–77.
2.   *G.P.;* K. 760. (The lines were added in the 1818 version.)
3.   *Annotations to Siris* 241; K. 775.
4.   *Proclus' Philosophical and Mathematical Commentaries*, I, xxx–xxxiv.
5.   Ibid., xxxiv.
6.   K. 97.
7.   *Essay concerning Humane Understanding*, Bk. I, Chap. 4, § 2, p. 27.
8.   *Annotations to Siris* 215, 212; K. 774.
9.   *All Religions Are One;* K. 97.
10.  *Essay*, Bk. II, Chap. 9, § 14, p. 64.
11.  *M.H.H.* 4; K. 149.
12.  *Essay*, Bk. II, Chap. 2, § 3, p. 46.
13.  Ibid.
14.  *Principles of Human Knowledge*, §47; *Works*, II, 60 ff.
15.  *J.* 34; K. 661, 55–59.
16.  *M.H.H.* 14; K. 154.
17.  *Doctrine of the New Jerusalem concerning the Lord*, § 3, pp. 6 ff.
18.  *Three Dialogues*, III; *Works*, II, 230–31.
19.  *Siris*, § 289; K. 773.
20.  *Pym.* II.1–12; pp. 7–9.
21.  *M.H.H.* 12–13; K. 153.
22.  *Essay*, Bk. IV, Chap. 19, § 10, p. 428.
23.  Ibid., pp. 427–28.
24.  *M.H.H.* 12–13; K. 153.
25.  *Essay*, Bk. IV, Chap. 19, § 12, p. 427.
26.  Ibid., § 6, p. 424.
27.  *Doctrine of the New Jerusalem*, § 16, p. 57.
28.  Ibid., § 2, p. 4.
29.  K. 810.
30.  Keynes, *Catalogue of Blake's Separate Engravings*, Dublin, 1956.
31.  *Mysterium Magnum*, Chap. 30, §§ 45–46; *Works*, III, 159. See our II, pp. 331 ff. Had Blake also read St. Augustine's *Civitas Dei*?
32.  *Mysterium Magnum*, Chap. 30, §§ 45–46; *Works*, III, 159.
33.  *J.* 3; K. 621.
34.  *Annotations to Reynolds;* K. 445.
35.  *Three Dialogues* I; *Works*, II, 183.
36.  Yeats, *Blood and the Moon*.
37.  *V.L.J.* 92–95; K. 617.
38.  *Auguries of Innocence;* K. 433, 107–10.
39.  *Three Dialogues* III; *Works*, II, 228–29.

40.  *Europe* iii; K. 237, 1–13.
41.  *Europe* iii; K. 237, 17–18.
42.  *D.C.* iii; K. 570.
43.  Blake may have been thinking of Dr. Johnson's tulip; but the tulip in *Rasselas* illustrates a different point—i.e. that a poet should generalize and not particularize:

> The business of a poet, said Imlac, is to examine, not the individual, but the species; to remark general properties and large appearances: he does not number the streaks of the tulip, or describe the different shades in the verdure of the forest. He is to exhibit in his portraits of nature such prominent and striking features, as recal the original to every mind; and must neglect the minuter discriminations, which one may have remarked, and another have neglected, for those characteristicks which are alike obvious to vigilance and carelessness.  [P. 50]

Blake does, of course, answer Johnson when he writes that to "generalize is to be an idiot. To particularize is the alone distinction of merit."

44.  *Three Dialogues* i; *Works*, ii, 194–95.
45.  Ibid., p. 197.
46.  *M.H.H.* 14; K. 154.
47.  Taylor, in a note to the Orphic Hymn to Apollo (*O.H.*, 1792 edn., pp. 161 ff.), describes the lyre of Apollo as it was understood in the Pythagorean tradition. It is the harmony of number, of which music, architecture, the solar system, and all arts within the limits of their materials are expressions. It is the ordering harmony of the universe, as Blake was doubtless aware when he wrote: "I touch the heavens as an instrument to the glory of God."
48.  *M.* 5; K. 484, 19–37.
49.  *V.L.J.* 92–95; K. 617.
50.  *D.L.W.*, § 46, p. 37.
51.  *Theaetetus* 184C; *Works*, iv, 61.
52.  *Pym.* x.84–85; p. 65.
53.  *Archidoxes*, Bk. i, pp. 6–7.
54.  *Europe* 10; K. 241, 10–15.
55.  See our i, pp. 49–53.
56.  *B.U.* 27; K. 236, 35–42.
57.  *Oxford Book of Modern Verse*, p. xxvii.
58.  *Three Dialogues* iii; *Works*, ii, 250–51.
59.  *M.* 3; K. 482–83, 2–21.
60.  See our ii, p. 89.
61.  *B.U.* 14; K. 230, 28–34.
62.  *V.D.A.* 2; K. 191, 31–34.
63.  *J.* 29; K. 655, 66–69.
64.  *F.Z.* viii; K. 348–49, 301–304.
65.  *Auguries of Innocence;* K. 431.
66.  *Essay*, Bk. ii, Chap. 23, § 13, p. 141.
67.  Ibid., § 12, p. 140.
68.  Berkeley writes in the same vein, no doubt taking up Locke's train of thought: "it is not only possible but manifest, that there actually are animals, whose eyes

are by Nature framed to perceive those things, which by reason of their minuteness escape our sight. What think you of those inconceivably small animals perceived by glasses? Must we suppose they are all stark Blind? . . . is it not evident, they must see particles less than their own bodies, which will present them with a far different view in each object, from that which strikes our senses?" (*Three Dialogues* I; *Works*, II, 185).

69.  *V.D.A.* 4; K. 192, 13–18.
70.  *V.D.A.* 4; K. 192, 22–24.
71.  *V.D.A.* 3; K. 191, 2–13.
72.  *M.H.H.* 7; K. 150. These lines paraphrase (and reverse?) a stanza from Chatterton's *The Dethe of Syr Charles Bawdin* (*Poems by Rowley*, p. 51):

> *Howe dydd I knowe thatt ev'ry darte,*
> *That cutte the airie waie,*
> *Myghte nott fynde passage toe my harte,*
> *And close myne eyes for aie?*

73.  *Principles of Human Knowledge*, § 81; *Works*, II, 75.
74.  *T.C.R.*, Vol. II, § 785, p. 417.
75.  *V.D.A.* 5–6; K. 193, 33–41, 1–3.
76.  *V.D.A.* 7–8; K. 195, 30, 1–10.
77.  *Eloisa*, Vol. III, Letter CXXXIX, pp. 277–78.
78.  *Tiriel* 8; K. 109, 10.
79.  *Tiriel* 8; K. 109, 11–15.
80.  *Tiriel* 8; K. 109, 36.

## 21.  *Visionary Time and Space*

1.  *Principles of Philosophy* II.iv; *Philosophical Works*, I, 255–56. A. N. Whitehead traces the fallacy, as Blake had done before him, to the imputing of separate substantial existence to body and mind; and he attributes the fallacy to Descartes:

> At this point the confusion commences. The emergent individual value of each entity is transformed into the independent substantial existence of each entity, which is a very different notion. . . . He implicitly transformed this emergent individual value, inherent in the very fact of his own reality, into a private world of passions, or modes, of independent substance. Also the independence ascribed to bodily substances carried them away from the realm of values altogether. They degenerated into a mechanism entirely valueless, except as suggestive of an external ingenuity. The heavens had lost the glory of God. [*Science and the Modern World*, pp. 272–73]

So Blake had realized long before:

> . . . . *Accident being formed*
> *Into Substance & Principle by the cruelties of Demonstration*
> *It became Opake & Indefinite.*
>
> [*M.* 29; K. 517, 35–37]

2.  *Siris*, § 271; *Works*, V, 127.

3.  *Principles of Human Knowledge*, § 67; *Works*, II, 70.
4.  *V.L.J.* 92–95; K. 617.
5.  *Principles*, § 4; *Works*, II, 42.
6.  *J.* 71; K. 709, 15–19.
7.  *Siris*, § 270; *Works*, V, 127.
8.  *Pym.* IX.55–58; p. 57.
9.  Ibid., §§ 117 ff., pp. 67 f.
10. *Essay concerning Humane Understanding*, Bk. II, Chap. 15, § 3, p. 94.
11. *E.P.T.*, p. 248.
12. *D.L.W.*, § 7, p. 8.
13. Ibid., p. 7.
14. K. 89.
15. *J.* 98; K. 746, 29–38.
16. *B.U.* 14; K. 230, 46–47.
17. Locke, *Essay*, Bk. II, Chap. 15, § 8, p. 95.
18. Ibid., Bk. II, Chap. 17, § 15, p. 106.
19. *B.U.* 15; K. 230–31, 5–12.
20. Locke, *Essay*, Bk. II, Chap. 15, § 5, p. 94.
21. *B.U.* 19; K. 231, 2–9.
22. *F.Z.* II; K. 284, 148–54.
23. *F.Z.* II; K. 284, 166–69.
24. *F.Z.* II; K. 286, 243–46.
25. *F.Z.* III; K. 294, 107–108.
26. *J.* 91; K. 738–39, 42–53. Cf. Taylor: "As little as the eye of a fly at the bottom of the largest of Egyptian pyramids sees of the whole of that pyramid, compared with what is seen of it by the eye of man, so little does the greatest experimentalist see of the whole of things, compared with what Plato and Aristotle saw of it, through scientific reasoning founded on self-evident principles." ("The Creed of the Platonic Philosopher," in *Miscellanies in Prose and Verse* (London, 1805), p. 30, n.)
27. *F.Z.* I; K. 270, 239–41.
28. *F.Z.* I; K. 271, 249–50.
29. *Pym.* X. 119–31; pp. 68–69. All the "Mosaic" philosophers regarded this as a key passage. Here is Fludd's version:

> There is nothing more capable than the incorporeall or spiritual nature; nothing more swift, and quick or nimble; nothing more strong or powerfull . . . Beginning thus with thy self, do thou meditate, and command thy soul, what thou pleasest, and it will flye sooner than thou commandest: Command it (I say) that it pass into the Ocean sea, and it will be there before thou bidst it. Again, command it that it flye into heaven, and it will want no wings; nothing will hinder her or stop her in her course, no not the heat of the Sun, nor the vast largeness of the heavenly or aethereall vault, nor the wheeling about of the starry orbs, nor yet the bodies of the other starrs, but peircing all these, it passeth quite through, even unto the highest body. Moreover, and if thou wilt have her to pass over the celestiall Globes, and to search out whatsoever is above, thou maist do it also. Mark therefore how great the power of the Soul is, and how swift and quick it is in its execution. [*Mosaicall Philosophy*, Sec. II, Bk. II, Chap. 5, p. 231]

And here are Thomas Vaughan's paraphrases:

> she spans Kingdoms in a Thought, and injoyes all that inwardly, which she misseth outwardly. In her are patterns and Notions of all things in the world. If she but fancies her self in the midst of the Sea, presently she is there, and hears the rushing of the Billowes: she makes an Invisible voyage from one place to another, and presents to her self things absent, as if they were present. The dead live to her, there is no grave can hide them from her thoughts. Now she is here in dirt and mire, and in a trice above the Moon:
>
> > *Celsior exurgit pluviis, auditque ruentes*
> > *Sub pedibus nimbos et coeca tonitrua calcat.*
> >             [*Anthroposophia Theomagica*, pp. 46–47; *Works*, p. 47]

The two lines of Latin verse ("She soars high above the storms, and hears the roaring of the clouds beneath her feet, and spurns the blind thunder") suggest that Blake's immediate source of the passage given may have been Vaughan. Coleridge uses the same image: "One travels along with the lines of a mountain. Years ago I wanted to make Wordsworth sensible of this. How fine is Keswick vale! Would I repose, my soul lies and is quiet upon the broad level vale. Would it act? it darts up into the mountain-top like a kite, and like a chamois-goat runs along the ridge—or like a boy that makes a sport on the road of running along a wall or narrow fence!" (*Anima Poetae*, p. 101.)

30.  *F.Z.* II; K. 288, 295–301.
31.  *J.* 55; K. 686–87, 36–46.
32.  *F.Z.* V; K. 305, 2–19.
33.  *D.L.W.*, § 160, pp. 129–30.
34.  *M.* 34–35; K. 525, 53–55, 1.
34a. *F.Z.* VII; K. 324, 172–76.
35.  *F.Z.* I; K. 278, 527–29.
36.  "Ozoth" seems to be a combination of "Azoth" and "Optic."
37.  *M.* 28; K. 515, 29–39.
38.  *M.* 28–29; K. 516, 44–63, 1–3.
39.  *Essay*, Bk. II, Chap. 15, § 9, p. 96.
40.  *Principles*, § 98; *Works*, II, 83.
41.  *Asiatick Researches*, II, 114.
42.  *Principles*, § 46; *Works*, II, 59.
43.  *Aphorism* 3; K. 65.
44.  *M.* 29; K. 516, 4–24.
45.  G. M. Tyrrell, in *Homo Faber*, develops a similar train of thought: man's mode of perceiving literally creates his universe.
46.  K. 775.
47.  *Siris*, § 300; K. 774.
48.  *Laocoön;* K. 776.
49.  Newton, *Mathematical Principles*, Bk. I, def. VIII, scholium IV; tr. Motte, Vol. I, pp. 12–14. Italics mine.
50.  *Timaeus* 37D–38A; *Works*, II, 491–92.
51.  *M.* 28; K. 516, 44–45. See our II, p. 143.
52.  *D.L.W.*, § 73, p. 62.
53.  *Pym.* XI. 100–103; pp. 78–79.

54.  Ibid. x. 104–105; pp. 66–67.
55.  *M.* 22; K. 505, 15–25.
56.  *J.* 16; K. 638, 61–67.
57.  *J.* 13–14; K. 634, 66, 1.
58.  Notebook 91; K. 614.
59.  *M.* 24; K. 509–10, 68–73. The Greeks also had the vision of time as in eternal youth, and Blake himself probably knew this. Of Phanes, the first born of all things, Taylor says in his introduction to the *Hymns of Orpheus* that "he has wings on his shoulders, and he is called *Undecaying Time*, and Hercules." Taylor, quoting Proclus, describes time as the "agent of all *process*." Hercules is invoked as time and also as the spirit of prophecy. Like Los he is an archer:

> *Almighty Titan, prudent and benign,*
> *Of various forms, eternal and divine,*
> *Father of Time . . .*
> *Magnanimous, in divination skill'd,*
> *And in the athletic labours of the field.*
> *'Tis thine strong archer, all things to devour,*
> *Supreme, all-helping, all producing pow'r;*
> *To thee mankind as their deliv'rer pray.*
> [*O.H.* (1792 edn.), p. 133]

60.  *J.* 30; K. 655, 1–4.
61.  There is also the speech of Shakespeare's Ulysses to Achilles (*Troilus and Cressida* iii.iii):

> *Achilles:*  What are my deedes forgot?
> *Ulysses:*   Time hath (my Lord) a wallet at his backe,
>              Wherein he puts almes for oblivion:
>              A great siz'd monster of ingratitudes:
>              Those scraps are good deedes past,
>              Which are devour'd as fast as they are made,
>              Forgot as soon as done . . .

## 22.  *The Opening of Centers*

1.  *F.Z.* I; K. 266, 94–102.
2.  See our I, p. 257.
3.  *J.* 69; K. 707, 19–26.
4.  *Paradiso* xiii.11–12, xxviii.42.
5.  Proclus' *Mathematical Commentaries*, I, 114 ff.
6.  Ibid., p. 114.
7.  Ibid., p. 117.
8.  Ibid., p. 118.
9.  *F.Z.* I; K. 270, 222–32. Why the Daughter of Beulah who creates the Spaces is Eno, it is hard to say. She is presumably the "Eno, aged Mother" of *The Book of Los*, and conceivably allied to the "Woman Old" of *The Mental Traveller*, whose "labyrinths" may be compared to the spaces of the created world. See our I, pp. 321 f.

*10.*   *M.* 28; K. 516, 48.
*11.*   See our II, p. 145.
*12.*   *M.* 35; K. 526, 42–45.
*13.*   *J.* 41; K. 668, 15–18.
*14.*   Perhaps Eno becomes Erin because lost Eden is in the West, sunk in the Atlantic vale; but one can only guess. The agedness of Eno and Erin perhaps relates to the age of the time-world, already far advanced upon its course of six or eight thousand five hundred years. Or it may be that Blake knew of Kathleen ni Houlihan, the tall imposing aged woman who personifies Ireland, for he speaks of "the Majestic form of Erin." The figure of Eno, the Aged Mother, who in all likelihood derives from Juno, might be described in similar words.

There may, in the figure of Erin, be an echo of Ossian: "The daughters of Morven come forth, like the bow of the shower; they look towards green Ullin for the white sails of the King." Perhaps they look toward the West in the hope of seeing there the vision of returning Eden, "those infinite mountains of light, now barr'd out by the atlantic sea" (*M.H.H.* 25–27; K. 159). Erin's rainbow is her constant attribute, as it is of Juno, in the form of her attendant and messenger, Iris.

The appearance of Dinah, "a youthful form of Erin," throws no light upon Blake's choice of Erin as the Daughter of Beulah who opens the centers. It is possible, however, to see why Dinah is so called if we take Erin, in a non-mythological sense, simply as a personification of Ireland. The clue to Dinah lies in Boehme's *Mysterium Magnum;* as will be shown in this chapter, the opening of the centers is a theme that Blake has taken from Boehme, and the appearance of Dinah, in this context, incidentally confirms Blake's preoccupation with Boehme's thought at this point of the myth. Since Dinah has been something of a puzzle, I quote the whole long passage that provides the key to her unexplained appearance:

But this *Christendom* would set her Heart upon the Kingdom of this World, and so in the Dress of a Virgin trim herself with *many* Churches, Priests and Ceremonies, under the Habit of a Virgin; but in this Departure from the Simplicity and Humility of Christ, she would but *gad* abroad in the World, and look after fleshly Whoredom, as *Dinah* did, which is a type of fleshly *Christendom*, which is always born *after* the true Children of Christ, as *Dinah* was born after the Twelve Patriarchs: That is,

When *Christendom* is born and manifested among a People, it *begets* in that Place, first the Twelve Patriarchs, *viz*, the *Ground* of the Apostolick Doctrine; but when she mixes again with the heathenish wise Men, and with the Lust of the Flesh, then that place begets a *Dinah*, *viz.* a Whoredom with Christ; that is, a *seeming* Christian, yet the Heart is but a Whore . . .

She seeks again the *heathenish* Ground, and mixes herself with the Heathens, and is with Child by the heathenish Philosophy, and brings forth a Bastard, half Christian, half Heathenish, *viz.* a *new* Sect or *Doctrine*, which doth not fully agree in Form with the first Customs of that People, among whom it did spring forth; and yet in her Heart is *no* whit better than they.

And then this People raise themselves up against that strange Opinion, and cry out in Anger, These have *deflowered* our Sister *Dinah*, and have made her a Whore, and are enraged against the new-found Opinion, as the Sons of *Jacob* against *Sichem*, and with Fighting, and the Sword, with Storming and Cursing, run on against the Deflowerer of their Sister *Dinah*, and *murder* him, and not only him, but all the Males that are with him, as *Jacob's* Sons did the *Hamorites:* And then the Innocent must thus suffer with the Guilty, to signify, that they all of them, both the one and the other, live in *such religious Whoredom:* For the Whore, for whose Sake they take Vengeance, is their Sister, and born of their Stock, as *Dinah* their Sister was, and they came of one Mother.

We see here eminently the Type of contentious *Christendom;* how *Christendom* would be *headstrong* and furious in Opinions, and that in great Blindness, and not know for what, and would not see themselves, that they thus rage in their *own* Whoredom, and strive not about the Power of true Christianity, as about the true Christian *Life*, but about their contrived Opinions. . . . As *Jacob's* Sons did not see how to help the Evil, that their Sister might save her Credit; and though *Hamor* and *Sichem* sent to them to *give her a Dowry, and he would marry their Sister*, and love her, *and be circumcised*, and *become one People with them*, and would perform all Love, Faithfulness and Friendship towards them, yet all this did not avail.

[*Mysterium Magnum*, Chap. 62, §§ 6–10; *Works*, III, 374]

Here we have the key to Blake's allusion to Dinah, which immediately follows upon an account of the divisions and failure of the twelve patriarchs:

*I see a Feminine Form arise from the Four terrible Zoas,*
*Beautiful but terrible, struggling to take a form of beauty,*
*Rooted in Shechem: this is Dinah, the youthful form of Erin.*
[*J.* 74; K. 715, 52–54]

Dinah is true religion corrupted by paganism; Blake seems to imply that this is also true of the religion of Ireland. His commentator Yeats might have taken exception to this view of the Irish wedding of ancient Celtic tradition with that of Christianity, which he himself so warmly supported.

The religious contentions of Israel with Sichem have doubtless their parallel in the turbulent relations between Protestant and Catholic in Ireland. So that whatever the mythological sense of Erin, we must attribute Dinah, rather, to Blake's observations upon the political events of his time.

15. *J.* 48; K. 678, 28–39.
16. *Mysterium Magnum*, Chap. 10, § 43; *Works*, III, 44.
17. Ibid., § 39; *Works*, III, 43.
18. *Mysteries of Creation*, Bk. I, text 22, p. 22.
19. Chap. 4, § 72; *Works*, I, 32.
20. *Auguries of Innocence;* K. 431, 1–4.
21. *The Threefold Life of Man*, Chap. 6, § 43; *Works*, II, 62–63.
22. *J.* 71; K. 709, 6–9.
23. *Mysterium Magnum*, Chap. 43, § 9; *Works*, III, 253.
24. *J.* 13; K. 633, 34–36.
25. *The Threefold Life of Man*, Chap. 6, § 62; *Works*, II, 65.

26. The Euclidean mathematics, as expounded by Proclus, does moreover constantly present the punctum as the source of infinite (mathematical) power, since from it proceeds all dimension, as all number from unity. Modern projective geometry is based upon a reciprocity of the infinities of point and plane. "A point source may spend itself outward into the infinite space, but at the same moment an opposite and less familiar picture arises, namely that a 'planar' source in the infinite periphery which spends and loses itself inward to a central point" (Adams and Whicher, *The Plant between Sun and Earth*). It is notable that Goethe's thought and Blake's converge on this, as on many other matters concerning the metaphysics of nature—both, to be sure, deriving from the same current of alchemical thought, with its central concept of an underlying polarity resolved in a "marriage" or unity.

27. Joyce understood Blake: "Space: what you damn well have to see. Through spaces smaller than red globules of man's blood they creepy-crawl after Blake's buttocks into eternity of which this vegetable world is but a shadow. Hold to the now, the here, through which all future plunges to the past."

[*Ulysses*, 1947 edn., p. 175]

28. *M*. 29; K. 516, 1–3.

29. *J*. 33; K. 659, 19.

30. See our II, pp. 78–80.

31. See our II, p. 174.

32. *Opticks*, Bk. II, Chap. 4, obs. 2.

33. *J*. 98; K. 745, 9.

34. *J*. 77; K. 717.

35. *M*. 35; K. 526, 48–58.

36. Yeats's *Leda and the Swan* envisages all human history flowing from "a shudder in the loins" when the eternal swan couples with the virgin Leda.

37. Og and Anak are giants (Deut. 3:10–14, 9:2) and for this reason associated by Blake with the spatiality of the Newtonian universe:

> *Seek not thy heavenly father then beyond the skies,*
> *There Chaos dwells & ancient Night & Og & Anak old.*
> [*M*. 20; K. 502, 32–33]

38. *M*. 31; K. 520, 46–60.

39. Lines 41–44.

40. Letter to Butts, April 25, 1803; K. 823.

41. *M*. 31; K. 520, 29–39.

42. Letter to Butts, July 6, 1803; K. 825.

43. *Ode on the Spring*. Blake's illustrations were reproduced in a folio edition, published by the Oxford University Press, 1922, ed. H. J. C. Grierson.

44. *S.E.;* K. 213. Is it possible that Blake was influenced by Plotinus in the philosophical substance of this poem? Taylor's translation of Plotinus' *On Felicity* was published in 1794. *The Fly* is one of the last entries in the Notebook—number 55 of the poems and fragments. It might conceivably have been written in 1794.

Plotinus argues that "to live well" and "to be happy" are the same thing:

> since we constitute felicity in life, if we should think life a term synonimous to vital beings, we ought to assign to all animals an ability of becoming happy, and should think that those beings live well in energy, to whom a life

one and the same is present and which all animals are naturally capable of receiving. Nor ought we, on such a supposition, so to distribute a matter of this kind as to allow an ability of happiness to the rational nature and not to the irrational; for life will be that common something which, whoever participates, ought to be capable of obtaining felicity, since beatitude would consist in a certain life. [*P.F.B.* pp. 12–13; *Ennead* 1.4.3]

I cannot but think that Wordsworth's *Lines Written in Early Spring* was inspired by the same essay. This is not at all improbable, since Coleridge declared himself an admirer of "Taylor the English Pagan" in a letter to Thelwall, Nov. 19, 1796: "Dreamers, from Thoth the Egyptian to Taylor the English pagan, are my darling studies." If Coleridge read Taylor, what more likely than that Wordsworth should have read him too? Wordsworth's poem attributes happiness especially to birds and plants:

> *Through primrose tufts, in that green bower,*
> *The periwinkle trailed its wreaths;*
> *And 'tis my faith that every flower*
> *Enjoys the air it breathes.*
>
> *The birds around me hopped and played,*
> *Their thoughts I cannot measure:—*
> *But the least motion which they made,*
> *It seemed a thrill of pleasure.*

Wordsworth's poem closely follows Plotinus' argument, which continues:

living well belongs to other animals as well as to man. Thus birds are well conditioned or enjoy a sound existence, and sing agreeable to the institutions of Nature in their formation, and after this manner they may appear to possess a desirable life. But if we constitute felicity as a certain end, which is something extreme in the appetite of nature, in this way, all animals will be happy when they arrive at this extreme, and which, when obtained, Nature in them makes a stop, as having accomplished the whole of their existence, and filled it with all that is wanting from beginning to end . . . in this case it must belong to creatures the most vile and abject, and to plants themselves, whose slender existence arrives at its proper end.

[*P.F.B.* pp. 4–5; *Ennead* 1.4.1]

45.   Notebook 101; K. 182.
46.   *M.* 20; K. 502, 27–33.
47.   *J.* 27; K. 651, 53–56.
48.   *Aurora*, Chap. 18, §§ 34–36; *Works*, 1, 174.
49.   *M.* 4; K. 483, 9–12.
50.   *J.* 15; K. 636, 14–20.
51.   *M.* 32; K. 521, 17–21.
52.   *Mathematical Principles*, Vol. 11, Bk. 111, p. 389. How this definition must have rankled in Blake's mind we may judge from the trouble he has been at to contradict its component parts, and this over a number of years. When in 1827 he annotated Thornton's *Lord's Prayer*, he certainly had Newton still in mind, and was replying to him no less than to Dr. Thornton when he wrote: "Every thing

has as much right to Eternal life as God, who is the Servant of Man." "So you See That God is just such a Tyrant as Augustus Ceasar," Blake wrote beside a remark by Thornton about necessity for obedience to the will and power of God; and on the flyleaf, "This is Saying the Lord's Prayer Backwards, which they say Raises the devil"; and the devil raised is Newton's "Universal Ruler," as Blake's paraphrase of Thornton makes very clear: "Our Father Augustus Ceasar, who art in these thy Substantial Astronomical Telescopic Heavens, Holiness to thy Name or Title, & reverence to thy Shadow. Thy Kingship come upon Earth first & then in Heaven . . . & deliver us from Poverty in Jesus, that Evil One. For thine is the Kingship, [or] Allegoric Godship, & the Power, or War, & the Glory, or Law, Ages after Ages in thy descendants; for God is only an Allegory of Kings & nothing Else." [*Annotations to Thornton;* K. 788–89]

Once and for all, to settle with Newton the point "we do not say my Eternal, your Eternal," etc., Blake adopts the phrase, which he first uses in *The Gates of Paradise,* "*My* Eternal Man":

> *My Eternal Man set in Repose,*
> *The Female from his darkness rose*
>                          [K. 770]

Albion is called "The Eternal Man," and after the Last Judgment, when the Imagination triumphs over the creation of the ratio, "Many Eternal Men sat at the golden feast," and:

> *Man liveth not by Self alone, but in his brother's face*
> *Each shall behold the Eternal Father. . . .*
>                          [*F.Z.* 9; K. 374, 641–42]

Newton's monstrous definition continues (p. 391):

He is utterly void of all body and bodily figure, and can therefore neither be seen, nor heard, nor touched; nor ought he to be worshipped under the representation of any corporeal thing. We have ideas of his attributes, but what the real substance of any thing is, we know not. In bodies we see only their figures and colours, we hear only the sounds, we touch only their outward surfaces, we smell only the smells, and taste the savours; but their inward substances are not to be known, either by our senses, or by any reflex act of our minds; much less then have we any idea of the substance of God. We know him only by his most wise and excellent contrivances of things, and final causes; we admire him for his perfections; but we reverence and adore him on account of his dominion. For we adore him as his servants; and a God without dominion, providence, and final causes, is nothing else but Fate and Nature.

This is the definition that Blake answers in the *Everlasting Gospel:*

> *Poor Spiritual Knowledge is not worth a button!*
> *For thus the Gospel Sir Isaac confutes:*
> *"God can only be known by his Attributes;*
> *And as for the Indwelling of the Holy Ghost*
> *Or of Christ & his Father, it's all a boast*

> *And Pride & Vanity of the imagination,*
> *That disdains to follow this World's Fashion."*
> *To teach doubt & Experiment*
> *Certainly was not what Christ meant.*
>                                          [K. 752, 40–50]

53.  *M.* 32; K. 521, 18.
54.  April 12, 1827; K. 878.
55.  *F.Z.* II; K. 287, 266–67.
56.  Blake seems to have conceived times and spaces as something very like White-head's epochal theory (*Science and the Modern World*). Berkeley certainly gave him the necessary basis upon which to build his conception of subjective space-time. Since "There is nothing," Berkeley says, "*abstracted from the succession of ideas in our minds*, it follows that the duration of any finite spirit must be estimated *by the number of ideas or actions succeeding each other in that spirit or mind*" (*Principles*, § 111).

   Einstein's theory of relativity has overthrown the Newtonian universe of fixed and absolute location and duration, and Whitehead (the philosopher of Einstein's mathematics, as Locke was of Newton's) praises Berkeley for having made the right criticisms of Newton's mechanistic view of the universe, mentioning in particular his overthrowing of the idea of simple *location* in space and time. Whitehead sets aside the ultimate question as to whether nature exists only in the mind, and is content with a "provisional realism in which nature is conceived as a complex of prehensive unifications" (p. 101). The realities of nature are, he says, "the events in nature" (p. 102). According to Whitehead, the unit of natural occurrence is what he calls the "event": "Accordingly, a non-material-istic philosophy of nature will identify a primary organism as being the emergence of some particular pattern as grasped in the unity of a real event" (p. 146). Each event has its own space-time system, which comes into existence with that event: "Thus an event in realising itself displays a pattern, and this pattern requires a definite duration . . . the actuality of the space-time systems is constituted by the realisation of the pattern" (p. 177). This realization requires a duration, involving a definite lapse of time; and the duration is "spatialised." Duration is "that which is required for the realisation of a pattern in the given event" (p. 177). Realization is "the becoming of time in the field of extension. Extension is the complex of events, *qua* their potentialities. In realisation the potentiality becomes actuality" (p. 179); and finally, "Temporalisation [is] the realisation of a complete organism. This organism is an event holding in its essence its spatio-temporal relationships . . . throughout the spatio-temporal continuum" (p. 180). So far as I can understand Whitehead's definition, it is very near Blake's "Canaan."
57.  *M.* 41; K. 534, 37–42.
58.  *M.* 9; K. 490, 34–35, 52.
59.  *M.* 13; K. 494, 13.
60.  *M.* 13; K. 494, 15–17.
61.  *M.* 8; K. 489, 42–44. Michael and Satan alike—Good and Evil—are prisoners of this state. "Neither the just nor the wicked is in the supreme state"; the world of duality is, *as a whole*, fallen.

62.  *F.Z.* VIII; K. 350, 370–73.
63.  *Europe* 9; K. 240, 1–5.
64.  *M.* 10; K. 490, 3–5.

## 23.   *The Shadowy Female*

1.  *Aurora*, Chap. 11, § 2; *Works*, I, 92.
2.  Ibid., Chap. 3, § 99; *Works*, I, 39.
3.  "The Pope supposes Nature & the Virgin Mary to be the same allegorical per-sonages, but the Protestant considers Nature as incapable of bearing a Child" (*Note in Cennini's "Trattato della pittura"*; K. 779). Blake is speaking as a Protestant.
4.  *Aurora*, Chap. 16, §§ 21–22; *Works*, I, 158.
     The "garden of Eden" is, in the symbolism of the cabala, the tenth (and lowest) of the sefiroth or divine potencies within the Tree of God. There are three higher and seven lower sefiroth; so that the "tenth" does correspond to Boehme's "seventh" fontal spirit of demiurgic manifestation, the higher Trinity not appearing in manifested being. Mr. R. J. Zwi Werblowsky, then of the Institute of Jewish Studies, Manchester, in a letter of 18 Jan. 1955, gave me the following information: " 'Eden,' when it occurs in the Zohar and allied writings, denotes the second sefirah, Hokhmah ('Wisdom,' also Abba, father) while the river that goes forth from Eden (Gen. 2:10) is the third sefirah, Binah, Mother, etc. The symbol 'garden of Eden,' however, denotes the tenth sefirah or She-khinah. The reason for this odd distinction is, I suspect, a rather simple one. Shekhinah is always the garden, i.e. the place where the waters, springs, ferti-lizing powers etc. of the higher potencies finally end up and bring forth their ultimate fruit. This whole sefirotic or pleromatic process begins with Hokhmah, which, although the second sefirah, is to all intents and purposes the first, Kether being the utterly transcendent 'Urgrund.' Gen. 2:8 and 10 seem to distinguish between the garden and Eden. The life-giving waters of Binah (the 'magna mater' of the whole sefirotic pleroma) thus proceed from Eden-Hokhmah to water, and finally end up in the 'garden.' So much for the purely cabalistic aspect of the matter. Of course, the original cabala has nothing to do with Christian post-Renaissance cabalism, which is a completely autonomous entity that has grown from misunderstandings and often erroneous translations of *kabbal,* texts. The way all this happened makes a fascinating study."
     Boehme also distinguishes between "Eden" (the Sophia, who corresponds to the "Wisdom," and also to the Christian Logos, who in Fludd replaces Hokhmah as the second numeration of the Tree) and the "garden," who is Boehme's seventh fontal spirit, and corresponds nearly enough to the Shekhinah (Malkuth) of the Tree. Boehme calls Eve Adam's "rose garden." See Chap. 8 for a further discussion of Boehme's Sophia.
5.  *F.Z.* VIIb; K. 339, 232–35.
6.  *Aurora*, Chap. 13, §§ 48, 57; *Works*, I, 123. Italics mine.
7.  *F.Z.* I; K. 271, 261–63.
8.  *F.Z.* VII; K. 326, 239–42.
9.  See our I, pp. 208, 212; [85, 86].
     Mr. Edward Lucie-Smith pointed out to me, and even sent me photographs

of, antique sarcophagi which may well have been among Blake's sources for the "veil" of Vala; an iconographic attribute of Diana, who is often depicted wearing her veil in much the same manner as Vala of *Jerusalem* plate 46. He gave me a reference to *Die Antiken Sarkophagreliefs*, which to my shame I did not follow up. I quote from his letter: "I have been doing a little detective work on my Blake drawing of 'Diana and Endymion', and thought you would like to see the results." [Sir Geoffrey Keynes, however, does not think the drawing is by Blake; I therefore did not pursue this aspect of Mr. Lucie-Smith's information.] "The enclosed photostats show a Roman sarcophagus of about A.D. 190–210. This is in the *Metropolitan Museum Bulletin* for January 1957. The sarcophagus at Dumbarton Oaks which I mentioned has a different subject. Counting fragments, there are about 70 Endymion sarcophagi known." The letter goes on to enumerate some of these; but since (if the drawing is, as Keynes believes, spurious) this fact is not in itself relevant, I omit the references. What is interesting, however, is the iconography of the floating veil of Diana, which Blake did undoubtedly derive, in one way or another, from the antique. It would be interesting to know from exactly what work he took this visual theme; probably several, not necessarily or only sarcophagi.

10. *F.Z.* I; K. 271, 271.
11. The Babylonian Ishtar, when she descends into Hades, is stripped of her garments by the doorkeepers of the successive gates.
12. See our I, p. 114.
13. *D.E.*, p. 98.
14. "And there appeared a great wonder in heaven; a woman clothed with the sun, and the moon under her feet, and upon her head a crown of twelve stars" (Rev. 12:1).
15. Tr. Adlington, Chap. 47, p. 222. This passage is also paraphrased by Taylor in *D.E.*, pp. 75 ff.
16. *Treatise of Isis and Osiris*, p. 106.
17. Ibid., p. 11.
18. *J.* 34; K. 660, 7–9.
19. *F.Q.* VII.vii.5. See also IV.x–xli ff., where the veiled hermaphrodite Venus is described.
20. Todd ("William Blake and the Eighteenth-Century Mythologists," in *Tracks in the Snow*) proved that Blake had read certain articles published in the *Proceedings of the Calcutta Society*, founded by Sir William Jones. Flaxman sculpted his memorial, in which Jones is depicted learning from Brahmans. The plaster model of this is in the Slade School of Art, University of London.
21. "On the Philosophy of the Asiaticks," *Asiatick Researches*, IV, 171–72. Reprinted in *Works*, III, 229 ff. The reference in the last sentence is obviously to Berkeley.
22. Introduction to the *Hymn to Narayena; Works*, XIII, 302. A prose paraphrase of this hymn is given in "On the Gods of Greece, Italy & India," *Asiatick Researches*, I (1788), 244–45.
23. *Asiatick Researches*, I, 223. See also *Works*, III, 322.
24. Cf. the mirror of Dionysus, our I, pp. 306 f.
25. "Brahm" and "Brahma" are not to be confused. The former is the supreme deity, the latter the lesser figure of the demiurge.

26.  *F.Z.* VII; K. 326, 230.
27.  *F.Z.* III; K. 292, 44–45.
28.  *J.* 83; K. 728, 35–48. The "self-existent invisible GOD . . . first created the *waters*, and impressed them with a power of motion: by that power was produced a golden Egg, blazing like a thousand suns, in which was born BRAHMA, self-existing, the great parent of all rational beings" (*Asiatick Researches*, I, 244). From the two halves of the eggshell, heaven and earth are formed. (See *G.P.* 6.)

In *The Gates of Paradise*, 6, Blake has depicted a child hatching from the two halves of an egg; presumably the Orphic egg, which would identify the child as the Orphic Phanes, or the Hindu Brahma. Beneath the drawing, Blake has written a line from Dryden's *Palamon and Arcite* (Bk. III, 1069) whose context is Theseus' speech on the decay of the individual and the propagation of the species:

> *So Man, at first a Drop, dilates with Heat,*
> *Then, form'd, the little Heart begins to beat;*
> *Secret he feeds, unknowing in the Cell;*
> *At length, for Hatching ripe, he breaks the Shell,*
> *And struggles into Breath, and cries for Aid;*

This is based on the passage in Chaucer's *Knight's Tale* beginning at line 2129; but Blake's line is in fact an addition by Dryden, which is why I had so much difficulty in tracking it down in Dryden's works, and was driven to putting an appeal for help in *The Times Literary Supplement* which was kindly answered by Miss Helen Spalding.

"Hatching," for Blake, always refers to the birth of the soul, the second birth, of winged psyche from wingless pupa. It is in keeping with Blake's constant practice that Dryden's charming line should illustrate symbolic meanings of which its author had no thought.
29.  Owen Barfield, in *Saving the Appearances*, puts forward, in simple terms, a similar view. Man's actual world evolves with his consciousness. See also Tyrrell's *Homo Faber*, based on René Guénon (*The Reign of Quantity*), who reminds us that the natural world may also degenerate and withdraw its qualities and powers from degenerate civilizations like our own, following the loss of certain faculties of (qualitative) perception.
30.  Letter to Dr. Trusler, Aug. 23, 1799; K. 793.
31.  *M.* 29; K. 518, 65.
32.  *J.* 36; K. 663–64, 51–55.
33.  *J.*15; K. 636, 14–17.
34.  *J.* 23; K. 646, 32.
35.  *J.* 24; K. 648, 61–62.
36.  *J.* 42; K. 671, 80–81.
37.  *M.* 38; K. 529, 26.
38.  *J.* 71; K. 711, 61.
39.  *J.* 59; K. 691, 2–9.
40.  *J.* 30; K. 656, 40.
41.  *J.* 55; K. 686, 16. The relations of the sexes are especially bedeviled by physicality and "the veil." We recall that, according to Boehme, Eve was created in the spiritual "sleep" of Adam.

42. See our II, pp. 74–77.
43. *J.* 20; K. 643, 36. See our I, pp. 211 f.

## 24. *Jesus the Imagination*

1. This is likewise the teaching of Sufism, whose "universal man" is likened to the face of God seen in his creatures. See Titus Burckhardt, *De l'Homme universel.*
2. *J.* 4; K. 622, 4–7.
3. *J.* 4; K. 622, 24–26.
4. *M.* 14; K. 495, 25–27.
5. *J.* 24, K. 647, 23–24.
6. *J.* 29; K. 653, 1–4.
7. *J.* 30; K. 656, 19–20.
8. *J.* 24; K. 648, 57–60.
9. *J.* 5; K. 624, 58–59.
10. *J.* 9; K. 628, 16–17.
11. *J.* 38, K. 664, 11–12.
12. *J.* 44; K. 674, 18–20.
13. *J.* 66; K. 702, 40–44.
14. The dismay that some Blake scholars have felt at the apparent savagery of Blake's Last Judgment arises from a failure to realize the nature of the Judge and of that which is to be judged. Margaret Bottrall (*The Divine Image*, p. 90) discusses the point. She argues that Blake's "thou art a Man, God is no more" is "the final temptation, the satanic Selfhood trying to assert its claims." If this reading is right, then Satan's temptation consists not in the falsehood of the concept of the "divine human" but in the attempt to deceive Jesus in his use of the word "man," here used of the spectral satanic humanity and not of the Divine Humanity. The passage then becomes a distorted, "satanic" version of the true nature of the Last Judgment. The Judge is the Divine Humanity; but Satan pictures a Judgment carried out by the natural "satanic" man:

> *Thou art a Man, God is no more,*
> *Thy own humanity learn to adore,*
> *For that is my Spirit of Life.*
> *Awake, arise to Spiritual Strife*
> *And thy Revenge abroad display*
> *In terrors at the Last Judgment day.*
> *God's Mercy & Long Suffering*
> *Is but the Sinner to Judgment to bring.*
> *Thou on the Cross for them shalt pray*
> *And take Revenge at the Last Day.*
> [E.G. d; K. 752–53, 75–84]

Blake certainly imagined a Last Judgment that should be a destruction of all the errors of the created world, burned up in the light of eternity, but "revenge" belongs to Satan's self-righteous condemnation of sin and sinners, not to the Last Judgment of Imagination upon "error, or creation," which "is Burnt up the Moment Men cease to behold it." There is nothing there to punish, since the sins all belonged to the "deadly dreams" of error and possess no essential and eternal reality.

15.   *Laocoön;* K. 776. He may have been answering a couplet quoted by Taylor, *O.H.* (1824 edn.), p. 49, n. 43:

> *Jove is a circle, trigon, and a square,*
> *Centre and line, and all things before all.*

16.   *An History of Early Opinions concerning Jesus Christ*, II, 3. Blake's strange statement that "the ear is the earth of Eden" is explicable when we remember that Jesus is the "word," and that therefore the organ of hearing is the recipient of the creative *logos*.

17.   *Annotation to Siris*, § 300; K. 774.

18.   And also, precariously, in the writings of Eckhart and other mystical theologians within the Church.

19.   *V.L.J.* 87; K. 615, 1–4.

20.   *J.* 77; K. 717.

21.   *On Nature, Contemplation, and the One; P.F.B.*, pp. 243–44; *Ennead* III.8.11. See also quotation from the Hermetica, our II, pp. 110 f.

22.   *V.L.J.* 82; K. 611.

23.   *On Nature, Contemplation, and the One; P.F.B.*, p. 245; *Ennead* III.8.11.

24.   *Laocoön;* K. 776.

25.   *Annotation to Siris*, § 289; K. 773.

26.   *Three Principles*, Chap. 25, § 81; *Works*, I, 276.

27.   *Treatise on the Incarnation*, Pt. II, Chap. 3, §§ 41–42; *Works*, III, 96–97.

28.   Ibid., §§ 24–25; *Works*, III, 95.

29.   *Biographia Literaria*, pp. 145–46.

30.   Orthodox Christianity has not done so, at least to the same extent.

31.   If, indeed, the name "Protestant" ought to be given to a mystic so normally traditional.

32.   *Three Principles*, Chap. 7, § 6; *Works*, I, 42.

33.   *P.L.* I.17–23.

34.   *P.R.* IV.285–365.

35.   Ibid. 286–90.

36.   Ibid. 293–312.

37.   Ibid. 343–50.

38.   P. 195; K. 473.

39.   *M.H.H.* 12–13; K. 153.

40.   *P.R.* IV.331–39.

41.   *D.C.* II; K. 565.

42.   *F.Z.* VII; K. 326, 270–71.

43.   *On Providence; P.F.B.*, pp. 116–17; *Ennead* III.2.1.

44.   Ibid., p. 118; *Ennead* III.2.2.

45.   *F.Z.* I; K. 277, 469–75.

46.   *D.C.* V; K. 578.

47.   Plotinus also uses the image of a tree (*Ennead* III.8.10).

48.   *Mosaicall Philosophy*, Sec. II, Bk. II, Chap. 2, p. 171.

49.   Notebook 82–84; K. 612.
      See Chap. 23, n. 4, for an extract from a letter from Mr. R. J. Zwi Werblow-

sky on the cabalistic symbolism of "Eden," which is used, as by Blake, as the world of the divine Wisdom, and in contrast to the "garden" of bodily life (Malkuth) symbolized by Blake as "Vala's garden." Where the cabala gives "Wisdom" (also Abba, "father") Blake gives the figure of the Logos, "Jesus the Imagination." Boehme gives the divine Sophia, which he personifies as a feminine principle.

50.  K. 480.
51.  *V.L.J.* 69–70; K. 605–606.
51a. J. 63, 16–17; K. 697.
52.  Morley, *Blake, Coleridge, etc.*, p. 5.
53.  Blake is not entirely consistent in his use of the name Jehovah, but what I have written is generally true. *The Ghost of Abel* is a vindication of Jehovah, who asks no sacrifice but "a Broken Spirit / And a Contrite Heart," as against the ghost of Abel, who is Satan, demanding vengeance and refusing forgiveness. Jehovah is "thou Spiritual Voice" who calls Adam, who refuses to hear; His is the voice that calls the "lapsed Soul" in the "evening dew" of Paradise. Satan is the Elohim and, as such, contrasted with Jehovah, who is identified with Jesus, in whom he is to be manifested:

> *Satan.*  I will have Human Blood & not the blood of Bulls or Goats,
> And no Atonement, O Jehovah! the Elohim live on Sacrifice
> Of Men: hence I am God of Men: Thou Human, O Jehovah!
> By the Rock & Oak of the Druid, creeping Mistletoe & Thorn,
> Cain's City built with Human Blood, not Blood of Bulls & Goats,
> Thou shalt Thyself be Sacrificed to Me, thy God, on Calvary.
> *Jehovah.*  Such is My Will that Thou Thyself go to Eternal Death
> In Self Annihilation, even till Satan, Self-subdu'd, Put off Satan
> Into the Bottomless Abyss, whose torment arises for ever & ever.

> *On each side a Chorus of Angels entering Sing the following:*
> The Elohim of the Heathen Swore Vengeance for Sin! Then
>                                                       Thou stood'st
> Forth, O Elohim Jehovah! in the midst of the darkness of the
>                                                       Oath, All Clothed
> In Thy Covenant of the Forgiveness of Sins . . .
> The Elohim saw their Oath Eternal Fire: they rolled apart
>                                                       trembling over The
> Mercy Seat, each in his station fixt in the Firmament by Peace,
>                                                       Brotherhood and Love.
>                                                       [K. 780–81]

54.  *D.L.W.*, § 11, pp. 10–11.
55.  Ibid., § 19, pp. 17–18.
56.  J. 27; K. 651, 57–64.
57.  J. 35; K. 662, 3–10.
58.  J. 91; K. 738, 19–31.
59.  *D.L.W.*, § 78, p. 65.
60.  See our I, pp. 214 f.
61.  *F.Z.* IX; K. 374, 638–42.
62.  *V.L.J.* 76–77; K. 607.

63.  *Laocoön;* K. 777.
64.  "Art and Sacrament," in *Epoch and Artist*, p. 168.
65.  *Laocoön;* K. 776.
66.  *J.* 77; K. 716–17.
67.  *V.L.J.* 92–95; K. 617.
68.  *Mysterium Magnum*, Chap. 31, § 45; *Works*, III, 167.
69.  *V.L.J.* 70; K. 604.
70.  *F.Z.* I; K. 279, 553–55.
71.  *F.Z.* VIII; K. 351, 398–406.
72.  Scholem, *Major Trends*.
73.  *M.* 13; K. 494, 17–26.
74.  *J.* 55; K. 686, 32–33.
75.  The more familiar current names of these numerations are: Binah, Hesed, Geburah, Tiphereth, Nezah, Hod, Iesod, and Malcuth. Agrippa gives these names also (*Three Books of Occult Philosophy*, Bk. III, pp. 368–70). It is perhaps odd that Blake nowhere makes use of them.

## 25.   Satan the Selfhood

1.   *F.Z.* VIIb; K. 340, 301.
2.   *T.C.R.*, Vol. II, § 504, p. 131.
3.   *F.Z.* VII; K. 329, 357–60.
4.   *H.H.*, § 158, p. 97.
5.   *A.C.*, Vol. V, § 3743, pp. 102–103.
6.   *D.L.W.*, § 117, p. 96.
7.   *J.* 52; K. 682.
8.   *D.L.W.*, § 114, p. 92.
9.   *H.H.*, § 160, p. 99.
10.  To Satan "Life delights in life" is the essence of selfishness, whereas the morality of the ego may have all the appearance of altruism.
11.  *M.* 32; K. 522, 29.
12.  *J.* 33; K. 659, 5–18.
13.  Notebook 71–72; K. 605.
14.  *Biographia Literaria*, Chap. 13, p. 146.
15.  Notebook 68; K. 604–605.
16.  *V.L.J.* 92–95; K. 617.
17.  *M.* 10; K. 491, 8–9.
18.  *M.* 10; K. 490, 1–2.
19.  Calvin's Five Points, formulated at the Synod of Dort.
20.  *M.* 11; K. 492, 21–23.
21.  *M.* 7; K. 486, 2–6.
22.  *M.* 11; K. 491–92, 19–21.
23.  *M.* 5; K. 484, 11–14.
24.  *M.* 40; K. 533, 32–36.
25.  *J.* 10; K. 629, 8–14.
26.  *J.* 17; K. 639, 33–35.
27.  *On the Nature and Origin of Evil; P.F.B.*, pp. 60–61, 63; *Enneads* I.8.2–3.
28.  Morley, *Blake, Coleridge, etc.*, p. 6.
29.  *J.* 10; K. 630, 55–58.

30.  Morley, *Blake, Coleridge, etc.*, p. 6.
31.  *M.* 5; K. 484, 11.
32.  *M.* 13; K. 494, 32–33.
33.  *M.* 4; K. 483, 18.
34.  *M.* 31; K. 519–20, 17–24.
35.  Morley, *Blake, Coleridge, etc.*, p. 10.
36.  *P.L.* III.183–212.
37.  Ibid.
38.  *M.* 25; K. 510–11, 31–36.
39.  *M.* 13; K. 494, 27.
40.  Luke 22:37.
41.  *M.* 9; K. 490, 26–29.
42.  *M.* 4; K. 483, 1–4.
43.  *M.* 4; K. 483, 9–18.
44.  *P.L.* III.194–97.
45.  Blake would have found this in Agrippa.
46.  Job 39: 9 ff. The *Oxford English Dictionary* defines the unicorn as "a fabulous and legendary animal usually regarded as having the body of a horse with a single horn projecting from its forehead."
47.  Pl. 46 (41 in the Blake Trust facsimile edition); K. 676, 14. The iconographic sources of this plate are discussed by Sir Anthony Blunt in an essay on "Blake's Pictorial Imagination" in the *Warburg Journal*, VI (1943), 190–212. He cites the man-headed bulls at Persepolis, but gives no explanation of the single horns. Blake did, however, draw the elephant-headed god (Ganesha), whose coiled trunk is suggestive.
48.  The traditional unicorn has a straight horn encircled by a spiral pattern. Blake's spiral horns are not, after all, so very unlike this.
49.  *F.Z.* I; K. 264, 12–13.
50.  *M.* 9; K. 490, 51–52.
51.  *M.* 7; K. 486, 6–17.
52.  *M.* 7; K. 487, 19–25.
53.  *M.* 7; K. 487, 47–49.
54.  *M.* 8; K. 488, 7–10.
55.  *M.* 7; K. 487, 41–42.
56.  *M.* 8; K. 489, 47–48.
57.  *Annotations to Boyd's Dante* 39–40, 38–39; K. 411–12.
58.  Ibid. 45–46; K. 412.
59.  *M.* 29; K. 517, 48–49.
60.  *M.* 9; K. 489, 21–26.
61.  *M.H.H.* 23–24; K. 158.
62.  *J.* 49; K. 679, 27–31.
63.  *E.G.*, Supplementary Passages 2; K. 759, 34–37.
64.  "Those Churches ever consuming & ever building by the Spectres" (*J.* 13; K. 634, 62).
65.  *M.* 22; K. 506, 41–45.
66.  *J.* 52; K. 682–83:

> O Deists! Deism, is the Worship of the God of this World by the means of what you call Natural Religion and Natural Philosophy, and of Natural Morality or Self-Righteousness, the Selfish Virtues of the Natural Heart. This

was the Religion of the Pharisees who murder'd Jesus. Deism is the same & ends in the same.

Voltaire, Rousseau, Gibbon, Hume, charge the Spiritually Religious with Hypocrisy; but how a Monk, or a Methodist either, can be a Hypocrite, I cannot concieve. We are Men of like passions with others & pretend not to be holier than others; therefore, when a Religious Man falls into Sin, he ought not to be call'd a Hypocrite; this title is more properly to be given to a Player who falls into Sin, whose profession is Virtue & Morality & the making Men Self-Righteous. Foote in calling Whitefield, Hypocrite, was himself one; for Whitefield pretended not to be holier than others, but confessed his Sins before all the World. Voltaire! Rousseau! You cannot escape my charge that you are Pharisees & Hypocrites, for you are constantly talking of the Virtues of the Human Heart and particularly of your own, that you may accuse others, & especially the Religious, whose errors you, by this display of pretended Virtue, chiefly design to expose. Rousseau thought Men Good by Nature: he found them Evil & found no friend. Friendship cannot exist without Forgiveness of Sins continually. The Book written by Rousseau call'd his Confessions, is an apology & cloke for his sin & not a confession.

But you also charge the poor Monks & Religious with being the causes of War, while you acquit & flatter the Alexanders & Caesars, the Lewis's & Fredericks, who alone are its causes & its actors. But the Religion of Jesus, Forgiveness of Sin, can never be the cause of a War nor of a single Martyrdom.

Those who Martyr others or who cause War are Deists, but never can be Forgivers of Sin. The Glory of Christianity is To Conquer by Forgiveness. All the Destruction, therefore, in Christian Europe has arisen from Deism, which is Natural Religion.

67.  *M.* 32; K. 521, 14–17.
68.  *J.* 90; K. 736, 28–38. See above, our II, pp. 114 f.
69.  *E.G.* 100–101; K. 749, 52–57.
70.  *E.G.* i; K. 756, 3–4.
71.  *E.G.* b; K. 749, 48–51.
72.  *Doctrine of the New Jerusalem concerning the Lord,* § 35.
73.  *E.G.,* e; K. 755, 81–94.
74.  *E.G.,* d; K. 753, 81–84.
75.  *E.G.,* d; K. 753, 87–90.
76.  *E.G.,* d; K. 753, 91–108.
77.  3:14.
78.  *Tracks in the Snow,* p. 50.
79.  *Abury, a Temple of the British Druids,* p. 60.
80.  *The Warburg Journal,* VI, 225.
81.  See Keynes, ed., *Blake's Illustrations to the Bible,* No. 45.
82.  *Abury,* pp. 60–61.
83.  *E.G.* e; K. 755, 81–84.
84.  *E.G.* e; K. 755, 91–96.
85.  See our II, pp. 38 ff.

86.  *Mythology*, I, 477.
87.  *Europe* 10; K. 241, 21–23.
88.  *F.Z.* III; K. 294, 97, 101.
89.  *J.* 98; K. 746, 44–45.

## 26.  States

1.   "Within Christendom" does not imply that, properly understood, Christian doctrine is false.
2.   *M.* 32; K. 522, 30–38.
3.   *H.H.*, § 158, p. 92.
4.   Ibid., § 155, p. 95.
5.   Ibid., § 52, p. 31.
6.   *V.L.J.* 76–77; K. 607.
7.   *V.L.J.* 82–84; K. 611.
8.   *M.* 32; K. 522, 40–43.
9.   *J.* 35; K. 662, 3–16.
10.  M. 32; K. 521, 22–29.
11.  *G.P.;* K. 771.
12.  See our II, p. 245 [183].
13.  *J.* 61; K. 695, 51–52.
14.  *D.C.;* K. 567.
15.  Edwin Muir called his autobiography *The Story and the Fable:* the story is the individual life, the fable the pattern to which every life tends and approximates. Joseph Campbell's *Hero with a Thousand Faces* attempts to trace, through many myths, the fable that every man's life attempts to relive.
16.  *J.* 70; K. 709, 17–18.
17.  *J.* 25; K. 648, 12–16.
18.  Morley, *Blake, Coleridge, etc.*, p. 9.
19.  See our II, pp. 219–21.
20.  *F.Z.* VIII; K. 351, 379–83.
21.  *M.* 10; K. 490, 1–2.
22.  *J.* 41 (reversed writing on design); K. 669.
23.  *J.* 73; K. 713, 29–30.
24.  *V.L.J.* 80; K. 606.
25.  *G.P.* 14; K. 769.
26.  Catholic doctrine teaches that there is an eternal hell, but we are not compelled to believe that there is anyone in it. Juliana of Norwich, in her vision of hell, writes that she "saw none there," and Blake, "Dante saw devils where I saw none" (in Morley, *Blake, Coleridge, etc.*, p. 6).
27.  *J.* 52; K. 681.
28.  *V.L.J.* 91–92; K. 614.
29.  *M.* 22; K. 506, 50–52.
30.  *J.* 49; K. 680, 60–75. The stones of fire refer to the covering cherub in Ezek. 28:14: "thou wast upon the holy mountain of God; thou hast walked up and down in the midst of the stones of fire."
31.  *M.* 32; K. 521–22, 26–29.

32.  *M.* 41; K. 533, 1–28.
33.  *M.* 13–14; K. 495, 50–51, 1–2.


## 27.  *The Sickness of Albion*


1.  *J.* 27; K. 649. This was perhaps suggested by Priestley's similar address to the Jews, which concludes his *Comparison of the Institutions of Moses with Those of the Hindoos* (pp. 393 ff.): "Be not offended that a Christian, who from his early years has entertained [for the Jewish religion] the greatest respect and veneration, and who in this work has endeavoured to . . . evince its superiority to all other ancient religions."
2.  *Aurora*, Chap. 2, §§ 31–39; *Works*, I, 29.
3.  Taylor, *O.H.* (1824 edn.) xv, p. 48 n.
4.  *M.* 6; K. 486, 26.
5.  *J.* 70; K. 709, 32. *J.* 76; K. 716, 27. *J.* 27; K. 649.
6.  K. 703, 70–84.
7.  *J.* 24; K. 647, 7–10.
8.  *J.* 17; K. 639, 31–32.
9.  *F.Z.* III; K. 294, 81–82.
10.  *F.Z.* I; K. 279, 557–59. The reference to Ephraim seems to be Swedenborgian. Ephraim represents the *understanding* of the spiritual church, Zion its *love*. Man is turning to rational thought (*A.C.*). The "nuptial song" of Los and Enitharmon (*F.Z.* I; K. 274, 385 ff.) opens with the lines:

> Ephraim *call'd out* to Zion: "*Awake, O Brother Mountain!*
> *Let us refuse the Plow & Spade* . . ."

It is reason that calls upon love to destroy humanity in the name of the new philosophy.
11.  *J.* 23; K. 646, 33–34.
12.  *F.Z.* VII; K. 326, 251–57.
13.  *F.Z.* IX; K. 359–60, 99–113. Repeated almost verbatim in *J.* 19; K. 641, 1–15.
14.  *J.* 18; K. 640, 13–26.
15.  *J.* 19; K. 641, 17–18.
16.  *J.* 26–27; K. 642, 34–35.
17.  *J.* 21; K. 643, 3–11.
18.  *J.* 40; K. 666–67, 1–24.
19.  *J.* 43; K. 671, 2–3.
20.  *J.* 42; K. 670, 24.
21.  *J.* 98; K. 746, 33–38.
22.  See our I, pp. 50 f.; II, p. 268.
23.  *J.* 54; K. 685, 6–8. Cf. "calling rocks the atomic origins of existence."
24.  *J.* 33; K. 659, 8.
25.  *F.Z.* IV; K. 301, 134–35.
26.  *M.* 15; K. 497, 36–40.
27.  See Jung, in Wilhelm and Jung, *The Secret of the Golden Flower* (also in *Collected Works*, vol. 13), for an exegesis of the mandala in terms of his psychology. See also Jung, "On Mandala Symbolism" (*Collected Works*, vol. 9, part I).

28. *F.Z.* I; K. 264, 9–11.
29. *F.Z.* I; K. 272, 302.
30. Ezek. 1:5–6, 12.
31. *J.* 98; K. 745, 24–27.
32. *J.* 98; K. 745, 12.
33. *J.* 12; K. 632, 54–58.
34. The city within the skull (Golgos).
35. Bunyan, *The Holy War.*
36. *T.C.R.*, Vol. II, § 809, p. 438. See also *A Continuation concerning the Last Judgment*, § 42, p. 35.
37. *J.* 12; K. 632, 45–53. The name presents the usual problem. One can detect the root *golgos* (a skull). Does the word *zoa* come into the termination? In that case, the name means "life within the brain," as from its nature we know Golgonooza to be.
38. *J.* 59; K. 691, 11–13. The reference is to the Book of Revelation: the four living creatures—bull, eagle, man, and lion.
39. *A Letter . . . to Mr. MacPherson*, p. 10.
40. Wilford published two contributions to *Asiatick Researches* on this subject ("On the Chronology of the Hindoos," *A.R.*, v [1798], 241–95), in the second retracting his former views. An obliging Brahmin, finding that Wilford wished to believe this theory, had invented evidence for him. See Todd, *Tracks in the Snow*, p. 34.
41. Pp. 148–49. A valley opening toward the west in one of the Hebrides is known by its Gaelic-speaking inhabitants as "the gate of the dead," for it is the way that the souls of the dead travel from their island to paradise.
42. *D.E.*, p. 118.
43. Anglesey, or possibly the Isle of Man.
44. Davies, *Celtic Researches*, p. 175.
45. *J.* 63; K. 696, 1–4.
46. *J.* 65; K. 699–700, 14–16. Throughout *Jerusalem* Blake is seeking for symbols that will wed his cosmic myth to the history and geography of Britain. The war on the Cheviots is presumably the Battle of Chevy Chase.
47. See above, our I, pp. 341 f.
48. *F.Z.* III; K. 294, 105.
49. *J.* 45; K. 675, 17.
50. *J.* 48; K. 678, 30–33. This is the meaning of the Vale of Rephaim, which is likewise a drowned country. Rephaim is the valley where David fought with the Philistines, and after his victory said: "The Lord hath broken forth upon mine enemies before me, as the breach of waters" (II Sam. 5:20). Is it because the Philistines were led by the giant Goliath that it seems to Blake appropriate that on ". . . Ireland's farthest rocks, where Giants builded their Causeway, / Into the Sea of Rephaim, but the Sea o'erwhelmed them all" (*J.* 89; K. 735, 50–51)? It may explain, if it fails to justify, this abstruse allegorical mode of expression (for allegory, in Blake's own pejorative sense, it must be called), the work of the Daughters of Memory. (The reference is to the Giant's Causeway of basalt columns, in Ulster. Cf. "The Giants who formed this world," *M.H.H.* 15–17; K. 155.) In this same valley of Rephaim, Isaiah (17:5) foretells the reaping of a harvest: "And it shall be as when the harvestman gathereth the corn, and

reapeth the ears with his arm; and it shall be as he that gathereth ears in the valley of Rephaim."

51.  Evans-Wentz, in *The Fairy Faith in Celtic Countries*, calls fairyland "the world of the subjective."

52.  By an Indian it would be taken for granted that the phenomena are of a mental and subjective nature.

53.  *J.* 13; K. 633, 6.

54.  *J.* 14; K. 635, 26–30.

55.  *J.* 13; K. 633, 6–11.

56.  *J.* 13; K. 633, 20–23.

57.  *J.* 98; K. 745, 16–22.

58.  *V.L.J.* 92–95; K. 617.

59.  Letter to Dr. Trusler, Aug. 23, 1799; K. 793.

60.  *J.* 45; K. 676, 33–36. "Bath" has just spoken through the "Western Porch" a warning against the mechanistic philosophy of Albion, whose "machines are woven with his life."

61.  *Morning*, Notebook 12; K. 421.

62.  *V.L.J.* 92–95; K. 616.

63.  *D.C.* v; K. 578.

64.  *F.Z.* vii; K. 329, 364–66.

65.  *J.* 13; K. 633, 24–25.

66.  *J.* 34; K. 661, 27.

67.  *V.L.J.* 82–84; K. 612.

68.  See above, our I, pp. 362 ff.

69.  *M.* 39; K. 531, 35–46.

70.  *Autobiographies* (1st edn.), p. 240.

71.  *M.* 1; K. 480, 1–2.

72.  *J.* 38; K. 665, 29–34.

73.  *J.* 38; K. 665, 40–43.

74.  *J.* 12; K. 632, 25–32.

75.  *J.* 41; K. 668, 16–18.

76.  Letter to Butts, Jan. 10, 1802; K. 811.

77.  Notebook 18–19; K. 600.

78.  *J.* 5; K. 624, 61.

79.  *J.* 44; K. 674, 1–7.

80.  African "idolatry" was so understood in those days. Blake would have found much imaginative meaning in the beliefs of these supposed idolaters, had he known them.

81.  *J.* 45; K. 675, 17–25.

82.  *J.* 65; K. 699–700, 12–28. To pretend, as some left-wing writers do, that Blake opposed the industrial revolution only because it had put many craftsmen out of work is impossible in the light of the reasons he himself states.

83.  *F.Z.* vi; K. 315, 134–38.

84.  *Annotation to Bacon* 75; K. 403.

85.  *Laocoön;* K. 777.

86.  *M.* 25, 26; K. 511–12, 66–71, 1–12.

87.  Letter to Dr. Trusler, Aug. 23, 1799; K. 793.

88.  *M.* 29; K. 516, 6.

# Selected Bibliography

A COMPLETE BLAKE BIBLIOGRAPHY would not be in place here; but I have listed some books not mentioned in the course of this work, for their interest and value. Apart from Blake's works published in his lifetime I have as a rule not referred to books published before 1900, or to works since superseded.

The disproportionate growth of critical apparatus has reached such dimensions that what once may have been an aid to readers has become a thorny barrier through which many young students are never able to penetrate to the treasure beyond—the poetry itself. Nevertheless some at least of the books listed have been to the present writer experiences of illumination on the way, and will doubtless be so to others.

The entries are arranged as follows:

I. (A) Blake Bibliographies. (B) Editions of the Written Works. (C) Works Published Separately. (Chronologically under each heading.)

II. (A) Biographies and Biographical Material. (B) Criticism and Interpretation.

III. Other Books Referred To.

# I

## A. *Blake Bibliographies*

*A Bibliography of William Blake.* By Geoffrey Keynes. New York (Grolier Club), 1921.

*William Blake's Illuminated Books: A Census.* Compiled by Geoffrey Keynes and Edwin Wolf 2nd. New York (Grolier Club), 1953.

*Notes for a Catalogue of the Blake Library at The Georgian House, Merstham.* By Kerrison Preston. Cambridge, 1960.

*A Blake Bibliography: Annotated Lists of Works, Studies, and Blakeana.* By G. E. Bentley, Jr., and Martin K. Nurmi. Minneapolis (University of Minnesota Press) and London, 1964.

## B. *Editions of the Written Works*

*The Works of William Blake, Poetic, Symbolic, and Critical.* Edited, with Lithographs of the Illustrated "Prophetic Books," and a Memoir and Interpretation, by Edwin J. Ellis and W. B. Yeats. London, 1893. 3 vols.

> Yeats was also the editor of the single-volume edition of the *Poems* in the Muses' Library (London, 1893) and Ellis of the *Poetical Works* (London, 1906, 2 vols.).

*The Writings of William Blake* [in verse and prose]. Edited by Geoffrey Keynes. With reproductions and a portrait. London, 1925. 3 vols.

> The best and most complete text, superseding John Sampson's *The Poetical Works* (London, 1913) and other earlier editions.

*The Prophetic Writings of William Blake.* Edited by D. J. Sloss and J. P. R. Wallis. Oxford, 1926. 2 vols.

> A fully annotated text, with a concordance to Blake's symbolism. The interpretation is not reliable.

*Poetry and Prose of William Blake.* Edited by Geoffrey Keynes. London and New York, 1927.

> A volume in the Nonesuch Press "compendious" series, containing a revised text of Keynes's edition of 1925, but without notes and variants.

*The Poems & Prophecies of William Blake.* Edited by Max Plowman. London and New York (Everyman's Library), 1927.

*The Complete Writings of William Blake.* With All the Variant Readings. Edited by Geoffrey Keynes. London and New York, 1957.

> This "Variorum" (bicentenary) edition is now the definitive edition, containing material previously unpublished. A new edition appeared in 1966, with a few corrections and amendments but otherwise identical with the 1957 edition, which remains the source for the texts quoted in the present work.

*William Blake's Vala: Blake's Numbered Text.* Edited by H. M. Margoliouth. Oxford, 1956.

> The text of the original poem of this name, before the additions and alterations made to the manuscript now entitled *The Four Zoas.* It is included here to complete the corpus of Blake's original works.

*Vala, or The Four Zoas.* A Facsimile of the Manuscript, a Transcript of the Poem, and a Study of its Growth and Significance. By G. E. Bentley, Jr. Oxford, 1963. See also *Vala*, ed. H. M. Margoliouth, above.

## c. *Works Published Separately*

Entries marked * were engraved, printed, and published in small editions by Blake himself as specimens of "illuminated printing." Facsimile editions before 1900 are not listed.

*Poetical Sketches* (1783). Facsimile edition, London (Noel Douglas), 1926.

* *All Religions are One* (c. 1788–94). Facsimile edition, ed. Frederick Hollyer. London, 1926.

* *There is No Natural Religion* (c. 1788). Facsimile edition, ed. Philip Hofer, Cambridge (Mass.), 1948.

* *Songs of Innocence* (1789). Facsimile edition, London (Trianon Press), 1954.

* *The Book of Thel* (1789). Facsimile edition, ed. Frederick Hollyer. London, 1924. Another, London and New York, 1928. Another, London (Trianon Press), 1965.

*Tiriel.* Not printed in Blake's lifetime. No edition with plates yet published.

\* *The Marriage of Heaven and Hell* (1790). Facsimile, with a Note by Max Plowman, London and New York, 1927. Facsimile edition, London (Trianon Press), 1960.

*The French Revolution: A Poem in Seven Books*. Book the First (1791). Not published in Blake's lifetime; the only recorded copy is probably a proof.

\* *Visions of the Daughters of Albion* (1793). Facsimile, with a Note by J. Middleton Murry, London and New York, 1932. Facsimile edition, London (Trianon Press), 1959.

\* *America: A Prophecy* (1793). Color facsimile edition, with a Foreword by Ruthven Todd. New York (United Book Guild), 1947.

*For Children: The Gates of Paradise* (1793).

*For the Sexes: The Gates of Paradise* (1818). A revised issue of *For Children: The Gates of Paradise* (1793), with text added.

\* *Songs of Innocence and Experience*. Shewing the Two Contrary States of the Human Soul (1794). Facsimile edition, London (Trianon Press), 1955.

\* *Europe: A Prophecy* (1794).

\* *The [First] Book of Urizen* (1794). With a Note by Dorothy Plowman, London and New York, 1929. Facsimile edition, London (Trianon Press), 1958.

\* *The Song of Los* (1795).

\* *The Book of Ahania* (1795). One copy only recorded.

\* *Milton* (1804 [?1808]).

\* *Jerusalem: The Emanation of the Giant Albion* (1804–20). Facsimile edition, in color, London (Trianon Press), 1951; idem, black and white, 1955. A simplified version prepared and edited by W. R. Hughes, London, 1964.

*Blake's Chaucer*. The Canterbury Pilgrims, The Fresco Picture, Representing Chaucer's Characters painted by William Blake, as it is now submitted to the Public, the Designer proposes to engrave, etc. [A prospectus]. (1809).

*A Descriptive Catalogue of Pictures*, Poetical and Historical Inventions, Painted by William Blake, in Water Colours, being the Ancient method of Fresco Painting Restored: and Drawings, for Public Inspection . . . (1809). Compiled by Blake for an exhibition of his work.

*The Letters of William Blake*. Edited by Geoffrey Keynes. London, 1956.

See also the editions of the Complete Works edited by Keynes, which contain the whole of the available correspondence to date.

*Letters from William Blake to Thomas Butts 1800–1803*. Printed in facsimile, with an Introductory Note by Geoffrey Keynes. Oxford, 1926.

*The Notebook of William Blake Called the Rossetti Manuscript*. Edited by Geoffrey Keynes. London, 1935. With facsimile.

Blake also designed and engraved illustrations for a number of books by other authors. Of these only those most relevant to the present work are listed.

*Lavater's Aphorisms on Man*. Translated from the original MS. of John Caspar Lavater. (Engraved by Blake.) London, 1788.

Salzmann, C. G. *Elements of Morality, for the Use of Children; with an Introductory Address to Parents*. (Translated from the German by Mary Wollstonecraft.) London, 1790, 2 vols. 2nd edn. (first with plates adapted by Blake from German originals), London, 1791, 3 vols.

Wollstonecraft, Mary. *Original Stories from Real Life*. London, 1791. Edited by E. V. Lucas, London, 1906.

Darwin, Erasmus. *The Botanic Garden*. A Poem. London, 1791. (Title-page of second part dated 1790.)

Cumberland, George. *Thoughts on Outline, Sculpture and the System that Guided the Ancient Artists in Composing their Figures and Groupes*. London, 1796.

Young, Edward. *Night Thoughts*. Edited by R. Edwards. London, 1797. See also *Illustrations to Young's Night Thoughts, Done in Water-Colour by William Blake*. Thirty pages reproduced from the original water colors in the library of W. White. With an introductory essay by Geoffrey Keynes. Cambridge (Mass.) and London, 1927.

Blair, Robert. *The Grave*. Illustrated by twelve etchings executed by Louis Schiavonetti from original inventions [of William Blake]. London, 1808. Reissued 1813; London, 1903; London, 1905.

Thornton, Robert John. *The Pastorals of Virgil*. London, 1821. 2 vols. (This edition is the first with Blake's woodcuts.) Also edited by Laurence Binyon, London, 1902. See also *The Illustrations of William Blake for Thornton's Virgil*. Introduction by Geoffrey Keynes. London, 1938.

*The Engravings of William Blake*. By A. G. B. Russell. London, 1912.

*William Blake's Designs for Gray's Poems*. Reproduced with an Introduction from the unique copy belonging to His Grace the Duke of Hamilton. With an Introduction by H. J. C. Grierson. London, 1922.

*The Paintings of William Blake.* By Darrell Figgis. London, 1925.

*The Engraved Designs of William Blake.* By Laurence Binyon. London and New York, 1926.

Milton, John. *Poems in English.* With illustrations by William Blake. London, 1926. 2 vols.

*Pencil Drawings by William Blake.* Edited by Geoffrey Keynes. London, 1927. See also *Blake's Pencil Drawings*, Second Series, below.

*Illustrations of the Book of Job.* Being all the Water-Colour Designs, Pencil Drawings and Engravings Reproduced in Facsimile. Introduction by Laurence Binyon and Geoffrey Keynes. New York, 1935. The engravings have been reproduced in a number of other editions, including ed. Laurence Binyon, London, 1906; ed. Kenneth Patchen, New York, 1947. See also *William Blake's Engravings* (ed. Keynes), below.

Bunyan, John. *The Pilgrim's Progress.* Twenty-nine Blake Illustrations in Colour. With introduction by Geoffrey Keynes. New York (The Limited Editions Club), 1941. Another edition: Twelve Illustrations in Colour. New York (Heritage Press), 1942.

*William Blake's Engravings.* Edited with an Introduction by Geoffrey Keynes. London, 1950.

*Blake's Illustrations to the Divine Comedy.* By Albert S. Roe. Princeton, 1953. With an excellent introductory essay and bibliography.

*Engravings by William Blake: The Separate Plates.* A Catalogue Raisonné. By Geoffrey Keynes. Dublin, 1956.

*Blake's Pencil Drawings.* Second Series. Edited by Geoffrey Keynes. London, 1956.

*William Blake's Illustrations to the Bible.* A Catalogue compiled by Geoffrey Keynes. London (Trianon Press), 1957.

# II

## A. *Biographies and Biographical Material*

[Calvert, Samuel C.] *A Memoir of Edward Calvert, Artist* by his Third Son. London, 1893.

Ellis, Edwin. *The Real Blake.* A Portrait Biography. London, 1907.

Gilchrist, Alexander. *Life of William Blake*. (Completed after the death of Gilchrist by D. G. Rossetti.) London and Cambridge, 1863, 2 vols. Revised and enlarged edn., London, 1880, 2 vols. (References in the text are to the 1880 edition.) The best working edition is that edited by Ruthven Todd for Everyman's Library (London and New York, 1942), with an excellent bibliography.

Malkin, B. H. *A Father's Memoirs of His Child*. London, 1806.

> Contains the earliest contemporary account of Blake.

Palmer, A. H. *The Life and Letters of Samuel Palmer*. London, 1892.

Swinburne, A. C. *William Blake:* A Critical Essay. London, 1868.

Symons, Arthur. *William Blake*. London, 1907.

> Reprints a number of early authorities.

Tatham, Frederick. "The Life of William Blake." In: A. G. B. Russell (ed.). *The Letters of William Blake*. London, 1906.

Wilson, Mona. *The Life of William Blake*. London, 1927. Rev. edn., with additional notes, London, 1948.

> The standard biography.

B. *Criticism and Interpretation*

Blackstone, Bernard. *English Blake*. Cambridge, 1949.

Blunt, Anthony. "Blake's 'Ancient of Days'; The Symbolism of the Compasses," *Journal of the Warburg and Courtauld Institutes*, II (1938), 53–63.

———. "Blake's 'Brazen Serpent,' " ibid., VI (1943), 225–27.

———. *The Art of William Blake*. New York, 1959.

———. "Blake's Pictorial Imagination," *Journal of the Warburg and Courtauld Institutes*, VI (1943), 190–212.

———. "Blake's Glad Day," ibid., II (1938), 65–68.

Bowra, C. M. *The Prophetic Element*. London, 1960.

> A presidential address to the English Association.

Bronowski, J. *William Blake, 1757–1827: A Man without a Mask*. London, 1944. (Penguin, 1954.)

Comyns-Carr, J. "Blake." In *Encyclopaedia Britannica*, 11th edn., IV, 36–38. Cambridge, 1910.

Damon, Samuel Foster. *William Blake, His Philosophy and Symbols*. Boston and London, 1924. Repr., New York, 1947.

Davies, John Langdon. *The Theology of William Blake*. Oxford, 1948.

Digby, C. Wingfield. *Symbol and Image in William Blake*. Oxford, 1957.

Erdman, David V. *Blake: Prophet against Empire*. A Poet's Interpretation of the History of His Own Times. Princeton, 1954.

Frye, Northrop. *Fearful Symmetry*. A Study of William Blake. Princeton, 1947. (Beacon paperback, 1962.)

Harper, George Mills. *The Neoplatonism of William Blake*. Chapel Hill, 1961.

Hirst, Désirée. *Hidden Riches: Traditional Symbolism from the Renaissance to Blake*. London, 1964.

*Huntington Library Quarterly, The*. Blake Bicentennial Issue, XXI (1957).

> Contains Northrop Frye, "Blake's Introduction to Experience"; Kathleen Raine, "Some Sources of *Tiriel*"; Albert S. Roe, "A Drawing of the Last Judgment"; Robert R. Wark, "A Minor Blake Conundrum."

Keynes, Geoffrey. *Blake Studies*. London, 1949.

> Contains a bibliography of Keynes's writings on Blake.

———. "Blake's Vision of the Circle of the Life of Man." In: Dorothy Miner (ed.). *Studies in Art and Literature for Belle da Costa Greene*. Princeton, 1954. (Pp. 202–208.)

Lowery, Margaret Ruth. *Windows of the Morning*. A Critical Study of William Blake's *Poetical Sketches*. New Haven and London, 1940.

Margoliouth, H. M. *William Blake*. Oxford, 1951.

Morton, A. L. *The Everlasting Gospel:* A Study in the Sources of William Blake. London, 1958.

Murry, John Middleton. *William Blake*. London, 1933.

Percival, Milton O. *William Blake's Circle of Destiny*. New York, 1938.

Pinto, V. de Sola (ed.). *The Divine Vision*. Studies in the Poetry and Art of William Blake. London, 1957.

> Contributions by S. Foster Damon, Northrop Frye, K. Kiralis, M. K. Nurmi, V. de S. Pinto, K. Raine, P. Nanavutty, H. M. Margoliouth, and W. de la Mare.

Plowman, Max. *An Introduction to the Study of Blake*. London and Toronto, 1927.

Preston, Kerrison. *Blake and Rossetti.* London, 1944.

[Robertson, W. Graham.] *The Blake Collection of W. Graham Robertson.* Described by the Collector. Edited with an Introduction by Kerrison Preston. London, 1952.

Saurat, Denis. *Blake and Milton.* Bordeaux, 1920. Reissue, London, 1935.

———. *Blake & Modern Thought.* London, 1929.

Schorer, Mark. *William Blake: The Politics of Vision.* New York, 1946. (Vintage paperback, 1959.)

Story, Alfred Thomas. *William Blake: His Life, Character and Genius.* London and New York, 1893.

Todd, Ruthven. "William Blake and the Eighteenth-Century Mythologists." In: *Tracks in the Snow.* Studies in English Science and Art. London, 1946.

Wicksteed, Joseph. *Blake's Innocence and Experience.* A Study of the Songs and Manuscripts. London, Toronto, and New York, 1928.

———. *Blake's Vision of the Book of Job.* London and New York, 1910. 2nd revised and enlarged edn., London and New York, 1924.

——— (ed.). *William Blake's "Jerusalem."* With a Foreword by Geoffrey Keynes. London, 1954.

> Text and Commentary on the Facsimile published by the Trianon Press for the William Blake Trust.

Yeats, William Butler. "William Blake and his Illustrations to the Divine Comedy" and "William Blake and the Imagination." In: *Ideas of Good and Evil.* London, 1903. Reprinted in *Essays and Introductions.* London, 1961.

# III

## *Other Books Referred To*

Aeschylus. *The Tragedies.* Translated by R. Potter. Norwich, 1777.

Agrippa von Nettesheim, Heinrich Cornelius. *Three Books of Occult Philosophy.* Translated by J. F. London, 1651.

Al-Jīlī, Qotb al-Dīn ʿabd al-Karim ibn Ibrahīm ibn Sibṭ ʿabd al-Qādir. *De l'Homme universel*. Extrait du livre: *Alinsôn al-Kâmil*. Translated from the Arabic (into French) and commented by Titus Burckhardt. Algiers and Lyons, 1953.

Apuleius, Lucius. *The .XI. Bookes of the Golden Asse*. Translated by William Adlington. London, 1566.

———. See also Taylor (12).

Armstrong, Edward Allworthy. *The Folklore of Birds*. London, 1958.

Bacon, Francis. *The New Atlantis*. In: *Sylva Sylvarum*, or, A Natural History. Published by William Rawley. London, 1627.

———. *The Wisedome of the Ancients*. Translated by Sir A. Gorges. London, 1619.

Bacon, Roger. *The Mirror of Alchimy*. Translated by Thomas Creede. London, 1597.

Barfield, Owen. *Saving the Appearances: A Study in Idolatry*. London, 1957.

Barrett, Francis. *The Magus, or Celestial Intelligencer*. London, 1801. 2 parts.

Bayley, Harold. *The Lost Language of Symbolism*. London, 1912. 2 vols.

Beer, John Bernard. *Coleridge the Visionary*. London, 1959.

Berkeley, George. *Works*. Edited by A. A. Luce and T. E. Jessop. London, 1948–57. 9 vols.

[Bhagavat Gita.] *The Geeta*. Translated by Shri Purohit Swami. London, 1935.

———. See also Wilkins.

Blackstone, Bernard. *The Consecrated Urn*. London and New York, 1959.

[Boehme, Jacob.] *The Works of Jacob Behmen*. [Edited by G. Ward and T. Langcake.] London, 1764–81. 4 vols.

> This is the edition commonly known under the name of William Law. Each work in each volume is separately paginated.

Bryant, Jacob. *A New System, or an Analysis of Ancient Mythology: Wherein an Attempt is made to divest Tradition of Fable, and to Reduce the Truth to its Original Purity*. London, 1774–76. 3 vols.

Bunyan, John. *The Holy War*. London, 1682.

Burckhardt, Titus. See Al-Jīlī.

Burnet, Thomas. *Archaeologiae Philosophicae: sive Doctrina antiqua de rerum originibus libri duo*. London, 1692.

———. *The Theory of the Earth, and of its Proofs*. London, 1690.

Campbell, Joseph. *The Hero with a Thousand Faces*. (Bollingen Series XVII.) New York, 1949.

Chatterton, Thomas. *Poems Supposed to have been Written at Bristol, by Thomas Rowley and others, in the 15th Century*. Edited by Thomas Tyrwhitt. London, 1777.

Clavigero, Francesco Saverio. *The History of Mexico*. Translated by Charles Cullen. London, 1787. 2 vols.

Coburn, Kathleen. See Coleridge, *Inquiring Spirit*.

Coleridge, Samuel Taylor. *Aids to Reflection*. London, 1825.

———. *Anima Poetae*. From the Unpublished Notebooks of Samuel Taylor Coleridge. Edited by Ernest Hartley Coleridge. London, 1895.

———. *Biographia Literaria*. London and New York (Everyman's Library), 1949.

———. *Inquiring Spirit*. Edited by Kathleen Coburn. London, 1951.

———. *The Statesman's Manual*. London, 1816.

Coomaraswamy, Ananda Kentish. *The Bugbear of Literacy*. London, 1949.

———. *The Christian and Oriental or True Philosophy of Art*. Newport, Rhode Island, 1939.

———. *Time and Eternity*. (Artibus Asiae, Supplement 8.) Ascona, 1947.

———. *The Transformation of Nature in Art*. Cambridge (Mass.), 1934.

———. *Why Exhibit Works of Art?* London, 1943.

Cumberland, George. *The Captive of the Castle of Sennaar*. London, 1798.

Daniel, Gabriel. See Descartes.

Dante Alighieri. *The Divina Commedia*. Translated into English Verse by the Rev. Henry Boyd. London, 1802. 3 vols.

———. *The Inferno*. Translated by H. F. Cary. London, 1805–6. 2 vols.

Davies, Edward. *Celtic Researches, on the Origin, Traditions, and Language of the Ancient Britons*. London, 1804.

———. *The Mythology and Rites of the British Druids*. London, 1809.

Demophilus. See Taylor (9).

Descartes, René. *Philosophical Works*. Translated by Elizabeth S. Haldane and G. R. T. Ross. Cambridge, 1911–12. 2 vols.

———. *Principles of Philosophy, and a Voyage to the World of Cartesius.* Written originally in French [by G. Daniel], and now translated into English [by T. Taylor]. London, 1692.

Diaz del Castillo, Bernal. *The True History of the Conquest of Mexico*. Translated by Maurice Keatinge. London, 1800.

Dryden, John. *The Poems*. Edited by John Sargeaunt. London and New York, 1925.

———. See also Ovid, *Metamorphoses;* Virgil.

Eliot, Thomas Stearns. *The Sacred Wood*. London, 1928 (first publ. 1920).

Empson, William. *The Structure of Complex Words*. London, 1951.

[Enoch, Book of.] *The Book of Enoch the Prophet* . . . now first translated from an Ethiopic MS. Translated by R. Laurence. Oxford, 1821.

Evans-Wentz, W. Y. *The Fairy Faith in Celtic Countries*. London, 1911.

———. (ed.). *The Tibetan Book of the Dead*. With a psychological commentary by C. G. Jung. 3rd edn., London, 1957. (1st edn., London, 1927.)

———. (ed.). *The Tibetan Book of the Great Liberation*. With a psychological commentary by C. G. Jung. London and New York, 1954.

Fludd, Robert. *Mosaicall Philosophy, grounded upon the essentiall truth or eternal sapience*. Written first in Latin, and afterwards thus rendered into English. London, 1659.

———. *Philosophia Sacra*. Frankfurt, 1626.

Freud, Sigmund. "The Theme of the Three Caskets." Translated by C. J. M. Hubback. In *Complete Psychological Works*, vol. 12. London, 1958.

Geoffrey of Monmouth. *The British History*. Translated by Aaron Thompson. London, 1817.

Gibbon, Edward. *The History of the Decline and Fall of the Roman Empire*, London, 1776–88. 6 vols.

Guénon, René. *The Reign of Quantity and the Signs of the Times*. Translated by Lord Northbourne. [London], 1953.

[Hermes Trismegistus.] *The Divine Pymander of Hermes Mercurius Trismegistus*. Translated from the Arabic by Dr. [John] Everard [1650]. With an introduction by Hargrave Jennings. London, 1884.

Herodotus. *The History*. Translated by Isaac Littlebury. London, 1709. 2 vols.

Hesiod. *Works*. Translated by Thomas Cooke. London, 1728. 2 vols.

Homer. *The Iliad and Odyssey*. Translated into English blank verse by W. Cowper. London, 1791. 2 vols.

———. *The Whole Works of Homer, Prince of Poetts, in his Iliads, and Odysses*. Translated according to the Greek. By George Chapman. London, [1612]. 2 parts.

Johnson, Samuel. *The History of Rasselas, Prince of Abissinia*. Edited by R. W. Chapman. Oxford, 1927.

Jones, David. "Art and Sacrament." In: *Epoch and Artist*. Edited by Harman Grisewood. London, 1959.

Jones, Sir William. *Works*. London, 1807. 13 vols.

———. "On the Gods of Greece, Italy, and India," *Asiatick Researches* (Calcutta), I (1788), 221–75.

Joyce, James. *Ulysses*. London, 1947. (Orig., Paris, 1922).

Jung, Carl Gustav. *Collected Works*. Translated by R. F. C. Hull. London and New York, 1953– . 18 vols.

———. *Psychological Types*. Translated by H. G. Baynes. London and New York, 1923.

——— and Kerényi, Carl. *Essays on a Science of Mythology*. Translated by R. F. C. Hull. New York, 1949. (Also published as *Introduction to a Science of Mythology*, London, 1950.)

Lardner, Joseph Nathaniel. *Works*. London, 1788. 11 vols.

Lewis, Clive Staples. *A Preface to Paradise Lost*. London, 1942.

Locke, John. *An Essay concerning Humane Understanding*. London, 1690.

Lowes, John Livingston. *The Road to Xanadu*. New York and London, 1927.

Macpherson, James. *An Introduction to the History of Great Britain and Ireland*. 2nd edn., enlarged, London, 1772.

———. *The Works of Ossian*. Translated by James Macpherson. 3rd edn., London, 1765. 2 vols.

Mahony, Capt. "On *Singhala*, or *Ceylon*, and the Doctrines of Bhooddha, from the Books of the *Singhalais*," *Asiatick Researches* (Calcutta), VII (1801), 32–56.

Mallet, Paul Henri. *Northern Antiquities*. Translated [by Bishop Percy]. London, 1770. 2 vols.

Mankowitz, Wolf. *The Portland Vase and the Wedgwood Copies*. London, 1952.

Mead, G. R. S. *Orpheus*. London, 1896.

Montfaucon, Bernard de. *L'Antiquité expliquée et représentée en figures*. Paris, 1719–24. 10 vols.

Morley, Edith J. (ed.). *Blake, Coleridge, Wordsworth, Lamb, etc.* Being Selections from the Remains of Henry Crabb Robinson. Manchester, London and New York, 1922.

Mosheim, Johann Lorenz von. *An Ecclesiastical History, Antient and Modern.* Translated by A. Maclaine. London, 1765. 2 vols.

Muir, Edwin. *An Autobiography*. London, 1954. (An enlarged and revised version of *The Story and the Fable*, London, 1940.)

Newton, Isaac. *The Mathematical Principles of Natural Philosophy*. Translated by Andrew Motte. London, 1729. 2 vols.

———. *Opticks*. London, 1704. 3rd edn., corrected, London, 1721.

Orpheus. See Taylor (2).

Ossian. See Macpherson.

Ovid (Publius Ovidius Naso). *Fasti or the Romans Sacred Calendar*. Translated by W. Massey. London, 1757.

———. *Metamorphoses*. In fifteen books. Translated by the most Eminent Hands [J. Dryden and others]. Edited by Sir Samuel Garth. London, 1717.

Paracelsus (Theophrastus Bombast of Hohenheim). *Archidoxes* [and other works]. Translated by J. H. [?James Howell]. London, 1661. 2 parts.

———. *Aurora and Treasure of the Philosophers*. Translated by J. H. London, 1659.

———. *Nine Books on the Nature of Things*. See Sendivogius.

———. *Of the Chymical Transmutation, Genealogy and Generation of Metals and Minerals. . . .* Translated by R. Turner. London, 1657.

Paracelsus. *Philosophy Reformed & Improved in four Profound Tractates* . . . *Discovering the Wonderfull Mysteries of the Creation, by Paracelsus: being his Philosophy to the Athenians*. Translated by R. Turner. London, 1657.

Percy, Thomas. *Reliques of Ancient English Poetry*. London, 1765. 3 vols.

———. See also Mallet.

Plato. See Taylor (5, 8, 16).

Plotinus. See Taylor (1, 11).

Plutarch. *Morals*. Translated from the Greek by Several Hands [M. Morgan, S. Ford, W. Dillingham, T. Hoy, etc.]. 4th edn., London, 1704. 5 vols. (1st edn., 1684–94.) ("Of the Face, appearing within the Orb of the Moon," tr. A. G., *Gent.*, vol. 5, pp. 217–74.)

———. *Treatise of Isis and Osiris*. Translated by Samuel Squire. Cambridge, 1744. 2 parts.

Porphyry. See Taylor (18).

Priestley, Joseph. *A Comparison of the Institutions of Moses with Those of The Hindoos*. Northumberland, Pennsylvania, 1799.

———. *An History of Early Opinions Concerning Jesus Christ*. Birmingham, 1786. 4 vols.

Prior, Matthew. *Poems on Several Occasions*. London, 1709.

Proclus. See Taylor (3, 9).

Robinson, Henry Crabb. See Morley.

Rogers, Neville. *Shelley at Work: A Critical Inquiry*. Oxford, 1956.

Rousseau, Jean-Jacques. *Eloisa: or, a Series of Original Letters*. Translated [by William Kenrick]. London, 1784. 4 vols.

Scholem, Gershom G. *Major Trends in Jewish Mysticism*. 3rd edn., New York, 1954; London, 1955.

Schuon, Frithjof. *Gnosis*. Translated by G. E. H. Palmer. London, 1959.

———. *Stations of Wisdom*. Translated by G. E. H. Palmer. London, 1961.

Sendivogius, Michael. *A New Light of Alchymie;* . . . *also Nine Books of the Nature of Things, written by Paracelsus* . . . etc. Translated out of the Latin by J[ohn] F[rench]. London, 1650.

Sophocles. *The Tragedies*. Translated by Thomas Francklin. London, 1759. 2 vols.

———. *The Tragedies*. Translated by Robert Potter. London, 1788.

Stedman, J. G. *Narrative of a five years' expedition, against the Revolted Negroes of Surinam*. London, 1796. 2 vols.

Stuart, James, and Revett, Nicholas. *The Antiquities of Athens, measured and delineated*. London, 1762–1816. 4 vols.

Stukeley, William. *Abury, A Temple of the British Druids*. London, 1743.

———. *Stonehenge, a Temple Restored to the British Druids*. London, 1740.

———. *A Letter . . . to Mr Macpherson on his Publication of Fingal and Temora*. London, 1763.

Swedenborg, Emanuel. *Arcana Coelestia*. Translated by a Society of Gentlemen [actually, John Clowes]. London, 1802–12. 13 vols.

———. *Concerning the Earths in our Solar System*. [Translated by John Clowes.] London, 1787.

———. *The Delights of Wisdom concerning Conjugial* [sic] *Love*. [Translated by John Clowes.] London, 1794.

———. *The Doctrine of the New Jerusalem concerning the Lord*. 3rd edn., London, 1791.

———. *The Heavenly Doctrine of the New Jerusalem*. London, 1792.

———. *A Treatise Concerning Heaven and Hell*. [Translated by W. Cookworthy and T. Hartley.] London, 1778.

———. *A Treatise concerning the Last Judgement*. London, 1788.

———. *A Continuation concerning the Last Judgement, and the Spiritual World*. London, 1791.

———. *A Treatise on the Nature of Influx*. London, 1798.

———. *True Christian Religion; containing the Universal Theology of the New Church*. London, 1781. 2 vols.

———. *The Wisdom of Angels concerning Divine Love and Divine Wisdom*. London, 1788.

———. *The Wisdom of Angels concerning the Divine Providence*. London, 1790.

Sydenham. See Taylor (15).

Taylor, Thomas. [Note: In view of the importance of Taylor as the source of
Blake's knowledge of the Platonic philosophy, I have listed all his relevant works published up to and including 1805, the date of Blake's *Milton*.
He continued to publish until 1834, but his later works do not seem to have
influenced Blake's thought.]

(1) *Concerning the Beautiful, or a paraphrased translation from the
Greek of Plotinus, Ennead I, Book 6.* London, 1787. (Reprinted as *An
Essay on the Beautiful,* London, 1792.)

(2) *The Mystical Initiations, or, Hymns of Orpheus. Translated from
the . . . Greek, with a Preliminary Dissertation on the Life and Theology of Orpheus.* London, 1787. (2nd edn., *The Hymns of Orpheus,* London, 1792; 3rd edn., *The Mystical Hymns of Orpheus,* London, 1824.)

(3) *The Philosophical and Mathematical Commentaries of Proclus
on the First Book of Euclid's Elements . . . to which are added, the History of the Restoration of the Platonic Theology by the Latter Platonists,
and a Translation . . . of Proclus' Elements of Theology.* London,
1788–89. 2 vols. (2nd edn., 1792; rev. edn., 1823: see below, no. 18.)
("On the Cave of the Nymphs," vol. 2, pp. 278–307.)

(4) *A Dissertation on the Eleusinian and Bacchic Mysteries.* Amster-
dam, [1790]. (Appeared also in *The Pamphleteer,* vol. 8, London, 1816.)

(5) (tr.) *The Phaedrus of Plato.* London, 1792.

(6) *The Rights of Brutes.* London, 1792.

(7) (tr.) *Two Orations of the Emperor Julian.* London, 1793.

(8) (tr.) *The Cratylus, Phaedo, Parmenides and Timaeus of Plato.*
London, 1793.

(9) (tr.) *Sallust on the Gods and the World; and the Pythagoric
Sentences of Demophilus, translated from the Greek; and Five Hymns by
Proclus . . . with a Poetical Version.* London, 1793.

(10) (tr.) *Pausanias: The Description of Greece.* London, 1794.

(11) (tr.) *Five Books of Plotinus.* London, 1794.

(12) (tr.) *The Fable of Cupid and Psyche, translated from . . .
Apuleius.* London, 1795.

(13) "A Concise Exposition of the Chaldaic Dogmas, by Psellus,"

*The Monthly Magazine* (London), III, suppl. no. XIX (June 1797).

(14) (tr.) *Metaphysics of Aristotle.* London, 1801.

(15) (tr.) *The Dissertations of Maximus Tyrius.* London, 1804.

(16) (tr.) *The Works of Plato.* Translated by Floyer Sydenham and Thomas Taylor. London, 1804. 5 vols.

(17) *Miscellanies in Prose and Verse.* . . . London, 1805. (Contains "The Creed of the Platonic Philosopher.")

(18) (tr.) *Select Works of Porphyry.* London, 1823. ("On the Cave of the Nymphs," pp. 171–200.)

Teresa, Saint. *The Life of the Holy Mother St Teresa, . . . together with a short account of the Foundations which she made.* The whole abridged from her own writings. London, 1757.

Tyrrell, George Nugent Merle. *Homo Faber: A Study of Man's Mental Evolution.* London, 1951.

[Vaughan, Thomas.] *Anima Magica Abscondita, or, A Discourse of the Universall Spirit of Nature.* By Eugenius Philalethes. London, 1650.

———. *Anthroposophia Theomagica; or a Discourse of the Nature of Man and his State after Death.* By Eugenius Philalethes. London, 1650.

———. *Aula Lucis, or The House of Light* . . . By S. N., a Modern Speculator. London, 1652.

———. *Coelum Terrae.* See *Magia Adamica,* below.

———. *Euphrates, or The Waters of the East.* By Eugenius Philalethes. London, 1655.

———. *Lumen de Lumine, or, A New Magicall Light.* By Eugenius Philalethes. London, 1651.

———. *Magia Adamica, or, The Antiquitie of Magic.* . . . whereunto is added. . . . *Coelum Terrae.* By Eugenius Philalethes. London, 1650.

———. *The Works of Thomas Vaughan: Eugenius Philalethes.* Edited by A. E. Waite. London, 1919.

Virgil. *Works: containing his Pastorals, Georgics, and Aeneis.* Translated into English Verse by John Dryden. London, 1697.

Voltaire. *The Metaphysics of Sir Isaac Newton; or a Comparison between the Opinions of Sir Isaac Newton and M. Leibnitz.* Translated by D. E. Baker. London, 1747.

Warburton, William. *The Divine Legation of Moses.* 4th rev. and enl. edn., London, 1755–65. 5 vols. in 7 parts.

Watts, Isaac. *Divine Songs attempted in Easy Language for the Use of Children.* 9th edn., London, 1728. Another edn., Kidderminster [?1790].

Whitehead, Alfred North. *Science and the Modern World.* Cambridge, 1926.

Wilford, Captain. "On the Chronology of the Hindoos," *Asiatick Researches,* V (1798), 241–95.

Wilhelm, Richard (tr.). *The Secret of the Golden Flower.* With a Foreword and Commentary by C. G. Jung. Translated from the German by Cary F. Baynes. Rev. edn., London and New York, 1962. (Jung's commentary in his *Collected Works,* vol. 13.)

Wilkins, Sir Charles (tr.). *The Bhagvat-Geeta, or Dialogues of Kreeshna and Arjoon.* London, 1785.

Wilson, F. A. C. *W. B. Yeats and Tradition.* London, 1958.

Winckelmann, J. J. *Reflections on the Paintings and Sculptures of the Greeks.* Translated by H. F[üssli]. London, 1765.

Wind, Edgar. *Pagan Mysteries in the Renaissance.* London, 1958.

Yeats, William Butler. *Autobiographies.* London, 1926; 2nd edn., 1955.

———. *Collected Plays.* London, 1934; 2nd edn., 1952.

———. *Collected Poems.* 2nd edn., London and New York, 1950.

———. (ed.). *The Oxford Book of Modern Verse, 1892–1935.* Oxford, 1936.

———. *A Vision.* London, 1925; 2nd edn., 1937.

# Indexes

# Index of Works by Blake

Italics are not used for titles of Blake's works, though the titles are italicized in the text; but titles of works he illustrated or annotated are in italic. Titles of individual works of visual art (paintings, drawings, etc.) are given in quotation marks. References to notes are of three kinds: 16n20 = note 20 for page 16; 16 & n20 = note 20, and also the text on page 16; 16 (n20) = on page 16, the quotation carrying note 20. Superior figures [1] and [2] = vol. I and vol. II.

Ah! Sun-flower, *see* Songs of Experience

All Religions Are One, [1]72; [2]103, 104, 109; quoted, [2]105

America: A Prophecy, [1]50n38, 73, 124n65, 274, 338; quoted, [1]171, 245, 339 (n16), 340 & n19; ill., [1]117, 171, 192, 345

Ancient Britons, The, *see* Descriptive Catalogue of Pictures, A

"Ancient of Days, The" (color print), [2]56; ill., [2]57

Angel, The, *see* Songs of Experience

annotations to:
  Bacon, quoted, [2]278 (n84)
  Berkeley's *Siris*, [2]109; quoted, [1]364 (n13); [2]102, 105, 146, 194 (n17), 196 (n25)
  Boyd's *Dante*, quoted, [2]230 (n57)
  Lavater's *Aphorisms*, quoted, [1]118 (n45), 122, 321; [2]145
  Reynolds' *Discourses*, quoted, [1]259 (n31), 260–61; [2]101, 115 (n34), 199
  Swedenborg's *Divine Love and Wisdom*, quoted, [1]7 (n9), 13 (n21); [2]134
  Dr. Thornton's *New Translation of the Lord's Prayer*, quoted, [2]168n52
  Watson's *Apology*, quoted, [1]52

Arlington Court painting, [1]75–98 & 75n11, 137, 138, 242; ill., [1]74, 79, 87

Auguries of Innocence, [1]331; quoted, [1]13–14 (n27), 49 (n36), 243 (n38); [2]116 (n38), 124 (n65), 157 (n20)

Book of Ahania, The, [1]150; quoted, [1]154, 155–56, 159–60; [2]50, 85 (n6), 86n13; ill., [1]151

Book of Los, The, [1]242; [2]154n9; quoted, [1]92n41, 229–30, 239–40; [2]67 (n37), 68 (n43); ill., [1]229

Book of Moonlight, [1]252

Book of Thel, The, [1]68, 73, 75, 94, 99–125 passim & 112n32 & 114n38, 133, 170, 180, 203, 360; quoted, [1]28, 99, 100, 102 & n7, 103, 105, 110, 111, 113, 114n36, 117, 119–20, 121, 124–25, 146, 169; ill., [1]104, 116, 117

Book of Urizen, The [First], [1]6, 10, 277; [2]11, 46, 56 & n7, 59, 84, 122, 219, 223, 228; quoted, [1]202, 213–14, 221 (n57), 341, 343–44; [2]45, 52, 58, 61–62, 63, 66–67, 68 & n44, 73 (n66), 76 (n73), 86 & n13, 90 (n20), 97, 121 (n56), 123, 134 (n16), 136, 137; ill., [1]9, 46, 51, 225, 344; [2]64, 65, 66, 75, 135

"Bowman, The" (pencil drawing), ill., [1]228

"Brazen Serpent, The" (Bible illustr.), [2]237

Chaucer's Canterbury Pilgrims (essay), *see* Descriptive Catalogue of Pictures, A

Chimney Sweeper, The, *see* Songs of Experience; Songs of Innocence

Christian Forbearance, *see* Notebook of William Blake, The

Clod & the Pebble, The, *see* Songs of Experience

Conversations with Crabb Robinson, quoted, [1]212, 228; [2]13, 169 & n56, 221, 223

Couch of Death, The, *see* Poetical Sketches

Cradle Song, A, *see* Songs of Innocence

"Creation of Adam" (color printed monotype), ill., [2]13

Crystal Cabinet, The, [1]274; quoted, [1]274–75, 276

Cupid and Psyche, [1]112; *see also* Illustrations: Cumberland's *Thoughts on Outline*

"Cycle of the Life of Man, The," *see* Arlington Court painting

345

# General Index

References to notes are of three kinds: 16n20 = note 20 for page 16; 16 & n20 = note 20, and also the text on page 16; 16 (n20) = on page 16, the quotation carrying note 20. Superior figures [1] and [2] = vol. I and vol. II.

Abel, ghost of, [2]204n53

Abraham, [1]53

*Abury, A Temple of the British Druids* (Stukeley), [1]53; [2]236n79, 261; quoted, [1]50; [2]237 (n82); ill., [1]50

Adam, [1]37, 57, 60n74, 84, 97, 130, 136, 164, 165, 213, 214 & n40, 216, 297, 324, 325, 326, 327, 329, 330, 335, 336, 338, 339; [2]13, 16, 28, 35, 36, 38, 40, 49, 55, 65, 78, 114, 158, 173n4, 184 & n41, 197, 204n53, 210, 212, 215, 229, 241; cabalistic name of, [1]48n33; in occult tradition, [1]242n32

*Adamah, see* Adam

Addison, Joseph, [1]359

Adonis, [1]105–8, 114n37; [2]41; in Milton, [1]105 & n15; in Spenser, [1]103; Thel and, [1]103, 105–8

*Adrastia*, law of, [1]59, 60

A.E. (G. W. Russell), [1]71; [2]273

*Aeneid* (Vergil/Dryden), [1]135, 145; quoted, [1]24, 25, 134–35

age: old age: Blake's attitude toward, [1]66;—in Norse mythology, [1]55–56;—symbolism of, [1]66; symbolic, [1]59

Agrippa, Cornelius, [1]35, 54, 94n47, 99, 103 & n12, 113, 219, 329, 361; [2]15, 74, 200, 212 & n75, 213, 226n45; on heaven and hell, [1]62n83; influence on *Tiriel*, [1]56–65; occult nature of air, [2]234n7; scale of cabalistic correspondences, [1]230n78

Ahania, [1]151, 154–63, 235, 291, 292n5, 298; [2]86, 92

air: "nourishing air" image, [1]297n26; occult nature of, [1]234n7

Albion, [1]92n41, 137, 204, 206, 207, 209, 211, 212, 213, 243, 257, 264, 280, 310, 311, 327, 340, 343; [2]14, 28, 29, 48, 116, 124, 155, 168n52, 174, 183–93 passim, 206, 212, 216, 217, 241, 247, 248, 251–71 & n60, 272–80; Daughters of, [1]86, 210, 238, 311; [2]169, 182, 254; Friends of, [2]259; sons of, [1]120, 210; [2]266; Spectre of Albion, [1]325, 326; wife of, [2]173

alchemy/alchemical, [1]xxvi, xxxi, 4, 99, 195n40, 299, 333; [2]5n4, 8, 19, 20, 91n25, 99; concept of matter, [1]63, 119, 121, 290; [2]155; descent of intellect myth, [1]271–89; *deus absconditus*, [1]271, 280, 298, 299, 302; generation concept, [1]286; Luna symbolism, [1]220, 223, 232; marriage, [1]146; *vs.* Neoplatonism, [1]118; philosophers' stone, [1]116n41; Sol symbolism, [1]220–30, 232; star symbolism, [1]152; and *Thel*, [1]114; and *Tiriel*, [1]35; unity and duality, [1]360, 363n9; white symbolism, [1]114n38; *see also* Smaragdine Table

Alcott, Bronson, [1]72

allegory, Coleridge on, [1]5n4

*Allegro, L'* (Milton), [2]161; ill., [2]153, 160

Ammon, [1]5

*Among School Children* (Yeats), quoted, [1]138n18

Anak, [2]161 & n37, 165 & n46

"Ancients, the," [2]103

*Anemone pulsatilla*, [1]105 & n15

angels, [1]26–27, 59–60, 66; fallen, [1]50n38, 57–58; [2]29, 173; Swedenborgian, [1]8, 26, 98, 338n14

*Anima Magica Abscondita* (Vaughan), [1]195n40, 276; quoted, [1]224 (n64), 275 (n13)

*Anima Poetae* (Coleridge), quoted, [2]140n29

animal: forms, [2]3–16, 19; perception, [2]125n68; *see also names of animals, e.g.,* lion

Annandale, [2]267, 268, 277

Antamon, [1]266–68

*Anthroposophia Theomagica* (Vaughan), quoted, [1]122 (n60), 195n40, 219–20, 272n4, 276n16, 363n6; [2]140n29

Antigone, [1]45

*Antigone* (Sophocles/Potter), quoted, [1]38

*Antiken Sarcophagreliefs, Die* (C. Robert), [2]174n9

Antinomianism, [1]335n4

*Antiquité expliquée, L'* (Montfaucon), [2]84n5